CROSSWORD
DICTIONARY

GILLIAN M. CLARK

ERIC DOBBY
PUBLISHING

First published in Great Britain 1993
Reprinted 11 times
This edition published 2007

Eric Dobby Publishing Ltd
Random Acres,
Slip Mill Lane
Hawkhurst
Cranbrook
Kent TN18 5AD

ISBN 978-1-85882-064-4

Text typeset in Courier by Kevin O'Connor
Printed and bound in Finland by
WS Bookwell Ltd

Contents

Contents

Contents

African countries

3 & 4
Chad
Mali
Togo
UAR

5
Benin
Congo
Egypt
Gabon
Ghana
Kenya
Libya
Niger
Sudan
Zaïre

6
Angola

Gambia
Guinea
Malawi
Rwanda
Uganda
Zambia

7
Algeria
Burkina
Burundi
Comoros
Eritrea
Lesotho
Liberia
Mayotte
Morocco
Namibia
Nigeria
Réunion
Senegal
Somalia

Tunisia

8
Botswana
Cameroon
Djibouti
Ethiopia
St. Helena
Tanzania
Zimbabwe

9
Mauritius
Swaziland

10
Ivory Coast
Madagascar
Mauritania
Mozambique

Seychelles

11
Burkina Faso
Côte d'Ivoire
Saint Helena
Sierra Leone
South Africa

12
Guinea-Bissau

15 +
Cape Verde Islands
Central African
  Republic
Equatorial Guinea
Sao Tomé and Prin-
  cipé

Air and space travel

3
ace
bay
fin
fly
gas
jet
rev
UFO
yaw

4
bank
bump

buzz
crew
dive
dope
drag
flap
hull
kite
land
lane
lift
loop
mach
nose
prop

roll
slip
span
spar
spin
tail
taxi
trim
wash
wing
zoom

5
apron

cabin
cargo
chock
chord
climb
Comet
craft
crash
crate
ditch
drift
flaps
glide
pitch
plane

prang
pylon
radar
range
rigid
slots
stage
stall
strut
stunt

6
aerial
airbus

air car
airman
airway
basket
beacon
bomber
canard
cruise
drogue
fanjet
flight
gas-bag
George
glider
hangar

intake
launch
module
nose-up
ramjet
refuel
rocket
rudder
runway
yawing

7

aileron
airbase
aircrew
air flow
air lane
air lift
airline
airport
airraid
airship
aviator
ballast
balloon
biplane
bale out
bomb bay
capsule
ceiling
charter
chassis
chopper
clipper
cockpit
co-pilot
cowling
ejector
fairing
fighter
flyover
flypast
gondola
Halifax
Harrier

Heinkel
jump-jet
Junkers
landing
lift-off
Mae West
missile
Mustang
nacelle
nose-cap
pancake
payload
re-entry
ripcord
shuttle
sponson
Sputnik
tail fin
take-off
twin-jet
wingtip

8

aerofoil
aeronaut
aerostat
air brake
aircraft
airfield
air force
air frame
airliner
airplane
airscrew
airspace
airspeed
airstrip
airwoman
altitude
anhedral
approach
autogiro
autogyro
aviation
Beaufort

Blenheim
bomb-rack
Canberra
Concorde
corridor
dihedral
elevator
envelope
fuselage
grounded
gyrostat
heliport
in-flight
intercom
jet plane
joystick
Jumbo jet
Moonshot
Mosquito
non-rigid
nose cone
nosedive
nose down
pulse jet
rotodyne
seaplane
sideslip
spaceman
Spitfire
squadron
stopover
subsonic
tail boom
tail skid
tail unit
terminal
triplane
turbofan
turbojet
warplane
wind cone
wind sock
wing flap
Zeppelin

9

aerodrome
aeroplane
air intake
air pocket
airworthy
altimeter
amphibian
astrodome
astronaut
autopilot
cabin crew
cargo hold
cosmonaut
countdown
crash-land
delta wing
dirigible
Gladiator
gyroplane
Hurricane
jet bomber
Lancaster
launch pad
longerons
low-flying
mail plane
monocoque
monoplane
navigator
nosewheel
overshoot
parachute
power dive
propeller
rudder bar
sailplane
satellite
semi-rigid
spaceship
spacesuit
spacewalk
sweepback
Swordfish
tailplane

test pilot
Tiger Moth
touchdown
turboprop
twin-screw

10

aerobatics
aero engine
aeronautic
air control
air defence
air hostess
air steward
air support
air traffic
anemometer
balloonist
cantilever
cargo plane
dive bomber
flight deck
flight path
flight plan
flying-boat
gas-balloon
gas turbine
ground crew
helicopter
Hindenberg
hovercraft
hydroplane
jet fighter
landing run
mach number
outer space
robot plane
slipstream
solo flight
spacecraft
space probe
splashdown
stabilizer
stewardess
streamline

supersonic
test flight
Wellington

11

aeronautics
aerostatics
afterburner
blind flying
ejector seat
fire-balloon
flying speed
ground speed
heat barrier
heavy bomber
laminar flow
landing deck
landing gear
leading edge
loop the loop
Montgolfier
Moon landing
ornithopter
retro-rocket
sesquiplane
slotted wing
soft landing
space centre
stabilizers
strike plane
stunt flying
vapour trail

12

aerodynamics
air-sea rescue
arrester gear
arrester wire
belly landing
control tower
crash landing
ejection seat
fighter pilot
flying circus
flying saucer

freight-plane
jet propelled
landing light
landing speed
launching pad
maiden flight
night fighter
pressure suit
pursuit plane
radial engine
sound barrier
space capsule
space station
space vehicle
trailing edge

13

airworthiness
control column
cruising speed
forced landing
ground control
hot-air balloon
radiolocation
stalling speed
Stratocruiser
undercarriage

14 +

aircraft carrier
decompression
escape velocity
flying bedstead
heavier-than-air
lighter-than-air
looping the loop
Montgolfier balloon
passenger plane
semiretractable
space traveller
troop transport
undercarriage
weightlessness

American Indian tribes

2 & 3

Fox
Gê
Ona
Uru
Ute

4

Arua
Cree
Crow
Cuna
Erie
Hare
Hopi
Hupa
Inca
Iowa
Lipe
Macú
Maya
Moki
Mojo
Mura
Pano
Pima
Pomo
Sauk
Taos
Tupi
Yumi
Zuma
Zuñi

5

Acona
Adena
Arara
Aztec
Blood

Caddo
Campa
Cañar
Carib
Chimu
Chocó
Chono
Creek
Guató
Haidi
Huron
Incas
Kansa
Karok
Kaska
Kiowa
Lenca
Lipan
Maidu
Mbaya
Miami
Modoc
Moqui
Nahau
Nazca
Olmec
Omaha
Osage
Otomi
Ponca
Sarsi
Sioux
Slave
Taino
Teton
Wappo
Yagua
Yaqui
Yuchi
Yunca
Zoque

6

Abipón
Abnaki
Apache
Apinai
Arawak
Atoara
Aymara
Aztecs
Beaver
Biloxi
Bororo
Calusa
Cariri
Cayapa
Cayapó
Cayuga
Cayuse
Chavin
Conibo
Dakota
Dogrib
Guaymí
Jivaro
Kayopo
Kichai
Laguna
Lenape
Lucayo
Mandan
Mataco
Micmac
Mixtec
Mohave
Mohawk
Mojave
Munsee
Navaho
Nootka
Oglala
Omagua
Oneida

Ostiak
Ottowa
Paiute
Papago
Panare
Pawnee
Pequot
Pericu
Piegan
Pueblo
Quapaw
Salish
Santee
Sarcee
Siwash
Seneca
Toltec
Tucuna
Tupina
Warrau
Wintun
Witoto
Yahgan
Zamuco

7

Abenaki
Arapaho
Araucan
Arikara
Atakapa
Bannock
Beothuk
Camacan
Catawba
Carrier
Charrua
Chibcha
Chilcal
Chinook
Chumash
Choctaw

Ciboney
Cochimi
Coroado
Dakotah
Fuegian
Goajiro
Gosiute
Guaraní
Guayaná
Hidatsa
Klamath
Kutchin
Kutenai
Koyukon
Luiseno
Mahican
Mapuche
Mohegan
Mohican
Naskapi
Natchez
Ojibway
Orejone
Payaguá
Puelche
Quechua
Shawnee
Sirionó
Tairona
Tanaina
Timbira
Timucua
Tlingit
Tonkawa
Waiguri
Wichita
Wyandot
Yankton
Yamasee
Zapotec

8

Aguarana
Alacaluf
Amahuaca
Arikaree
Barbacoa
Caingang
Cherokee
Cheyenne
Chibchan
Chippewa
Colorado
Comanche
Delaware
Diaguita
Diegueño
Illinois
Iroquois
Jirajara
Kickapoo
Klikitat
Kootenai
Kwakiutl
Malecite
Maricopa
Menomini
Missouri
Mosquito
Muskogee
Nez
 Percé
Onondaga
Powhatan
Puebloan
Puelches
Querandi
Quichuan
Quileute
Quinault
Seminole
Sherente
Shoshone

Shoshoni
Shushwap
Sihasapa
Silksika
Sisseton
Subtaino
Tarascan
Tutchone
Yamamadi

9
Algonkian
Algonquin
Apalachee
Ashluslay
Ashochimi
Blackfoot
Chickasaw

Chilcotin
Chipewyan
Conestoga
Flatheads
Guaranian
Harasupai
Hoochinoo
Karankawa
Menominee
Motilones
Mundurucú
Penobscot
Puelchean
Taulipang
Tehuelche
Tsmishian
Tupinambá
Tuscarora
Wampanoag
Winnebago

10
Alacalufan
Algonquian
Araucanian
Assiniboin
Athabascan
Bella Coola
Chitimacha
Chiviguano
Coahuiltec
Gabrielino
Gros Ventre
Leni-Lenapé
Miccosukee
Minnetaree
Montagnais
Nambicuara
Patagonian

Potawatomi
Tarahumara

11
Narraganset
Susquehanna
Tupi-guaraní
Yellowknife

12
Pasamaquoddy
San Ildefonso

13
Massachusetts

American presidents

4
Bush, George H.W.
Bush, George W.
Ford, Gerald R.
Polk, James K.
Taft, William H.

5
Adams, John & John Quincy
Grant, Ulysses S.
Hayes, Rutherford B.
Nixon, Richard M.
Tyler, John

6
Arthur, Chester A.
Carter, James E.
Hoover, Herbert C.
Monroe, James

Pierce, Franklin
Reagan, Ronald W.
Taylor, Zachary
Truman, Harry S.
Wilson, Woodrow

7
Clinton, William J. (Bill)
Harding, Warren G.
Jackson, Andrew
Johnson, Andrew & Lyndon B.
Kennedy, John F.
Lincoln, Abraham
Madison, James

8
Buchanan, James
Coolidge, Calvin
Fillmore, Millard

Garfield,   James A
Harrison,   Benjamin &
            William H.
McKinley,   William
Van Buren, Martin

9
Cleveland, Grover

Jefferson, Thomas
Roosevelt, Franklin D. &
            Theodore

10
Eisenhower, Dwight D.
Washington, George

American state capitals

5
Boise	(Idaho)
Dover	(Delaware)
Pierre	(South Dakota)
Salem	(Oregon)

6
Albany	(New York)
Austin	(Texas)
Boston	(Massachusetts)
Denver	(Colorado)
Helena	(Montana)
Juneau	(Alaska)
Lincoln	(Nebraska)
St Paul	(Minnesota)
Topeka	(Kansas)

7
Atlanta	(Georgia)
Augusta	(Maine)
Concord	(New Hampshire)
Jackson	(Mississippi)
Lansing	(Michigan)
Madison	(Wisconsin)
Olympia	(Washington)
Phoenix	(Arizona)

Raleigh	(North Carolina)
Santa Fe	(New Mexico)
Trenton	(New Jersey)

8
Bismarck	(North Dakota)
Cheyenne	(Wyoming)
Columbia	(South Carolina)
Columbus	(Ohio)
Honolulu	(Hawaii)
Richmond	(Virginia)

9
Annapolis	(Maryland)
Des Moines	(Iowa)
Frankfort	(Kentucky)
Nashville	(Tennessee)

10
Baton Rouge	(Louisiana)
Carson City	(Nevada)
Charleston	(West Virginia)
Harrisburg	(Pennsylvania)
Little Rock	(Arkansas)
Montgomery	(Alabama)
Montpelier	(Vermont)

Providence   (Rhode Island)
Sacramento   (California)

11

Tallahassee   (Florida
Springfield   (Illinois)

12

Indianapolis   (Indiana)
Oklahoma City   (Oklahoma)
Salt Lake City   (Utah)

13

Jefferson City   (Missouri)

American States

(including abbreviations and ZIP codes)

4

Iowa (Ia., Io)		IA
Ohio (O.)		OH
Utah (Ut.)		UT

5

Idaho (Id., Ida.)		ID
Maine (Me.)		ME
Texas (Tex.)		TX

6

Alaska		AK
Hawaii		HI
Kansas (Kans.)		KA
Nevada (Nev.)		NV
Oregon (Ore., Oreg.)		OR

7

Alabama (Ala.)		AL
Arizona (Ariz.)		AZ
Florida (Fla.)		FL
Georgia (Ga.)		GA
Indiana (Ind.)		IN
Montana (Mont.)		MT
New York (N.Y.)		NY
Vermont (Vt.)		VT

Wyoming (Wyo.)		WY

8

Arkansas	(Ark.)	AR
Colorado	(Colo.)	CO
Delaware	(Del.)	DE
Illinois	(Ill.)	IL
Kentucky	(Ken,Ky.)	KY
Maryland	(Md.)	MD
Michigan	(Mich.)	MI
Missouri	(Mo.)	MO
Nebraska	(Neb.,Nebr.)	NE
Oklahoma	(Okla.)	OK
Virginia	(Va.)	VA

9

Louisiana (La.)		LA
Minnesota (Minn.)		MN
New Jersey (N.J.)		NJ
New Mexico (N. M.,N.Mex.)		NM
Tennessee (Tenn.)		TN
Winconsin (Wis.)		WI

10

California (Cal.,Calif.)		CA
Washington (Wash.)		WA

11

Connecticut (Conn.)   CT
Mississippi (Miss.)   MS
North Dakota (N.D.,N.Dak)   ND
Rhode Island (R.I.)   RI
South Dakota (S.D.,S.Dak.)
 SD

12

New Hampshire (N.H.)   NH
Pennsylvania (Pa,Penn.)   PA

West Virginia (W.Va.)   WV

13

Massachusetts (Mass)   MA
North Carolina (N.C)   NC
South Carolina (S.C)   SC

15 +

District of Columbia (D.C)
                              DC

Animal groups

3

gam (whales)
mob (kangaroos)
nye (pheasants)
pod (seals,
  whales,whiting)
rag (colts)

4

army (frogs)
bale (turtles)
bevy (larks,
  quails, swans)
cast (hawks)
cete (badgers)
down (hares)
dule (doves,
  turtles)
fall (woodcock)
gang (elk)
haul (fish)
herd (antelope,
  asses, buffalo,
  cattle, cranes,
  deer, elephants,
  giraffes, goats,
  oxen, pigs,
  sheep, swine)
hive (bees)
host (sparrows)
husk (hares)
knob (pochards,
  teal, toads,
  widgeon)
leap (leopards)
lepe (leopards)
loft (pigeons)
mute (hounds)
nest (mice,
  rabbits,wasps)
nide (pheasants)
pace (asses)
pack (grouse,
  hounds,hyenas,
  wolves)
rush (pochards)
rout (wolves)
sord (mallards)
sute (mallards,
  wildfowl)
team (draught
  animals,oxen,
  young ducks)

walk (snipe)
wing (plovers)
wisp (snipe)
yoke (oxen)

5

brood (chickens,
  hens)
catch (fish)
charm (finches)
cloud (gnats)
covey (grouse,
  partridges)
crash (rhinos)
drift (swine)
drove
  (cattle,oxen)
flock (geese,
  goats, pigeons,
  sheep)
flush (mallards)
grist (bees)
plump (waterfowl)
pride (lions)
sedge (bitterns,
  cranes,herons)

shoal (fish)
siege (cranes,
  herons)
skein (flying
  geese)
skulk (foxes)
sloth (bears)
smuck (jellyfish)
swarm (bees, flies)
tribe (goats)
troop (antelopes,
  kangaroos, monkeys)
watch
  (nightingales)
wedge (swans)

6

clutch (hens)
colony (ants,
  gulls, herons)
covert (coots)
desert (lapwings)
flight (doves,
  ducks, pigeons,
  swallows)
gaggle (geese)
kennel (hounds,
  raches)
kindle (kittens)

labour (moles)
litter (cubs, kit-
  tens, pigs, pups)
murder (crows)
muster (peafowl)
school (fish,
  porpoises, whales)
sleuth (bears)
spring (teal)
warren (rabbits)

7

badling (ducks)
draught (fish)
clamour (rooks or
  starlings)
clouder (cats)
clowder (cats)
cluster (cats)
company (widgeon)
dopping (sheldrake)
rookery (penguins,
  rooks, seals)
sounder (pigs)

8

building (rooks)
fesnying (ferrets)
paddling (ducks)
richesse (martens)
singular (boars)

9

badelynge (ducks)
mustering (storks)

10

chattering
  (choughs)
exaltation (larks)
shrewdness (apes)
unkindness
  (ravens)

11

murmuration
  (starlings)

12

congregation
  (plovers)

Architectural terms

3	4			attic	inlay
bay	ambo	dado	pele	conge	Ionic
cap	anta	dais	peel	crown	lobby
die	apse	dome	stoa	crypt	newel
eye	arch	fret		Doric	niche
key	band	frog	**5**	foils	ogive
	bead	fust	aisle	gable	ovolo
	bell	jamb	ambry	glyph	Roman
		nave	arris	helix	scape
		ogee			

Architectural terms

shaft
shank
socle
talon
tenia
torus
Tudor
verge

6

abacus
access
alcove
almery
arcade
ashlar
atrium
attick
aumbry
aumery
belfry
bonnet
broach
canopy
chevet
column
corbel
corona
crenel
cupola
dagger
dentil
diaper
facade
fillet
finial
flèche
fresco
frieze
gablet
gazebo
Gothic
guttae
heroic
impost

lancet
lesene
lierne
lintel
lintol
loggia
louvre
mantel
metope
Minoan
mutule
Norman
oculus
patera
pillar
plinth
pulpit
quadra
regula
rococo
scapus
screen
scroll
sedile
soffit
Tuscan
trophy
urella
vestry
volute
wreath
xystus
zig-zag

7

annulet
arch rib
astylar
balcony
baroque
bastion
boultin
butment
calotte
capital

cavetto
chancel
chebron
cornice
crochet
crocket
distyle
Eastern
echinus
encarpa
entasis
eustyle
festoon
fleuron
fluting
gadroon
galilee
gallery
Grecian
lacunar
lantern
lattice
lequear
lunette
narthex
nulling
obelisk
oratory
parvise
portail
portico
postern
pteroma
redding
regency
reredos
rosette
rotunda
roundel
scallop
Spanish
systyle
tessara
tondino
tracery
transom

trumeau
zikurat

8

abutment
acanthus
astragal
aedicula
apophyge
arenated
astragal
atlantes
baluster
bartizan
basilica
beak head
buttress
caryatid
cimborio
cincture
crenelle
cresting
cymatium
diastyle
dipteral
dog-tooth
edge roll
Egyptian
extrados
formeret
gargoyle
intrados
Jacobean
keel arch
keystone
lich gate
lych gate
miserere
pavilion
pedestal
pediment
pilaster
predella
pulpitum
rocaille

spandrel
spandril
spirelet
Sumerian
torching
transept
triglyph
tympanum
verandha
vignette
voussoir
wainscot
zikkurat
ziggurat

9

acropolis
antefixae
anthemion
apex stone
arabesque
arch brick
archivolt
attic base
bird's
  beak
Byzantine
campanile
canephora
cartouche
castellum
caulicoli
cloisters
colonnade
Composite
decorated
dripstone
foliation
hexastyle
hypocaust
hypostyle
ingle nook
label stop
lacunaria
linenfold

mezzanine
mouldings
octastyle
Palladian
refectory
sgraffito
stanchion
strapwork
stylobate
trabeated
triforium
trilithon
vestibule
zoophorus

10

acroterion
abmulatory
araeostyle
architrave
baldachino

ball flower
balustrade
battlemen
caryatides
cinquefoil
colonnette
Corinthian
egg and dart
enrichment
hagioscope
Lady chapel
lancet arch
misericord
modillions
pietra dura
presbytery
pycnostyle
quatrefoil
Romanesque
rood screen
rose window
sexpartite

tetrastyle
trachelion

11

castellated
entablature
fan vaulting
harelip arch
leaded light
mantelpiece
mantelshelf
oriel window
rectilinear
Renaissance
reticulated

12

amphitheatre
blind tracery
cockle stairs

Early English
egg and
  tongue
lancet window
porte-cochère
superimposed
transitional

13

amphi-pros-
  tyle
Perpendicular

14

angular capi-
  tal
flying but-
  tress
hypotrache-
  lion

Arthurian legend

(Kn = knight)

3

Amr
Cai   (Kn)
Cei   (Kn)
Kay   (Kn)

4

Anna
Bors   (Kn)
Bran
Bron
Drem
Erec   (Kn)
Loth
Lugh
Mark   (King)

Menw
Urry   (Kn)

5

Annwn
Balan
Balin
Cabal
Clust
Damas
Ector   (Kn)
Eidyn
Enide
Gorre
Grail
Gwair

Gwynn
Hélie
Linet
Llwch
Lucan   (Kn)
Mabon
Mador   (Kn)
Olwen
Owain   (Kn)
Troit
Urien   (King)
Uther
Yvain   (Kn)

6

Arthur
Avalon
Bedwyr (Kn)
Boarte (Kn)
Brisen
Cafall
Cedric
Elaine
Evrain
  (King)
Gareth
  (Kn)
Gawain
  (Kn)
Gildas
Helake

Helias
Lionel   (Kn)
Logres
Lunete
Meliot   (Kn)
Melwas
Merlin
Modred   (Kn)
Morgan
Pelles   (King)
Pisear   (King)
Yseult

7

Accolon
Astolat
Brewnor
Caer Gai
Camelot
Camille
Camlann
Culhwch
Dinodan   (Kn)
Escolat
Ettarde
Gaheris   (Kn)
Galahad   (Kn)
Galigan
Ganadin
Gorlois
Guiomar   (Kn)
Gwythyr
Lamorak
Lyonors
Medraut
Morholt
Mordred   (Kn)
Niniane
Niviene
Pelleas   (Kn)
Pryderi
Prydwen
Tristan   (Kn)
Viviane
Viviene

Ygraine

8

Afarnach
Agravain   (Kn)
Amesbury
Avallach
Bedivere   (Kn)
Bercilak
Brangane
Caerleon
Caer Wydr
Corbenic
Galahalt   (Kn)
Hellawes
Lancelot   (Kn)
Leodegan   (King)
Morgause
Perceval
Rhiannon
Sangreal
Taliesin
Tintagel
Tristram   (Kn)

9

Agravaine
Alexander   (Kn)
Caer Siddi
Excalibur
Gornement
Grail King   (The)
Gringolet
Guinevere
Guinglain   (Kn)
Guingmars
Gwalchmei
Hermaunce   (King)
Holy Grail   (The)
Holy Lance   (The)
La Pucelle
Launcelot   (Kn)
Manawydan
Meleagant

Palug's Cat
Palomides   (Kn)
Pellinore   (King)
Trebuchet
Vortigern
Waste Land

10

Baudemagus   (King)
Belle Garde
Black Witch   (The)
Blanchflor
Caledfwlch
Creiddylad
Cup of Llwyr
Fisher King   (The)
Gwenhwyfar
Joyous Isle
Lost Forest
Maimed King   (The)
Rich Fisher
Round Table   (The)
Ysbadadden

11

City of Glass
Fair Unknown
Glastonbury
Grail Bearer (The)
Grail Keeper (The)
Green Chapel
Green Knight (The)
Isle of Glass
Joyous Garde
Lady Laudine
Mabonagrain
Morgan le Fay
Perilous Bed
Twrch Trwyth

12

Caer Feddiwid
Golden Island

Isle of Apples
Isle of Avalon
Lady Lyonesse
Orgueilleuse
Perilous Ford

Mound of Arberth
Perilous Forest
Queen of Denmark
Uther Pendragon

13

Blonde Esmerée
Drwst Iron Fist
Fairy Fortress
Glass Fortress
Isle of Maidens
Lady of the Lake (The)
Loathly Damsel (The)
Questing Beast (The)
Siege Perilous
Weeping Castle
Yseult the Fair

14

Boar of Cornwall (The)
Bran the Blessed
Castle Perilous
Esclados the Red
Mador de la Porte (Kn)

15 +

Alexander the Orphan (Kn)
Battle of Camlann
Broceliande Forest
Castle of Evil Adventure
Castle of Maidens
Castle of Wonders
Cauldron of Diwrnach
Demon Cat of Lausanne (The)
Drinking Horn of Gwlgawd
Echel Pierced Thigh
Fortress of Carousel
Harbin of the Mountain
King Mark of Cornwall
Knight with the Lion
Magic Cauldron of Annwn
Maiden of the White Hands
Table of Gwyddneu Long Leg
Valley of No Return
Waste City of Senaudon
Yseult of the White Hands

Artists

3	Key	**4**	Caro	Dufy	Gere	Hand
Arp	Lam	Adam	Cima	Dyce	Gill	Hare
Apt	Lee	Ager	Cole	Dyck	Goes	Hart
Cox	Low	Agam	Colt	Earl	Gogh	Heba
Baj	Mor	Ball	Cuyp	East	Good	Hemy
Bol	May	Bell	Dadd	Etty	Gore	Herp
Dix	Nay	Bird	Dali	Eves	Goya	Holl
Dou	Pot	Bone	Deas	Eyck	Graf	Home
Egg	Poy	Both	Dick	Faed	Gray	Hone
Fry	Puy	Boyd	Dine	Falk	Gris	Hook
Fyt	Ryn	Burn	Dodd	Fehr	Gros	Huet
Gay	Vos	Bush	Doré	Feke	Guys	Hunt
Gow	Wit	Carr	Dove	Ford	Hall	Ives
			Duca	Gabo	Hals	Jack

Jorn	Rizi	**5**	Cione	Gaddi	Le Vau
John	Rohe		Clark	Gallo	Lewis
Judd	Rops	Aalto	Clint	Gaudí	Lippi
Juel	Ross	Abbey	Cohen	Gaunt	Lotto
Kalf	Rush	Adams	Cooke	Genga	Lowry
Kane	Sage	Adler	Corot	Gibbs	Lucas
Katz	Sant	Allan	Cossa	Giles	Manet
Kaus	Shaw	Allen	Costa	Golub	Maris
Kent	Shee	Amiet	Cotes	Gorky	Mason
Kerr	Shin	Amman	Craig	Gotch	Mauve
King	Sime	Andre	Crane	Goyen	Mense
Klee	Sims	Ajlak	Credi	Greco	Metso
Koch	Smet	Arman	Crome	Grant	Mills
Koen	Soto	Appel	Curry	Grosz	Milne
Laer	Spee	Auger	Dalou	Gully	Mochi
Lamb	Swan	Avery	Danby	Haden	Moira
Lane	Tait	Bacon	David	Haghe	Monet
Lear	Todd	Baily	Davie	Hayes	Moore
Leck	Toft	Bakic	Davis	Healy	Muche
Lely	Tome	Balla	Degas	Heron	Munch
Lion	Tosi	Banks	Denny	Hicks	Myron
Long	Town	Barry	Devis	Holty	Nebot
Luks	Troy	Barye	Dixon	Hooch	Neefs
Mack	Tuke	Bates	Dolci	Huber	Nervi
Maes	Turo	Beale	Dosse	Inman	Nicol
Mara	Ubac	Beham	Doyle	Innes	Noble
Marc	Uden	Bevin	Drury	Itten	Nolde
Meit	Uhde	Bezzi	Dürer	Jacob	North
Mena	Vien	Bigot	Dulac	Jance	Okada
Miró	Vita	Birch	Dupré	Johns	Orley
Mola	Wade	Blake	Elias	Jones	Orpen
Nash	Wain	Blume	Ensor	Keene	Oudry
Nast	Ward	Boehm	Ernst	Keith	Pajou
Neer	Watt	Bolgi	Estes	Kelly	Palma
Nost	Webb	Bosch	Evans	Kitja	Pater
Opie	Weir	Bough	Exter	Klein	Payne
Orsi	West	Breer	Ferri	Klimt	Peale
Owen	Witz	Brett	Finui	Kolbe	Penny
Page	Wols	Brock	Flint	Kraft	Piper
Pane	Wood	Brown	Foley	Kroll	Plaas
Peto	Wren	Bundy	Freud	Kurin	Platt
Post	Wyck	Burra	Frink	Laing	Ponte
Pyne	Zick	Caffa	Frith	Lance	Ponti
Reid	Zorn	Carra	Frost	Leech	Poole
Reni		Cesar	Fuger	Leger	Prout
Rich		Chase	Furse	Lemon	Proot

Pryde	Vivan	Braque	Ferber	Isabey
Pryse	Vonet	Briggs	Ferren	Ivanon
Puget	Watts	Brough	Fildes	Jagger
Pugin	Wells	Brunel	Finlay	Jarvis
Pynas	White	Buchel	Fisher	Jennys
Rabin	Wiens	Burnet	Flavin	Joseph
Redon	Woods	Burton	Floris	Kantor
Ricci	Wyatt	Butler	Forbes	Kaprow
Riley	Wyeth	Bylert	Foster	Kessel
Rodin	Wylie	Calder	Fraser	Kettle
Rooke	Yanes	Callow	French	Keyser
Rossi	Yeats	Campin	Fuller	Knight
Ryder	Zoppo	Carter	Fuseli	Kramer
Ryman		Casson	Geddes	Kruger
Sands		Chabot	Gellée	Laroon
Saura	**6**	Claude	Gérard	Laszlo
Scott		Clouet	Gerome	Latham
Segna	Aachen	Clovie	Gibson	Lavery
Short	Abbate	Colton	Gilman	Lawson
Siloe	Abbott	Conder	Ginner	Leader
Sleap	Aikman	Cooper	Giotto	Lebrun
Small	Albers	Copley	Girtin	Ledoux
Smith	Allori	Corbet	Glover	Legros
Soane	Antigo	Cotman	Goethe	Le Nain
Soest	Archer	Cowper	Gordon	Le Witt
Somer	Arnold	Cozens	Graham	Leslie
Speed	Ashbee	Currie	Greuze	Linton
Staël	Ashton	Dahmen	Guardi	Lurcat
Stark	Ayrton	Davies	Gulich	Mabuse
Steen	Barker	Dawson	Hacker	McEvoy
Steer	Barton	Deacon	Hanson	Manson
Stone	Baskin	Derain	Harral	Marden
Stott	Bawden	De Wint	Haydon	Marini
Studd	Behnes	Dobson	Heckel	Martin
Sully	Benson	Dobell	Helion	Massys
Tacco	Benton	Donner	Hilton	Merida
Tassi	Berman	Draper	Holmes	Mesdac
Testa	Bettes	Du Bois	Hodges	Millet
Tobey	Bewick	Duccio	Hopper	Miller
Tonks	Biddle	Dunbar	Howard	Monaco
Towne	Birley	Dunlop	Hudson	Morley
Udine	Bishop	Eakins	Hughes	Morone
Unwin	Blanch	Elwell	Hunter	Morris
Uwins	Blythe	Ellard	Ingles	Morrow
Vanni	Bodley	Erlach	Ingres	MÜller
Velde	Boudin	Eworth	Inness	Murphy
	Boxall			

Murray	Romney	Verrio	Bearden	Cortona
Mytens	Rothko	Vertue	Beechey	Courbet
Neagle	Rouault	Vignon	Belcher	Cranach
Negret	Rubens	Villon	Bellini	Cundell
Newman	Ruskin	Walker	Bellows	Currier
Newton	Saachi	Waller	Bennett	Dalziel
Nisbet	Sadler	Wallis	Bercham	Daniell
Noland	Sandby	Walton	Bernard	Daumier
Obrist	Sandys	Wardle	Bernini	Da Vinci
Oliver	Savery	Warhol	Bianchi	De Hooch
Olsson	Scully	Watson	Bingham	Deineka
O'Neill	Seddon	Weekes	Boamyer	Dekkers
Ostade	Serres	Weenix	Boldini	Delvaux
Paalen	Seurat	Weight	Bomberg	De Lazlo
Palmer	Signac	Weyden	Bonnard	Dicksee
Panini	Sisley	Wilkie	Boshier	Diderot
Parker	Sluter	Wilson	Boucher	Dighton
Parton	Smirke	Wittel	Bramley	Dorazio
Paxton	Smythe	Windus	Brauner	Douglas
Pegram	Sodoma	Wright	Bridell	Downman
Pellan	Spagna	Wyllie	Brouwer	Duchamp
Penley	Spence	Wynter	Burlink	Edridge
Pereda	Stokes	Yeames	Calvert	Edwards
Perret	Storck	Yvaral	Camargo	El Greco
Pettie	Storey	Zenale	Cameron	Emanuel
Pierce	Strang	Zucchi	Campion	Epstein
Pignon	Strube		Carraci	Falcone
Piombo	Stuart		Cellini	Ferrari
Pimmer	Stubbs	**7**	Cennini	Flaxman
Pisano	Tadema		Cézanne	Fontana
Potter	Tamayo	Acconci	Chagall	Fouquet
Powers	Tanguy	Aersten	Chardin	Fox-Pitt
Predis	Tatlin	Alberti	Charles	Francia
Raffet	Tayler	Algardi	Cheston	Francke
Ramsay	Taylor	Allston	Chirico	Froment
Renoir	Thomas	Amigoni	Christo	Furniss
Ribera	Tissot	Andrews	Chryssa	Gabriel
Riccio	Titian	Appleby	Cimabue	Gallego
Ridley	Tocque	Aretino	Clausen	Garstin
Rimmer	Troyon	Arundel	Cockram	Gauguin
Rivera	Turner	Baldung	Cocteau	Gertler
Rivers	Vacher	Balthos	Collier	Gertlin
Robbia	Valdes	Barlach	Collins	Gibbons
Robert	Van Ryn	Barocci	Connard	Gifford
Rogers	Varley	Bassano	Corinth	Gilbert
Romano	Vernet	Bateman	Cornell	Gillray
		Bazille		

Goodall	Klinger	Mueller	Raphael	Van Dyck
Goodwin	Knapton	Murillo	Rattner	Van Eyck
Gozzoli	Kneller	Nasmith	Resnick	Van Gogh
Greaves	Knights	Nattier	Reveron	Valadon
Gregory	Kooning	Neumann	Richier	Vaughan
Grimmer	Kossoff	Noguchi	Riviere	Vecchio
Gropius	Krasner	O'Connor	Roberts	Vellert
Guarini	La Fosse	O'Gorman	Rouault	Vermeer
Guevara	Lambert	Olitzki	Roussel	Vischer
Guthrie	Lancret	Onushto	Russell	von Elst
Haberle	Lanteri	Orcagna	Rustici	Vostell
Hackert	Laurens	Orchard	Samaras	Warburg
Harding	Lemoyne	Osborne	Sanchez	Watteau
Hartley	Lenbach	Ordonez	Sargent	Webster
Hartung	Lessore	Pacchia	Schetky	Westall
Hayward	Levitan	Pacheco	Schiele	Whiting
Herbert	Linnell	Parrish	Sedgely	Whitley
Herring	Llander	Parsons	Seghers	Wildens
Hillier	Lochner	Pasmore	Seymour	Woolner
Hobbema	Lombard	Peacock	Shannon	Wootton
Hockney	Lorenzo	Penrose	Shields	Wynants
Hodgkin	Lucidel	Perreal	Sickert	Yunkers
Hofland	Macbeth	Peruzzi	Siddall	Zadkins
Hofmann	Maccoli	Pevsner	Simpson	Zoffany
Hogarth	Maclise	Phidias	Smetham	Zuccaro
Hokusai	Maderno	Philips	Snyders	
Holbein	Maillol	Phillip	Solomon	
Holland	Maistre	Philpot	Spencer	**8**
Holroyd	Mancini	Picabia	Stanley	Aaltonen
Hoppner	Mansart	Picasso	Stevens	Agostini
Hopwood	Maratti	Pickard	Stimmer	Albright
Horsley	Martini	Pigalle	Strozzi	Allinson
Hoskins	Matisse	Pinwell	Tanning	Amberger
Housman	Meadows	Pittoni	Teniers	Angelico
Humphry	Memlinc	Polenus	Tenniel	Annesley
Indiana	Merritt	Pollock	Thirtle	Annigoni
Isakson	Metcalf	Pomeroy	Thomson	Armitage
Israels	Meunier	Pourbus	Tibaldi	Armstead
Jackson	Michaux	Poussin	Tiepolo	Atkinson
Jaggers	Millais	Poynter	Tiffany	Augustin
Jenkins	Mitchel	Prinsep	Torelli	Aumonier
Jespers	Morales	Preston	Tunnard	Avercamp
Johnson	Morandi	Pucelle	Uccello	Basissio
Joulett	Morisot	Quellan	Ugolino	Bauchant
Kallela	Morland	Rackham	Utamaro	Beaumont
Kensett	Morrice	Raeburn	Utrillo	Beckmann

Beerbohm	Dubuffet	Jordaens	Palladio	Terbosch
Bellange	Dufresne	Kaufmann	Papworth	Tidemand
Bellotto	Eastlake	Kaulbach	Paolozzi	Tinguely
Boccioni	Eggeling	Kienholz	Passmore	Topolski
Boffraud	Etchelle	Kirchner	Paul Nash	Tournier
Boughton	Evergood	Kokoshka	Pederson	Turnbull
Brabazon	Falconet	Kollwitz	Perugino	Vanbrugh
Bramante	Fancelli	Kruseman	Phillips	Van Cleve
Brancusi	Ferguson	Kupetszky	Pissarro	Van Goyen
Brangwyn	Fielding	Lachaise	Pomodoro	Van Steen
Brearley	Flanagan	Landseer	Pontormo	Vasarely
Breitner	Fontaine	Lawrence	Pynacker	Verbeeck
Bronzine	Frampton	Leighton	Raimondi	Vermeyen
Brooking	Garofalo	Leonardo	Redgrave	Veronese
Breughel	Gerhaert	Logsdail	Regnault	Vigeland
Caffière	Ghiberti	Lombardo	Reynolds	Vittoria
Calderon	Gibbings	Lariondu	Richmond	Vlaminck
Callcott	Giordand	Macallum	Ricketts	Vuillard
Calthorp	Giovanni	Macquoid	Robinson	Waterlow
Cappelle	Goldberg	Magnelli	Rockwell	Wheatley
Carducci	Gonzales	Magritte	Romanino	Whistler
Carracci	Gottlieb	Maitland	Rombouts	Willcock
Carrière	Granacci	Mantegna	Rossetti	Williams
Chambers	Greenway	Marshall	Rousseau	Willinck
Champney	Grimaldi	Masaccio	Rugendas	Woodward
Chandler	Grimshaw	Melville	Rushbury	Zakharov
Chantrey	Hamilton	Melondez	Saarinen	Zurbarán
Christus	Hartwell	Millares	Salviati	
Colville	Hartigan	Mondrian	Sassetta	**9**
Cousteau	Hepworth	Montalba	Scamozzi	Ackermann
Crawford	Herkomer	Montanes	Scheffer	Alexander
Crawhall	Highmore	Montegna	Schinkel	Antonella
Creswick	Hilliard	Mortimer	Segonzac	Appleyard
Crivelli	Hitchens	Moynihan	Severini	Ardizzone
Darboven	Hodgkins	Muirhead	Simmonds	Armstrong
Daubigny	Holloway	Mulready	Smithson	Aston Webb
De Keyser	Houghton	Munnings	Solimena	Baizerman
De Laszlo	Hultberg	Nadelman	Solrenson	Bakhinzen
Delaunay	Ibbetson	Nanteuil	Spinello	Beardsley
Del Prete	Inchbold	Naviasky	Springer	Bickerton
Delville	Ironside	Nesfield	Stanhope	Biederman
Desnoyer	Jacobsen	Nevinson	Stothard	Blackburn
Deverell	Jamesone	Niemeyer	Streeter	Blakelock
Dietrich	Jan Steen	Oliveira	Stringer	Blanchard
Domenico	John Opie	Overbesk	Sullivan	Bonington
Dressler	Johnston	Ozenfant	Taiebaut	Botticini

Boulicant	Hitchcock	Poliakoff	Brockhurst
Branwhite	Honthorst	Portinari	Burchfield
Brustolon	Houbraken	Ravilious	Burne-Jones
Caldecott	Hurlstone	Reinharot	Carraciole
Caulfield	Immendorf	Rembrandt	Caravaggio
Canaletto	Jacobello	Remington	Carmichael
Cavallini	Jawlensky	Romanello	Cattermole
Collinson	Josephson	Roubillac	Chasseriau
Colquhoon	Kandinsky	Salisbury	Courturier
Constable	Kauffmann	Sansovino	Cruikshank
Cornelius	Kemp-Welch	Schafener	D'Arcangelo
Correggio	Kiprensky	Schalcken	Del Pacchia
Courtauld	Kokoschka	Segantini	Diebenkorn
De Fresnov	Kreighoff	Singleton	di Giovanni
Delacroix	Lancaster	Stanfield	Eilshemius
Delaroche	Lanfranco	Steenwyck	Epiphanius
d'Erlanger	La Thangue	Steinberg	Everdingen
Dominguez	Laurencin	Stevenson	Fiddes-Watt
Donaldson	Lee-Hankey	Strudwick	Finoguerra
Donatello	Lightfoot	Telemaque	Freundlich
Elsheimer	Llewellyn	Thornhill	Friedenson
Everdiner	Lundquist	Tischbein	Fulleylove
Fahlstrom	Lundstrom	Trevisani	Giacometti
Farington	MacDonald	Woodville	Glendening
Feininger	MacGregor	Velazquez	Goncharova
Fergusson	MacKennal	Verrochio	Grandville
Fernandez	McLachlan	Waterford	Guillaumin
Flannagan	McWhirter	Whitcombe	Hammershoi
Fragonard	Maleevich	Yamaguchi	Heartfield
Friedrich	Martineau	Yoshihara	Hildebrand
Fromentin	Maundrell		Holman-Hunt
Gastineau	Mazzolino		Hornebottle
Generalic	Mestrovic	**10**	Huntingdon
Géricault	Metzinger	Alechinsky	Ipousteguy
Gillespie	Mondriaan	Alma-Tadema	Isenbrandt
Giorgione	Mortenson	Altichiero	Jan van Eyck
Greenhill	Multscher	Archipenko	Kennington
Greenough	Nicholson	Arcimsoldo	La Brocquey
Griffiths	Norhtcote	Baddelaire	La Fresnaye
Grünewald	Oldenburg	Bandinelli	Lethbridge
Guido Reni	Oppenheim	Bellegambi	Liebermann
Halswelle	Pechstein	Berrucuete	Lienberger
Hatherell	Peselling	Blashfield	Lorenzetti
Haussmann	Pettoruti	Botticelli	Mackintosh
Hawksmoor	Peverelli	Bramantino	Macmonnies
Henderson	Pisanello	Breenbergh	Marcoussis

Haynes-Williams
Riccidi Lorenzo
Schmidt Rutluff

15 +
Arnold di Cambo
Augustino de Duccio
Baranoff Russine
Cornetille de Lyon
Giovanni da Milano

Giovanni di Bondone
Lawes Witteronge
Leonardo da Vinci
Pietro de Cortonia
Puvis de Chavannes
Rembrandt van Ryn
Theodoric of Prague
Theophanes the Greek
Toulouse-Lautrec
Van Huchenburgh
Vitale da Bolugna

Australian Prime Ministers

4
Cook,   Sir J.
Holt,   Harold
Page,   Sir Earle
Reid,   Sir G.

5
Bruce, Stanley M.
Forde, F.M.
Hawke, Robert
Lyons, Joseph A.

6
Barton, Sir Edmund
Curtin, John
Deakin, Alfred
Fadden, A.W.
Fisher, Andrew
Fraser, Malcolm
Gorton, J.G.
Howard, John
Hughes, William M.
McEwen, John
Watson, John

7
Chifley, J.B.
Keating, Paul
McMahon, William
Menzies, Sir
  Robert G.
Scullin, J.H.
Whitlam, Gough

Authors, philosophers, poets and playwrights

2 & 3
Ady
Aho
Arp
Ash
Dam
Fry
Gay
Hay
Kyd

Lee
Paz
Poe
Sue
Vas

4
Agee
Alan
Amis

Asch
Ayer
Ayme
Ball
Bana
Baum
Beer
Benn
Blok
Blox
Boll

Bolt
Boye
Buck
Bull
Cats
Cary
Char
Cruz
Dahl
Dons
Dues

Du Fu
Eich
Folz
Ford
Frug
Fust
Gide
Glyn
Gray
Grey
Hein

Heym
Hoel
Hood
Hope
Hugo
Hume
Hunt
Ilie
Jens
Kant
Kirk

Authors, philosophers, poets and playwrights

Kiss	Vraz	Brant	Harte	Meyer	Rozov
Koch	Wain	Broch	Hasek	Milne	Sachs
Kock	Ward	Bunin	Hauff	Monti	Sagan
Lamb	Webb	Burns	Haugh	Moore	Scene
Lang	West	Butor	Hegel	Murry	Scott
Lear	Wood	Byron	Heine	Musil	Seton
Lenz	Wren	Camus	Henry	Myers	Shute
Livy	Wyss	Capek	Henty	Nashe	Simms
Lobb	Zola	Carew	Hertz	Nazor	Simon
Loos	Zech	Clare	Hesse	Novak	Smart
Mann		Colum	Heyse	Noyes	Smith
Marx		Cople	Homer	Odets	Spark
Melo	**5**	Cosie	Hooft	O'Hara	Staël
Mill	Abell	Craik	Hulme	Olsen	Staff
More	Aboab	Crane	Ibsen	Opitz	Stein
Muir	Acton	Croce	Imber	Orczy	Storm
Munk	Acuna	Dante	Jahnn	Orton	Stowe
Nash	Adams	Dario	James	Otway	Svevo
Nexo	Aesop	Defoe	Jarry	Ouida	Swift
Obey	Agnon	Deval	Jasik	Paine	Synge
Oles	Ahlin	Donne	Jones	Pan Gu	Szabo
Ovid	Albee	Doyle	Joyce	Pater	Talev
Perk	Arany	Dumas	Kafka	Paton	Tasso
Pope	Arden	Duras	Kaleb	Peake	Testi
Read	Arnim	Dutch	Keats	Peele	Thoor
Renn	Asnyk	Eeden	Kemal	Peguy	Tieck
Rhys	Auden	Eliot	Kesey	Pepys	Tompa
Rode	Ayres	Elyot	Kidde	Perse	Tuwim
Roth	Barry	Ewald	Kinck	Piron	Twain
Rowe	Barth	Freud	Kraus	Plath	Tynan
Ruiz	Bates	Frost	Larra	Plato	Tzara
Rung	Bazin	Gatti	Leino	Pliny	Udall
Saar	Beets	Genet	Lewis	Pound	Urban
Sade	Behan	Gogol	Locke	Powys	Vadja
Sa'Di	Bello	Gorki	Lodge	Prati	Varro
Saki	Belyl	Gosse	Logue	Preti	Verde
Sand	Bembo	Gower	Lorca	Prior	Verne
Shaw	Benda	Grass	Lowry	Pulci	Vidal
Smaj	Benet	Green	Lucan	Raabe	Vigny
Snow	Berni	Greig	Lucas	Raine	Virta
Soya	Bette	Grimm	Macha	Ramuz	Waley
Stub	Blake	Guidi	Marot	Reade	Waugh
Toth	Bloem	Hacks	Marsh	Rezac	Weiss
Tate	Bolto	Halbe	Marti	Ridja	Wells
Urfe	Bojer	Halle	Mason	Rilke	White
Vega	Bowen	Hardy	Matos	Rolfe	Wilde

Wolfe	Belloc	Coppee	Hebbel	Ludwig	Pinter
Woolf	Bellow	Coward	Heller	Lu Hsun	Piozzi
Wyatt	Becque	Cowley	Hesiod	Lytton	Plomer
Yeats	Ben-Ami	Cowper	Hierro	Machen	Porter
Yonge	Benson	Crabbe	Hilton	Mailer	Potter
Zesen	Besant	Cretin	Hobbes	Malory	Prados
Zeyer	Bialik	Cronin	Hoddis	Marino	Proust
Zorin	Bierce	Curtis	Hojeda	Marner	Racine
Zweig	Binyon	Daumal	Holmes	Mendes	Ramlar
	Blyton	Daniel	Horace	Mercer	Ramsay
	Bocage	Daudet	Hudson	Millay	Ransom
6	Borges	Davies	Hughes	Miller	Raynal
Accius	Borrow	Dehmel	Huxley	Milton	Reizen
Adamov	Brecht	Dekker	Illyes	Moberg	Restif
Alcott	Bremer	de Sade	Irving	Modena	Reuter
Aldana	Breton	Donnay	Isaacs	Molnar	Rhigas
Aldiss	Bridie	Dowson	Ivanov	Morgan	Roland
Aleman	Brieux	Dryden	Jammes	Morike	Rowley
Alfasi	Brontë	Dunbar	Jensen	Muller	Runyon
Algren	Brooke	Durych	Jonson	Munthe	Ruskin
Ambler	Brophy	Ekelof	Jotuni	Murger	Samain
Andres	Browne	Eluard	Jovine	Murray	Sandel
Andric	Bryant	Empson	Kaiser	Musset	Sapper
Aprily	Buchan	Ennius	Kallas	Nechun	Sappho
Aquino	Bunyan	Evelyn	Kalvos	Neruda	Sardou
Aragon	Burger	Falcao	Keller	Nemeth	Sartre
Archer	Burney	Fichte	Kleist	Nerval	Savage
Arnold	Butler	Fouque	Kostic	Nesbit	Sayers
Ascham	Caesar	Fowles	Kramer	Njegos	Scribe
Aseyeu	Camoes	France	Krieza	Norwid	Seneca
Asimov	Capote	Frisch	Kumick	O'Brien	Sereni
Aubrey	Carson	Fugard	Laclos	O'Casey	Sidney
Austen	Castro	Fuller	Landor	Olesha	Silone
Azorin	Cayrol	Gaiser	Lanier	O'Neill	Singer
Azuela	Cavafy	Gibbon	Lao-Tse	Onerva	Smiles
Balzac	Celine	Gibran	Larkin	Orwell	Sponde
Barbey	Celaya	Goethe	Larney	Pagnal	Stampa
Barham	Celtis	Grabbe	Lateur	Parker	Steele
Barker	Chekov	Graham	Lawler	Pascal	Sterne
Barnes	Cibber	Graves	Le Fanu	Pavese	Stoker
Baroja	Clarke	Greene	Lefort	Pereda	Storey
Barres	Clough	Grossi	Leonov	Perron	Stramm
Barrie	Coffin	Guitry	Lesage	Petofi	Surrey
Basile	Colman	Habana	Lidman	Picard	Symons
Baudri	Conrad	Hamsun	London	Pindar	Tagore
Bellay	Cooper	Harris	Lowell	Pinero	Talvio

Tarsis	Anouilh	Centina	Foscolo	Kerouac
Thomas	Aquineas	Chamson	Freneau	Kipling
Toller	Arbuzon	Chapman	Freytag	Kirshon
Torres	Aretino	Chaucer	Froding	Klinger
Toulet	Arghezi	Chekhov	Gabirol	Knudsen
Traven	Ariosto	Chenier	Gallico	Labiche
Uhland	Arrabal	Chu Yuan	Garnier	Lardner
Elevic	Azevedo	Clauden	Garrett	Layamon
Undset	Babusse	Cleland	Gaskell	Leacock
Updike	Balchin	Cocteau	Gautier	Le Carre
Uppdal	Baldwin	Cobbett	Gilbert	Lehmann
Valery	Barbour	Colette	Gippius	Lessing
Vesaas	Baretti	Collins	Gissing	Lindsay
Vidric	Beckett	Conetti	Golding	Lydgate
Villon	Beddoes	Corelli	Grahame	Machaut
Virgil	Belleau	Crashaw	Gresser	McKenna
Vondel	Bellman	Creeley	Guarini	Malamud
Wagner	Bennett	da Ponte	Gunther	Malraux
Walden	Bentham	Deledda	Haggard	Manzoni
Waller	Bentley	Delille	Hammett	Marceau
Walser	Bergman	Desnick	Hansson	Marlowe
Walton	Bergson	de Vigny	Hartley	Marryat
Warton	Bernard	Dickens	Hartman	Marston
Werfel	Blunden	Diderot	Hazlitt	Martial
Wesker	Boiardo	Dinesen	Heiberg	Martins
Wilder	Boileau	Dodgson	Hellman	Marvell
Wilson	Boreman	Douglas	Herbert	Masters
Wolker	Boswell	Drabble	Hermans	Maugham
Wotton	Bousono	Drayton	Herrick	Mauriac
Wright	Boutens	Dreiser	Heywood	Maurois
Yovkou	Bo Zhu Yi	Duhamel	Holberg	Medrona
	Bradley	Dunsany	Hopkins	Mencken
	Brandao	Durrell	Housman	Mercier
7	Bridges	Ekelund	Huygens	Merimée
	Bronson	Emerson	Ibn Ezra	Mishima
Aakjeer	Buchner	Ercilla	Iffland	Mistral
Addison	Burgess	Eupolis	Ionesco	Molière
Aelfric	Burnett	Ferrier	Jeffers	Montagu
Aguilar	Buzzati	Feullet	Jimenez	Montale
Aksakov	Cadalso	Feydeau	Jodelle	Moravia
Alarcon	Caedmon	Firbank	Johnson	Morante
Alberti	Campana	Flecker	Juvenal	Moretti
Alcaeus	Cao Chan	Fleming	Kassack	Murdoch
Aldanov	Carossa	Folengo	Kastner	Nabokov
Aldrich	Carroll	Fontane	Kaufman	Naevius
Alegria	Cernuda	Forster	Kendall	Nagibin
Aneirin				

Naipaul	Spencer	Andersen	De la Mare	Leopardi
Neumann	Spender	Anderson	De Musset	Lockhart
Novalis	Spenser	Annensky	Disraeli	Longinus
Obaldia	Spinoza	Apuleius	Donleavy	Lovelace
O'Connor	Stevens	Asturias	Du Bartas	Macaulay
Osborne	Surtees	Atterbom	Elsschot	Macleish
Palacio	Tacitus	Bandeira	Etherege	Macneice
Patmore	Tardieu	Banville	Faulkner	Majerova
Peacock	Terence	Barbusse	Fielding	Malherbe
Piovene	Thespis	Bataille	Figueroa	Mallarmé
Plautus	Thomson	Beaumont	Firdausi	Manninen
Prevert	Thoreau	Beckford	Fischart	Marivaux
Pushkin	Thurber	Beerbohm	Flaubert	Marquand
Pynchon	Todorov	Belinsky	Fletcher	Melville
Queneau	Tolkein	Benchley	Fontaine	Menander
Quental	Tolstoy	Beranger	Fontanes	Meredith
Radnoti	Travers	Berkeley	Forester	Michelet
Ransome	Trenyov	Bernanos	Ginsberg	Mirabeau
Regnier	Tristan	Bertrand	Goncourt	Mitchell
Reymont	Tutuola	Betjeman	Gonzales	Mustapaa
Richler	Unamuno	Bjornson	Gryphius	Naogeorg
Rimbaud	Ustinov	Bradbury	Heinesen	Nekrasov
Rolland	Vaughan	Brancati	Henryson	Nicolson
Romains	Veldeke	Brentano	Hochhuth	Overland
Ronsard	Vicente	Browning	Hoffmman	Palgrave
Rostand	Volodin	Calderon	Holstein	Pasolini
Rousell	Wallace	Campbell	Huysmans	Pearlman
Russell	Walpole	Carducci	Imperial	Perrault
Rydberg	Webster	Carrillo	Jacobsen	Petrarch
Sarment	Weinert	Castilho	Kalidasa	Phaedrus
Sassoon	Wharton	Catullus	Kavanagh	Philemon
Scarron	Whitman	Chandler	Kingsley	Pichette
Schaper	Wieland	Chartier	Kirsanov	Plutarch
Seferis	Winkler	Christie	Koestler	Quintana
Shaffer	Wittlin	Claudian	Kornilov	Rabelais
Shapiro	Yesenin	Claussen	Kotzebue	Radiguet
Shelley	Yavarov	Congreve	Kualmann	Rankovic
Simenon		Conquest	Laforgue	Rattigan
Simonov		Constant	Lagerlöf	Remarque
Sitwell	**8**	Corbiere	Langland	Richards
Siwertz	Abulafia	Crompton	Las Cases	Rossetti
Skelton	Abu Nuwas	Cummings	La Taille	Rousseau
Sosyura	Agricola	Cynewulf	Lawrence	Runeberg
Southey	Anacreon	Dagerman	Leibnitz	Salinger
Staring	Anchieta	Davenant	Leopardi	Sandburg
Soyinka	Andersch	Day Lewis	Lehtonen	San Pedro

Sarraute
Scaliger
Scheffel
Schiller
Shadwell
Sheridan
Sillitoe
Sinclair
Slowacki
Smollet
Spillane
Stendhal
Stoppard
Strachey
Stricker
Suckling
Su Dong Po
Taliesin
Tansillo
Tennyson
Thompson
Timeneda
Tourneur
Traherne
Trilling
Trollope
Tulsidas
Turgenev
Tyutcher
Ukrainka
Vailland
Vanbrugh
Verlaine
Vennberg
Villegas
Voltaire
Voronsky
Vonnegut
Wedekind
Welhaven
Williams
Zapolska
Zamyatin
Zorilla

9

Abravenel
Aeschylus
Ainsworth
Akhmatova
Aldington
Alexandre
Allingham
Angilbert
Arbuthnot
Aristotle
Berkowitz
Bernardes
Bernstein
Bidermann
Blackmore
Blackwood
Bobrowski
Boccaccio
Borchardt
Bulatovie
Burroughs
Cervantes
Cesarotti
Charteris
Churchill
Ciminelli
Coleridge
Compaomor
Corneille
Dabrowski
D'Annunzio
de la Roche
de Quincey
Descartes
Deschamps
Doolittle
Dos Passos
Drachmann
Du Guillet
Du Maurier
Eckermann
Edgeworth
Ehrenberg
Euripides

Fridegard
Froissart
Giraudoux
Goldsmith
Goncharov
Gottsched
Greenwood
Guerrazzi
Hauptmann
Hawthorne
Hemingway
Hernandes
Herodotus
Highsmith
Holderlin
Immermann
Isherwood
Jefferies
Jorgenson
Kisfaludy
Klopstock
La Bruyere
La Fayette
Lamartine
Lampedusa
Laurenyou
Lermontov
Linklater
Llewellyn
Lomonosov
Lovecraft
Lucretius
Lundkuist
Mackenzie
Malaparte
Mansfield
Marinette
Martineau
Martinson
Masefield
Massinger
McCullers
Middleton
Michaelis
Monsarrat
Montaigne

Mutanabbi
Nordstrom
Nietzsche
O'Flaherty
Osterling
Ostrovsky
Parkinson
Pasternak
Perzynski
Poliziano
Pratolini
Pratchett
Priestley
Pritchett
Radcliffe
Rochester
Rodriguez
Rosenhane
Sackville
Schickele
Schreiner
Sebastian
Shenstone
Sholokhov
Slaveykov
Sodergran
Sophocles
Steinbeck
Sternheim
Stevenson
Sturluson
Suetonius
Sumarokov
Swinburne
Thackeray
Theotokas
Trevelyan
Tsvetaeva
Ungaretti
Velichkov
Verhaeren
Vinokorov
Vittorini
Wergeland
Wildenvey
Witkewicz

Wodehouse
Woestjine
Wycherley
Zhukovsky
Zimorovic
Zuckmayer

10

Achterberg
Albertinus
Alecsandri
Ballantyne
Baudelaire
Bilderdijk
Brassilach
Bregendahl
Campanella
Cavalcanti
Chatterjee
Chatterton
Chesterton
Clenfuegos
Colliander
Conan Doyle
Conscience
Courteline
Czechowiez
Dazai Osamu
de Beauvoir
Della Vale
Destouches
Dio Cassius
Dostoevsky
Drinkwater
Dürrenmatt
Ebrenstein
Fitzgerald
Fontanella
Galsworthy
Guinizelli
Hallgrimur
Heidenstam
Henningsen
Ignjatovic
Kasprovicz

Khlebnikov
La Fontaine
Lagerkvist
Lohenstein
Longfellow
Macdiarmid
Mandelstam
Maupassant
McGonagall
Metastasio
Mickiewicz
Obstfelder
Ostrovskii
Peyrefitte
Pirandello
Prevalakis
Propertius
Quintilian
Richardson
Rutherford
Saint-Simon
Schnitzler
Shevchenko
Spielhagen
Strindberg
Tannhauser
Tendryakou
Theocritus
Thucydides
Van Der Post
Vishnevsky
Wassermann
Williamson
Wordsworth
Zabolotsky
Zamfiresco

11

Ankerlarsen
Anzengruber
Apollinaire
Archilochus
Bacchylides
Beer-Hofman
Blessington

Bontempelli
Callimachus
Castiglione
Champfleury
de la Bruyère
Dostoyevski
Eichendorff
Friis Muller
Garcia Lorca
Grillparzer
Gyllenstein
Kazantazkis
Kochanowski
Lautréamont
Lo-Johansson
Maeterlinck
Matsuo Basho
Mayakovskii
Montherlant
Omar Khayyam
Palazzeschi
Perez Galdos
Pontoppidan
Shakespeare
Sienkiewicz
Stuckenberg
Superveille
Veselinovic
Valdivielso
Yevtushenko
Weyssenhoff

12

Aristophanes
Beaumarchais
Dahlistjerna
Ferlinghetti
Feuchtwanger
Gabrie y Ga-
lan
Hartzenbusch
Hofmannsthal
Lichtenstein
Lopez de
Ayala

Martin Du Gard
Matthew Paris
Nastasijevc
Perez de Ayala
Robbe-Grillet
Saint-Exupery
Solzhenitsyn
Tocqueville
Viele-Griffin
Voznesenskii
Wittgenstein

13

Castelo Branco
Chateaubriand
Csokonai Vitez
Harishchandra
Marie de France
Montchristien
Paludan-Muller
Sep-Szarzynski
Tirso de Molina
Villchardouin
Zeami Motokiyo

14

Avarez Quintero
Brillat-Savarin
Compton-Burnett
Dafydd Ap Gwilym
Dante Alighieri
Droste-Hulshoff
Gongora y Argote
Grimmelshausen
Herrmann-Neisse
Jacopone da Todi
Leconte de Lisle
Lopez de Mendoza
Martinez Sierra
Ochlenschlager
Prévost de'exiles
Sully-Prudhomme
Tchernichowski
Wollstonecraft

Velez de Guevara
Zorrilla y Moral

15

Alarcon y Mendoza
Bores D'Hauterive
Diodorus Siculus
Garcia Gutierrez
Granville Barker
Guittone D'arezzo
Kaden-Brandrowski
Pliny The Younger
Villiers de Lisle

16

Bosboom-Toussaint
Chretien de Troyes
Christine de Pison
Cyrano de Bergerac
Garcilas de la Vega
Hedenvind-Erksson
Kawabata Yasunari
Petronius Arbiter
Platen-Hallemunde
Rojas Villandrano

17 +

Andreas Capellanus
Apollonius of Rhodes
Benoit de Sainte-Maure
Bernardin de Saint-Pierre
Calderon de la Barca
Chikamatsu Monzaemon
Dionysius of Halicarnassus
Drummond of Hawthornden
Echegaray y Eizaguirre
Friederich von Hausen
Gottfried von Strassburg
Guillaume de Lorris
Heinrich von Melsson
Heinrich von Neustade
Heinrich von Witten Weller
Helinand de Fradmont
Kakinomoto Hitomaro
Sanchez de Badojoz
Tanizaki Jun-Ichiro
Thomas of Erceldoune
Ulrich von Lichenstein
Villiers de l'Isle-Adam
Walter of Chatillon
Walter von der Vogelweide
Ziegler und Kliphausen

Battles and sieges

3	Agra	Nile	Alton	Calvi	Lewes
Kut	Alma	Rhur	Anzio	Crécy	Liege
Lys	Amoy	Taku	Arcot	Crete	Ligny
Tet	Caen	Troy	Arras	Delhi	Maida
Ulm	Gaza	Yser	Basra	El Teb	Malta
	Ivry	Zama	Blitz	Eylau	Marne
	Jena		Boyne	Genoa	Meuse
4	Laon		Bulge	Herat	Miami
Acre	Loos	**5**	Burma	Issus	Paris
Aden	Maas	Aisne	Cadiz	Kabul	Pusan
	Mons	Alamo	Cairo	Kandy	Rhine

Sedan
Selby
Selle
Shilo
Somme
Tagus
Texel
Tours
Valmy
Ypres

6

Actium
Amiens
Arbela
Argaon
Arnhem
Assaye
Atbara
Bagdad
Barnet
Bastia
Bataan
Berlin
Burgos
Busaco
Calais
Camden
Cannae
Chusan
Coruna
Dargai
Delium
Dieppe
Dyrham
Dunbar
Exeter
Ferrol
Guarda
Gujrat
Havana
Hexham
Isonzo
Jattoo
Jhansi

Lutzen
Madras
Madrid
Majuba
Malaga
Manila
Mantua
Masada
Midway
Mileto
Minden
Moscow
Nagpur
Narvik
Naseby
Oporto
Orthez
Ostend
Peking
Pinkie
Plevna
Quebec
Rhodes
Rivoli
Rocroi
Sadowa
Saints
Shiloh
Tarifa
Tobago
Tobruk
Toulon
Towton
Tudela
Tugela
Ushant
Verdun
Vienna
Wagram
Warsaw

7

Aboukir
Abu Klea
Alamein

Albuera
Almansa
Almeida
Antwerp
Ashdown
Atlanta
Badajoz
Baghdad
Bapaume
Bautzen
Bousaco
Brienne
Britain
Bull Run
Cambrai
Cape Bon
Cassino
Chalons
Chester
Coimbra
Colenso
Concord
Cordova
Coronel
Corunna
Dresden
Dunkirk
Edgecot
Edghill
El Obeid
Evesham
Falkirk
Flodden
Granada
Gwalior
Iwo Jima
Jutland
La Hogue
Leipzig
Lemberg
Lepanto
Leuthen
Lucknow
Magdala
Magenta
Marengo

Matapan
Megiddo
Minorca
Moselle
Moskowa
Nations
Newbury
Nivelle
Okinawa
Orléans
Plassey
Plataea
Ploesti
Poltava
Preston
St. Kitts
St. Lucia
Salamis
Salerno
Sobraon
Solebay
Taranto
Trenton
Vimiera
Vitoria
Wareham

8

Antietam
Ardennes
Atlantic
Bastille
Benfleet
Beresina
Blenheim
Bhurtpur
Borodino
Bosworth
Brooklyn
Calcutta
Carthage
Cawnpore
Coral Sea
Cowperis
Culloden

Edgehill
Edington
Flanders
Flushing
Fontenoy
Fort Erie
Granicus
Guernica
Hastings
Hydaspes
Inkerman
Kandahar
Khartoum
Lake Erie
Lansdown
Le Cateau
Langside
Mafeking
Malakoff
Marathon
Maubeuge
Medellin
Messines
Metaurus
Mohne Dam
Montreal
Navarino
Nieuport
Normandy
Omdurman
Philippi
Poitiers
Potidaea
Pretoria
Przemysl
St. Albans
St. Mihiel
St. Pierre
Salsette
Saratoga
Spion Kop
Stirling
Suvla Bay
Syracuse
Talavera
Tenerife

Tiberias
Toulouse
Valencia
Waterloo
Yorktown
Zaragoza

9

Agincourt
Aldershot
Algeciras
Ashingdon
Balaclava
Belle Isle
Caporetto
Chaeronea
Champagne
Charleroi
Ctesiphon
Dettingen
Eddington
El Alamein
Falklands
Festubert
Friedland
Gallipoli
Gaugamela
Gibraltar
Hyderabad
Kimberley
Ladysmith
Laing's Nek
Leningrad
Lexington
Leyte Gulf
Louisburg
Mauritius
Melagnano
Mobile Bay
Otterburn
Oudenarde
Pharsalus
Port Mahon
Ramillies
Rochester

Rodriguez
Saragossa
St. Quentin
St. Vincent
Salamanca
Sedgemoor
Solferino
Stormberg
Stromboli
Tarragona
Tourcoing
Trafalgar
Vicksburg
Vimy Ridge
Wakefield
Walcheren
Worcester
Zeebrugge

10

Adrianople
Ahmednagar
Alexandria
Appomattox
Austerlitz
Beachy Head
Brandywine
Brownstown
Brunanburh
Bunker Hill
Camperdown
Charleston
Chevy-chase
Chichester
Cold Harbor
Copenhagen
Corregidor
Dogger Bank
Fort George
Fort Hudson
Fort Sumter
Germantown
Gettysburg
Goose Green
Gravelotte

Guadeloupe
Heligoland
Imjin River
Kut-el-Amara
La Rochelle
Les Saintes
Malplaquet
Martinique
Montevideo
Montfaucon
New Orleans
Nördlingen
Paardeburg
Petersburg
Port Arthur
Porto Praya
Quatre Bras
River Plate
River Stour
Sevastopol
Shrewsbury
Solway Moss
Stalingrad
Tannenberg
Tel-el-Kebir
Tewkesbury
Tinchebray
Wilderness

11

Albuquerque
Bannockburn
Breitenfeld
Chattanooga
Chilianwala
Dardanelles
Dien Bien Phu
Fort Niagara
Guadalcanal
Halidon Hill
Hedgley Moor
Hohenlinden
Isandhlwana
Jameson Raid
Lostwithiel

Marston Moor
Pearl Harbor
Philiphaugh
Philippines
Pieter's Hill
Pondicherry
Prestonpans
Quiberon Bay
Rorke's Drift
Schoneveldt
Schweinfurt
Sheriffmuir
Thermoplyae
Ticonderoga
White Plains

12

Adwalton Moor
Belville Wood
Bloemfontein
Flodden Field
Gainsborough
Harper's Ferry
Homildon Hill
Maiden Castle
Northallerton
Radcot Bridge
Roundway Down
San Sebastian
Seringapatam
Trichinopoly
Turnham Green

13

Antietam Creek
Boroughbridge
Bosworth Field
Cape St. Vin-
  cent
Ciudad Rodrigo
Lake Champlain
Little Bighorn
Losecoat Field
Magersfontein

Messines Ridge
Neuve Chapelle
Neville's Cross
Passchendaele
Spanish Armada
Stow-on-the-Wold
White Mountain

14
Chalgrove Field
Constantinople
Cropredy Bridge
Fredericksburg
Mortimer's Cross
Stamford Bridge
Tsushima Strait

15 +
Battle of Britain
Brandywine River
Countisbury Hill
Falkland Islands
Guilford Court
 House
Heights of Abraham
Plains of Abraham

Bays (b), capes (c), channels (ch), firths (f), gulfs (g) and straits (s)

3 & 4

Aden	(g)
Bass	(s)
Cod	(c)
Cook	(s)
East	(c)
Horn	(c)
Luce	(b)
Lyme	(b)
Oman	(g)
Race	(c)
Riga	(g)
Suez	(g)

5

Aqaba	(g)
Cabot	(s)
Cadiz	(g)
Clyde	(f)
Corfu	(s)
Davis	(s)
Dover	(s)
Forth	(f)
Fundy	(b)
Gabes	(g)
Genoa	(g)
Hawke	(b)
Kerch	(s)
Kutch	(g)
Lions	(g)
Lorne	(f)
Maine	(g)
Menai	(s)
Moray	(f)
North	(c,ch)
Papua	(g)
Paria	(g)
Sable	(c)
Salem	(g)
Scott	(c)
Sirte	(g)
Start	(b)
Tunis	(g)
Verde	(c)

6

Alaska	(g)
Anadyr	(g)
Baffin	(b)
Bantry	(b)
Barrow	(b)
Beauly	(f)
Bering	(s)
Biscay	(b)
Botany	(b)
Cambay	(g)
Colwyn	(b)
Danzig	(g)
Dingle	(b)
Dublin	(b)
Hormuz	(s)
Hudson	(b,s)
Mannai	(g)
Masira	(g)
Mexico	(g)
Mounts	(b)
Naples	(g)
Panama	(g)
Parita	(g)
Plenty	(b)
Solway	(f)
St.Ives	(b)
Tasman	(b)

Tonkin (g)
Torbay (b)

7

Aboukir (b)
Bigbury (b)
Boothia (g)
Bothnia (g)
Bristol (b, ch)
Chidley (c)
Corinth (g)
Denmark (s)
Donegal (b)
Dornoch (f)
Dundalk (b)
Dundrum (b)
English (ch)
Finland (g)
Florida (s)
Formosa (s)
Foveaux (s)
Killala (b)
Malacca (s)
Persian (g)
Salerno (g)
Sandown (b)
Swansea (b)
Taranto (g)
Totland (b)
Trieste (g)
Trinity (b)
Wigtown (b)
Yucatan (ch)

8

Amundsen (g)
Bideford (b)
Blacksod (b)
Campeche (g)
Cardigan (b)
Chiriqui (g)
Colombia (c)
Cromarty (f)
Delaware (b)
Farewell (c)
Flamingo (b)
Flattery (c)
Good Hope (c)
Hammamet (g)
Hatteras (c)
Honduras (g)
Makassar (s)
Martaban (g)
Pentland (f)
Quiberon (b)
San Jorge (g)
Sembilan (s)
St. Bride's (b)
Tremadoc (b)
Valencia (g)

9

Belle Isle (s)
Capricorn (ch)
Discovery (b)
Frobisher (b)

Gibraltar (s)
Guayaquil (g)
Liverpool (b)
Mendocino (c)
Morecambe (b)
Mosquitos (g)
Notre Dame (b)
Placentia (b)
St. Bridges (b)
St. Vincent (c)
Trafalgar (c)
Trearddur (b)

10

Bridgwater (b)
Byam Martin (ch)
Carmarthen (b)
California (g)
Conception (b)
Coronation (g)
Freshwater (b)
St. Lawrence (g)
Van Diemen (g)

11

Carpentaria (g)
Tehuantepec (g)

12 +

Morrosquillo (g)
Joseph
  Bonaparte (g)

Biblical characters

2 & 3

Asa
Buz
Eli
Eve
Gad
God
Gog
Ham
Huz
Job
Lot
Og

4

Abel
Adah
Adam
Ahab
Ahaz
Amos
Aner
Aser
Baal
Boaz
Cain
Cush
Enos
Esau
Ezra
Heth
Irad
Jael
Jehu
Joab
Joel
John
Jude
Leah
Levi
Luke
Magi
Mark
Mary
Moab

Noah	Jeran	Andrew	Nahath	Goliath
Onan	Jesse	Apphra	Nathan	Havilah
Paul	Jesus	Balaam	Nimrod	Ishmael
Phut	Joash	Belial	Philip	Japheth
Ruth	Jonah	Bilhah	Pilate	Jehovah
Saul	Joram	Cainan	Raamah	Jezebel
Seba	Joses	Canaan	Rachel	Jezreel
Seth	Jubal	Christ	Reuben	Joiakim
Shah	Judah	Daniel	Reumah	Keturah
Shem	Judas	Darius	Rizpah	Lazarus
	Laban	Dismas	Sabtah	Lucifer
	Linus	Dorcas	Salome	Malachi

5

	Lucas	Elijah	Samson	Malchus
Aaron	Lydia	Elisha	Samuel	Maneses
Abiah	Madai	Ephron	Shelah	Matthew
Abihu	Magog	Eschol	Simeon	Meshach
Abner	Mamre	Esther	Sisera	Michael
Abram	Micah	Eunice	Thomas	Mizraim
Annas	Moses	Festus	Uzziah	Obadiah
Barak	Nahor	Gehazi	Yahweh	Ogarmah
Caleb	Nahum	Gideon	Zillah	Pharoah
Cyrus	Naomi	Gilboa	Zilpah	Philcol
Dagon	Ophir	Haggai	Zimran	Phineas
David	Peter	Hannah	Zophar	Raphael
Dedan	Rahab	Isaiah		Rebekah
Demas	Sarah	Israel		Riphath
Devil	Satan	Jairus	**7**	Scechem
Dinah	Sheba	Jethro		Shallum
Elias	Sihon	Joseph	Abigail	Solomon
Elihu	Silas	Joshua	Abraham	Stephen
Enoch	Simon	Josiah	Absalom	Timothy
Gaham	Tamar	Jotham	Ananias	Zebedee
Gaius	Tebah	Judith	Antipas	Zebulon
Gomer	Tirus	Kemuel	Apolyon	
Hagar	Titus	Kittim	Azariah	
Haman	Tubal	Kohath	Bethual	**8**
Hamor	Uriah	Lamech	Clement	
Herod	Uriel	Marcus	Cleopas	Abednego
Hiram	Zadok	Martha	Deborah	Abinadab
Hosea	Zimri	Milcar	Delilah	Adonijah
Isaac		Miriam	Didymus	Alphaeus
Jabel		Mizpah	Dodanim	Archipus
Jacob	**6**	Naamah	Eleazer	Barabbas
James		Naaman	Elkanah	Barnabas
Jarod	Abadon	Naboth	Ephraim	Benjamin
Javan	Abijah	Nahash	Ezekiel	Caiaphas
	Amalek		Gabriel	Ebenezer

Gamaliel
Habakkuk
Herodius
Hezekiah
Immanuel
Isacchar
Iscariot
Issachar
Jephthah
Jeremiah
Jeraboam
Jonathan
Josedech
Maccabee
Manasseh
Matthias
Mehujael
Mordecai
Naphtali
Nehemiah
Onesimus
Philemon
Potiphar
Rehoboam
St. Dismas
Sabtecha
Sapphira
Shadrach
Zecharia
Zedekiah
Zipporah

9

Abimelech
Ahasuerus
Barachias
Bathsheba
Boanerges
Cornelius
Demetrius
Elisabeth
Jehoiakim
Magdalene
Methusael
Nathanael
Nepthalim
Nicodemus
Sephamiah
Shealtiel
Thaddaeus
Tubal-Cain
Zacchaeus
Zachariah
Zacharias
Zephaniah

10

Bartimaeus
Belshazzar
Holofernes
Methuselah
Mahalaleel
Theophilus
Virgin Mary

11

Aristarchus
Bartholomew
Jehoshaphat
Jesus Christ
Melchisedec
Melchizedek
Sennacherib

12

James the Less
Witch of Endor

13

Judas Iscariot
Mary of Bethany
Mary Magdalene
Pontius Pilate

14

John the Baptist
Nebuchadnezzar

15 +

James's the Greater
John's the Evangelist
Joseph of Arimathea
Philip of Bethsaida
Philip the Evangelist
Simon the Caananite

Birds

2				4		
ka	cob	maw	poe		coly	fowl
oo	daw	mew	roc	barb	coot	gawk
	emu	moa	tit	baya	crow	gowk
	ern	nun	tui	bubo	dodo	guan
	hen	owl	wry	chat	dove	gull
3	jay	pau		cirl	duck	hawk
	kea	pen		cock	erne	hern
auk	mao	pie			eyas	huia

huma	amsel	loxia	saker	wonga	dopper
ibis	annet	lyrie	sally	yacou	drongo
jack	argus	macaw	sarus		ducker
kagu	biddy	madge	sasia		duiker
kaka	bongo	maneh	saury	**6**	dunlin
kite	booby	mavis	scape	Adelie	eaglet
kiwi	bowet	merle	scarf	aiglet	einack
knot	brant	minah	scaup	aigret	elanet
koel	brent	miner	scoby	alcedo	falcon
kora	bucco	molly	scops	alcyon	fulmar
lark	capon	monal	scout	Amazon	galeen
loon	chick	murre	scray	ananas	gambet
lory	claik	mynah	scull	ancona	gander
mina	colin	nandu	senex	argala	gannet
monk	crake	nelly	serin	auklet	garrot
myna	crane	noddy	shama	avocet	gentoo
nene	creak	ornis	sitta	avoset	godurt
nias	curre	ortyx	skite	bantam	godwit
nyas	daker	ousel	snipe	barbet	gorhen
pauw	didus	ouzel	solan	bishop	goslet
pavo	diver	owlet	soree	bonxie	grakle
pern	drake	oxeye	spink	bowess	grouse
pica	dunne	paauw	squab	brahma	guinea
piet	dunny	pewet	stare	brolga	hacket
poll	eagle	pewit	stilt	budgie	hagden
rail	egret	picus	stint	buffel	hareld
rhea	eider	piper	stork	bulbul	hermit
rook	finch	pipit	strix	cagmag	hoazin
ruff	frank	pitta	swift	canary	hoopoe
rype	galah	poaka	tarin	chough	hoopoo
shag	ganza	poker	terek	chukar	houdan
skua	glede	polly	tiddy	chukor	jabiru
smee	goose	poult	topau	citril	jacana
smew	grebe	prion	topet	cochin	jaeger
swan	gripe	purre	twite	condor	jerkin
taha	harpy	quail	umbre	corbie	kakapo
teal	henny	radge	urile	corvus	keltis
tern	heron	ralph	urubu	coucal	kiddow
tody	hobby	raven	veery	cuckoo	kondor
weka	homer	reeve	vireo	culver	lanner
wren	imber	robin	virgo	curlew	leipoa
xema	jager	rodge	wader	cushat	linnet
yite	junco	rotch	wagel	cygnet	loriot
	larus	rudge	wavey	cygnus	magpie
5	layer	ryper	whaup	darter	marrot
agami	lowan	sacre	whilk	dipper	martin

menura
merlin
merops
merula
missel
mistle
monaul
mopoke
mot-mot
musket
nandoo
nandow
nestor
nicker
oriole
osprey
ouzlem
oxbird
parrot
parson
pastor
pavone
peahen
peeper
peewit
pernis
petrel
phoebe
pigeon
plover
poulet
pouter
powter
puffin
pullet
pygarg
queest
quelea
quezal
ratite
redcap
reeler
roberd
rocker
roller
rotche

ruddoc
rumkin
runner
sappho
scaury
scobby
scoter
sea-bar
sea-cob
sea-hen
sea-mew
sea-pie
serula
shrike
shrite
sicsac
simbil
siskin
smeath
soland
sorage
sparve
strich
strick
sultan
surrey
takahe
tarsel
tatler
tercel
tewhit
thrush
tirwit
tomtit
toucan
towhee
tringa
trogon
turaco
turbit
turkey
turner
turtle
tystie
waggel
weaver

whidah
whydah
wigeon
willet
witwal
xenops
yaffle
yaffil
ynambu
yucker
zicsac
zivola
zoozoo

7

antbird
apteryx
attagas
attagen
awl-bird
babbler
barn owl
bee-bird
bee-kite
bittern
blue-cap
blue-eye
blue jay
bluetit
boobook
buceros
bull-bat
bummalo
bunting
buphaga
bush-tit
bustard
butcher
buzzard
cackler
caponet
cariama
carvist
cat-bird
chewink

chicken
ciconia
coal tit
cob-swan
colibri
columba
corella
cotinga
courlan
courlin
courser
cow-bird
cracker
creeper
crombec
cropper
dididae
dorhawk
dorking
dottrel
doucher
dovekie
dovelet
dun-bird
dunnock
egg-bird
emu-wren
fantail
fen duck
fern owl
fig-bird
finfoot
fish owl
flapper
flicker
flusher
gadwall
gavilan
gobbler
gorcock
gorcrow
goshawk
gosling
grackle
grallae
graylag

greyhen
greylag
grey hen
grey owl
hacklet
halcyon
harfang
harrier
hatcher
hawk owl
hickway
hoatzin
horn owl
ice-bird
impeyan
jacamar
jacinth
jackass
jackdaw
jacksaw
jacobin
jashawk
jedcock
kamichi
kestrel
killdee
kinglet
lagopus
lapwing
laugher
lavrock
Leghorn
lentner
lich-owl
lorilet
mallard
manakin
manikin
marabou
maracan
martlet
may-bird
megamys
migrant
minivet
minorca

modwall	royston	vulture	bobolink	fire-bird
moorhen	ruddock	vulturn	bob-white	firetail
motacil	sakeret	wagtail	bockelet	fish-hawk
moth-owl	sawbill	wapacut	bockeret	flamingo
mudlark	sawwhet	warbler	brancher	forktail
muggent	scammel	waxbill	brevipen	gairfowl
noctule	scooper	waxwing	brown owl	gamebird
oilbird	sea-bird	whooper	bush chat	gamecock
ortolan	sea-crow	widgeon	bush lark	gang-gang
ostrich	sea-dove	willock	cage bird	garefowl
oven-tit	sea-duck	wimbrel	calandra	garganey
pandion	sea-fowl	witlock	calangay	great tit
partlet	seagull	witwall	call-bird	greenlet
peacock	sea-hawk	wood owl	caneroma	grey teal
peafowl	senegal	wren-tit	capuchin	grosbeak
pelican	seriema	wrybill	caracara	guachero
penguin	serinus	wryneck	cardinal	hackbolt
percher	shorley	wyandot	cargoose	hangbird
peterel	simargh	yeldrin	churn owl	hangnest
phaeton	sirgang		clot-bird	hawfinch
phoenix	skimmer	**8**	cockatoo	hazel-hen
pinnock	skylark	aasvogel	cock bird	heath-hen
pintado	snow-owl	accentor	cockerel	hemipode
pintail	sparrow	adjutant	coquimbo	hernshaw
pinnock	squacco	aigrette	corn bird	hickwall
pintado	staniel	alcatras	curassow	hoactzin
pochard	stannel	amadavad	cursores	hornbill
poe-bird	stanyel	amadavat	cutwater	horseman
poulard	stumpie	arapunga	dabchick	hula-bird
poultry	sturnus	avadavat	daker-hen	keskidee
poy-bird	sunbird	bald-coot	dandy-hen	killdeer
puttock	swallow	bald ibis	didapper	kingbird
quabird	swimmer	baldpate	dinornis	king-crow
quetzel	tandora	barnacle	dipchick	landrail
raddock	tanager	bateleur	dotterel	langshan
rainbow	tarrock	beam-bird	duck-hawk	lanneret
rantock	tattler	becafico	duckling	laverock
ratitae	tiercel	bee-eater	duckmole	lingbird
redhead	tinamou	bell-bird	dun-diver	lorikeet
redpoll	tinamus	berghaan	eagle-owl	lovebird
redtail	titlark	blackcap	estridge	lyrebird
redwing	titling	bluebird	falconet	mannikin
robinet	touraco	bluewing	fauvette	man-of-war
rooster	trochil	blue-wren	fen-goose	maori hen
rosella	tumbler	boat-bill	fig-eater	marabout
rotchie	turakoo	boat-tail	finnikin	marsh-hen

marsh tit	ringtail	umbrette	black swan	gallinazo
megapode	rock dove	water-hen	blacktail	gallinule
mire-crow	rocketer	wheatear	black tern	gerfalcon
mire-drum	rubecula	whimbrel	blood-bird	gier-eagle
moorcock	sage-cock	whinchat	blue crane	glaucopis
moorfowl	sand-bird	whip-bird	bowerbird	goldcrest
moorgame	sand-cock	whistler	brambling	goldeneye
more-pork	sand-lark	whitecap	broadbill	goldfinch
morillon	sarcelle	white-ear	brown hawk	goldspink
murrelet	scops owl	white-eye	bullfinch	goosander
musk duck	screamer	wildfowl	buzzardet	grassbird
mute swan	scrub tit	woodchat	campanero	grass wren
mynabird	sea-eagle	woodcock	cassowary	great skua
nestling	sea-quail	wood duck	cedar-bird	grey goose
nightjar	sea-raven	wood ibis	cereopsis	grey heron
night-owl	sea-snipe	woodlark	chaffinch	grossbeak
notornis	sedge-hen	woodwale	chatterer	guillemot
nuthatch	shelduck	wood-wren	chevalier	guinea hen
ovenbird	shoebill	wrannock	chickadee	gyrfalcon
oxpecker	shoveler	xanthura	chickling	hatchling
palm dove	silktail	yeldring	coal-mouse	heathbird
parakeet	sittella	yeldrock	cockatiel	heathcock
paraquet	snowbird	yoldring	cock robin	hen-driver
paroquet	snowy owl	zopilote	columbine	heronshaw
peachick	songbird		cormorant	hirundine
penelope	songster	**9**	corncrake	honey-bird
percolin	starling	accipiter	crossbill	horned owl
petchary	struthio	albatross	currawong	jack-snipe
pheasant	swamp-hen	abdorinha	dandy-cock	Jenny wren
philomer	swiftlet	ant-thrush	deinornis	jerfalcon
pickerel	tanagers	autophagi	dicky bird	kittiwake
plungeon	tantalus	bald eagle	dowitcher	lint-white
poorwill	tapaculo	baldicoot	eagle-hawk	little auk
popinjay	tawny owl	baltimore	eider duck	little owl
puffbird	tell-tale	bean goose	field-duck	log-runner
pygmy owl	tercelet	beccafico	fieldfare	lorrikeet
rainbird	thrasher	beefeater	field wren	malee hen
redshank	thresher	bell-minah	fig parrot	mallemuck
redstart	throstle	bergander	figpecker	mango bird
reed-bird	titmouse	birgander	firecrest	marshbird
reedling	titterel	blackbird	fledgling	merganser
reed-wren	tomnoddy	black cock	flute-bird	meropidan
rice-bird	toucanet	black duck	francolin	merulidan
rifleman	tragopan	black game	friarbird	mire-snipe
ringbill	trembler	black gull	fringilla	moundbird
ring dove	troupial	blackhead	frogmouth	mousebird

mousehawk
mud-sucker
muscipaca
natatores
night-fowl
night hawk
ossifraga
ossifraga
owl-parrot
paradisea
paraquito
pardalote
parrakeet
parroquet
partridge
peregrine
petaurist
phalarope
pied-goose
pine finch
ptarmigan
quachilto
razorbill
redbreast
red grouse
rhynchops
riflebird
ring-ousel
rock-pipit
rosefinch
rossignol
sabrewing
salangane
sandpiper
sapsucker
satin-bird
scald-crow
scratcher
scrub-bird
scrubfowl
scrub-wren
sea-parrot
secretary
sedge-bird
sedge wren
shearbill

sheldrake
shitepoke
shoveller
shrike-tit
silver-eye
skunk-bird
snake-bird
snow-finch
snow goose
sooty tern
solitaire
spinebill
spoonbill
stick-bird
stilt-bird
stink-bird
stock dove
stonechat
stone-hawk
storm-bird
swamp-hawk
swartback
swordbill
talegalla
tetraonid
thickhead
thick-knee
thornbill
tiercelet
trochilus
trumpeter
turkey-hen
turnstone
umber-bird
waterbird
water-cock
waterfowl
water-rail
wedgebill
whale-head
wheat-bird
whiteface
whitehead
whitetail
whitewing
widow-bird

willow tit
windhover
woodspite
wyandotte

10

aberdevine
Andalusian
ant-catcher
Arctic skua
Arctic tern
bearded tit
bell-magpie
bird of prey
bishop bird
black stork
blight-bird
blue-bonnet
bluebreast
bluethroat
boobook owl
brent goose
bronze-wing
budgerigar
budgerygah
bufflehead
burrow-duck
bush-shrike
butter-bird
butterbump
canary bird
canvasback
Cape pigeon
chiffchaff
chittagong
common gull
cow-bunting
crested tit
crow-shrike
demoiselle
dickcissel
didunculus
dishwasher
diving duck
dollar-bird

dung-hunter
dusky minah
dusky robin
ember goose
eurylaimus
fallow-chat
fledgeling
flycatcher
fratercula
goatmilker
goatsucker
goldhammer
gooney-bird
grassfinch
greenfinch
greenshank
grey falcon
grey parrot
grey plover
ground dove
ground lark
ground robin
guinea fowl
gymnocitta
hammerhead
harpy eagle
heath-poult
hen-harrier
herald duck
honeyeater
honeyguide
hooded crow
jungle-fowl
kingfisher
king parrot
kookaburra
magpie-lark
mallee bird
mallee fowl
maned goose
meadow-lark
missel-bird
mutton-bird
night heron
night raven
nutcracker

parson-bird
peewee-lark
pettichaps
pick-cheese
piping crow
prairie hen
pratincole
quaker-bird
racket-tail
rafter-bird
rain plover
ramphastos
reed thrush
regent-bird
ring-plover
road runner
rock-hopper
rock parrot
rock pigeon
ruby-throat
sacred ibis
saddleback
sage grouse
salpinctes
sanderling
sand grouse
sandmartin
sassorolla
scoter duck
screech-owl
sea-swallow
shearwater
sickle-bill
silver gull
solan goose
song-shrike
songthrush
summer-duck
spirit-duck
stone-snipe
sun bittern
tailor-bird
talegallus
tit-warbler
tree-runner
tropic bird

turkey-cock
turtle dove
tyrant-bird
water-ousel
water pipit
wattle-bird
weasel-coot
weaverbird
whidah-bird
whydah-bird
white brant
white egret
white stork
willow wren
wonga-wonga
wood grouse
woodpecker
wood pigeon
wood-shrike
wood-thrush
yaffingale
yellow-bird
yellowlegs
zebra finch

11

Alpine swift
apostle bird
banded stilt
black falcon
black grouse
black martin
blackthroat
bonebreaker
bristle-bird
brush turkey
buffalo bird
bush-creeper
butcherbird
Canada goose
carrion crow
cattle egret
chanticleer
cirl bunting
cock-sparrow

conirostres
corn bunting
diamondbird
dragoon-bird
fairy martin
fallow finch
flock pigeon
frigate-bird
fruit pigeon
gallows-bird
game-chicken
gnatcatcher
gnat-snapper
golden eagle
grallatores
green linnet
grey wagtail
ground-robin
harrier-hawk
hazel grouse
herring gull
hooded robin
honey-sucker
house martin
hummingbird
Java sparrow
kestrel-hawk
king penguin
king vulture
lammergeier
lammergeyer
leatherhead
leptodactyl
lily-trotter
magpie-goose
meadow pipit
mockingbird
moor buzzard
mulga parrot
Muscovy duck
nightingale
Pacific gull
procellaria
pterodactyl
punchinello
purple finch

quail-thrush
querquedule
rainbow-bird
reed bunting
reed sparrow
reed warbler
rock warbler
scarlet ibis
scissorbill
scissortail
screech-hawk
scrub turkey
sea dotterel
sea-pheasant
shell-parrot
shrike-robin
singing bird
snow bunting
soldier-bird
sparrowhawk
stone curlew
stone falcon
stone plover
storm petrel
swallowtail
treecreeper
wallcreeper
weaver-finch
white stork
whitethroat
whooper swan
wood swallow
wood warbler
wren babbler
yellow robin

12

Adele penguin
Alpine chough
adjutant bird
bramble finch
bronze pigeon
burrowing owl
capercaillie
cardinal bird

cow blackbird
crested grebe
cuckoo-shrike
curvirostral
dabbling duck
dentirostres
drongo-cuckoo
drongo-shrike
elephant bird
Eskimo curlew
fairy penguin
fighting cock
fissirostres
flowerpecker
glaucous gull
golden oriole
golden plover
grass warbler
great bustard
greylag goose
ground cuckoo
ground pigeon
ground thrush
hedge sparrow
hedge warbler
homing pigeon
honey-buzzard
honeycreeper
house sparrow
lanner falcon
mandarin duck
man-of-war bird
mandarin duck
marsh harrier
marsh warbler
missel thrush
mistle thrush
mound-builder
mourning-dove
nutmeg-pigeon
painted quail
painted snipe
pallid cuckoo
peaceful dove
perching duck
pink cockatoo

Plymouth rock
razor-grinder
reed-pheasant
rifle warbler
sage-thrasher
sandwich tern
sapphire-wing
sedge warbler
serpent-eater
shoveler duck
shrike-thrush
stone-chatter
stormy petrel
stubble-goose
stubble-quail
swamp harrier
tachydromian
tiger-bittern
turbit-pigeon
turner pigeon
umbrella-bird
velvet-scoter
water wagtail
whippoorwill
white goshawk
willow grouse
yellowhammer

13

adjutant stork
American eagle
American robin
archaeopteryx
argus pheasant
Baltimore bird
barnacle goose
black cockatoo
boatswain-bird
brown thrasher
buff Orpington
carrier pigeon
chaparral cock
cock-of-the-rock
crested pigeon
crocodile bird

Egyptian goose
fantail pigeon
harlequin duck
Hawaiian goose
Iceland falcon
imperial eagle
little bunting
little bustard
long-tailed tit
mistletoe-bird
musk parrakeet
owlet-nightjar
oystercatcher
plantain-eater
red-wattle bird
rock partridge
rosella parrot
sandhill crane
screech-martin
screech-thrush
secretary bird
shell-parakeet
shining parrot
spidercatcher
stink-pheasant
swallow-shrike
tumbler pigeon
turkey-buzzard
whistling duck
white cockatoo
whooping crane
willow-warbler
wood-sandpiper
yellow bunting
yellow wagtail
zebra parakeet

14

babbling thrush
bearded vulture
bird of paradise
canvasback duck
Darwin's finches
diamond sparrow
double-bar finch

emperor penguin
golden pheasant
griffon vulture
horned screamer
king-lory parrot
long-tailed duck
long-tailed skua
Mank shearwater
mountain thrush
nankeen kestrel
oriental cuckoo
plains-wanderer
prairie chicken
rhinoceros bird
Rhode Island red
ring-tailed duck
robin redbreast
satin bowerbird
silver pheasant

sociable plover
spotted harrier
tawny frogmouth
welcome swallow
whistling eagle

15

American bittern
Baltimore oriole
Dartford warbler
fire-crested wren
gold-crested wren
laughing jackass
passenger pigeon
peacock-pheasant
peregrine falcon
pink-footed goose
spotted redshank
white-headed duck

16 +

American redstart
great crested
  grebe
great spotted
  woodpecker
ivory-billed wood-
  pecker
lesser spotted
  woodpecker
spotted flycatcher
tyrant flycatcher
wandering alba-
  tross
white-fronted
  goose
yellow-headed
  blackbird

Birthstones

Note: Not all sources agree, so some months appear twice

4

opal (October)
ruby (July)

5

agate (June)
pearl (June)
topaz (November)

6

garnet (January)

7

diamond (April)
emerald (May)
peridot (August)

8

amethyst (February

sapphire (September)
sardonyx (August)

9

turquoise (December)

10

aquamarine (March)

Boats and ships

(including nautical terms)

2					
AB	TBD	furl	pram	abaft	fluyt	sheet
PO	top	gaff	prau	abeam	foggy	shell
RM	tow	gale	proa	about	fusta	shoal
RN	tub	gang	prow	afore	gauge	shore
OS	tug	grog	punt	after	grave	siren
SS	USN	hand	quay	ahead	gusty	skeid
	USS	hank	raft	aloft	hatch	skiff
	way	hard	rail	avast	haven	sloop
	yaw	haul	rake	awash	hawse	smack
		haze	reef	badan	heads	sound
3		hazy	ride	balam	hitch	sprit
aak		head	roll	balsa	hoist	steer
aft	**4**	helm	rope	barge	jetty	stern
ark	ahoy	hold	rove	beach	kayak	storm
bay	alee	hove	sail	belay	kedge	swell
bow	back	hulk	salt	below	ketch	thole
cat	beam	hull	scud	bells	kevel	tidal
cay	beat	jack	ship	berth	lay-to	tramp
cog	bend	jagt	sink	bight	lay up	U-boat
cox	bitt	junk	spar	bilge	leaky	umiak
CPO	boom	keel	stay	block	liner	watch
ebb	bows	knot	stem	board	misty	weigh
FOB	brig	land	surf	brace	naval	wharf
gig	bunk	lead	swab	briny	oakum	wheel
guy	buoy	leak	tack	cabin	ocean	winch
HMS	calk	line	tide	cable	oiler	windy
hoy	calm	list	toss	canal	orlop	wreck
jib	capt.	load	trim	canoe	pitch	xebec
jig	comb	luff	veer	cargo	prize	yacht
kof	crew	mast	wake	caulk	radar	zaruk
lee	deck	mate	warp	chart	radio	zebec
log	dhow	mess	wave	cleat	refit	
man	dive	mine	wear	craft	roads	
MTB	dock	mist	wind	davit	ropes	**6**
aor	doni	mole	wing	depth	rower	aboard
ram	dory	moor	yawl	drift	royal	adrift
rig	eddy	navy	yard	E-boat	sally	afloat
RMS	fend	neap	yarn	eight	salvo	anchor
sea	flag	oars		ferry	sands	armada
SOS	floe	peak	**5**	fleet	screw	ashore
sub	flow	poop	aback	float	scull	astern
tar	foam	port		fluke	sheer	baghla
	fore					

Boats and ships

barque
batten
beacon
billow
bireme
boejer
bojort
bonnet
bridge
bunker
caique
canvas
careen
convoy
course
cruise
cutter
debark
dinghy
dromon
dugout
embark
engine
ensign
escort
fathom
fender
flukes
fo' c' sle
funnel
galley
gromet
gunnel
hawser
hooker
hove-to
inship
jetsam
jigger
lading
lateen
launch
lay-off
league
leeway
Lloyd' s

locker
lugger
marina
marine
marker
maroon
mashwa
masted
master
may day
mizzen
mutiny
offing
on deck
outfit
packet
paddle
patrol
pay off
pay out
pennon
piracy
pirate
raider
reefer
rigged
rigger
rudder
sailor
saloon
sampan
sambuk
sculls
seaway
sheets
shroud
sinker
slaver
splice
squall
stormy
strake
strand
stream
tackle
tanker

tender
thwart
tiller
towage
trader
undock
unfurl
unlade
unload
unship
vessel
voyage
whaler
wherry
zebeck

7

aground
athwart
bale out
ballast
beached
bearing
beating
boarder
bollard
bowline
bow wave
breaker
bulwark
bumboat
buoyage
capsize
capstan
caracor
caravel
carrack
cast off
catfall
catwalk
channel
charter
chebeck
clipper
coaling

coaming
coaster
cockpit
collier
compass
conning
coracle
corsair
cruiser
currach
curragh
cyclone
deadeye
deep-sea
dismast
dockage
drakkar
draught
dredger
drifter
dry dock
ease off
ebb tide
embargo
felucca
fishery
flotsam
fog bank
foghorn
foretop
forward
founder
frigate
futtock
galliot
galleon
gangway
gimbals
go about
go below
gondola
grapnel
graving
grommet
gudgeon
gunboat

gun-deck
gun port
gun room
gunwale
hagboat
halyard
harbour
harpoon
haul off
head off
headway
heave to
horizon
inboard
iceberg
ice floe
inboard
inshore
Jack Tar
jib boom
keelage
keelson
landing
lanyard
latches
leaking
lee side
lee tide
leeward
lighter
listing
loading
log book
lookout
luffing
lugsail
man o'
war
mariner
marines
marline
minisub
mistral
monitor
monsoon
moorage

mooring
oarsman
old salt
on board
painter
pennant
pinnace
piragua
pirogue
polacca
pontoon
quarter
rations
ratline
reefing
ride out
rigging
rollers
rope-end
rowboat
rowlock
sailing
salvage
sculler
scupper
scuttle
sea lane
sea-legs
sea room
seasick
seaward
set sail
sextant
shipper
shrouds
sick bay
sinking
skipper
skysail
slipway
spanker
steamer
steward
stowage
tacking
tempest

tonnage	bulkhead	hornpipe	nautical	stranded
top deck	bulwarks	hull-down	navigate	submerge
top mast	buntline	icebound	neap tide	surfboat
topsail	car ferry	ice-field	outboard	tacking
topside	castaway	Indiaman	paravane	taffrail
tornado	caulking	ironclad	pattamar	thole pin
torpedo	coasting	jackstay	pierhead	tranship
towline	cockboat	jettison	pilotage	trimaran
towpath	corvette	jury mast	poop deck	unbuoyed
towrope	crossing	keelhaul	porthole	under way
transom	cruising	keel over	portside	vanguard
trawler	cutwater	landfall	pump room	wardroom
trireme	dead slow	landmark	put about	waterman
trysail	deckhand	landsman	put to sea	windlass
tugboat	derelict	landward	quarters	windward
typhoon	ditty-bag	larboard	reef knot	wreckage
unladen	ditty-box	lead-line	re-embark	yachting
veering	dockyard	leeboard	sail loft	
ward off	dog watch	lee shore	sail room	**9**
warping	doldrums	lifebelt	sail yard	
warship	downhaul	lifeboat	salvable	admiralty
whistle	drifting	lifebuoy	salvager	afterdeck
wrecked	even keel	lifeline	sandbank	all aboard
wrecker	faltboat	load line	schooner	alongside
yardarm	flagship	longboat	scudding	amidships
	floating	long haul	scuppers	anchorage
8	flotilla	longship	seaborne	anchoring
	fogbound	low water	sea chest	bargepole
ambatche	foldboat	magazine	seafarer	below deck
anchored	foot-rope	mailboat	seagoing	bilge-keel
at anchor	foremast	main boom	shallows	bilge pump
backstay	forepeak	main deck	sheer off	Blue Peter
backwash	foresail	mainmast	ship ahoy	boat drill
baidarka	forestay	mainsail	shipmate	bomb ketch
barbette	free port	mainstay	ship oars	broadside
bargeman	gaffsail	main yard	shipping	canal boat
barnacle	go aboard	make sail	showboat	captaincy
beam-ends	go ashore	man of war	squadron	cargo boat
becalmed	gunsloop	maritime	spy-glass	catamaran
berthage	halliard	masthead	squadron	chartroom
berthing	halyards	mastless	standard	close haul
binnacle	hatchway	messmate	stand off	cock-boat
boatdeck	head into	midships	staysail	craftsman
boathook	headwind	moorings	steerage	crosstree
bowsprit	high seas	mutineer	sternway	crosswind
broach to	high tide	mutinous	stowaway	crow's
				nest

4 5

Davy Jones
dead water
deck cargo
departure
destroyer
discharge
disembark
dress ship
driftwood
Elmo's fire
ferryboat
fire drill
flood tide
flying jib
foreshore
foundered
freeboard
freighter
gangplank
half-hitch
hard aport
high water
hoist sail
holystone
houseboat
house flag
hurricane
hydrofoil
jack-staff
jolly boat
kentledge
lightship
lower deck
maelstrom
mainbrace
mainsheet
midstream
minefield
minelayer
mizzentop
motorboat
navigable
navigator
orlop deck
outrigger
overboard

periscope
pilot boat
powerboat
press gang
privateer
prize crew
quicksand
red ensign
revictual
riverboat
roadstead
Royal Navy
rum runner
sailcloth
seafaring
seaworthy
semaphore
shipboard
ship's
  boat
ship's
  crew
shipshape
shipwreck
shoreward
sick berth
sidelight
sou'wester
speedboat
spindrift
spinnaker
spritsail
stanchion
starboard
stateroom
steamship
steersman
sternpost
stokehold
stromsail
submarine
tarpaulin
telescope
tide table
trade wind
troopship

twin-screw
two-decker
upper deck
waterline
whaleboat
whirlwind
yachtsman

10

aboard ship
alongshore
anchor buoy
banana boat
barkentine
batten down
battleship
Bermuda rig
bilge water
blue ensign
bluejacket
breakwater
bootlegger
brigantine
cargo space
cast anchor
catch a
  crab
charthouse
coal bunker
crosstrees
deadlights
degaussing
diving bell
diving suit
dockmaster
downstream
drop anchor
drop astern
engine room
fathomless
figurehead
fore-and-
  aft
forecastle
full-rigged

gaff-rigged
heavy-laden
high and
  dry
hovercraft
ice-breaker
Jolly Roger
jury-rigged
jury rudder
landlocked
landlubber
lateen sail
lay a
  course
liberty-man
life jacket
lighterage
lighthouse
marker buoy
martingale
middle deck
midshipman
mizzen mast
mizzen sail
narrow boat
navigating
navigation
night watch
ocean-going
packetboat
paddleboat
pipe aboard
port of
  call
powder room
prize money
prisonship
quadrireme
quarantine
raking fire
reduce sail
rendezvous
rope ladder
rowing boat
rudderless
rudder post

seamanship
ship broker
shipwright
slack water
spring tide
square-sail
stern-board
sternsheet
submariner
take in sail
tea clipper
tidal basin
tidal river
topgallant
tea clipper
unfathomed
upperworks
water-borne
waterspout
watertight
wheel-house
windjammer

11

abandon ship
barquantine
beachcomber
belaying pin
capital ship
captainship
centreboard
close-hauled
cockleshell
compass card
compass rose
contact mine
debarkation
depth charge
dreadnought
echo-sounder
embarkation
escape hatch
factory ship
fishing boat
galley-slave

get under way
go alongside
graving dock
ground-swell
harbour dues
hug the shore
keelhauling
landing deck
lifeboatman
make headway
merchantman
middle watch
minesweeper
motor launch
naval rating
paddle-wheel
port of entry
quarterdeck
quinquereme
racing eight
rangefinder
riding light
sailing date
sailing ship
searchlight
seasickness
sheet anchor
shipbreaker
ship's doctor
ship's papers
spring a leak
standing off
steam launch
steerage-way
stern-chaser
submersible
supertanker
support ship
three-decker
three-master
thwartships
torpedo boat
torpedo tube
unballasted
unnavigable

waterlogged
weather ship
weather side
weigh anchor
white ensign

12

air-sea rescue
between-decks
bill of lading
breeches buoy
cabin cruiser
cable's-length
change course
clinker-built
collision mat
companionway
conning tower
displacement
East Indiaman
escort vessel
fishing fleet
floating dock
futtock-plate
ground tackle
hospital ship
Jacob's ladder
landing craft
liberty ship
line of battle
longshoreman
magnetic mine
maiden voyage
man overboard
marine engine
marline spike
merchant ship
minesweeping
nautical mile
navigability
outward-bound
Plimsoll line
privateering
recommission

ride at anchor
ship chandler
shipping lane
square-rigged
starboard bow
studding sail
tourist class
training ship
tramp steamer
transhipment
Trinity House
undercurrent
unfathomable
weatherglass
will-o'-the-wisp

13

battle cruiser
cat-o'-nine-tails
close quarters
container ship
dead reckoning
grappling iron
high-water mark
hurricane deck
life-preserver
naval dockyard
order of battle
paddle steamer
passenger ship
quartermaster
re-embarkation
royal dockyard
ship of the line
starboard beam

14

channel steamer
circumnavigate
compass bearing
disembarkation
letter of marque
Lloyd's Register

naval architect
powder magazine
prevailing wind
schooner-rigged
screw propeller
ship's carpenter
superstructure
topgallant mast

15 +

aircraft carrier
Davy Jones' locker
mariner's compass
motor torpedo boat
pocket battleship
through-deck cruiser

Books of the Bible

Old Testament

Genesis	Gen.	I. Kings	I Kgs.
Ecclesiastes	Eccles.	Obadiah	Obad.
Exodus	Exod.	II. Kings	II Kgs.
Song of Solomon	S. of S.	Jonah	Jonah
Leviticus	Lev.	I. Chronicles	I Chr.
Isaiah	Isa.	Micah	Mic.
Numbers	Num.	II. Chronicles	II Chr.
Jeremiah	Jer.	Nahum	Nahum
Deuteronomy	Deut.	Ezra	Ezra
Lamentations	Lam.	Habakkuk	Hab.
Joshua	Josh.	Nehemiah	Neh.
Ezekiel	Ezek.	Zephaniah	Zeph.
Judges	Judg.	Esther	Esther
Daniel	Dan.	Haggai	Hag.
Ruth	Ruth	Job	Job
Hosea	Hos.	Zechariah	Zech.
I. Samuel	I Sam.	Psalms	Ps.
Joel	Joel	Malachi	Mal.
II. Samuel	II Sa.	Proverbs	Prov.
Amos	Amos		

New Testament

Matthew	Matt.	John	John
I. Timothy	I Tim.	Philemon	Philem.
Mark	Mark	The Acts	Acts
II. Timothy	II Tim.	To the Hebrews	Heb.
Luke	Luke	The Romans	Rom.
Titus	Titus	Epistle of James	Jas.
		I. Corinthians	I Cor.

I. Peter	I Pet.	III. John	III John
II. Corinthians	II Cor.	Colossians	Col.
II. Peter	II Pet.	Jude	Jude
Galatians	Gal.	I. Thessalonains	I Thes.
I. John	I John	Revelation	Rev.
Ephesians	Eph. II.	II. Thessalonians	II Thes.
John	II John		
Philippians	Phil.		

Apocrypha

I. Esdras	I Esd.
II. Esdras	II Esd.
Tobit	Tobit
Judith	Judith
The Rest of Esther	Rest of Esth.
The Wisdom of Solomon	Wisd.
Ecclesiasticus	Ecclus.
Baruch, with the Epistle of Jeremiah	Baruch
The Song of the Three Holy Children	S. of III Ch.
The History of Susanna	Sus.
Bel and the Dragon	Bel & Dr.
The Prayer of Manasses	Pr. of Man.
I. Maccabees	I Macc.
II. Maccabees	II Macc.

Old Testament

3 & 4
Amos
Ezra
Job
Joel
Ruth

5
Hosea
Jonah
Kings
Micah
Nahum

6
Daniel
Esther
Exodus
Haggai
Isaiah
Joshua
Judges
Psalms
Samuel

7
Ezekiel
Genesis
Numbers
Obadiah

Malachi
Solomon

8
Habakkuk
Jeremiah
Nehemiah
Proverbs

9
Leviticus
Zechariah
Zephaniah

10
Chronicles

11
Deuteronomy

12
Ecclesiastes
Lamentations

13
Song of Solomon

New Testament

4
Acts
John
Jude
Luke
Mark

5
James
Peter

Titus

6
Romans

7
Hebrews
Matthew
Timothy

8
Philemon

9
Ephesians
Galatians

10
Colossians
Revelation

11
Corinthians
Philippians

13
Thessalonians

Bottles and barrels

3
keg = 5-10 galls
nip = $^1/_6$ bottle
pin = $4^1/_2$ galls
tun = 210 galls
vat = variable

4
baby = $^1/_8$ bottle
back = variable
butt = 110 galls
cask = variable
pipe = 105 galls

6
barrel = 36 galls
bushel = 8 galls
carafe = variable
carboy = variable
firkin = 9 galls
magnum = 2 bottles

8
demijohn = variable
hogshead = 54 galls
Jeroboam = 4 bottles
puncheon = 72 galls
Rehaboam = 6 bottles

9
Balthazar = 16 bottles
kilderkin = 18 galls

10 +
double magnum = 4 bottles
Methuselah = 8 bottles
Nebuchadnezzar = 20 bottles
Salmanazar = 12 bottles

Boxing weights

9
flyweight

11
heavyweight
lightweight

12
bantamweight

middleweight
welterweight

13
cruiserweight
featherweight

14
light-flyweight
super-flyweight

15 +
light-heavyweight
light-middleweight
light-welterweight
super-bantamweight
super-feather-
  weight
super-heavyweight
super-lightweight
super-middleweight
super-welterweight

British and Irish counties and regions

(including abbreviations, former county names and island areas of Scotland)

3 & 4
Avon
Ayr
Beds
Bute
Cork
Down
Fife
Kent
Leix
Mayo
Oxon
Ross
York

5
Angus
Banff
Berks
Bucks
Cambs
Cavan

Clare
Clwyd
Derby
Devon
Dyfed
Elgin
Essex
Flint
Gwent
Hants
Herts
Hunts
Kerry
Lancs
Louth
Meath
Moray
Nairn
Notts
Perth
Powys
Salop
Sligo

Wilts

6
Antrim
Argyll
Armagh
Border
Brecon
Carlow
Dorset
Dublin
Durham
Forfar
Galway
Lanark
London
Offaly
Orkney
Oxford
Radnor
Staffs
Surrey

Sussex
Tyrone

7
Bedford
Berwick
Central
Cumbria
Denbigh
Donegal
Gwynedd
Kildare
Kinross
Leitrim
Lincoln
Lothian
Norfolk
Peebles
Renfrew
Rutland
Selkirk
Suffolk
Tayside

Warwick
Wexford
Wicklow
Wigtown

8
Aberdeen
Anglesey
Ayrshire
Cardigan
Cheshire
Cornwall
Cromarty
Dumfries
Grampian
Hereford
Hertford
Highland
Kilkenny
Limerick
Longford
Monaghan

Monmouth
Pembroke
Roxburgh
Shetland
Somerset
Stafford
Stirling

9

Berkshire
Caithness
Cambridge
Cleveland
Connaught
Dunbarton
Edinburgh
Fermanagh
Fifeshire
Glamorgan
Hampshire
Inverness
Leicester
Merioneth
Middlesex
Northants
Roscommon
Tipperary
Waterford
Westmeath
Wiltshire
Worcester
Yorkshire

10

Banffshire
Buckingham
Caernarvon
Carmarthen
Cumberland
Derbyshire
East Sussex
Flintshire
Gloucester
Haddington

Humberside
Huntingdon
Kincardine
Lancashire
Linlithgow
Merseyside
Midlothian
Montgomery
Morayshire
Nottingham
Perthshire
Shropshire
Sutherland
West Sussex

11

Argyllshire
Clackmannan
Dorsetshire
East Lothian
Forfarshire
Isle of Wight
King's County
Lanarkshire
Londonderry
Northampton
Oxfordshire
Radnorshire
Strathclyde
Tyne and Wear
West Lothian
Westmorland

12

Bedfordshire
Berwickshire
Denbighshire
Kirkudbright
Lincolnshire
Mid Glamorgan
Queen's County
Renfrewshire
Rutlandshire
Warwickshire

Western Isles
West Midlands

13

Aberdeenshire
Cardiganshire
Dumfriesshire
Herefordshire
Hertfordshire
Monmouthshire
Pembrokeshire
Staffordshire
Stirlingshire
West Glamorgan
West Yorkshire

14

Brecknockshire
Cambridgeshire
Dunbartonshire
Glamorganshire
Inverness-shire
Leicestershire
Merionethshire
Northumberland
North Yorkshire
South Glamorgan
South Yorkshire
Worcestershire

15 +

Buckinghamshire
Caernarvonshire
Carmarthenshire
Clackmannanshire
Dumfries and Galloway
Gloucestershire
Huntingdonshire
Kircudbrightshire
Montgomeryshire
Northamptonshire
Nottinghamshire
Ross and Cromarty

British Prime Ministers

4

Bute, (Lord)
Eden, Sir Anthony
Grey, Lord
Peel, Sir Robert
Pitt, William

5

Blair, Anthony
Brown, Gordon
Derby, (Earl of)
Heath, Edward R.
Major, John
North, (Lord)

6

Attlee, Clement R.
Wilson, (J.) Harold

7

Asquith, Herbert H.
Baldwin, Stanley
Balfour, Arthur J.
Canning, George
Russell, Lord John

8

Aberdeen, (Earl of)
Bonar Law, Andrew

Disraeli Benjamin
Goderich, (Viscount)
Perceval, Spencer
Portland, (Duke of)
Rosebery, (Earl of)
Thatcher, Margaret H.

9

Addington, Henry
Callaghan, (L.) James
Churchill, Winston S.
Gladstone, William E.
Grenville, (Lord)
Liverpool, (Earl of)
MacDonald, (James) Ramsay
Macmillan, Harold
Melbourne, (Viscount)
Salisbury, (Marquess of)
Shelburne, Lord

10

Palmerston, (Viscount)
Rockingham, (Earl of)
Wellington, (Duke of)

11

Chamberlain, Neville
Douglas-Home, Sir Alec
Lloyd-George, David

12

Campbell-Bannerman, Sir

Canadian Prime Ministers

4
King, William M.

5
Clark, Joseph

6
Abbott, Sir John
Borden, Sir Robert
Bowell, Sir Mackenzie
Harper, Stephen
Martin, Paul
Tupper, Sir Charles
Turner, John

7
Bennett, Richard B.
Laurier, Sir Wilfrid

Meighen, Arthur
Pearson, Lester B.
Trudeau, Pierre E.

8
Campbell, Kim
Chrétien, Jean
Thompson, Sir John
Mulroney, Brian

9
Macdonald, Sir John
Mackenzie, Alexander
St. Laurent, Louis S.

11
Diefenbaker, John

Canadian provinces and territories

Provinces

Alberta
British Columbia
Manitoba
New Brunswick
Newfoundland

Nova Scotia
Ontario
Prince Edward Island
Quebec
Saskatchewan

Territories

Northwest Territories
Yukon Territory

Capital cities and towns

4

Aden
Apia
Baku
Bern
Dili
Doha
Kiev
Lima
Lome
Malé
Oslo
Riga
Rome
San'a
Suva
Vila

5

Abuja
Accra
Agaña
Ajman
Alofi
Amman
Berne
Cairo
Dacca
Dakar
Dehli
Dhaka
Dubai
Hanoi
Kabul
Koror
La Paz
Macao
Minsk
Nauru
Paris
Praia
Quito

Rabat
Sana'a
Seoul
Sofia
Sucre
Tokyo
Tunis
Vaduz
Zagreb
Zomba

6

Ankara
Asmara
Astana
Athens
Avarua
Bagdad
Bamako
Bangui
Banjul
Beirut
Belice
Belize
Berlin
Bissau
Bogotá
Brunei
Dodoma
Dublin
Erevan
Habana
Harare
Havana
Kigali
Kuwait
Lisbon
London
Luanda
Lusaka
Madrid
Majuro

Malabo
Manama
Manila
Maputo
Maseru
Masqat
Mexico
Monaco
Moroni
Moscow
Muscat
Nassau
Naimey
Noumea
Ottawa
Panama
Peking
Prague
Riyadh
Roseau
Saigon
Saipan
Skopje
Taipei
Tarawa
Tehran
Thimbu
Thimpu
Tirana
Vienna
Warsaw

7

Abidjan
Algiers
Andorra
Baghdad
Bangkok
Beijing
Belfast
Caracas
Cardiff

Cayenne
Colombo
Conakry
Cotonou
Douglas
El Aaiun
Gangtok
Honiara
Jakarta
Kampala
Kolonia
Managua
Mata-Utu
Mbabane
Nairobi
Nicosia
Papeete
Rangoon
St. Denis
St. John's
San José
San Juan
Santiago
Sao Tomé
Sharjah
Stanley
Tallinn
Tbilisi
Thimphu
Tripoli
Valetta
Vatican
Vilnius
Yaoundé
Yerevan

8

Abu Dhabi
Ashgabat
Asunciòn
Belgrade
Belmopan

Bishkek
Brasilia
Brussels
Budapest
Canberra
Cape Town
Castries
Chinisau
Damascus
Djibouti
Dushanbe
Freetown
Fujairah
Funafuti
Gaborone
Hamilton
Helsinki
Katmandu
Khartoum
Kingston
Kinshasa
Laayoune
Lilongwe
Monrovia
N'Djamena
New Delhi
Pago Pago
Plymouth
Pretoria
Pristina
Road Town
St. Helier
St. Pierre
Santiago
Sarajevo
Tashkent
The Hague
Valletta
Victoria
Windhoek

9

Amsterdam
Bucharest
Bujumbura
Edinburgh
Gaberones
Gibraltar
Grand Turk
Guatemala
Islamabad
Jamestown
Jerusalem
Kathmandu
Kingstown
Ljubjlana
Mogadishu
Naypyidaw
Nuku'alofa
Phnom Penh
Podgorica
Port Louis
Porto Novo
Pyongyang
Reykjavik
St George's
Salisbury
San Marino
Singapore
Stockholm
The Valley
Thorshavn
Ulan Bator

Vientiane

10

Addis Ababa
Basse-Terre
Bratislava
Bridgetown
Copenhagen
East Berlin
Georgetown
George Town
Kuwait City
Libreville
Luxembourg
Mamoundzou
Mexico City
Montevideo
Nouakchott
Oranjestad
Panama City
Paramaribo
Quezon City
Tananarive
Washington
Willemstad
Wellington

11

Brazzaville
Buenos Aires
Dar es Salaam

Kuala Lumpur
Monaco-ville
Ouagadougou
Port Moresby
Port of Spain
St. Peter Port
San Salvador
Santa Isabel
Tegucipalpa
Vatican City

12

Antananarivo
Luang Prabang
Port au Prince
Ras al-Khaimah
Santo Domingo
Umm al-Qaiwain

13

Guatemala City
Medina as-Shaab
Uaboe District

14

Andorra la Vella

15 +

Bandar Seri Begawan
Charlotte Amalie

Castles (British) and fortification

(including some fictional)

3		**4**					**5**	
Hay	Oer		Deal	Fast	Pool	Udny	Borve	
May			Doon	Holt	Raby	York	Boyne	
Mey			Dore	Leod	Rait		Burgh	
Moy		Acre	Dote	Maol	Ring		Carew	
Odo		Bere	Drum	Maud	Roch	Blair	Chirk	
			Duns	Peel	Star		Clare	

Coity
Corfe
Cowes
Croft
Cutra
Donne
Dover
Drogo
Duart
Elcho
Ewloe
Flint
Fyvie
Gylen
Hawen
Hever
Hurst
Keiss
Keldy
Knock
Leeds
Lewes
Lymne
Mylor
Powis
Riber
Slane
Sween
Tenby
Zenda

6

Aboyne
Airlie
Auchen
Bodiam
Bolton
Brecon
Brodie
Brough
Builth
Cawdor
Conway
Cornet
Dudley

Duffus
Dundee
Dunure
Durham
Edzell
Exeter
Floors
Forter
Fraser
Glamis
Gordon
Gwrych
Gwydir
Hailes
Hoddom
Howard
Huntly
Kendal
Ludlow
Maiden
Midmar
Millom
Morton
Newark
Nunney
Ogmore
Oxford
Picton
Raglan
Raheen
Rowton
Spynie
Strame
Walmer
Walton
Yester

7

Adamant
Affleck
Alnwick
Appleby
Ardross
Arundel
Balloch

Barholm
Barnard
Beeston
Belvoir
Blarney
Braemar
Bramber
Bratton
Brodick
Cadbury
Caister
Cardiff
Chester
Cooling
Compton
Cowdray
Crathes
Culzean
Denbigh
Douglas
Dunluce
Dunskey
Dunster
Duntulm
Dynevor
Finavon
Guthrie
Harlech
Huntley
Kanturk
Kennedy
Kielder
Kilmory
Kinkell
Lincoln
Lochnaw
Lowther
Mingary
Narwick
Naworth
Newport
Niddrie
Norwich
Penrhyn
Penrice
Penrith

Rattray
Rossend
Ruthven
Saddell
St. Denis
St. Mawes
Seagate
Sizergh
Skipton
Stalker
Sudeley
Swansea
Taunton
Threave
Tilbury
Tutbury
Uisdein
Warwick
Wigmore
Windsor
Wressle

8

Aberdour
Amberley
Ardvreck
Ardmaddy
Balmoral
Balvenie
Bamburgh
Baynard's
Berkeley
Bothwell
Brougham
Bruckley
Burleigh
Campbell
Cardigan
Carlisle
Carsluth
Chepstow
Cigerran
Corgarff
Crawford
Crichton

Darnaway
Delgatie
Dirleton
Doubting
Dryslwyn
Drummond
Dunottar
Duntrune
Dunvegan
Finlarig
Goodrich
Hawarden
Helmsley
Hertford
Kidwelly
Kilchurn
Langwell
Maxstoke
Mountjoy
Muchalls
Neidpath
Nottland
Pembroke
Pevensey
Pitcaple
Pitsligo
Pittulie
Plymouth
Rhuddlan
Richmond
Rothesay
Roxburgh
St. Donats
Sandwich
Southsea
Stirling
Stokesay
Stormont
Sycharth
Tamworth
Thetford
Tintagel
Urquhart
Walworth
Yarnbury

9

Allington
Beaumaris
Blackness
Borthwick
Broughton
Cambridge
Cardoness
Carlswith
Caulfield
Cilgerran
Claypotts
Clitheroe
Comlongon
Craignish
Criccieth
Crookston
Dalhousie
Dalnaglar
Dinas Bran
Donnamore
Drumminor
Dumbarton
Dundonald
Dunnottar
Earlshall
East Cowes
Edinburgh
Findlater
Glasclune
Greystoke
Haverford
Hedingham
Hermitage
Keissimul

Kildrummy
Kilkerran
Killochan
Kilracock
Kimbolton
Lancaster
Lochleven
Manorbier
Middleham
Muncaster
Newcastle
Old Slains
Pembridge
Pendennis
Pickering
Powderham
Restormel
Rochester
St. Andrews
Scalloway
Sherborne
Skenfrith
Tantallon
Tregennis
Ulzieside
Warkworth

10

Auchindown
Caernarfon
Caerphilly
Carmarthen
Colchester
Craigievar

Donnington
Fort George
Inverlochy
Kenilworth
Launceston
Linlithgow
Lochindore
Lough Cutra
Okehampton
Pontefract
Porchester
Portsmouth
Rockingham
St. Briavels
Sutherland
Winchester

11

Abergavenny
Aberystwyth
Armathwaite
Aughentaine
Carisbrooke
Carnasserie
Castlecraig
Chillingham
Cockermouth
Conisbrough
Craignethan
Dolwyddelan
Fort William
Framlingham
Harry Avery's
Lindisfarne

Llantrisant
Llanstephan
Painscastle
Ravensburgh
Ravenscraig
Scarborough
Tattershall

12

Berry Pomeroy
Caerlaverock
Carreg Cennen
Castel Y Bere
Christchurch
Dunstanburgh
Eilean Donnan
Fotheringhay
Fraoch Eilean
Hertsmonceux
Huntingtower
Inverallochy
Kinlochaline
Tower of London

13

Kaim of Mathers
Kirkcudbright
Smaitham Tower

14

Ashby de la
Zouche

Some technical terms

3 & 4

cob
rib
apse
arch
bay

berm
bond
hall
hood
jamb
keep

loop
moat
pier
rath
yett

5

aisle
fosse
gable
joist
light

mural
rewel
oriel
pitch
scarp
shaft

solar
splay
vault

6

abacus
arcade
ashlar
aumbry
bailey
batter
clunch
course
crenel
donjon
dormer
fillet
fresco
impost
lancet
louvre
merlon
oolite
plinth
rubble
soffit
squint
turret

7

bastion
bratice
chamfer

chevron
cornice
curtain
gallery
groined
mullion
oratory
parados
parapet
piscina
postern
rampart
ravelin
saltire
tracery
transom
trefoil

8

barbican
bartizan
bivalate
buttress
dogtooth
dressing
drystone
foliated
footings
hillfort
mangonel

moulding
nailhead
palisade
pediment
pilaster
pinnacle
pitching
ring-work
voussoir
wing-wall

9

castellan
constable
crosswall
drum-tower
embattled
embrasure
freestone
garderobe
half-shaft
nookshaft
openjoint
refectory
revetment
roofridge
shell-keep
trebuchet
vitrified
wall-stair

10

ambulatory
battlement
diaper work
drawbridge
meutrieres
portcullis
quadrangle
Romanesque
weathering

11

castellated
counterfort
herringbone
motte-bailey
rustication

12 +

castellation
counterscarp
forebuilding
great chamber
multivallate
stringcourse
machicolation

Cathedrals, abbeys and priories

Cathedrals

3 4, & 5

Ely
Derby
Elgin
Ripon
Truro

Wells

6

Bangor
Brecon
Durham

Exeter
Oxford

7

Brechin
Bristol

Chester
Dornoch
Dunkeld
Glasgow
Lincoln
Norwich
St. Asaph

St. Paul's

St. David's
St. Woolos

Salisbury
Sheffield
Southwark
Southwell
Wakefield
Worcester

Manchester
Portsmouth
Winchester

8
Aberdeen
Bradford
Carlisle
Coventry
Dunblane
Hereford
Kirkwall
Llandaff
St. Albans

9
Blackburn
Edinburgh
Guildford
Leicester
Lichfield
Liverpool
Newcastle
Rochester
St. Andrews

10
Birmingham
Canterbury
Chichester
Chelmsford
Gloucester

11
York Minster

12
Peterborough

13
Bury St. Edmunds

Abbeys and priories

3 & 4
Bath
Dale
Iona
Kyme
Usk

5
Blyth
Kelso
Selby
Swine
Tilty
Torre

6
Battle
Bayham
Binham
Bourne
Boxley
Bungay
Byland
Elstow
Ewenny

Hexham
Hurley
Ingham
Jarrow
Knaith
Lapley
Launde
Lenton
Margam
Milton
Owston
Pamber
Penmon
Pilton
Ramsey
Romsey
St. Bees
Whitby
Witham

7
Alnwick
Cartmel
Culross
Dunster
Leiston
Marrick

Melrose
Minster
Monkton
Paisley
Royston
Thorney
Tintern
Tutbury
Waltham
Worksop
Wroxall

8
Amesbury
Arbroath
Augustus
Beaulieu
Boxgrove
Cardigan
Chepstow
Chirbury
Croyland
Dalkeith
Dryburgh
Fairwell
Freiston
Glenluce

Holyrood
Jedburgh
Kidwelly
Merevale
Newstead
Nuneaton
Pershore
Rumburgh
St. Clears
Whithorn
Woodkirk

9
Abbey Dore
Beauchief
Blackmore
Brinkburn
Bromfield
Cranborne
Davington
Deerhurst
Haughmond
Kirkstall
Kirkstead
Lancaster
Lanercost
Newbattle

Old Malton
Prinknash
St. Germans
Sherborne
Stogursey
Stranraer
Up Holland
Weybourne
Wymondham

10

Ardchattan
Atherstone
Birkenhead
Blanchland
Dorchester
Dundrennan
Inchmahome
Lastingham
Leominster
LLangenith
Malmesbury
Monk's Kirby
Nun Monkton

Polesworth
Shrewsbury
Sweetheart
Tewkesbury
Thurgarton

11

Abergavenny
Bridlington
Canons Ashby
Carisbrooke
Crossraguel
Dunfermline
Glastonbury
Holm Cultram
West Malling
Westminster

12

Christchurch
Fort Augustus
Great Bricett
Great Malvern
Letheringham

Little Dunmow
Redlingfield

13

Cambuskenneth
Little Malvern
Monk Wearmouth

14

Bristol, St. James
Deeping St. James
Leonard Stanley
LLanbadarn Fawr
Hatfield Peveral
York, Holy Trinity
St. Michael's
  Mount

16

Breedon-on-the-
  Hill
Hatfield Broad Oak
Little Coggeshall

Cheeses

4

blue
Brie
curd
Edam
tome

5

banon
brick
caboc
comte
cream
danbo
Derby
Dutch

6

asiago
bagnes
bondon
bresse

fetta
Gouda
herve
leigh
molbo
murol
niolo
Swiss
tamie
toucy

cachat
cantal
cendre
Dunlop
fourme
gapron
Gerome
halumi
hrasma
laruns
leiden
morven
olivet
rollot
salers
samsoe
sbrinz

surati
tilsit
venaco

7

bondard
boursin
brinzen
broccio
brocciu
brousse
brucciu
bryndza
cabecou
Cheddar
cottage

crowdie
dauphin
demi-sel
fontina
gaperon
Gruyère
jonchee
langres
levroux
limburg
livarot
macquée
mont-d'or
morbier
munster
mycella
nantais

picodon
pyramid
quargel
ricotta
sapsago
Stilton
vendôme

8

auvergne
Ayrshire
beaufort
beauvoir
bel paëse
bergkase
boulette

brickbat
chaource
Cheshire
Cotswold
edelpilz
emmental
epoisses
manchego
Parmesan
pecarino
pelardon
remoudou
rigottes
scamorze
taleggio
vacherin
valencay

9

appenzall
blue vinny
broodkass
Caithness
cambozola
Camembert
Chabichou
chevreton
emmenthal
excelsior
gambozola
gammelost
jarlsburg
la bouille
la gougère
Leicester
limburger
lymeswold
mâconnais
maroilles
mimolette

pave d'auge
port-salut
provolone
reblochon
roquefort
sage Derby

10

belle paese
Caerphilly
Danish blue
dolcelatte
Gloucester
gorgonzola
Lancashire
mozzarella
neufchatel
pithiviers
poivre d'ane
red Windsor
saingorlon
stracchino

11

carre de l'est
coeur de bray
coulommiers
croute rouge
katshkawalj
petit-suisse
pont-l'eveque
Saint Maurie
Saint Paulin
schabzieger
schlosskase
tête-de-moine
tome au raisin
triple cream
weisslacker

Wensleydale

12

bleu de bresse
blue Cheshire
caciocavallo
red Leicester
soumaintrain
tome de savoie

13

bleu d'auvergne
Saint-Nectaire
selles-sur-cher

14

bleu des causses
brillat-savarin
feuille de dreux
laguiole-aubrac
nantais dit cure
Saint-Florentine
Saint-Marcellin
trappistenkase

15 +

boulette d'avenes
bouton-de-culotte
chevrotin des aravis
crottin de chavignol
double Gloucester
pouligny-Saint-
  Pierre
rigotte de pelussin
valencay levroux
Westminster blue

Chemical elements

(alphabetical list, with symbols)

actinium	Ac	hafnium	Hf	promethium	Pm
aluminium	Al	hahnium	Ha	protactinium	Pa
americium	Am	Hassium	Hs	radium	Ra
antimony	Sb	helium	He	radon	Rn
argon	Ar	holmium	Ho	rhenium	Re
arsenic	As	hydrogen	H	rhodium	Rh
astatine	At	indium	In	rontgenium	Rg
barium	Ba	iodine	I	rubidium	Rb
berkelium	Bk	iridium	Ir	ruthenium	Ru
beryllium	Be	iron	Fe	rutherfordium	Rf
bismuth	Bi	krypton	Kr	samarium	Sm
bohrium	Bh	lanthanum	La	scandium	Sc
boron	B	lawrencium	Lr	seaborgium	Sg
bromine	Br	lead	Pb	selenium	Se
cadmium	Cd	lithium	Li	silicon	Si
caesium	Cs	lutetium	Lu	silver	Ag
calcium	Ca	magnesium	Mg	sodium	Na
californium	Cf	manganese	Mn	strontium	Sr
carbon	C	meitnerium	Mr	sulphur	S
cerium	Ce	mendelevium	Md	tantalum	Ta
chlorine	Cl	mercury	Hg	technetium	Tc
chromium	Cr	molybdenum	Mo	tellurium	Te
cobalt	Co	neodymium	Nd	terbium	Tb
copper	Cu	neon	Ne	thallium	Tl
curium	Cm	neptunium	Np	thorium	Th
darmstadtium	Ds	nickel	Ni	thulium	Tm
dubnium	Db	niobium	Nb	tin	Sn
dysprosium	Dy	nitrogen	N	titanium	Ti
einsteinium	Es	nobelium	No	tungsten	W
erbium	Er	osmium	Os	uranium	U
europium	Eu	oxygen	O	vanadium	V
fermium	Fm	palladium	Pd	xenon	Xe
fluorine	F	phosphorus	P	ytterbium	Yb
francium	Fr	platinum	Pt	yttrium	Y
gadolinium	Gd	plutonium	Pu	zinc	Zn
gallium	Ga	polonium	Po	zirconium	Zr
germanium	Ge	potassium	K		
gold	Au	praeseodymium	Pr		

3
tin

4
gold
iron
lead
zinc

5
argon
boron
radon
xenon

6
barium
carbon
cerium
cobalt
copper
curium
erbium

helium
iodine
nickel
osmium
oxygen
radium
silver
sodium

7
arsenic
bohrium
bismuth
bromine
cadmium
caesium
calcium
dubnium
fermium
gallium
hafnium
hahnium
holmium
iridium
krypton
lithium

mercury
niobium
rhenium
rhodium
silicon
sulphur
terbium
thorium
thulium
uranium
yttrium

8
actinium
antimony
astatine
chromium
europium
francium
hydrogen
lutetium
nitrogen
nobelium
platinum
polonium
rubidium

samarium
scandium
selenium
tantalum
thallium
titanium
tungsten
vanadium

9
aluminium
americium
berkelium
beryllium
germanium
lanthanum
magnesium
manganese
neodymium
neptunium
palladium
potassium
ruthenium
strontium
ytterbium
zirconium

10
dysprosium
gadolinium
lawrencium
meitnerium
molybdenum
phosphorus
promethium
rontgenium
seaborgium
technetium

11
californium
einsteinium
mendelevium

12
darmstadtium
praseodymium
protactinium

13
rutherfordium

Chinese calendar

Rat	1924	1936	1948	1960	1972	1984	1996	2008
Ox	1925	1937	1949	1961	1973	1985	1997	2009
Tiger	1926	1938	1950	1962	1974	1986	1998	2010
Hare	1927	1939	1951	1963	1975	1987	1999	2011
Dragon	1928	1940	1952	1964	1976	1988	2000	2012
Snake	1929	1941	1953	1965	1977	1989	2001	2013
Horse	1930	1942	1954	1966	1978	1990	2002	2014
Sheep	1931	1943	1955	1967	1979	1991	2003	2015
Monkey	1932	1944	1956	1968	1980	1992	2004	2016
Fowl	1933	1945	1957	1969	1981	1993	2005	2017
Dog	1934	1946	1958	1970	1982	1994	2006	2018
Pig	1935	1947	1959	1971	1983	1995	2007	2019

Cinque Ports

3
Rye

Hythe

6
Romney

8
Hastings
Sandwich

10
Winchelsea

5
Dover

Cities and towns

3	4 (cont.)			
Abo	Caen	Luta	Waco	Blyth	Enugu

3	4	4	4	4	4
Abo	Caen	Luta	Waco	Blyth	Enugu
Aix	Cali	Lvov	Ware	Boise	Epsom
Ava	Cobh	Lydd	Wick	Boyle	Errol
Ayr	Cork	Lyon	Yarm	Bowen	Essen
Ely	Deal	Male	York	Brest	Evian
Fez	Diss	Metz		Bronx	Filey
Pau	Doha	Mold	**5**	Brora	Flint
Rye	Duns	Muff	Abuja	Bunaw	Fowey
Ufa	Elie	Nice	Aaiun	Butte	Frome
Usk	Eton	Oban	Accra	Cairo	Gavle
Wem	Gaza	Omsk	Ajmer	Calne	Genoa
Wye	Gera	Oran	Akron	Ceres	Galle
	Giza	Oslo	Alloa	Chard	Ghent
4	Graz	Pécs	Alofi	Cheam	Goole
Aden	Hilo	Pisa	Alton	Clare	Gorky
Agra	Holt	Reno	Alwar	Colne	Gurst
Albi	Homs	Rhyl	Amman	Cowes	Hague
Alva	Hove	Riga	Annan	Crail	Haifa
Apia	Hull	Roma	Arhus	Crewe	Halle
Baku	Hyde	Rome	Arles	Cupar	Hanoi
Bala	Ince	Rona	Arras	Cuzco	Hedon
Bâle	Kano	Ross	Aswan	Dacca	Herat
Bari	Kiel	Ryde	Avaru	Dakar	Hythe
Barr	Kiev	Sana	Ayton	Delft	Izmir
Bath	Kirn	Shap	Bacup	Delhi	Jaffa
Bern	Kobe	Sian	Balla	Denny	Kabul
Bonn	Köln	Stow	Banff	Derby	Kandy
Bray	Lamu	Suez	Basra	Dijon	Kazan
Brno	Leek	Suhl	Basse	Doagh	Keiss
Bude	Lima	Suva	Basel	Dover	Keith
Bury	Linz	Troy	Basle	Egham	Kells
	Looe	Tyre	Berne	Elgin	Kelso
	Lodz	Vasa		Ellon	Koror
	Lome	Vigo		Ellon	Kotah

6 5

Kyoto	Perth	Vaduz	Bayeux	Cromer	Hexham
Lagos	Pinsk	Varna	Beauly	Crieff	Hobart
Lairg	Poole	Vilna	Bedale	Cullen	Howrah
La Paz	Poona	Visby	Beirut	Dairen	Huntly
Largo	Posen	Wells	Belcoo	Dallas	Ibadan
Larne	Praia	Wigan	Belize	Danzig	Ilford
Leeds	Pskov	Worms	Belper	Darwen	Ilkley
Leigh	Quito	Wuhan	Beragh	Darwin	Imphal
Leith	Rabat	Yalta	Berber	Dayton	Indore
Lewes	Reims	Yaren	Bergen	Denver	Irvine
Liege	Ripon	Ypres	Berlin	Dieppe	Jaipur
Lille	Risca		Bhopal	Dinant	Jarrow
Louth	Rosas		Biggar	Dodoma	Jeddah
Luton	Rouen	**6**	Bilbao	Dollar	Jhansi
Luxor	Rugby	Aachen	Biloxi	Dublin	Juarez
Lyons	Salem	Abadan	Bissau	Dudley	Kanpur
Macon	Salen	Aboyne	Bochum	Dunbar	Kassel
Mâcon	Selby	Agadir	Bodmin	Dundee	Kaunas
Mainz	Selma	Albany	Bognor	Dunlop	Kendal
Malmo	Seoul	Aleppo	Bogotá	Dunnet	Kigali
March	Sidon	Alford	Bolton	Dunoon	Killin
Mecca	Siena	Amalfi	Bombay	Durban	Kohima
Miami	Simla	Amiens	Bo'ness	Durham	Krakow
Milan	Sligo	Ancona	Bootle	Eccles	Kuwait
Minsk	Sofia	Ankara	Boston	El Paso	Lanark
Mosul	Split	Anshan	Bourne	Epping	Lahore
Nairn	Stoke	Alston	Brecon	Erfurt	Lauder
Namur	Stone	Antrim	Bremen	Eugene	Leiden
Nancy	Sucre	Arklow	Bruges	Exeter	Le Mans
Natal	Tampa	Arnhem	Bruton	Forfar	Leslie
Neath	Tanta	Ashton	Buckie	Forres	Leyden
Nevin	Tenby	Athens	Builth	Fresno	Linton
Newry	Thame	Austin	Bungay	Fushun	Lisbon
Nimes	Tokyo	Babani	Burton	Galatz	Lobito
Olney	Toome	Balboa	Buxton	Galway	London
Omagh	Tours	Bamako	Cairns	Geneva	Luanda
Omaha	Trent	Bangor	Calais	Gdansk	Lubeck
Osaka	Trier	Banjul	Callan	Goring	Lublin
Ostia	Tring	Bantry	Cannes	Hanley	Ludlow
Otley	Troon	Barnet	Canton	Harare	Lurgan
Ozark	Truro	Barvas	Carlow	Harbin	Lusaka
Padua	Tulle	Baroda	Cashel	Harlow	Lynton
Palma	Tulsa	Barrow	Cassel	Havana	Lytham
Paria	Tunis	Barton	Comrie	Havant	Madras
Paris	Turin	Batley	Conway	Hawick	Madrid
Parma	Utica	Battle	Cracow	Henley	Malabo

Malaga	Oxford	Strood	**7**	Bowmore
Maldon	Peking	Stroud		Braemar
Malton	Penryn	Sutton	Abilene	Brandon
Manama	Peoria	Sydney	Airdrie	Brechin
Manila	Pewsey	Tabriz	Ajaccio	Breslau
Maputo	Pinner	Tacoma	Alençon	Bristol
Marlow	Pilsen	Taipei	Algiers	Brixham
Margam	Pladda	Tarana	Alma-Ata	Brodick
Masham	Potosi	Tetuan	Alnwick	Bromley
Meerut	Prague	Tehran	Anaheim	Buffalo
Meknes	Pudsey	Thebes	Andover	Burnham
Mobile	Puebla	Thirsk	Antwerp	Burnley
Moffat	Quebec	Thorne	Appleby	Burslem
Morini	Quetta	Thurso	Arundel	Bushire
Morley	Rampur	Tiflis	Ashford	Caistor
Moscow	Ramsey	Tirana	Athinai	Calgary
Moskva	Recife	Tobruk	Athlone	Canobie
Mukden	Redcar	Toledo	Atlanta	Caracas
Munich	Reggio	Topeka	Avignon	Carbury
Muscat	Regina	Totnes	Aylsham	Cardiff
Mysore	Repton	Toulon	Badajoz	Cargill
Nagoya	Rheims	Treves	Baghdad	Carluke
Nagpur	Ripley	Tromso	Balloch	Carrick
Naples	Riyadh	Tsinan	Bampton	Catford
Nantes	Romney	Tucson	Banbury	Cawston
Napier	Romsey	Urbana	Bandung	Cayenne
Narvik	Rosyth	Verdun	Bangkok	Chatham
Naseby	Roseau	Venice	Barking	Cheadle
Nassau	Rothes	Verona	Bay City	Cheddar
Nelson	Ruabon	Vienna	Bayonne	Chesham
Neston	Ruthin	Walton	Beccles	Chester
Newark	St. Ives	Warsaw	Bedford	Chicago
Newent	St. Malo	Weston	Begawan	Chorley
Newlyn	St. Paul	Whitby	Beijing	Clacton
Newton	Santos	Widnes	Belfast	Clifton
Norham	Seaham	Wigton	Belfort	Clogher
Noumea	Seaton	Wilton	Benares	Clonmel
Oakham	Selsey	Wishaw	Bendigo	Colombo
Odense	Settle	Witham	Berwick	Coblenz
Odessa	Shotts	Witney	Bewdley	Cologne
Oldham	Shrule	Wooler	Bexhill	Conakry
Oporto	Skopje	Yarrow	Bickley	Concord
Ossett	Smyrna	Yeovil	Bilston	Cordoba
Ostend	Snaith	Zagreb	Blarney	Corinth
Ottawa	Soweto	Zurich	Bologna	Corunna
Oundle	Sparta		Boulder	Cottbus

Cities and towns

Crawley	Gwalior	Lemberg	Padstow	Sao Tomé
Croydon	Halifax	Leyburn	Paisley	Sapporo
Cumnock	Hamburg	Limoges	Palermo	Saxelby
Cwmbran	Hanover	Lincoln	Palmyra	Seaford
Datchet	Harwich	Lisburn	Papeete	Seattle
Dawlish	Haworth	Livorno	Peebles	Selkirk
Denbigh	Helston	Lourdes	Penrith	Setubal
Detroit	Heywood	Lucknow	Phoenix	Seville
Devizes	Hitchin	Lucerne	Piraeus	Shannon
Donetsk	Hoboken	Macduff	Pompeii	Shifnal
Dongola	Honiara	Madison	Portree	Shipley
Dorking	Honiton	Maesteg	Portsoy	Shipton
Douglas	Hornsea	Malines	Potsdam	Silloth
Dresden	Hornsey	Malvern	Poulton	Spandau
Dundalk	Horsham	Managua	Prescot	Spilsby
Dundrum	Houston	Mansura	Preston	Spokane
Dunedin	Ipswich	Margate	Rainham	Staines
Dunkeld	Irkutsk	Mashhad	Raleigh	Stanley
Dunkirk	Isfahan	Massawa	Rangoon	Stilton
Dunster	Jackson	Masseru	Ravenna	Strathy
Dursley	Jakarta	Mata-utu	Reading	Sudbury
Elstree	Jodhpur	Matlock	Redhill	Sunbury
Entebbe	Kalinin	Maybole	Redruth	Swanage
Erzerum	Kampala	Mbabane	Reigate	Swansea
Esbjerg	Karachi	Melrose	Renfrew	Swindon
Estoril	Kerkira	Memphis	Retford	Swinton
Evanton	Keswick	Messina	Roanoke	Taiyuan
Everton	Key West	Modesto	Romford	Tallinn
Evesham	Kharkov	Mombasa	Rosario	Tangier
Exmouth	Kildare	Morpeth	Rostock	Taranto
Falkirk	Kilmory	Munchen	Royston	Tarbert
Fareham	Kilsyth	Mycenae	Rugeley	Taunton
Farnham	Kington	Nairobi	Runcorn	Tayport
Finedon	Kinross	Nanking	Saginaw	Tbilisi
Fintona	Kintyre	Newbury	St. Asaph	Tel Aviv
Firenze	Koblenz	Newport	St. Louis	Telford
Fukuoka	Kolonia	New York	St. Neots	Tenbury
Glasgow	Kunming	Nicosia	St. Johns	Tetbury
Glossop	Lanchow	Norfolk	Salerno	Thaxted
Godthab	Lamlash	Norwich	Salford	Tilbury
Golspie	La Plata	Oakland	Saltash	Toronto
Gosport	Larbert	Oldbury	Sandown	Torquay
Gourock	Ledbury	Orlando	San José	Tranent
Granada	Leghorn	Orleans	San Juan	Trieste
Granton	Le Havre	Ormesby	San Remo	Tripoli
Grimsby	Leipzig	Overton	Santa Fe	Twyford

Uppsala	Axbridge	Cardigan	Grantown	Lampeter
Utrecht	Auckland	Carlisle	Grenoble	Langholm
Ventnor	Aycliffe	Castries	Greenbay	Las Vegas
Vilnius	Bakewell	Caterham	Greenlaw	Lausanne
Walsall	Ballarat	Cawnpore	Greenock	Lavenham
Wantage	Ballater	Chartres	Guilford	Lechlade
Wareham	Ballybay	Chepstow	Hadleigh	Leuchars
Warwick	Banchory	Chertsey	Hailsham	Limerick
Watchet	Barmouth	Cheyenne	Halstead	Liskeard
Watford	Barnsley	Columbus	Hamilton	Llanelly
Weobley	Barrhill	Clevedon	Hannibal	Llanrwst
Wexford	Bathurst	Clontarf	Hartford	Loanhead
Wicklow	Bayreuth	Clovelly	Hastings	Longtown
Windsor	Bedworth	Coventry	Hatfield	Lynmouth
Winslow	Belgrade	Crediton	Hay-on-Wye	Mafeking
Wisbeck	Benguela	Creetown	Helsinki	Mannheim
Worksop	Besançon	Cromarty	Helmsley	Markinch
Wrexham	Beverley	Damascus	Hereford	Maryport
Yaounde	Biarritz	Dalkeith	Herne Bay	Mandalay
Yakutsk	Bicester	Daventry	Hertford	Maynoath
Yerevan	Bideford	Dearborn	Hinckley	Midhurst
Yonkers	Blantyre	Deptford	Holbeach	Minehead
Youghal	Bolsover	Dewsbury	Honolulu	Moniaive
Zagazig	Bordeaux	Dingwall	Holyhead	Monmouth
	Boulogne	Djibouti	Holywell	Monrovia
	Brackley	Dortmund	Hunmanby	Montreal
8	Bradford	Drogheda	Ilkeston	Montrose
	Brampton	Dufftown	Ismailia	Monymusk
Aalesund	Brasilia	Dumfries	Istanbul	Muirkirk
Aberavon	Bridgend	Dunbeath	Jamalpur	Murmansk
Aberdare	Bridport	Dunblane	Jeantown	Nagasaki
Aberdeen	Brighton	Dungiven	Jedburgh	Nantwich
Abingdon	Brindisi	Earlston	Kandahar	Neilston
Abu Dhabi	Brisbane	Ebbw Vale	Katmandu	Newburgh
Acapulco	Bromyard	Egremont	Khartoum	New Delhi
Adelaide	Brooklyn	Eyemouth	Keighley	New Mills
Agartala	Broseley	Fakenham	Kidwelly	Newhaven
Alfreton	Brussels	Falmouth	Kilbride	Novgorod
Alicante	Budapest	Findhorn	Kilkenny	Nuneaton
Amesbury	Burghead	Florence	Kilrenny	Nurnburg
Ampthill	Calcutta	Fortrose	Kingston	Oak Ridge
Amritsar	Camborne	Freetown	Kinshasa	Omdurman
Arbroath	Canberra	Gisborne	Kirkwall	Ormskirk
Armadale	Canisbay	Glenluce	Knighton	Oswestry
Arrochar	Canonbie	Goteburg	La Guaira	Palo Alto
Asunción	Cape Town	Grantham	Lambourn	Pamplona
Augsburg				

Pasadena	Shenyang	Veracruz	Blackburn	Des Moines
Pembroke	Shillong	Victoria	Blackburn	Devonport
Penicuik	Shipston	Wallasey	Blackpool	Dolgellau
Penzance	Sidmouth	Wallsend	Blandford	Doncaster
Pershore	Skegness	Westbury	Blisworth	Donington
Peshawar	Sleaford	Winnipeg	Bracadale	Dordrecht
Peterlee	Smolensk	Worthing	Bracknell	Droitwich
Petworth	Srinagar	Yarmouth	Braintree	Dronfield
Pevensey	Soissons	Yokohama	Brentwood	Dubrovnik
Pitsligo	Sorrento	Zanzibar	Brighouse	Dumbarton
Plaistow	Southend	Zaragoza	Broughton	Dungannon
Plymouth	Spalding		Brunswick	Dunkerque
Pnom Penh	Stafford		Bucharest	Dunstable
Portrush	Stamford	**9**	Buckhaven	Edinburgh
Port Said	Stanhope	Abbeville	Bushmills	Eindhoven
Portland	Stockton	Aberaeron	Byzantium	Ellesmere
Pretoria	Strabane	Aberdovey	Cairntoul	Fairbanks
Przemysl	Stratton	Aberfeldy	Callander	Faversham
Pwllheli	Strichen	Aberfoyle	Cambridge	Ferintosh
Ramsgate	Surabaja	Agrigento	Carnarvon	Festiniog
Redditch	Surbiton	Ahmedabad	Carnforth	Fishguard
Rhayader	Swaffham	Aldeburgh	Carstairs	Fleetwood
Richmond	Syracuse	Aldershot	Cartagena	Fort Wayne
Ringwood	Takoradi	Allahabad	Champaign	Fort Worth
Rochdale	Talgarth	Alresford	Changchun	Frankfurt
Rothbury	Tamworth	Ambleside	Charlotte	Galveston
Rothesay	Tangiers	Amsterdam	Cherbourg	Gateshead
St. Albans	Tashkent	Anchorage	Cherkessk	Gibralter
St. Helens	The Hague	Annapolis	Chesilton	Godalming
St. Helier	Thetford	Ardrossan	Chihuahua	Gravesend
St. Pierre	Thornaby	Arlington	Chingford	Greenwich
St. Tropez	Tientsin	Ashbourne	Chungking	Grinstead
Salonika	Timbuktu	Ashburton	Cleveland	Guildford
Saltburn	Tiverton	Astrakhan	Clitheroe	Guayaquil
Salzburg	Toulouse	Avonmouth	Coleraine	Harrogate
San Diego	Tredegar	Aylesbury	Congleton	Haslemere
Sandwich	Tregaron	Ballymena	Connemara	Haverhill
Santa Ana	Trillick	Ballymore	Constanza	Hiroshima
Santiago	Trujillo	Baltimore	Cookstown	Hollywood
Sao Paulo	Tunstall	Banbridge	Cranbrook	Holmfirth
Sarajevo	Uckfield	Bangalore	Crewkerne	Hyderabad
Savannah	Ullapool	Barcelona	Criccieth	Ilchester
Schwerin	Uxbridge	Beaumaris	Cricklade	Immingham
Sedbergh	Valencia	Beersheba	Cuckfield	Innsbruck
Shanghai	Valletta	Belturbet	Darmstadt	Inveraray
Shanklin	Varanasi	Bethlehem	Dartmouth	Inverness

Inverurie	Marrakesh	Rotterdam	Vadi Halfa
Islamabad	Marseille	St. Andrews	Vancouver
Jamestown	Mauchline	St. Austell	Vientiane
Jerusalem	Melbourne	St. Etienne	Volgograd
Johnstone	Middleton	Salisbury	Wainfleet
Johnstown	Milwaukee	Saltcoats	Wakefield
Kalamazoo	Mogadishu	Saltfleet	Walvis Bay
Karaganda	Montauban	Samarkand	Warkworth
Karlsruhe	Monterrey	San Marino	Waterbury
Kettering	Morecombe	Santander	Waterford
Killarney	Nashville	Saragossa	Welshpool
Kimberley	Newcastle	Saskatoon	Weybridge
King's Lynn	New London	Sherborne	Wiesbaden
Kingstown	Newmarket	Singapore	Wimbledon
Kingswear	New Radnor	Slamannan	Wincanton
Kingussie	New Romney	Smethwick	Wokingham
Kirkcaldy	Northwich	Southport	Woodstock
Knutsford	Nuremburg	Southwell	Worcester
Krivoi Rog	Otterburn	Southwold	Wuppertal
Kuibyshev	Palembang	Stavanger	Wymondham
Ladysmith	Panmunjon	Starcross	Ypsilanti
Lambourn	Pembridge	Stevenage	Zeebrugge
Lancaster	Penistone	Stewarton	
Las Palmas	Penkridge	Stockholm	
Leicester	Penyghent	Stockport	**10**
Leningrad	Perpignan	Stokesley	Accrington
Lexington	Peterhead	Stourport	Addis Ababa
Lichfield	Phnom Penh	Stranraer	Alexandria
Liverpool	Pickering	Stratford	Altrincham
Ljubljana	Pitlochry	Stuttgart	Anstruther
Llandudno	Pontypool	Sundsvall	Ardrishaig
Lochgelly	Portadown	Tarporley	Atomic City
Lochinvar	Porthcawl	Tavistock	Auchinleck
Lockerbie	Port Louis	Tenterden	Baden Baden
Long Beach	Portmadoc	Tipperary	Bad Homburg
Longridge	Prestwick	Tobermory	Ballantrae
Lowestoft	Princeton	Todmorden	Ballybofir
Lyme Regis	Rasharkin	Tonbridge	Ballyclare
Lymington	Reykjavik	Toowoomba	Ballyhaise
Macau City	Riccarton	Towcester	Ballymoney
Magdeberg	Rio Grande	Trondheim	Barnstaple
Maidstone	Rochester	Tynemouth	Baton Rouge
Mansfield	Ronaldsay	Ulan Bator	Bedlington
Manhattan	Roscommon	Ulverston	Billericay
Maracaibo	Rostrevor	Uppingham	Birkenhead
Marrakech	Rotherham	Uttoxeter	Birmingham

Cities and towns

Bratislava	Eccleshall	Konigsberg	Paramaribo
Bridgnorth	Evansville	La Rochelle	Patrington
Bridgwater	Ffestiniog	Launceston	Peacehaven
Broken Hill	Folkestone	Leamington	Pernambuco
Bromsgrove	Fray Bentos	Lennoxtown	Pittenweem
Broxbourne	Galashiels	Leominster	Pittsburgh
Buckingham	Georgetown	Lesmahagow	Pontefract
Caernarfon	Gillingham	Libreville	Pontypridd
Caernarvon	Glengariff	Linlithgow	Portaferry
Canterbury	Glenrothes	Littleport	Port Arthur
Carmarthen	Gloucester	Little Rock	Portishead
Carnoustie	Gothenburg	Livingston	Portsmouth
Carsphairn	Greensboro	Llandovery	Port Talbot
Carshalton	Greenville	Llanfyllin	Presteigne
Casablanca	Guantanamo	Llangadock	Providence
Castelderg	Halesworth	Llangollen	Ravenglass
Castelfinn	Harrisburg	Llanidloes	Rawalpindi
Castletown	Hartlepool	Long Branch	Rutherglen
Chandigarh	Haslingden	Los Angeles	Sacramento
Charleston	Heathfield	Lubumbashi	Saintfield
Chelmsford	Heidelberg	Louisville	St. Leonards
Cheltenham	Horncastle	Luxembourg	Saint Louis
Chichester	Hornchurch	Maidenhead	Saxmundham
Chippenham	Hungerford	Malmesbury	Sevastapol
Chittagong	Hunstanton	Manchester	Shepperton
Cincinatti	Huntingdon	Marseilles	Sheringham
Chulmleigh	Huntsville	Mexborough	Shrewsbury
Coggeshall	Ilfracombe	Mexico City	Simonstown
Coatbridge	Jamshedpur	Miami Beach	Stalbridge
Colchester	Jersey City	Micheldean	Stalingrad
Coldingham	Johnshaven	Middlewich	Stonehaven
Coldstream	Kalgoorlie	Mildenhall	Stonehouse
Copenhagen	Kansas City	Milnathort	Stoneykirk
Crickhowel	Kenilworth	Monte Carlo	Strangford
Cullompton	Kilconnell	Montelimar	Strasbourg
Cushenhall	Kilcreggan	Montevideo	Strathavon
Dalbeattie	Killenaule	Montgomery	Strathearn
Darjeeling	Kilmainham	Motherwell	Stowmarket
Darlington	Kilmalcolm	Nailsworth	Sunderland
Donaghadel	Kilmarnock	New Bedford	Sverdlovsk
Dorchester	Kilwinning	New Orleans	Tanderagee
Dukinfield	Kincardine	Nottingham	Teddington
Dusseldorf	Kingsbarns	Okehampton	Teignmouth
Eastbourne	Kirkmaiden	Palmerston	Tewkesbury
East Linton	Kirriemuir	Pangbourne	Thunder Bay
East London	Kitakyushu	Panama City	Torrington

Townsville
Trivandrum
Trowbridge
Tweedmouth
Valparaiso
Versailles
Walsingham
Warminster
Warrington
Washington
Wednesbury
Wellington
West Calder
Westward Ho
Whitchurch
Whitehaven
Whitstable
Whittlesey
Willemstad
Willenhall
Willington
Wilsontown
Winchelsea
Winchester
Windermere
Windlesham
Wirksworth
Withernsea
Woodbridge
Workington
Youngstown

11

Aberchirder
Abergavenny
Aberystwyth
Albuquerque
Antofagasta
Armentieres
Bahia Blanca
Ballycastle
Ballygawley
Ballymurphy
Balquhidder
Bannockburn

Basingstoke
Blairgowrie
Bognor Regis
Bournemouth
Brassaville
Bridlington
Builth Wells
Buenos Aires
Brandenburg
Bhubaneswar
Buntingford
Campbeltown
Carrickmore
Cedar Rapids
Charlestown
Chattanooga
Cleethorpes
Cockermouth
Crossmaglen
Cumbernauld
Dar-es-Salaam
Downpatrick
Draperstown
Dunfermline
Enniskillen
Fettercairn
Fort William
Fraserburgh
Fredericton
Glastonbury
Grahamstown
Grand Rapids
Guadalajara
Guisborough
Helensburgh
Haltwhistle
Hatherleigh
Helsingborg
High Wycombe
Ingatestone
Invergordon
Kaliningrad
Kuala Lumpar
Letterkenny
Llantrisant
Londonderry

Lossiemouth
Lostwithiel
Lutterworth
Mablethorpe
Machynlleth
Magherafelt
Manningtree
Market Rasen
Marlborough
Marl de Plata
Maxwelltown
Minneapolis
Montpellier
Much Wenlock
Musselburgh
New Brighton
Newport News
Newton Abbot
Northampton
Novosibirsk
Palm Springs
Petersfield
Port D'Allegre
Port Glasgow
Portglenone
Porto Alegre
Port of Spain
Port Patrick
Port Moresby
Port Stanley
Pultneytown
Rathfryland
Rawtenstall
Rockhampton
Saarbrucken
St. Peter Port
San Salvador
Scarborough
Shaftesbury
Sharpeville
Southampton
South Molton
Springfield
Stalybridge
Stourbridge
Tantanarive

Cities and towns

Trincomalee
Vladivostok
Wallingford
Walthamstow
Whitechurch
Vatican City

12

Alice Springs
Atlantic City
Attleborough
Auchterarder
Barranquilla
Beverley Hills
Bexhill-on-Sea
Bloemfontein
Burnham-on-Sea
Castle Dawson
Chesterfield
Christchurch
Clacton-on-Sea
East Kilbride
Fayetteville
Five Mile Town
Fort Augustus
Forte-de-France
Gainsborough
Great Grimsby
Great Malvern
Huddersfield
Independence
Indianapolis
Inishtrahull
Innerleithen
Jacksonville
Johannesburg
Laurencekirk
Loughborough
Macclesfield
Milton Keynes
Niagara Falls
New Brunswick
Newton Abbott
North Berwick
North Sheilds

North Walsham
Oklahoma City
Peterborough
Philadelphia
Port-au-Prince
Poughkeepsie
Rio de Janeiro
St Petersburg
Salt Lake City
San Francisco
San Sebastian
Santa Barbara
Santo Domingo
Shoeburyness
South Shields
Stewartstown
Stoke-on-Trent
Strathpeffer
Tenbury Wells
Tillicoultry

13

Aix-la-Chapelle
Auchtermuchty
Barnard Castle
Berkhamstead
Belo Horizonte
Bishop's Castle
Boroughbridge
Brightlingsea
Brookeborough
Burton-on-Trent
Bury St Edmunds
Carrickfergus
Castle Douglas
Charlottetown
Dalmellington
East Grinstead
Godmanchester
Great Yarmouth
Guatemala City
Haverfordwest
Higham Ferrers
Inverkeithing
Inverkeithnie

Kidderminster
Kirkby Stephen
Kirkcubbright
Kirkintilloch
Knaresborough
Leamington Spa
Littlehampton
Lytham St Annes
Market Deeping
Market Drayton
Melton Mowbray
Middlesbrough
Merthyr Tydfil
Newark-on-Trent
Newton Stewart
Northallerton
Port Elizabeth
Saffron Walden
St Petersburgh
Shepton Mallet
Southend-on-Sea
Wolverhampton
Wootton Basset

14

Bishop Auckland
Bishops Waltham
Chipping Barnet
Chipping Norton
Constantinople
Fort Lauderdale
Grantown-on-Spey
Hemel Hempstead
Henley-on-Thames
Kirkby Lonsdale
Market Bosworth
Newtown Stewart
Poulton-le-Fylde
Stockton-on-Tees
Stony Stratford
Tunbridge Wells
Wellingborough

15 +

Ashton-under-Lyne

Barrow-in-Furness
Berwick-upon-Tweed
Bishop's Stortford
Burnham-on-Crouch
Burton-upon-Trent
Castle Donington
Claremont Ferrand
Colorado Springs

Kingstown-upon-Hull
Leighton Buzzard
Newcastle-on-Tyne
Santiago de Chile
Stratford-on-Avon
Stratford-upon-Avon
Sutton Coldfield
Welwyn Garden City
Weston-Super-Mare

Clergy and religious followers

2
DD
Fr
RR

3
Dom
Fra
nun
Rev.

4
abba
abbé
bapu
curé
dean
guru
imam
lama
mage
monk
Papa
Pope
sufi
yogi

5
abbot

bonze
canon
chela
clerk
druid
elder
fakir
frate
friar
hadji
magus
mahdi
minim
mufti
padre
prior
rabbi
sadhu
swami
vicar
yogin

6
abbess
beadle
bishop
cantor
clergy
cleric
curate
custos

datary
deacon
divine
doctor
eparch
exarch
Father
flamen
frater
hermit
lector
martyr
Mother
mullah
mystic
novice
nuncio
palmer
parson
pastor
priest
primus
reader
rector
scribe
server
sexton
sister
verger
votary
warden

7
acolyte
apostle
ascetic
brahman
brahmin
brother
caloyer
chanter
chorist
dervish
dignity
dominie
Holy Joe
hymnist
intoner
muezzin
ordinee
ostiary
pilgrim
Pontiff
prelate
primate
prophet
provost
recluse
sacrist
shriver
stylite
sub-dean

8
antipope
bacchant
beadsman
bedesman
brethren
canoness
canonist
cardinal
cenobite
chaplain
choirboy
choirman
choragus
co-bishop
Corybant
crucifer
ecclesia
eminence
exorcist
holiness
incenser
initiate
lay vicar
lectress
man of God
marabout
prioress
mathurin
minister
neophyte
ordainer

ordinand
ordinant
ordinary
organist
penitent
pontifex
preacher
prioress
Reverend
seminary
sidesman
sky-pilot
squarson
subprior
superior
thurifer
vicaress
vice-dean
votaress

9

anchoress
anchorite
archdruid
ayatollah
baccanite
bishopess
black monk
catechist
celebrant
cellarist
chantress
chorister
churchman
clergyman
coenobite
confessor
cordelier
Dalai Lama
deaconess
dignitary
grey friar
incumbent
lay reader

lay rector
lay sister
liturgist
mendicant
missioner
moderator
monsignor
novitiate
observant
officiant
Orangeman
patriarch
pillarist
postulant
precentor
predicant
prelatess
presbyter
priestess
recollect
rectoress
rural dean
sacristan
sextoness
shaveling
suc-cantor
sub-deacon
succentor
suffragan
theologer
vestryman

10

archbishop
archdeacon
archflamen
archpriest
beadswoman
bedeswoman
black friar
camerlengo
catechumen
cloisterer
conclavist

cloistress
covenanter
ecclesiast
enumerator
evangelist
high priest
lay brother
licentiate
limitarian
minor canon
missionary
prebendary
prolocutor
psalmodist
sanctifier
seminarian
seminarist
sermoniser
solemniser
sub-chanter
theologian
theologist
white friar

11

arch-prelate
churchwoman
class leader
clergywoman
commendator
consecrator
intercessor
internuncio
interventor
lord provost
monseigneur
Panchen Lama
papal legate
papal nuncio
parish clerk
precentress
probationer
sub-prioress
vicar-forane

12

canon regular
canon secular
churchwarden
ecclesiastic
low-churchman
metropolitan
parish priest
penitentiary
Prince-Bishop
Vicar-General

13

archimandrite
archpresbyter
church officer
high-churchman
high priestess
knight templar
local preacher
sister of mercy
spiritual peer
titular bishop

14

apostolic vicar
church organist
Devil's advocate
mother superior
parish minister
preaching friar
Reverend Mother
Superintendent
vicar-apostolic

15

suffragan bishop
whirling dervish

Colours

3
bay
dun
hue
jet
red
tan

4
anil
bice
blue
buff
cyan
dark
drab
ebon
écru
fawn
gold
gray
grey
iris
jade
kohl
lake
navy
noir
onyx
opal
pale
pied
pink
plum
puce
roan
rose
ruby
rust
sage
sand
vert

woad

5
amber
ashen
azure
beige
black
blond
brown
camel
cocoa
coral
cream
delft
flame
flesh
green
hazel
helio
henna
ivory
jaspé
khaki
light
lilac
livid
loden
maize
mauve
ocher
ochre
olive
peach
pearl
prune
rouge
ruddy
sable
sandy
sepia
shade

slate
snowy
stone
straw
taupe
tawny
topaz
umber
white

6
acajou
annato
archil
argent
auburn
bister
bistre
blonde
bronze
burnet
cerise
cherry
chroma
citron
claret
cobalt
copper
flaxen
garnet
golden
indigo
jasper
madder
maroon
motley
orange
orchil
oyster
pastel
pearly
purple

reseda
russet
sallow
salmon
sienna
silver
titian
violet
yellow

7
apricot
aureate
biscuit
caramel
carroty
carmine
chamois
citrine
crimson
cudbear
dark red
emerald
filbert
filemot
fuchsia
grizzle
heather
jacinth
jonquil
magenta
mottled
mustard
natural
neutral
old gold
old rose
piebald
red lead
ruby red
saffron
scarlet
sea blue

sky blue
tea rose
thistle
tile red

8
alizarin
amaranth
amethyst
ash blond
baby blue
baby pink
blood red
blue-grey
bordeaux
brunette
burgundy
chestnut
cinnamon
cyclamen
dark blue
dove grey
eau de nil
eggshell
grizzled
gun metal
hazel nut
hyacinth
iron grey
jet black
lavender
mahogany
mole grey
mulberry
navy blue
nut brown
off white
pale blue
pea green
pistache
poppy red
primrose

raw umber
red ochre
rose pink
sanguine
sapphire
saxe blue
sea green
spectrum
viridian
xanthein

9

alice blue
aubergine
azure blue
blue-black
blue-green
burnt lake
cadet blue
cadet grey
cameo pink
carnation
carnelian
champagne
cherry red
chocolate
chrome red
coal black
cochineal
dark green
dark brown
delph blue
duck green
dusky pink
Dutch blue
Dutch pink
flesh pink
green-blue
Indian red
jade green
leaf green
light blue
lily white
lime green
livid pink

madder red
moss green
mouse grey
Naples red
Nile green
olive drab
pale green
parchment
pearl grey
raspberry
raw sienna
royal blue
Saxon blue
slate grey
smoke grey
solferino
steel blue
tangerine
tomato red
turkey red
turquoise
verdigris
vermilion

10

acid yellow
apple green
aquamarine
Berlin blue
beryl green
burnt umber
brown ochre
café au lait
Chinese red
cobalt blue
congo brown
ensign blue
fiesta pink
flake white
French grey
French navy
grass green
green ochre
heliotrope
indigo blue

Irish green
ivory white
light green
liver brown
marine blue
olive brown
olive green
Oxford blue
Oxford grey
oyster pink
pale yellow
Paris green
Persian red
petrol blue
polychrome
powder blue
salmon pink
silver-grey
smoked grey
Spanish red
stone ochre
strawberry
terracotta
zenith blue

11

bottle green
brown madder
burnt almond
burnt orange
cardinal red
carmine lake
chrome green
chrome yellow
cinnamon red
cyanine blue
Dresden blue
forest green
horizon blue
hunting pink
Japanese red
lapis lazuli
lemon yellow
peacock blue
Persian blue

pomegranite
Prussian red
Russian jade
stone colour
straw colour
ultramarine
Venetian red
walnut brown
winter white
yellow ochre

12

air force
  blue
ball park
  blue
canary yellow
castilian red
Chinese white
chrome yellow
Egyptian blue
eggshell blue
electric blue
emerald green
golden yellow
hyacinth blue
lavender blue
Lincoln green
midnight blue
Naples yellow
pastel colour
pillar box
  red
Prussian blue
sapphire blue
solferino red
Spanish black
Spanish brown
Tyrian purple
Vandyke brown
verdant green
Wedgwood blue

13

bishop's purple
Cambridge blue
cadmium yellow
chestnut brown
mother-of-pearl
multicoloured
particoloured
pepper-and-salt
primary colour
Scheele's green
straw-coloured
sulphur yellow

tortoiseshell
turquoise blue
Tyrian purple

14

Brunswick black
Brunswick green
cornflower blue
heather mixture
imperial purple
periwinkle blue

pistachio green
platinum blonde
primrose yellow
strawberry roan
turquoise green

15 +

caledonian brown
chartreuse green
chartreuse yellow
secondary colour

Commonwealth countries

4
Fiji

5
Ghana
India
Kenya
Malta
Nauru
Tonga

6
Belize
Brunei
Canada
Cyprus
Gambia
Guyana
Malawi
Tuvalu
Uganda
Zambia

7
Bahamas
Grenada
Jamaica

Lesotho
Namibia
Nigeria
Vanuatu

8
Anguilla
Barbados
Botswana
Cameroon
Dominica
Kiribati
Malaysia
Maldives
Pakistan
Sri Lanka
Tanzania
Zimbabwe

9
Australia
Mauritius
Singapore
Swaziland

10
Bangladesh
Mozambique

New Zealand
Saint Lucia
Seychelles

11
Sierra Leone
South Africa

12
Western Samoa

13
United Kingdom

14
Papua New Guinea
Solomon Islands

15 +
Antigua and Barbuda
Saint Christopher and
  Nevis
Saint Vincent and the
  Grenadines
Trinidad and Tobago

Composers and musicians

3

Bax
Cui

4

Adam
Arne
Bach
Bart
Berg
Bing
Blow
Bohm
Bolt
Bull
Bush
Butt
Byrd
Cage
Cahn
Doss
Goss
Hart
Hess
Ives
John
Lalo
Lill
Lind
Monk
Nono
Orff
Wolf
Wood

5

Alkan
Arrau
Auber
Auric

Baker
Barry
Berio
Bizet
Bliss
Bloch
Beohm
Boult
Boyce
Bream
Bruch
Bulow
Croft
Davis
D'Indy
Dufay
Dukas
Dupré
Dykes
Elgar
Evans
Falla
Fauré
Field
Freni
Friml
Gedda
Gigli
Gluck
Gobbi
Grieg
Grove
Hallé
Hatch
Haydn
Henze
Holst
Ibert
Lehar
Liszt
Locke
Lully
Melba

Mehta
Moffo
Moore
Munch
Ogdon
Parry
Patti
Pears
Ravel
Reger
Satie
Sharp
Smart
Solti
Sousa
Spohr
Stern
Suppé
Szell
Teyte
Verdi
Webbe
Weber
Weill
Widor

6

Arnold
Barber
Barnby
Bartok
Berlin
Bishop
Boulez
Brahms
Bridge
Burney
Busoni
Callas
Carter
Caruso
Casals

Chopin
Clarke
Coates
Cortot
Cowell
Curwen
Curzon
Davies
de Falk
Delius
Dibdin
Duparc
Du Pres
Dvorak
Enesco
Flotow
Franck
Galway
Glinka
Gounod
Gretry
Groves
Gruber
Halevy
Handel
Harris
Hawles
Hotter
Hummel
Imbrie
Jochum
Joplin
Kirbye
Kodaly
Krenek
Lassus
Lennon
Ligeti
Maazel
Mahler
Milnes
Morley
Mozart

Porter
Previn
Purday
Rameau
Rogers
Rubbra
Sankey
Schutz
Sedaka
Stefer
Tallis
Varese
Wagner
Walter
Walton
Webern
Wesley

7

Albeniz
Allegri
Antheil
Arriaga
Babbitt
Bantock
Bartock
Beecham
Bellini
Bennett
Berlioz
Borodin
Brendel
Britten
Caballé
Caccini
Campion
Cavalli
Copland
Corelli
Debussy
Delibes
Domingo

Dowland
Farnaby
Ferrier
Gabriel
Galuppi
Gibbons
Giulini
Hammond
Hassler
Hofmann
Ireland
Janacek
Karajan
Kennedy
Kubelik
Lambert
Lehmann
Lehmann
Malcolm
Martinu
Mancini
Menotti
Menuhin
Milhaud
Monteux
Nicolai
Nielsen
Nikisch
Nilsson
Novello
Okeghem
Orbison
Ormandy
Perotin
Poulenc
Puccini
Purcell
Redhead
Richter
Rodrigo
Rossini
Rouseel
Ruggles

Salieri
Sargent
Schuman
Smetana
Solomon
Stainer
Stamitz
Strauss
Tartini
Thibaud
Thomson
Tippett
Vivaldi
Warlock
Weelkes
Wellesz
Xenakis

8

Albinoni
Ansermet
Berkeley
Bjorling
Bruckner
Carreras
Chabrier
Chausson
Cimarosa
Clementi
Couperin
Dohnanyl
Flagstad
Gershwin
Gesualdo
Ghiaurov
Glazunov
Goossens
Grainger
Granados
Honegger
Horowitz
Kreisler
Maconchy
Marenzio

Mascagni
Massenet
Melchoir
Messager
Messiaen
Milstein
Musgrave
Oistrakh
Paganini
Philidor
Phillips
Reinagle
Respighi
Schnabel
Schubert
Schumann
Scriabin
Sessions
Sibelius
Stanford
Sullivan
Taverner
Te Kanawa
Telemann
Teschner
Williams
Zabaleta

9

Addinsell
Ashkenazy
Bacharach
Balakirev
Barenboim
Beethoven
Bernstein
Boulanger
Buxtehude
Chaliapin
Cherubini
Christoff
Dolmetsch
Donizetti
Dunstable

Gauntlett
Hindemith
Hoddinott
Kaempfert
Klemperer
Landowska
Maccartney
Mackerras
Malipiero
Meyerbeer
Offenbach
Pavarotti
Pergolesi
Prokofiev
Scarlatti
Stokowski
Tortelier
Toscanini

10

Barbirolli
Birtwistle
Boccherini
Galli-Curci
Los Angeles
Mengelberg
Monteverdi
Moszkowski
Mussorgski
Paderewski
Palestrina
Penderecki
Praetorius
Rawsthorne
Rubinstein
Saint-Saens
Sammartini
Schoenberg
Skalkottas
Stradivari
Stravinsky
Sutherland
Tetrazzini
Villa-Lobos
Wainwright

11

Charpentier
Furtwangler
Hammerstein
Humperdinck
Leoncavallo
Leschetizky
Lloyd-Webber
Lutoslawski
Mendelssohn
Moussorgsky
Rachmaninov
Ravenscroft
Schwarzkopf
Stockhausen
Szymanowski
Tchaikovsky
Wolf-Ferrari

12

Dallapiccola
de Los Angeles
Guido d'Arezzo
Khachaturian
Koussevitsky
Rachmaninoff
Shostakovich

13

Rouget de l'Isle
Vassilievitch

14

Fischer-Dieskau
Jaques-Dalcroze
Josquin des Prez
Rimsky-Korsakov

15 +

Coleridge-Taylor
Strauss the
  Younger
Vaughan Williams

Constellations

3

Ara
Box
Cup
Fly
Fox
Leo
Net
Ram

4

Apus
Argo
Bull
Crab
Crow
Dove
Foal
Goat
Grus
Hare
Keel
Lion
Lynx
Lyra
Lyre
Pavo
Poop
Rule
Sail
Swan
Vela
Wolf

5

Altar
Aries
Arrow
Cetus
Clock

Crane
Draco
Eagle
Hydra
Indus
Lepus
Libra
Lupus
Mensa
Musca
Norma
Orion
Pyxis
River
Stern
Table
Twins
Virgo
Whale

6

Antila
Aquila
Archer
Auriga
Boötes
Caelum
Cancer
Carina
Corvus
Crater
Cygnus
Dorado
Dragon
Fishes
Fornax
Gemini
Hydrus
Indian
Lizard
Octans
Octant

Pictor
Pisces
Plough
Puppis
Scales
Scutum
Shield
Taurus
Toucan
Tucana
Virgin
Volans

7

Air pump
Balance
Centaur
Cepheus
Columba
Dolphin
Furnace
Giraffe
Lacerta
Lion cub
Painter
Peacock
Pegasus
Perseus
Phoenix
Sagitta
Serpens
Serpent
Sextans
Sextant
Unicorn

8

Aquarius
Circinus
Equuleus
Eridanus

Great dog
Hercules
Herdsman
Leo minor
Scorpion
Scorpius
Sculptor
Triangle

9

Andromeda
Big dipper
Centaurus
Chameleon
Compasses
Delphinus
Great bear
Little dog
Monocerus
Ophiuchus
Reticulum
Swordfish
Telescope
Ursa Major
Ursa Minor
Vulpecula

10

Canis Major
Canis Minor
Chamaeleon
Charioteer
Compass box
Flying fish
Horologium
Little bear
Microscope
Triangulum
Water snake

11

Capricornus
Cassiopoeia
Hunting dogs
Little snake
Sagittarius
Telescopium
Water-bearer

12

Camelopardus
Microscopium

13 +

Berenice's hair
Bird of Paradise
Canes Venatici
Coma Berenices
Corona Australis
Corona Borealis
Crux Australis
Northern crown
Piscis Austrinus
Sculptor's chisel
Serpent bearer
Southern cross
Southern crown
Southern fish
Southern triangle
Triangulum Austral

Countries

(including names of former countries)

3

DDR
GDR
UAR
USA

4

Aden
Anam
Bali
Chad
Cuba
Eire
Fiji
Guam
Iran
Iraq
Java
Laos
Mali
Nejd
Niue
Oman
Peru
Siam
Togo
USSR

5

Annam
Aruba
Benin
Burma
Chile
China
Congo
Crete
Egypt
Fiume
Gabon

Ghana
Haiti
India
Italy
Japan
Kandy
Kenya
Khmer
Korea
Libya
Lydia
Macao
Malta
Natal
Nauru
Nepal
Niger
Palau
Papua
Qatar
Spain
Sudan
Syria
Tchad
Texas
Tibet
Timor
Tonga
Wales
Yemen
Zaïre

6

Angola
Arabia
Azores
Belice
Belize
Bhutan
Bosnia
Brazil

Brunei
Canada
Ceylon
Cyprus
Epirus
Europe
France
Gambia
Greece
Guinea
Guyana
Hawaii
Israel
Johore
Jordan
Kuwait
Latvia
Malawi
Malaya
Mexico
Monaco
Muscat
Norway
Panama
Persia
Poland
Russia
Rwanda
Serbia
Servia
Sicily
Sikkim
Soudan
Sweden
Taiwan
Tobago
Turkey
Tuvalu
Ulster
Uganda
Urundi
Zambia

7

Albania
Algeria
America
Andorra
Antigua
Armenia
Ashanti
Assyria
Austria
Bahamas
Bahrain
Bavaria
Belarus
Belgium
Bermuda
Bohemia
Bolivia
Britain
Burkina
Burundi
Comoros
Corsica
Croatia
Dahomey
Denmark
Ecuador
England
Eritrea
Estonia
Faeroes
Finland
Formosa
Georgia
Germany
Grenada
Holland
Hungary
Iceland
Ireland
Jamaica
Lebanon

Lesotho
Liberia
Livonia
Macedon
Mayotte
Moldavia
Morocco
Myanmar
Namibia
Nigeria
Prussia
Réunion
Romania
Rumania
St. Kitts
St. Lucia
Sao Tomé
Sarawak
Senegal
Somalia
Sumatra
Sumeria
Surinam
Tartary
Tunisia
Ukraine
Uruguay
Vanuatu
Vatican
Vietnam

8

Anguilla
Barbados
Botswana
Bulgaria
Burgundy
Cambodia
Cameroon
Colombia
Djibouti

Dominica
Ethiopia
Honduras
Hong Kong
Kiribati
Malaysia
Maldives
Mongolia
Pakistan
Paraguay
Portugal
Rhodesia
St. Helena
Salvador
Sardinia
Scotland
Slovakia
Slovenia
Sri Lanka
Tanzania
Tasmania
Thailand
Togoland
Trinidad
Zanzibar
Zimbabwe
Zululand

9

Abyssinia
Argentina
Argentine
Australia
Babylonia
Caledonia
Cameroons
Costa Rica
Gibraltar
Greenland
Guatemala
Hindustan
Indonesia
Kampuchea
Kazakstan
Lithuania
Luxemburg

Macedonia
Manchuria
Mauritius
New Guinea
Nicaragua
Nyasaland
Palestine
Patagonia
Pondoland
San Marino
Singapore
Swaziland
Transvaal
Venezuela
West Timor

10

Bangladesh
Basutoland
California
Cape Colony
Damaraland
Elba Island
El Salvador
Guadeloupe
Ivory Coast
Kyrgyzstan
Luxembourg
Madagascar
Martinique
Mauretania
Mauritania
Montenegro
Montserrat
Mozambique
New Zealand
North Korea
Puerto Rico
Seychelles
Shan States
Somaliland
South Korea
South Yemen
Tajikistan
Tanganyika

Uzbekistan
Upper Volta
Yugoslavia

11

Afghanistan
Baluchistan
Burkina Faso
Cochin China
Cook Islands
Côte d'Ivoire
Dutch Guiana
East Germany
French Congo
Malay States
Mashonaland
Mesopotamia
Namaqualand
Netherlands
New Hebrides
Phillipines
Saudi Arabia
Sierra Leone
South Africa
Soviet Union
Switzerland
Transjordan
Vatican City
West Germany

12

Bechuanaland
Belgian Congo
Cocos Islands
Eastern Samoa
French Guiana
Great Britain
Guinea-Bissau
Liechenstein
Malta and Gozo
Matabeleland
New Caledonia
Newfoundland

North America
North Vietnam
Ruanda-Urundi
South Georgia
South Vietnam
Turkmenistan
United States
Western Samoa

13

Afars and Issas
Barbary States
Canary Islands
Cayman Islands
Comoro Islands
Czech Republic
Faeroe Islands
Khmer Republic
Liechtenstein
Muscat and Oman
Norfolk Island
Trucial States
United Kingdom
Virgin Islands

14

Balearic Islands
Cape of Good Hope
Congo Free State
Czechoslovakia
Gilbert Islands
Irish Free State
Leeward Islands
Maldive Islands
Mariana Islands
Papua New Guinea
Pitcairn Island
Society Islands
Solomon Islands

15

Ascension Island

British Honduras
Caroline Islands
Christmas Island
Cyclades Islands
Dutch East Indies
Falkland Islands
French Polynesia
Holy Roman Empire
Marshall Islands
Northern Nigeria
Northern Ireland
Orange Free State
Southern Nigeria
South-West Africa

Cape Verde Islands
Central African Republic
Congolese Republic
Dominican Republic
Equatorial New Guinea
Malagasy Republic
Martinique Island
Netherlands Antilles
Sao Tomé and Principe
St. Christopher and Nevis
St. Pierre and Miquelon
St. Vincent and the Grenadines
Trinidad and Tobago
Turks and Caicos Islands
United Arab Emirates
United Arab Republic
United States of America
Vatican City State

16 +

Antigua and Barbuda
Bosnia and Herzegovina

Dance

(including ballet terms)

3	**4**				
act	ahir	kolo	bulba	lundu	trata
arc	ball	loop	carol	mambo	twirl
bob	beat	piva	conga	nazun	twist
bop	bump	pogo	cueca	numba	valse
bug	cana	pony	dansa	okina	velal
dog	clam	reel	debka	pavan	volta
fly	crab	shag	disco	polka	waltz
gig	drag	slop	fling	poule	
hay	fado	step	galop	round	
hey	fish	swim	gavot	rueda	**6**
hop	fris	Toby	gigue	rumba	abuang
jig	frug	trip	glide	samba	almain
olé	haka	trot	gopak	sarba	amener
pas	hora	turn	grind	shake	Apache
set	itch	vira	haloa	sibel	atinga
son	jerk		hopak	sibyl	ballet
tap	jive	**5**	kummi	skate	batuta
	jota	baris	l' ag-ya	stomp	bolero
	juba	bebop	limbo	strut	boogie
		brawl	Lindy	tango	boston
			loure	Ta-tao	bourée

branle	stroll	gombeys	twinkle	habanera
brante	rirana	gondhal	two-step	hand jive
calata	valeta	goshiki	wakamba	hey-de-guy
canary	Watusi	halling	ziganka	hornpipe
cancan	Weller	himinau		huapango
canter	yumari	hoedown		hula-hula
carole	zig-zag	jabadao	**8**	hunt ball
cebell		jon-nuke		Irish jig
cha-cha		knees-up	alegrias	jazz roll
chassé	**7**	lamento	a moleson	Judy walk
contra		lambada	assemble	kantikoy
coupee	ahidous	lancers	attitude	lace step
danzon	aparima	landler	aurresku	La Marche
djoged	arnaout	Languas	ballroom	Lulu-Fado
do-si-do	baborak	La Rueda	balztanz	mailehen
eixida	ball pla	La Volta	Basilino	merengue
El Ocho	bambuco	llorona	big apple	mohobelo
fading	banjara	madison	blue beat	moonwalk
figuer	batuque	maillot	boogaloo	moresque
friska	beguine	maypole	bull-foot	mutchico
frisky	bharang	mazurka	bunny-hug	nizzarda
gangar	bourrée	measure	cabriole	orchesis
gienys	Cacucha	milonga	cachucha	oxdansen
hustle	canarie	moresco	cakewalk	pachanga
kick-up	canario	morisco	canacuas	pantalon
jacara	carioca	muneira	Canaries	pea straw
jarabe	chicken	old time	candiote	pericote
jarana	cinq pas	one-step	ceilidhe	race-ball
kagura	classic	pasillo	chaconne	rigadoon
kalela	Coranto	pericon	charrada	rigaudon
masque	courdant	planxty	cinq pace	rutuburi
maxina	Csardas	polacca	coryphée	saraband
maxixe	dos-a-dos	purpuri	courante	skipping
minuet	El Corte	ragtime	Dionysia	slow drag
monkey	El Passo	romaika	egg-dance	stomping
morris	estampe	roundel	ensemble	tap-dance
pavane	farruca	routine	fallaway	tea-dance
pessah	feather	sardana	fan dance	telemark
pointe	footing	satacek	fandango	Texas rag
polska	forlana	saunter	filly dog	the walks
redowa	fouetté	shuffle	fishtail	Trescone
Reigen	foxtrot	sikinik	fish walk	Tsamikos
Rogero	furiant	tandava	flamenco	waltzing
shimmy	furlana	tantara	flip-flop	war dance
spring	gavotte	traipse	galliard	
sousta	geranos	trenise	Guarjira	
	glocsen		gymnaska	

9

allamande
arabesque
bacchanal
baguettes
bailecito
barn dance
Bauertanz
bergamask
bossa nova
boulanger
breakaway
break dance
breakdown
bull-dance
camel walk
cardadora
cha-cha-cha
clog dance
cotillion
Drehtanza
eagle rock
Ecossaise
elevation
entrechant
Fanny bump
farandole
folk-dance
formation
funky butt
gallegada
gallopade
hajdutanc
hitch-hike
horn dance
horse trot
jitterbug
kathakali
kolomejka
Malaguena
mistletoe
mokorotlo
pas de deux
paso doble
passepied

Paul Jones
pirouette
polonaise
poussette
promenade
quadrille
quick-step
renningen
ring-dance
River Cree
rock 'n' roll
roundelay
sand-dance
sarabande
sateckova
saut major
Schwalmer
siciliana
siciliano
slow waltz
spot dance
stag-dance
step-dance
tamborito
tambourin
threesome
tripudium
troyanats
variation
Yale blues
zapateado

10

atnumokito
bandltantz
basse dance
baton dance
belly-dance
Bergamasca
bergeretta
Bonnie Kitty
carmagnole
castle walk
chaniotiko
charleston

cinque-pace
corroboree
demi-vuelta
epaulement
espringale
fackeltanz
farandoulo
furry dance
gay Gordons
grand march
haute dance
Havanagila
hokey-cokey
hully-gully
Kemp's jigge
Kibby dance
kyndaldans
Las Tijeras
lauterbach
locomotion
Monferrina
running set
masked ball
masquerade
orchestics
petronella
pigeon-wing
repertoire
roundabout
round dance
salterello
seguidilla
seven veils
Scotch reel
snake dance
Strathspey
strip tease
suruvakary
sword dance
tap-dancing
tarantella
thé dansant
torch-dance
trenchmore
turkey trot
tyrolienne

walk-around

11

antistrophe
babaroschka
black bottom
bumps-a-daisy
buzzard lope
contredanse
choreograph
circle dance
cracovienne
dansuringur
dinner-dance
discothèque
dithyrambos
figure-dance
floral dance
folk dancing
grizzly bear
kangaroo dip
Lambeth walk
lamb skinner
La Media Luna
Los Huapango
Los Negritos
monkey dance
Morris dance
Old Noll's Jig
palais glide
pamperruque
pas de basque
Passacaglia
pas redouble
pastourelle
Peggy Ramsey
performance
Quadernaria
rock and roll
rotary waltz
Royal Boston
schottische
semibradoras
shimmy-shake
slow foxtrot

square-dance
tewrdannckh
varsity drag
varsovienne

12

American spin
Bacchic dance
boogie-woogie
break dancing
Brechin Fancy
chassé-croisé
cheer-leading
chestnut tree
choreography
country dance
Court Masques
creux de vervi
damhsa nam boc
danse du salon
danse macabre
divertimento
double Boston
foursome reel
funky chicken
green garters
Hull's victory
Kalamationos
labanotation
mashed potato
mid-way rhythm
novelty dance
passy-measure
reel o' Tulloch
roulli-roilli
ruffty-tuffty
schuhplatter
Scottish reel
siebensprung
skating waltz
skirt-dancing
triple Boston
tripudation
Virginia reel
Yankee tangle

13

Admiral Nelson
baile con corte
Boston two-step
Church dancing
country dancing
double-shuffle
eightsome reel
ghillie callum
Hamilton house
Highland fling
Latin American
Mairi's wedding
Morris dancing
orchesography
palais de dance
Paseo con Golpe
pepper-is-black
Ronds de Jambes
Schwarzwalder
square dancing
Viennese waltz

14

babbity bowster
basic throwaway
country bumpkin
country dancing
Cumberland reel
Jack-in-the-green
milkmaid's dance
Mrs. Grant's Fancy
regel-quadrille
strip the willow
The Duke of Perth

15

ballroom dancing
Campbell's frolic
chasse à trois pas
cinderella-dance
college hornpipe
hesitation waltz

invitation waltz
military two-step
Roger de Coverley
sailor's hornpipe
sellinger's round
sequence dancing
soft-shoe shuffle
The White Cockade

16 +

All the flowers of the broom
Appalachian mountain dance
British Grenadiers
Circassian circle
Country and Western
Flowers of Edinburgh
Sir Roger de Coverley

Ballet terms

3
bas
cou
dos
lié
pas

4
bras
côté
demi
face
haut
jeté
levé
pied
plié
port
posé
rond
saut
tour
tutu
volé

5
arqué
avant
barre
battu
beats
brisé

collé
corps
coupé
couru
croix
début
décor
élève
fondu
grand
jambe
ligne
passé
permé
petit
piqué
pivot
porté
poser
rosin
sauté
scène
serré
temps
tendu
terre
tombé

6
aplomb
à terre
attack
baissé

ballon
cambré
chaîné
changé
chassé
croisé
cuisse
dedans
dégagé
dehors
dessus
détiré
devant
double
droite
écarté
effacé
élancé
en l'air
entrée
épaulé
étendu
étoile
failli
flèche
gauche
glissé
jarret
marche
Maître
monter
ouvert
penché
pointé

relevé
retiré
stance
voyagé

7
allongé
arrière
arrondi
attaque
balance
comique
danseur
déboîté
déboulé
dessous
échappé
emboîté
épaulée
étendre
fouetté
jarreté
leotard
maillot
marquer
posture
ramassé
répéter
retombé
seconde
sissone
soutenu
taqueté

turn out

8
assemblé
attitude
back bend
ballonné
batterie
cabriole
cagneaux
coryphée
courdone
couronne
danseuse
demi-plié
derrière
détourné
glissade
pistolet
première
renversé
serpette
spotting
stulchik
tonnelet
tournant

9
arabesque
ballerina
ballabile
battement

cou de pied
cinquième
développé
élévation
entrechat
entrelace
enveloppé
équilibre
grotesque
hortensia
juponnage
limbering
marcheuse
pas de deux
pirouette
quatrième
raccourci
révérence
révoltade
troisième

10

balançoire
changement
choreology
enlèvement
épaulement
port de bras
répétition
soubresaut
taquèterie

11

contretemps
double tours
grand jettés
pas de basque
sur la pointe

12

choreography
danseur noble

enchainement
gargouillade

13

corps de ballet
demi-character

14

closed position
divertissement
grand battement
prima ballerina

15 +

autour de la salle
l' expression corporelle
régisseur-géneral

Deserts

4

Gila
Gobi
Kara
Thar

5

Dahna
Namib
Nafud
Nazca
Nefud
Negev
Olmos
Ordoś
Sinai
Sturt

6

Arunta
Barren
Gibson
Indian
Kerman
Libyan
Mohave
Mojave
Nubian
Sahara
Somali
Syrian
Zirreh

7

Alashan

An Nafud
Arabian
Atacama
Eastern
Kara Kum
Morrope
Painted
Qara Qum
Sechura
Shamiya
Simpson
Sonoran

8

Colorado
Kalahari
Kyzyl Kum
Muyunkum

Vizcaino

9

Anatolian
Black Rock
Black Sand
Dasht-e-Lut
Dasht-i-Lut
Dzungaria
Great Salt
Mongolian
Turkestan

10

Australian
Bet-Pak-Dala

Great Sandy
Patagonian
Rub' al Khali
Takla Makan

Dasht-e-Margo
Death Valley

14
Bolson De Mapimi

11
Dasht-I-Kavir
Dasht-e-Kavir
Dasht-I-Margo

13
Great Salt Lake
Great Victoria

16
Turfan Depression

Charles Dickens

Books by Charles Dickens

9
Chimes, The
Hard Times

10
Bleak House
Edwin Drood

11
Oliver Twist

12
Barnaby Rudge
Dombey and Son
Little Dorrit

13
Haunted Man,
The

Mugby Junction
Sketches by Boz

14
No Thoroughfare
Pickwick Papers

15
Battle of Life,
The
Christmas Carol, A
Mudfog Papers, The
Our Mutual Friend

16 +
Cricket on the
Hearth, The

David Copperfield
George Silverman's
Explanation
Great Expectations
Martin Chuzzlewit
Master Humphrey's Clock
Message From The Sea, A
Mrs. Lirriper's Legacy
Mrs. Lirriper's Lodgings
Nicholas Nickleby
Old Curiosity Shop, The
Poor Relation's Story,
The
Tale of Two Cities, A
Uncommercial Traveller,
The

Dickensian characters

2 & 3
Bet
Bob
Gay
Jip

Jo
Joe
Kit
Liz
Mat

Meg
Pip
Tim
Tom

4
Aged (The)
Anny
Bell
Bill

Bray
Bray (Miss)
Bung
Clem
Clem (Mrs.)
Cobb
Cute
Dick
Duff
Fang
Fern
Fips
Fogg
Gamp (Mrs.)
Grip
Grub
Hawk
Heep
Heep (Mrs.)
Hugh
Jane
Jink
John
Jowl
Jupe
Kags
Kate
Klem
Klem (Miss)
Knag
Knag (Miss)
Mann (Mrs.)
Mary
Nell
Muff
Nemo
Omer
Peak
Peel
Pell
Peps (Dr.)
Pott
Pott (Mrs.)
Prig
Pyke
Riah

Rosa
Rugg
Ruth
Slug
Slum
Tigg
Tope (Miss)
Veck
Wade
Wade (Miss)
Wegg

5

Agnes
Alice
Alick
Bates
Becky
Betsy
Bevan
Biddy
Bloss
Bloss (Mrs.)
Boxer
Brass
Brick
Brown
Caddy
Carlo
Casby
Chick
Chips
Choke
Clare
Crupp
Crupp (Mrs.)
Daisy
Diver
Drood
Dumps
Emily
Evans
Fagin
Filer
Fixem

Flite
Giles
Gills
Gowan
Gowan (Mrs.)
Grace
Green
Green (Mrs.)
Gride
Grime
Grove
Guppy
Gwynn
Hardy
Henry
Hicks
Jacob
Janet
Jenny
Jerry
Jinks
Jones
Jones (Mrs.)
Joram
Kenge
Krook
Lobbs
Lorry
Lupin
Lupin (Mrs.)
Maggy
Marks
Mercy
Miggs
Mills
Minns
Mitts (Mrs.)
Molly
Monks
Mould
Nancy
Neddy
Noggs
Pedro
Perch
Perch (Mrs.)

Pinch
Pluck
Price
Pross
Quale
Quilp
Quilp (Mrs.)
Rudge
Rudge (Mrs.)
Sarah
Scott
Short
Slurk
Slyme
Smart
Smike
Sophy
Squod
Stagg
Sykes
Tibbs
Tipps (Mrs.)
Toots
Tozer
Trabb
Trent
Trott
Tuggs
Twist
Venus
Wosky (Dr.)

6

Alfred
Babley
Badger
Badger (Mrs.)
Bagman
Bagnet
Bagnet (Mrs.)
Bailey
Bamber
Bantam
Barker
Barkis

Bobster	Groffin	Redburn
Boldwig	Heyling	Richard
Britain	Hopkins	Saggers (Mrs.)
Brooker	Jackman	Sampson
Browdie	Jackson	Scadder
Bullamy	Jaggers	Scrooge
Charity	Jeddler (Dr.)	Simpson
Charley	Jellyby	Skewton
Chester	Jellyby (Mrs.)	Skewton (Mrs.)
Chiggie	Jiniwin	Slammer (Dr.)
Chillip	Jiniwin (Mrs.)	Slowboy
Chivery	Jinkins	Slunkey
Chivery (Mrs.)	Jobling (Dr.)	Smangle
Chuffey	Jorkins	Smauker
Cleaver	Kenwigs	Snagsby
Clenham	Kenwigs (Mrs.)	Snagsby (Mrs.)
Clenham (Mrs.)	Larkins	Snawley
Crackit	Lewsome	Snubbin
Creakle	Loggins	Snuffin
Creakle (Mrs.)	Macklin	Sowerby (Mrs.)
Crewler	Macklin (Mrs.)	Sparsit
Crewler (Mrs.)	Mallard	Sparsit (Mrs.)
Dawkins	Manette (Dr.)	Spenlow
Dedlock	Manners	Squeers
Defarge	Meagles	Squeers (Mrs.)
Drummle	Meagles (Mrs.)	Stryver
Dubbley	Mercury	Sweeney (Mrs.)
Durdles	Mowcher	Swidger
Edmunds	Nadgeth	Swidger (Mrs.)
Edmunds (Mrs.)	Neckett	Taunton
Estella	Newcome	Taunton (Mrs.)
Evenson	Nubbles	'The Aged'
Fleming	Nubbles (Mrs.)	Tickler
Gargery	Nupkins	'Tiny Tim'
Gargery (Mrs.)	O' Bleary	Tippins
Garland	Overton	Todgers
Garland (Mrs.)	Parsons (Mrs.)	Todgers (Mrs.)
Gaspard	Pawkins	Tom Cobb
Gazingi	Peecher	Tomkins
General	Pipchin	Toughey
General (Mrs.)	Pipchin (Mrs.)	Trotter
Granger	Plummer	Trundle
Gridley	Podsnap	Wackles
Grimwig	Podsnap (Mrs.)	Wackles (Mrs.)
Grudden (Mrs.)	Nupkins (Mrs.)	Wemmick
Grinder	Quinion	Whimple

Whimple (Mrs.)
Whisker
Wickham
Wickham (Mrs.)
Wilkins
Wobbler

8

Ada Clare
Alphonse
Anderson (Mrs.)
Aunt Jane
Bachelor
Bagstock
Barnacle
Beckwith
Beverley
Blathers
Brandley
Brandley (Mrs.)
Bravassa
Brittles
Brownlow
Bull' s Eye
Carstone
Chadband (Rev.)
Chadband (Mrs.)
Chitling
Claypole
Cleriker
Cluppins
Cluppins (Mrs.)
Craddock (Mrs.)
Cratchit
Cratchit (Mrs.)
Crummles
Crummles (Mrs.)
Crumpton
Cruncher
Cruncher (Mrs.)
Crushton
Dark Jack
Dingwall
Dingwall (Mrs.)
Diogenes

Fielding
Fielding (Mrs.)
Finching
Finching (Mrs.)
Fladdock
Flammell
Fledgeby
Flornish
Gamfield
Gashford
Gliddery
Gummidge (Mrs.)
Haredale
Harleigh
Havisham
Hortense
Humphrey
Jarndyce
Jem Grove
Jennings
John Owen
La Creevy
Langdale
Langford
Ledbrain
Ledbrook
Lenville
Limbkins
Littimer
Lobskini
Losberne
Magwitch
Micawber
Micawber (Mrs.)
Miss Bray
Miss Klem
Miss Knag
Miss Tope
Miss Wade
Nicholas
Nickleby
Nickleby (Mrs.)
Old Lobbs
Old Sally
Peggotty
Petowker

Pickwick
Plornish
Plornish (Mrs.)
Quickear
Robinson
Roger Cly
Sharpeye
Skettles
Skiffins
Skimpole
Slinkton
Smithers
Snitchey
Sparkins
Sparkler
Sparkler (Mrs.)
Stiggins (Rev.)
Tetterby
Tetterby (Mrs.)
Toby Veck
Tom Green
Tom Pinch
Tom Scott
Tom Smart
Traddles
Trotters
Trotwood
Uncle Tom
Westlock
Whiffers
Will Fern
Woolford

9

Amy Dorrit
Belvawney
Betsy Prig
Billickin (Mrs.)
Bill Sykes
Blackpool
Bob Sawyer
Bounderby
Bullfinch
Charlotte
Cheeryble

Chickweed
Chuckster
'Cleopatra'
Compeyson
Doctor Peps
Evremonde
Fleetwood
Flipfield
Flipfield (Mrs.)
Gattleton
Gradgrind (Mrs.)
Gregsbury
Grewgious
Harthouse
Headstone
Isaac List
Jem Hutley
Jem Groves
Joe Specks
Joe Willet
Kindheart
Leo Hunter
Lightwood
Lillyvick
'Lord Peter'
Malderton
Mantalini
Maplesone
Maplesome (Mrs.)
Markleham
Miss Flite
Miss Gwynn
Miss Miggs
Miss Mills
Miss Pross
Murdstone
Ned Dennis
Nell Trent
Oakun Head
Old Chuffy
Old Orlick
Pardiggle
Pardiggle (Mrs.)
Pecksniff
Phil Squod
Potterson

Riderhood
Ruth Pinch
Sam Weller
Sarah Gamp
Silas Wegg
Sludberry
Smallweed
Snodgrass
Spruggins
Swiveller
Tackleton
Tappertit
'The Bagman'
'The Cherub'
'The Fat Boy'
Tom Codlin
Towlinson
Uncle Bill
Uriah Heep
Veneering
Veneering (Mrs.)
Verisopht
Walter Gay
Wickfield
Will Marks
Wiltshire
Wisbottle
Witherden
Woodcourt
Wrayburne

10

Alice Brown
Aunt Martha
Ayresleigh
Banjo Jones
Betsy Clark
Bevis Marks
Bill Barker
Bill Barley
Bitherston
Chevy Slyme
Chuzzlewit
Crisparkle (Mrs.)
'Cymon' Tuggs

Dame Durden
Doctor Peps
Edwin Drood
Emma Porter
Flintwinch
Heathfield
Henry Gowan
'Honest John'
Jack Bamber
Jack Bunsby
Jack Maloon
Jack Martin
Jem Larkins
Jesse Hexam
Job Trotter
Joe Gargery
John Basard
John Carker
John Dounce
John Grueby
John Harman
John Jasper
John Willet
Jonas Mudge
Julia Mills
'Kit' Nubbles
Kittlebell
Knight Bell
Little Dick
Little Paul
MacStinger
MacStinger (Mrs.)
Maria Lobbs
Mark Tapley
Mary Graham
Minnie Omer
Miss Benton
Miss Cheggs
Miss Wilfer
Onewenever (Mrs.)
Parker Peps (Dr.)
Paul Dombey
Phil Parkes
Rosa Dartle
Rose Maylie
Rouncewell

Rouncewell (Mrs.)
Sally Brass
Sempronius
Signor Jupe
Simon Tuggs
Sliderskew
Sowerberry
Sowerberry (Mrs.)
Spottletoe
Spottletoe (Mrs.)
Stareleigh (Justice)
Steerforth
Steerforth (Mrs.)
Tony Weller
Turveydrop
Williamson
Williamson (Mrs.)
Wititterly

11

Abel Garland
Annie Strong (Mrs.)
Anthony Humm
Arthur Gride
Balderstone
Bella Wilfer
Betsey Quilp
Betty Higden (Mrs.)
Bob Cratchit
Cecilia Jupe
Charles Well
Copperfield
Copperfield (Mrs.)
Daniel Doyce
Daniel Quilp
Deputy 'Winks'
Doctor Payne
Doctor Wosky
Dodge Orlick
Dora Spenlow
Edith Dombey
Emily Wardle
Emma Peecher
Fanny Dombey

Fanny Dorrit
Frank Milvey (Rev.)
Gabriel Grub
'Game Chicken', The
Grandfather
Ham Peggotty
Harry Maylie
Horace Kinch
Jack Hopkins
Jack Redburn
Jacob Barton
James Carker
Jane Wackles
Jarvis Lorry
Jemima Evans
Jesse Hexham
John Browdie
John Chivery
John Dawkins
John Edmunds
John Evenson
John Jobling (Dr.)
John Podsnap
John Smauker
John Wemmock
Joseph Tuggs
Lady Clubber
Lady Dedlock
Lady Tippins
Linkinwater
Little Emily
Lizzie Hexam
Louisa Chick
Lucretia Fox
Lucy Crewler
Malta Bagnet
Mark Gilbert
Mary Heyling
Marchioness
Misses Brown
Miss Crewler
Miss Edwards
Miss Gazingi
Miss Larkins

Miss Mowcher
Miss Peecher
Miss Wackles
Monflathers
Newman Noggs
Oliver Twist
Peerybingle
Peerybingle (Mrs.)
Percy Noakes
Peter Magnus
Polly Toodle (Mrs.)
Pumblechook
Robin Toodle
Slackbridge
Snevellicci
Snevellicci (Mrs.)
Solomon Peel
Solomon Pell
Susan Nipper
Susan Weller
Sweedlepipe
'The Bachelor'
Tim Cratchit
Toby Crackit
Tom Chitling
Tony Jobling
Tracy Tupman
Tulkinghorn
Uncle George
Uncle Robert
Witherfield (Miss)
Young Bright

12

Abel Magwitch
Agnes Fleming
Alderman Cute
Alfred Jingle
Alfred Lammie
Amelia Martin
'Artful Dodger', The
Aunt Margaret
Barnaby Rudge

Bayham Badger
Bully Globson
Bully Stryver
Charles Tuggs
Charley Bates
Charley Hexam
Colonel Diver
Dick Datchery
Doctor Lumbey
Doctor Strong
Duke Humphrey
Edith Granger
Edward Cuttle
Edward Dorrit
Elijah Pogram
Emily Taunton
Emma Haredale
Emma Micawber
Esther Hawdon
Fanny Cleaver
Fanny Squeers
Feenix cousin
George Gordon
Grace Jeddler
Honeythunder
Horace Hunter
Jessie Jobson
Job Potterson
Joe, the 'Fat Boy'
John Anderson
John Jarndyce
John Westlock
Julia Manners
Kate Nickleby
Koeldwethout
Little Dorrit
Little Swills
Lord Barnacle
Lucie Manette
Madeline Bray
Major Pawkins
Martha Endell
Martha Varden (Mrs.)
Mary Fielding
Matilda Price
Mathew Bagnet

Milly Swidger
Miss Bravassa
Miss Havisham
Miss La Creevy
Miss Ledbrook
Miss Skiffins
Miss Willises
Miss Woolford
Montague Tigg
Mulberry Hawk
Noah Claypole
'Peepy' Jellyby
Philip Pirrip
Philip Quarll
Philip Redlaw
Prince Blabud
Sampson Brass
Samuel Briggs
Samuel Weller
Sarah Crewler
Solomon Daisy
Solomon Gills
Solomon Pross
Sophy Crewler
Stoney Briggs
Straudenheim
Sydney Carton
The Clergyman
The Vengeance
Thomas Sapsea
Tilly Slowboy
Tite Barnacle
Tom Flipfield
Tom Gradgrind
Tom Malderton
William Guppy

13

Alfred Tomkins
Anastasia Rugg
Arabella Allen
Arthur Clenham
Augustus Minns
Belinda Pocket
Belinda Waters

Benjamin Allen
Benjamin Stagg
Bertha Plummer
Betty Clubbins
  (Mrs.)
'Bob the Grinder'
Brook-Dingwall
Captain Bunsby
Captain Cuttle
Captain Dowler
Captain George
Captain Hawdon
Captain Purday
Captain Waters
Charles Darnay
Charles Timson
Charley Hexham
Clara Peggotty
Colonel Bulder
Colonel Gordon
Daniel Grummer
Dick Swiveller
Doctor Blimber
Doctor Jeddler
Doctor Jobling
Doctor Manette
Doctor Slammer
Dodson and Fogg
Dorothy Dibble
  (Mrs.)
Edward Chester
Edward Plummer
Emily Peggotty
Emily Smithers
Ernest Defarge
Flora Finching
Gabriel Varden
General Conway
George Heyling
George Nupkins
George Sampson
George Swidger
Harriet Beadle
Harriet Carker
Herbert Pocket
Horace Crewler

(Rev.)
Horatio Fizkin
Jane Murdstone
Jerry Cruncher
Joseph Overton
Judy Smallweed
Lavinia Wilfer
Lord Verisopht
Louisa Crewler
Madame Defarge
Maria Crumpton
Marion Jeddler
Martha Bardell
Mary Ann Raddle
Matthew Bagnet
Matthew Pocket
Melvin Twemlow
Michael Bumple
Michael Warden
Minnie Meagles
(Mrs.)
Miss Belvawney
Miss Flipfield
Misses Crewler
Misses Kenwigs
Misses Wackles
Miss Lillerton
Miss Potterson
Miss Woodcourt
Mistress Alice
Peg Sliderskew
Philip Swidger
Professor Muff
Rachael Wardle
Ralph Nickleby
Richard Babley
Sally Flanders
Sally Tetterby
Samson Dribble
Samuel Slumkey
Samuel Wilkins
Septimus Hicks
Seth Pecksniff
Sophie Wackles
Thomas Groffin
Tumley Snuffim

Watkins Tottle
William Barker
William Dorrit

14

Abbey Potterson
Agnes Wickfield
Alexander Trott
Allen Woodcourt
Amelia Crumpton
Anthony Jeddler
Augustus Cooper
Augustus Moddle
Barnet Skettles
Bentley Drummle
Betsey Cluppins
Betsey Trotwood
Captain Boldwig
Caroline Jellby
Caroline Wilson
Cecilia Bobster
'Charlotta' Tuggs
Chickenstalker
Daniel Peggotty
'Dot' Peerybingle
Edward Sparkler
Edwin Cheeryble
Eugene Wrayburn
Florence Dombey
Francis Spenlow
Frank Cheeryble
Fam Grewgious
Honoria Dedlock
Isabella Wardle
Jefferson Brick
Johnny Tetterby
Lady Snuohanuph
Lavinia Spenlow
Master Humphery
Mercantile Jack
Mercy Pecksniff
'Merry' Pecksniff
Miss Julia Mills
Miss Monflather
Miss Twinkerton
Monsieur Rigaud

Nicodemus Dumps
Octavius Budden
Olympia Squires
Reginald Wilfer
Reuben Haredale
Roger Riderhood
Samuel Pickwick
Serjeant Buzfuz
Signor Lobskini
Simon Tappertit
Sir John Chester
Solphia Tetterby
'The Game Chicken'
Therese Defarge
Thomas Traddles
Tim Linkinwater
Toby Chuzzlewit
Watt Rouncewell
William Swidger
Woolwich Bagnet

15

Alexander Briggs
Alexander Budden
Alfred Mantalini
Anastasia Weedle
Benjamin Britain
Captain Murderer
Caroline Crewler
Caroline Jellyby
'Cherry' Pecksniff
Clarissa Spenlow
Clemency Newcome
Conkey Chickweed
Cornelia Blimber
David Copperfield
Doctor Mannette
'Dolphus Tetterby
Dora Copperfield
Ebenezer Scrooge
Edward Murdstone
Estella Havisham
Esther Summerson
Eugene Wrayburne
Frederick Dorrit
General Fladdock

Georgina Podsnap
Godfrey Nickleby
Hannibal Chollop
Henrietta Boffin
Henry Wititterly
Hon. Elijah Pogram
Horatio Sparkins
'Horatio St. Julien'
Inspector Bucket
James Steerforth
John Edward Nandy
John Peerybingle
Jonas Chuzzlewit
Josephine Sleary
Josiah Rounderby
Julia Wititterly
Lavinia Dingwall
Louisa Gradgrind
MacChoakumchild
Madame Mantalini
Margaret Crewler
Mary Peerybingle
Miss Snevellicci
Monsieur Defarge
Mrs. Joseph Porter
Nathaniel Pipkin
Nathaniel Winkle
Neville Landless
Nicodemus Boffin
Ninetta Crummles
Paul Sweedlepipe
Professor Mullet
Richard Carstone
Serjeant Snubbin
Sir Joseph Bowley
Sir Mulberry Hawk
Smallweed Family
Sophronia Sphynx
Teresa Malderton
'The Artful Dodger'
Vincent Crummles
Volumnia Dedlock
Wilkins Micawber
William Cleverly

16 +

Affery Flinchwinch (Mrs.)
Alexander Grazinglands
Alexander Mannette (Dr.)
Angelo Cyrus Bantam
Augustus Snodgrass
Bartholomew Smallweed
Bradley Headstone
Chancery prisoner, The
Charles St. Evremonde
Charlotte Neckett
Christopher Casby
Christopher Nubbles
Chuzzlewit Fawkes
Clara Copperfield
Clarence Barnacle
Doctor Honeythunder
Doctor Parker Peps
Doctor John Jobling
Ferdinand Barnacle
Geoffrey Haredale
George Chuzzlewit
George Rouncewell
Georgiana Podsnap
Giovanni Carlavero
Grandfather Smallweed
Grandmother Smallweed
Gregory Chuzzlewit
Hamilton Veneering
Henrietta Nupkins (Mrs.)
Henrietta Simmons
Indignation Cocker
Jeremiah Flintwinch
John Baptiste Cavalletto
Lady Honoria Dedlock
Lawrence Boythorne
Lieutenant Tappleton
Lieutenant Tartar
Lord George Gordon
Lucie St Evremonde
Luke Honeythunder (Dr.)
Mademoiselle Hortense
Marquis St Evremonde
Master Tommy Bardell
Monsieur Ernest Defarge

Monsieur The Face Maker
Monsieur Theophile Gabelle
Mortimer Lightwood
Nicholas Nickleby
Pleasant Riderhood
Prince Turveydrop
Septimus Crisparkle (Rev.)

Sir Leicester Dedlock
Sir Thomas Clubber
Sophronia Akershem
Susannah Cleverly
Theophile Gabelle (Monsieur)
The Ventriloquist (Monsieur)
Young John Chuvery

Dogs (breeds)

3 & 4

chow
peke
pug
puli

5

Akita
boxer
corgi
hound
husky
spitz

6

Afghan
basset
beagle
borzoi
briard
collie
Kuvasz
poodle
Saluki
setter
shelty

7

basenji
bulldog
griffon

harrier
lowchen
lurcher
Maltese
mastiff
pointer
Samoyed
shih-tzu
spaniel
terrier
whippet

8

Airedale
Alsatian
chow-chow
Doberman
elkhound
foxhound
keeshond
komondor
Labrador
Malinois
papillon
Sealyham
sheepdog

9

Chihuahua
dachshund
Dalmatian
deerhound

Dobermann
Great Dane
greyhound
Kerry blue
lhasa apso
Pekingese
red setter
retriever
St. Bernard
schnauzer
Tervueren
wolfhound

10

Bedlington
bloodhound
fox terrier
Jack Russel
otter hound
Pomeranian
Rottweiler
schipperke
Weimaraner
Welsh corgi

11

Afghan hound
basset hound
bichon frise
bull mastiff
bull terrier
Groenendael

Ibizan hound
Irish setter
rough collie
Skye terrier

12

border collie
cairn terrier
field spaniel
Finnish spitz
gazelle hound
Gordon setter
Irish terrier
Japanese Chin
Newfoundland
Pharoah hound
silky terrier
smooth collie
Welsh terrier

13

affenpinscher
bearded collie
border terrier
Boston terrier
cocker spaniel
Dandie Dinmont
Dutch barge dog
English setter
French bulldog
Hungarian puli
Japanese spitz

Siberian husky
Sussex spaniel

14
Chinese crested
Clumber spaniel
giant schnauzer
Irish wolfhound
Maltese terrier
Norfolk terrier
Norwich terrier
Tibetan spaniel
Tibetan terrier
Wheaten terrier

15 & 16
Airedale terrier
Alaskan Malamute
Brittany spaniel
Doberman pinscher
golden retriever
Hungarian Vizsla
Italian greyhound
Kerry blue terrier
Lakeland terrier
Mexican hairless
Norwegian buhund
Persian greyhound
Russian wolfhound
Scottish terrier
Sealyham terrier
Shetland sheepdog
springer spaniel
Swedish vallhund
Tosa fighting dog
Yorkshire terrier

17 & 18
American foxhound
American toy terrier
Australian cattle dog
Australian terrier

Bedlington terrier
Bernese mountain dog
Belgian shepherd dog
black and tan terrier
Bouvier des Flandres
Cardigan Welsh corgi
English toy spaniel
English toy terrier
German shepherd dog
griffon Bruxellois
Irish water spaniel
King Charles spaniel
Labrador retriever
large Munsterlander
Manchester terrier
Miniature pinscher
Old English sheepdog
Pembroke Welsh corgi
Pyrenean mountain dog
Rhodesian ridgeback

19 +
American cocker spaniel
American pit bull terrier
American Staffordshire
  terrier
American water spaniel
Australian silky terrier
Cavalier King Charles
  spaniel
Chesapeake Bay retriever
Curly-coated retriever
Dandie Dinmont terrier
English cocker spaniel
English springer spaniel
flat-coated retriever
German shorthaired pointer
German wirehaired pointer
miniature bull terrier
Staffordshire bull terrier
Welsh springer spaniel
West Highland white terrier
wirehaired pointing griffon

Domestic animals

3

ass
bay
cat
cow
cur
dam
dog
dun
ewe
hog
kid
nag
pet
pig
pup
ram
rex
rip
sow
teg
tom
tup

4

boar
bull
byre
calf
cavy
colt
duck
foal
fowl
gilt
grey
goat
hack
kine
jack
jade

lamb
Manx
mare
moke
mule
mutt
neat
plug
pony
roan
runt
sire
Soay
stot
stud
tike
tyke
urus
zebu

5

billy
bitch
bluey
brach
burro
chick
cuddy
Duroc
dogie
filly
goose
hinny
horse
hound
hutch
Jacob
jenny
Kerry
kitty
mount
nanny

pacer
Pekin
pooch
puppy
screw
sheep
shire
shoat
slink
steed
steer
swine
tabby
whelp

6

agouti
albino
Angora
bantam
barton
bayard
bovine
bronco
cattle
canine
chaser
cayuse
Dexter
donkey
entire
equine
Exmoor
farrow
feline
gerbil
gun-dog
heifer
hogget
hunter
hummel
jennet

Jersey
jumper
kitten
lap-dog
maiden
merino
onager
piglet
porker
rabbit
racker
ratter
roarer
ringer
sorrel
tomcat
wether

7

aurochs
Beveren
bighorn
bird-dog
bovidae
brachet
brindle
bullock
Burmese
caracul
catling
cattalo
charger
Cheviot
chicken
courser
equidae
gelding
gosling
hackney
hamster
harrier
hircune

jackass
karakul
Leghorn
Manx cat
mongrel
Muscovy
mustang
palfrey
Persian
piebald
pit pony
porcine
poultry
Red Poll
rosette
Siamese
sumpter
trotter

8

Ayrshire
cavicorn
chestnut
coach dog
Cotswold
dairy cow
Dartmoor
Devon rex
duckling
Friesian
Galloway
Guernsey
guide dog
Hereford
Herdwick
Highland
landrace
longhorn
maverick
pack mule
palomino
polo pony

103

ruminant
Shetland
skewbald
stallion
Tamworth
tortoise
war horse
watchdog
water dog
yearling

9

Angora cat
badger dog
billy goat
brood mare
buckhound
cart-horse
dray-horse
gazehound
grimalkin
guinea pig
Jersey cow
Judas goat
Kent Marsh
Kerry Hill
nanny goat
New Forest
Orpington
pack-horse
police dog
racehorse
Rough Fell
seal-point
shorthorn
Southdown
staghound
stud-horse
Swaledale
Wyandotte

10

Abyssinian
Angora goat

Barnvelder
bellwether
blue heeler
Burmese cat
chinchilla
Clun Forest
Clydesdale
coach-horse
Cornish rex
dapple grey
Dorset horn
Exmoor pony
free-marten
guinea fowl
hunting dog
Indian game
Maltese cat
lilac-point
Jacob sheep
Persian cat
saddleback
sausage dog
shaft-horse
shire horse
Siamese cat
South Devon
sucking pig
tabby-point
tracker dog

11

badger-hound
Belgian hare
blue Burmese
carriage dog
Cheshire cat
colourpoint
Dutch rabbit
dwarf rabbit
English game
Highland cow
Light Sussex
Romney Marsh
saddle-horse

silver tabby
sorrel horse
sumpter mule

12

Berkshire pig
Black Norfolk
Black Leghorn
Blue Imperial
brown Burmese
cashmere goat
Dartmoor pony
draught-horse
Flemish giant
Havana rabbit
Plymouth rock
Polish rabbit
quarter-horse
Suffolk sheep
sumpter horse
thoroughbred
water spaniel
White Leghorn
Yorkshire pig

13

Aberdeen Angus
Aylesbury duck
Beveren rabbit
Buff Orpington
carriage-horse
Cotswold sheep
English rabbit
golden hamster
Hampshire Down
khaki Campbell
Large black pig
Large white pig
New Forest pony
red Abyssinian
steeplechaser
tortoiseshell
Welsh mountain

14

blackface sheep
chocolate-point
Japanese rabbit
lop-eared rabbit
Rhode Island Red
Southdown sheep
strawberry roan
tortie-and-white

15 & 16

British Friesian
Copenhagen rabbit
Dorset Horn sheep
Himalayan rabbit
red-point Siamese

Shropshire sheep

17 +

blue-pointed Siamese
Border Leicester sheep
chocolate-pointed Siamese
English Leicester sheep
Gloucester Old Spot
lilac-pointed Siamese
Lincolnshire Curly-coat
Lincoln Red Shorthorn
New Zealand White rabbit
Peruvian guinea-pig
Scottish blackface
seal-pointed Siamese
Wensleydale longwool

Dress

3	alba	hood	tabi	Blake	dicky
aba	apex	hose	toga	boina	dress
alb	baju	izar	togs	boots	ephod
bal	barb	jama	topi	burka	fichu
bat	beck	képi	tutu	busby	frock
bib	belt	kilt	vamp	cabas	gansy
bra	boot	mask	veil	cappa	get-up
cap	benn	maxi	vest	chale	gilet
cop	bota	midi	wrap	chaps	gippo
fez	busk	mini		choga	glove
fur	cape	mink	**5**	choli	habit
hat	clog	mitt		cloak	irham
kit	coat	muff	abnet	clogs	jabot
lei	cope	mule	Acton	clout	jamah
mac	cote	pump	aegie	cordy	jeans
obi	cowl	robe	amice	cotta	jelab
tam	cuff	ruff	ampyx	cotte	jupon
tie	daps	sari	apron	crest	lammy
top	dido	sash	arcan	crown	Levis
	duds	saya	armor	curch	lodeb
4	garb	shoe	Ascot	cylas	lungi
	gear	slip	Barbe	cymar	mitre
abba	geta	sock	Barry	Derby	mitts
agal	gown	spat	Benjy	dhoti	mufti
	haik	suit	beret		nappy

pagne
pagri
palla
pants
parka
pilch
pinny
pumps
sabot
scarf
shako
shawl
shift
shirt
skirt
smock
snood
spats
stock
stole
strip
tammy
tails
teddy
tiara
tongs
topee
toque
train
trews
tunic
V-neck
visor
vizor
weeds

6

abolla
almuce
anadem
analav
anklet
anorak
arctic
armlet

armour
artois
Balkan
banyan
barret
barvel
basque
bautta
beanie
beaver
bertha
bicorn
bietle
biggin
bikini
binder
bishop
blazer
bliaud
blouse
boater
bodice
bolero
bonnet
bootee
bowler
bow tie
boxers
bracae
braces
bragas
braies
breton
briefs
brogan
brogue
buskin
bustle
burnie
caftan
calash
calcie
caliga
calpac
camail
camisa

camise
capote
capuce
caputi
caraco
casque
castor
causia
cestus
chadar
chiton
choker
cilice
cimier
claque
cloche
cobcab
cocket
cornet
corona
corset
cothum
covert
cravat
diadem
diaper
dickey
dirndl
dolman
domino
fuster
farcap
fedora
fillet
flares
gaiter
gansey
garter
gaucho
girdle
guimpe
halter
helmet
hennin
huipil
jacket

jelick
jerkin
jersey
jubbah
jumper
kabaya
kaftan
kersey
kimono
kirtle
kittel
lammie
livery
loafer
lungee
Magyar
mantee
mantle
Mantua
mitten
mobcap
moggan
muller
nylons
outfit
Panama
patten
peg-top
peplos
peplum
pileus
pinner
pirnie
poncho
pop-sox
pugree
puttee
raglan
reefer
ruffle
sandal
sarong
serape
shimmy
shorts
shroud

slacks
smalls
sontag
square
step-in
sun hat
sun top
tabard
tamise
tartan
thongs
tights
tippet
top hat
topper
trilby
trunks
t-shirt
tucker
turban
tuxedo
tweeds
ulster
undies
uplift
vampay
vestee
waders
whites
wimple
woolly
Zouave

7

amictus
apparel
arisard
armband
baboosh
baldric
balteus
bandana
bandeau
bandore
Barbour

barbute	chuddar	loafers	surcoat	body coat
baroque	chudder	Mae West	surtout	body suit
bashlyk	clobber	maillot	sweater	bombards
basinet	commode	manteau	tank top	boot-hose
bavette	coronel	montero	tea gown	bottekin
bavolet	coronet	muffler	top boot	bottine
bedizen	corsage	necktie	topcoat	breeches
belcher	cossack	negligé	traheen	Burberry
berdash	costume	nightie	tricorn	burgonet
beretta	coxcomb	olivers	tunicle	burnoose
betsies	crepida	overall	twinset	burnouse
biretta	crispin	Oxfords	uniform	bycocket
blouson	cuculla	paletot	veiling	cabasset
blucher	cuirass	panties	watteau	camisole
bottine	culotte	parasol	wedgies	canotier
box cape	curchef	pattern	wellies	cape coat
box coat	cutaway	pelisse	wing tie	capeline
brimmer	dopatta	petasos	woollen	capriole
broigne	doublet	pierrot	wrapper	capucine
bustier	drawers	pillbox	xurqana	caputium
burnous	earmuff	pluvial	yashmak	carcanet
busskin	epaulet	puggree	Y-fronts	cardigan
calecon	Eton cap	puttees	zimarra	cardinal
calette	fanchon	pyjamas		Caroline
camorro	fashion	raiment		casaquin
canezou	filibet	regalia	**8**	catercap
cape hat	flat cap	rompers		chandail
capuche	flat hat	rubbers	abbé cape	chaperon
capulet	foulard	sarafan	all-in-one	chaqueta
casaque	fur coat	scogger	analabos	charshaf
cassock	gaiters	shalwar	antelope	chasuble
casuals	garment	silk hat	babouche	chausses
catskin	ghillie	singlet	babushka	chef's hat
caubeen	G-string	ski boot	baladran	chongsam
cerevis	gumboot	slip-ons	ball gown	cloth cap
chainse	gumshoe	slipper	Balmoral	codpiece
chalwar	gym shoe	slyders	bandanna	colobium
chaplet	gym slip	smicket	barbette	copatain
chemise	handbag	sneaker	basquine	corselet
chevron	high-low	socklet	bathrobe	couch hat
chimere	homburg	soutane	bearskin	coverall
chip hat	hosiery	spencer	bed socks	crew neck
chlamys	jodhpur	sporran	benjamin	crush hat
chopine	klompen	stetson	biggonet	cucullus
chou hat	layette	sultain	binnogue	culottes
chrisom	leotard	sunsuit	black tie	dalmatic
			bloomers	dance set

dandy hat
djellaba
dom pedro
dormeuse
duck-bill
dunce cap
dust coat
dutch cap
earmuffs
Eton suit
faldetta
flannels
flimsies
footwear
galoshes
gamashes
gauntlet
golf shoe
golf sock
goloshes
Guernsey
gumboots
gym shoes
half-hose
half slip
headgear
hipsters
host coat
hot pants
jackboot
judo coat
judo robe
jump suit
kerchief
knickers
knitwear
larrigan
lala-lava
leggings
lingerie
liripipe
mantelet
mantilla
moccasin
nightcap
negligée

nightcap
oilskins
opera hat
overalls
overcoat
overshoe
pantsuit
parament
peasecod
peignoir
philibeg
pileolus
pinafore
plastron
platinum
plimsole
plimsoll
pullover
raincoat
sabotine
scapular
ski pants
skull-cap
slip-over
slippers
sneakers
snowshoe
sombrero
stocking
straw hat
sun dress
surplice
swimsuit
swimwear
tail coat
tailleur
tarboosh
toquette
trainers
trencher
tricorne
trousers
two-piece
white tie
woollens
woollies

zoot suit

9

afterwelt
alice band
alpargata
alpine hat
ankle boot
ankle sock
armilausa
baby-dolls
baby skirt
balaclava
balayeuse
ball dress
balmacaan
bambin hat
bandalier
bandoleer
beach wrap
beavertop
bed jacket
beegum hat
bell skirt
billicock
blousette
blue jeans
body linen
bourrelet
bowler hat
brassiere
broadbrim
brodequin
cabriolet
caparison
cape dress
cape stole
cartwheel
casentino
casquette
cassimere
chemiloon
chin-cloth
chivarras
cholo coat
coat dress

coat shirt
cocked hat
comforter
coolie hat
copataine
copintank
cornercap
cothurnus
court shoe
cowboy hat
creedmore
crinoline
dog collar
dominical
dress coat
dress shoe
dress suit
dungarees
epaulette
fleshings
flip-flops
forage cap
frock coat
full dress
gabardine
gaberdine
garibaldi
ghonnella
glengarry
greatcoat
headdress
headpiece
headscarf
helmet cap
high heels
hoop skirt
houri-coat
house-coat
hula skirt
jackboots
jockey cap
Juliet cap
kid gloves
knee socks
loincloth
long johns

macintosh
millinery
miniskirt
neckcloth
nightgown
night wear
outerwear
overdress
overshirt
overskirt
panama hat
pantaloon
pantelets
pantoffle
pantyhose
pea jacket
peaked cap
petticoat
pilot coat
plimsolls
plus fours
polonaise
polo shirt
Quaker hat
redingote
round neck
sack dress
sailor hat
sanbenito
school tie
separates
shaksheer
shellsuit
shintiyan
shovel hat
shower cap
shower hat
sloppy joe
slouch hat
snowshoes
sou'wester
stomacher
string tie
sunbonnet
surcingle
tent dress

thigh boot
trousseau
trunk-hose
undercoat
undergown
undervest
underwear
vestments
victorine
waistband
waistcoat
waist slip
watch coat
white coat
wide-awake
witch's hat
wyliecoat

10

Angelus cap
apron dress
apron tunic
baby bonnet
basic dress
bathing cap
beer jacket
bellboy cap
berrettino
bibi bonnet
bicycle bal
blouse coat
bobby socks
body-shaper
body-warmer
boiler suit
bosom shirt
boudoir cap
bridal gown
brigandine
brunch coat
bucket tops
bumper brim
bush jacket
button boot
calzoneras

canvas shoe
cape collar
cappa magna
carmagnole
cerveliere
chatelaine
chemisette
chignon cap
chouquette
clock-mutch
coolie coat
coqueluche
corps pique
cossack cap
cote-hardie
court shoes
couvre-chef
coverchief
covert coat
crepe soles
crosscloth
cummerbund
dance dress
deshabille
dinner suit
diploidian
douillette
drainpipes
dress plain
dress shirt
dress shoes
duffel coat
eclipse tie
espadrille
Eton collar
Eton jacket
Eugenie hat
fancy dress
fascinator
feather boa
flying suit
fore-and-aft
fustanella
garmenture
grass skirt
halter neck

harem skirt
hug-me-tight
jiffer coat
lederhosen
leghorn hat
liripipium
lounge suit
lumberjack
mackintosh
mess jacket
nightdress
nightshirt
opera cloak
overblouse
overgaiter
Oxford bags
Oxford gown
pantaloons
party dress
pettipants
picture hat
pith helmet
plastic mac
poke bonnet
pork pie hat
riding boot
riding-hood
sailor suit
service cap
showercoat
shirtwaist
slumber cap
smoking cap
sports coat
sport shirt
sportswear
sticharion
string vest
Sunday best
suspenders
sweat shirt
swirl skirt
three-piece
trench coat
underdress
underlinen

underpants
undershirt
underskirt
veldschoen
waterproof
windjammer
Windsor tie
wing collar

11

Alsatian bow
baby clothes
ballet dress
ballet shoes
bathing suit
battle dress
bellbottoms
bespoke suit
bib-and-brace
boiled shirt
bovver boots
boxer shorts
braçonnière
breechcloth
British warm
cancan dress
cavalier hat
chapeau bras
chapel de fer
circassiene
co-ordinates
corset cover
cowboy boots
dancing clog
deerstalker
dinner dress
dirndl skirt
drape jacket
empire skirt
espadrilles
evening gown
evening slip
evening wear
farthingale
flared skirt
formal dress

galligaskin
hand-me-downs
hobble skirt
hostess gown
houppelande
hunting boot
leisure suit
matinee coat
middy blouse
morning suit
mortar-board
neckerchief
overgarment
panty girdle
pencil skirt
Phrygian cap
puffa-jacket
rah-rah skirt
ready-to-wear
riding habit
rubber apron
running shoe
Russian boot
safari dress
sewing apron
shawl collar
snap-brim-hat
soup-and-fish
southwester
spatterdash
stocking cap
string glove
swagger coat
Tam-O' Shanter
tennis skirt
trouser suit
tunic blouse
Tyrolean hat
undergirdle
underthings
vagabond hat
walking shoe
wedding gown
wedding veil
wellingtons
widow's weeds

windbreaker
windcheater

12

Amish costume
Balkan blouse
balloon skirt
baseball boot
battle jacket
belly doublet
bloomer dress
body stocking
bomber jacket
business suit
camicia rossa
cami-knickers
cardigan suit
cartwheel hat
cavalier boot
chastity belt
chemise dress
chemise frock
chesterfield
chukker shirt
cigarette mit
collar and tie
college scarf
combinations
corset bodice
cottage cloak
crusader hood
dinner jacket
divided skirt
donkey jacket
dress clothes
dressing gown
Easter bonnet
English drape
evening dress
evening shoes
evening skirt
handkerchief
headkerchief
helmet bonnet
jockey shorts

knee-breeches
lounging robe
lumber jacket
manadrin coat
monkey jacket
morning dress
motoring viel
pedal pushers
penitentials
Quaker bonnet
roll-on girdle
safari jacket
sailor collar
Scotch bonnet
shirtwaister
sleeping coat
sleeping suit
smallclothes
stiletto heel
stovepipe hat
sweater dress
ten-gallon hat
tennis shorts
trouserettes
underclothes
undergarment
wide-awake hat
Zouave jacket

13

acrobatic shoe
apres-ski socks
Beefeater's hat
bellboy jacket
Bermuda shorts
circular skirt
coachman's coat
combing jacket
cottage bonnet
cropped jacket
culotte shorts
cut-away jacket
dressing saque
elevator shoes
football scarf
hacking jacket

Hawaiian skirt
liberty bodice
maternity wear
matinee jacket
Mother Hubbard
mourning dress
nofs ghonella
Norfolk jacket
nurse's uniform
peek-a-boo waist
period costume
pinafore dress
platform shoes
princess dress
puffball skirt
Sam Brown belt
school uniform
slingback shoe
smoking jacket
sports clothes
sugar-loaf suit
suspender-belt
teddybear coat
trunk-breeches
underclothing
winkle-pickers

14

afternoon dress
barefoot sandal
bathing costume
bicycle clip hat
cabbage-tree hat
cache-poussiere
camouflage suit
cardigan bodice
clerical collar
congress gaitor
continental hat
dressing jacket
dressmaker suit
Egyptian sandal
evening sweater
French knickers
knickerbockers
longline jacket

shooting jacket
straight-jacket
travelling suit

15

boudoir slippers
bridesmaid dress
brothel-creepers
Cardigan sweater
chapeau Francais
chemise à la reine
Chevalier bonnet
Christening robe
double-duty dress
envelope chemise
Fair Isle sweater
Gainsborough hat
Hungarian blouse
Montgomery beret
national costume
Wellington boots
wrap-around skirt

16 +

Ballerina costume
Bethlehem Headdress
butcher boy blouse
camel's hair shawl
Charlotte Corday cap
chemise a l'anglaise
Chesterfield coat
chicken skin glove
coal scuttle bonnet
Confirmation Dress
directoire knickers
Eisenhower jacket
Elbert Hubbard tie
foundation garment
going-away costume
Salvation Army bonnet
swaddling clothes
swallow-tailed coat
thermal underwear

Drinks and beverages

3

ale
BDV
bub
cha
Elk
fix
Flu
gin
HPW
IPA
KCB
kir
nog
pop
RAC
Roy
rum
rye
sec
tea
Wow

4

Ante
arak
asti
Auto
Balm
Bass
beer
bock
Bolo
bols
brut
Cape
char
coke
cola
Cota
Club
Crow
Darb
Dawn
dram
fizz
flip
grog
Hell
hock
Inca
Jo-jo
kava
Kina
Kups
kas.
Lily
malt
marc
mate
mead
mild
milk
Moll
Navy
mumm
must
ouzo
Peto
Polo
port
raki
reid
Rosé
sack
sake
saki
soda
Soho
So-so
sour
Star
stum
tent
Ture
wine
wort
Yale
Zaza

5

Abbey
Allen
anise
anram
arack
Araki
Aurum
ayala
Baron
Biffy
Bijou
Blues
bohea
Bronx
broth
bumbo
Byrrh
capri
chica
choum
cider
cocoa
congo
cream
Cuban
Cupid
cyser
daisy
Dandy
Davis
Derby
Diana
Dinah
Dixie
Dream
Duppy
Ethel
Fancy
Fieth
Gypsy
Hakam
H and
H
Hasty
hooch
hyson
Irish
irroy
Jewel
julep
kvass
lagbi
lager
Lasky
lassi
Luigi
Mamie
Melba
Melon
mobby
morat
negus
noyau
Opera
padra
Pansy
pekoe
perry
Pimms
Pinky
Plaza
plonk
punch
purre
quass
Royal
Savoy
shrub
sirop
sling
smash
stout
tafia
Tango
toddy
tonic
Tuica
vichy
vodka
water
winox
Yeres
Zamba

6

Adonis
Alaska
alegar
Allies
Angler
arrack
Bamboo
Bennet
Big Boy
bitter
Beadle
Bishop
Bombay
boukha
Bovril
branca
brandy
Brazil
Bridal
Butler
bubbly
canary
Carrol
Caruso
Casino
cassis
caudle
chicha
Choker
coffee
Cognac
Cooper
Creole
Degree
Devil's
Dunlop
egg-nog
elixir
Empire
Fernet
finkel
Floupe
Froupe
Gasper
Geneva
Gibson
Gilroy
gimlet
Glider
grappa
Graves
Guards
Harry's
Havana
Hoopla
Hotcha
Joburg
junora
Kicker
kirsch
kummel
Ladies
lambic
Lerina
liquor
Lisbon
London
Malaga
Masdeu
mastic
meliss
mescal
Metaxa
muscat
Nicado
noggin
Old
Pal
oolong
orgeat
pastis
perkin
Pernod
pimint
pontac
porter
posset
poteen
Presto
ptisan
pulque
qetsch
Queens
rickey
Rob
Roy
Saumur
Scotch
scubac
shandy
sherry
Silver
Snyder
spirit
squash

stingo	Cabaret	Lawhill	Spokane	Cape Town	lager top
Strega	Cachiry	mace ale	Stinger	Chambery	Leap Frog
Striep	Campari	Madeira	Sunrise	charneco	lemonade
Suisse	catawba	Malmsey	tea bags	China tea	limeade
Sunset	Cat's-	Manyann	Tempter	cider cup	Linstead
swipes	eye	martini	tequila	ciderkin	Lone Tree
Tavern	Charles	Maurice	tintara	Claridge	Magnolia
tisane	Chicago	Mayfair	twankay	Cliquot	Mah-Jongo
Trilby	Classic	Mexican	Twin Six	coca-cola	Martinez
Tuxedo	cobbler	mint tea	vibrona	cocktail	Midnight
Victor	cordial	Morning	Vie Rose	Cornwell	montilla
Virgin	Cordova	Newbury	Waldorf	daiquiri	nightcap
volnay	Culross	New Life	wassail	Diki-Diki	Nick's
wherry	curacao	New York	Wembley	Drambuie	Own
whisky	Deep Sea	Oh Henry	whiskey	Dubonnet	Night Car
	Dempsey	Oom Paul	Whisper	Earl Grey	oopak tea
	Devonia	pale ale	Whoopee	eau-de-vie	Olivette
7	Diabalo	Perfect	Xanthia	espresso	Oriental
	Doctor's	Perrier	Yolande	falernum	Ovaltine
akvavit	Douglas	Pimento		Fairbank	padra tea
alcamas	Douzico	pink gin		Fantasio	Pall Mall
alcohol	dry wine	Pooh-Bah	**8**	Florence	Palmetto
ale-gill	Du Barry	Pomerol	absinthe	Fox River	Paradise
Alfonso	Duchess	Pommard	Advocaat	fruit cup	pekoe tea
alicant	Eclipse	pulchra	Affinity	gin and It	persicot
allasch	egg-flip	Putitan	anisette	gin-sling	Peter Pan
Approve	escubac	Quakers	Apparency	green tea	Philomel
aquavit	Falerno	Rainbow	Apple Car	Guinness	Planters
Astoria	Foxtrot	ratafia	apple tea	Habitant	pilsener
Atta Boy	Gazette	Red Flag	aperitif	Handicap	Ping Pong
Aviator	gimblet	red wine	Armangnac	Hawaiian	Pink Baby
Bacardi	gin fizz	rickeys	Assam tea	Hercules	Pink Lady
Bailey's	gin sour	Roc-a-Coe	Atom Bomb	Highball	Pol Roger
Banjino	Glad Eye	sage tea	Aviation	Honolulu	Poop Deck
Barbara	Guarozo	sambuca	Baracchs	Hollands	pouchong
beef tea	Harvard	samshoo	bee's wing	Hoots Mon	prasites
bee wine	herb tea	sangria	beverage	Horlicks	prunelle
Belmont	Hop Toad	schnaps	block tea	hot toddy	Pruneaux
Bentley	Hot Deck	scrumpy	Blue Bird	hydromel	punt y
bitters	koumiss	seltzer	bock-beer	Jack Pine	mes
Blanche	iced tea	Sevilla	brick tea	Jack Rose	ramboose
Blenton	liqueur	sherbet	Brooklyn	King Cole	red biddy
Booster	low-wine	Sidecar	Bunny Hug	Kingston	red wines
boukhra	Jackson	sloe gin	Calvados	Klondyke	roederer
bourbon	Jeypack	spirits	Canadian	Knock Out	root beer
Bulldog					

ruby port
rum-punch
rum-shrub
sangaree
schnapps
Shamrock
sillabub
skim-milk
Snowball
souchong
Soul Kiss
sour milk
Spion Cop
Sunshine
Swizzles
syllabub
The Comet
Tia Maria
Tropical
Up-to-date
Valencia
Velocity
verjuice
vermouth
van de Ham
vin blanc
Which Way
Whiz Bang
wish-wash

9

Addington
Albertine
Alexander
Alice Mine
altar wine
angostura
Angel Face
Angel's Tip
Applejack
arquebuse
Artillery
aqua vitae
barley pop

Beautiful
Beaux Arts
Bee's Knees
Berry Wall
birch wine
bitter ale
bitter top
black beer
Blue Devil
Blue Train
Boomerang
brandewyn
Breakfast
Brunelle
Buck Jones
Buck's Fizz
Cablegram
Ceylon tea
chocolate
Cointreau
Commodore
Copa de Oro
cream soda
Cuba Libre
Deauville
Depth Bomb
De Rigueur
Diplomate
dry ginger
East India
elder wine
Eve's Apple
Eye Opener
Fairbanks
Falernian
framboise
Genevieve
ginger ale
ginger pop
Grape Vine
Grand Slam
grenadine
guignolet
Gun Cotton
Halls' wine

Harrovian
hermitage
Heidsieck
hippocras
Homestead
honey beer
Honeymoon
Indian tea
lager beer
limejuice
Lusitania
Manhattan
metheglin
milk punch
milkshake
Minnehaha
mint julep
mirabelle
Moonlight
Moonraker
moonshine
mulled ale
muscadine
oolong tea
orangeade
orange gin
Palm Beach
Pink Pearl
President
Quelle Vie
rice water
Rosington
Royal Mile
salutaris
San Martin
Scotch ale
Secrestat
Sensation
shandy gaff
slivovitz
small-beer
soda water
soft drink
South Side
still hock

sweet wine
sundowner
tarragona
tawny port
Tipperary
triple sec
Trocedero
whisky mac
White Baby
White Lady
White Lion
white port
white wine
Whizz Bang
Wincarnis
Union Jack

10

Abricotine
Angel's Kiss
Angel's Wing
angosturas
Archbishop
barley beer
barley wine
Biltong Dry
bitter beer
Blackthorn
Black Maria
black-strap
Blood Hound
Bloody Mary
Blue Monday
Bobby Burns
Bonnie Scot
Brain Storm
Broken Spur
Bush-Ranger
buttermilk
brou de noix
café-au-lait
calcavella
cappuccino
Charleston

chartreuse
Chorus Lady
clary-water
Clementine
Clover Club
camomile tea
coconut milk
constantia
Co-operation
Corn Popper
Coronation
crème de ciel
Crème Wette
Dolly O' Dare
dry martini
Earl Grey tea
Earthquake
Eddie Brown
Eton Blazer
Fairy Belle
Fascinator
Fifty-fifty
frontiniac
fruit juice
Gene Corrie
Gene Tunney
genevrette
ginger beer
ginger wine
Golden Dawn
Golden Gate
goldwasser
Green Briar
Hanky Panky
Hesitation
Horse' s Neck
Jabberwock
Jack Kearns
Jamaica rum
Jimmy Blanc
Jockey Club
Journalist
lime squash
London Buck
malt liquor

malted milk
malt whiskey
mango mamba
maraschino
Merry Widow
mickey finn
Monte Carlo
Montpelier
Moselle cup
mulled wine
Munich beer
nettle beer
pale sherry
parsley tea
peppermint
Piccadilly
Pina Colada
Poet' s Dream
raisin wine
Rolls Royce
Rum Collins
Sleepy Head
Tom Collins
rum and coke
rye whiskey
sack posset
shandygaff
soft drinks
spruce beer
still wines
Stone Fence
sweet wines
tanglefoot
Temptation
toast water
tonic water
twankey tea
usquebaugh
Vanderbilt
vichy water
Washington
whisky sour
white capri
white wines
Widow' s Kiss

11

aguardiente
amontillado
apollinaris
apple brandy
barley broth
barleywater
Beachcomber
benedictine
Black Velvet
Bronx Silver
Bud' s Special
Café de Paris
Chanticcleer
cider-brandy
citron water
Coopers Town
Courvoisier
cowslip wine
crème de moka
Depth Charge
dry monopole
Eagle' s Dream
Fallen Angel
Fifth Avenue
Franken Jack
Froth Blower
Gloom Chaser
Gloom Raiser
Great Secret
Green Dragon
half and half
Hildebrande
Irish coffee
Irish whisky
John Collins
Johnnie Mack
Kiss-me-quick
lager shandy
Leave-it-to-
me
lemon squash
Little Devil
Lord Suffolk
Loud Speaker

Millionaire
Mississippi
Modder River
montefiasco
mountain-dew
Moulin Rouge
orange-pekoe
peach brandy
Pat' s special
Plymouth gin
potash water
pouchong tea
Quarter Deck
Rattlesnake
Screwdriver
Self-starter
Silver Bells
slivervitza
soda and milk
souchong tea
spring water
Swazi Freeze
tomato juice
Toby Special
Tom and Jerry
Third Degree
Thunder Clap
Trappistine
vintage wine
wassail bowl
Yellow Daisy

12

Barbary Coast
Bich' s Special
bitter shandy
Block and Fall
Blood and Sand
Brandy Blazer
brandy coffee
Bronx Express
Cameron' s Kick
cherry brandy

Church Parade
Churchwarden
crème de cacao
Crystal Bronx
Cyprus sherry
Desert Healer
dry ginger ale
Elephant's Ear
Fernet-Branca
Fine and Dandy
Fourth Degree
Gaelic coffee
gin and French
ginger brandy
Golden Ermine
Grand Marnier
hair of the dog
Hoffman House
Holland House
ice-cream soda
India pale ale
Irish whiskey
kirschwasser
Maiden's Blush
Malvern water
mineral water
Mule's Hind Leg
mulled claret
Old Fashioned
orange brandy
orange squash
peach bitters
Perrier-Jouet
Prince's Smile
red wine punch
Rhenish wines
sarsaparilla
Scotch whisky
seltzer water
Silver Streak
treacle water
Treble Chance
Wedding Belle
whisky and dry
white gin sour
Yankee Prince

Yellow Special

13

aerated waters
aperitif wines
apricot brandy
Barney Barnato
Barton Special
Bijou cocktail
Broadway Smile
Bronx cocktail
Champagne Buck
Champselysees
Cherry Blossom
Cherry Heering
Contrexeville
Corpse Reviver
crème-de-menthe
dandelion wine
Darjeeling tea
decaffeinated
Eau de Vie de Lie
Everything But
Fluffy Ruffles
ginger cordial
Golden Slipper
Grace's Delight
fortified wine
instant coffee
liqueur brandy
liqueur whisky
Knickerbocker
Maiden's Prayer
Mazato of Perou
orange bitters
Orange Blossom
pineapple fizz
pink champagne
Planters Punch
Prairie Oyster
seidlitz water
Seventh Heaven
sherry cobbler
sparkling hock
sparkling wine

Spring Feeling
Veuve Clicquot
vino ordinaire
whisky and soda
Yellow Rattler

14

Bacardi and coke
Bamboo cocktail
blended whiskey
champagne cider
champagne punch
Dam-the-weather
French vermouth
Johannisberger
Logan Princess
Lulu's Favourite
Lutkins Special
Newton's Special
Pink Peccadillo
Piper-Heidsieck
Rob Roy cocktail
sparkling wines
vermouth cassis
white wine punch

15

blackcurrant tea
Cascade cocktail
champagne cognac
champagne frappé
Duchess cocktail
Everybody's Irish
grapefruit juice
green chartreuse
Italian vermouth
Jersey Lightning
Martini-cocktail
Peychaud bitters
sacramental wine
Southern Comfort
tintara burgundy
Welcome Stranger
West Country mint

16 +

Amaretto di Saranno
American dry ginger
Between the Sheets
blackcurrant juice
Book-seller's Special
Chambery Quetsch of Alsace
Danziger Goldmasser
dandelion and burdock

decaffeinated coffee
drinking chocolate
granulated coffee
Green-eyed Monster
Harvey Wallbanger
Lapsang souchong tea
raspberry leaf tea
Schwarzwald Kirsh Wasser
Thunder and Lightning
whisky and American

European Union members

5
Italy
Malta
Spain

Poland
Sweden

Ireland
Romania

10
Luxembourg

6
Cyprus
France
Greece
Latvia

7
Austria
Belgium
Bulgaria
Denmark
Estonia
Germany
Hungary

8
Portugal
Slovakia
Slovenia

9
Lithuania

11
Netherlands

13
Czech Republic
United Kingdom

Fabrics/materials

3
aba
abb
fur
net
PVC
rep

4
abba
baft
cony

drab
felt
gimp
gros
hide
jute
lace
lame
lawn
leno
mink
repp
silk
wool

5
abaya
baize
batik
braid
cloth
crape
crêpe
denim
drill
gauze
gunny
khaki

lacet
linen
lisle
lurex
mungo
ninon
nylon
orris
plaid
plush
rayon
sable
satin
serge

stuff
suede
surah
tabby
tamin
tasar
tulle
tweed
twill
tulle
voile

6
alpaca
angora
beaver
boucle
broche
burlap
byssus
calico
camlet
canvas
chintz
cotton

dacron
damask
dimity
dowlas
ermine
faille
fleece
foxfur
gurrah
hodden
jersey
Kendal
linsey
lustre
marmot
merino
mohair
moreen
muslin
poplin
ratine
samite
sateen
sendal
shoddy
soneri
tamine
tartan
ticken
tissue
toison
tusser
velour
velure
velvet
wincey
winsey

7

abb wool
acrilan
art-silk
baracan
batiste
brocade

buckram
cambric
chagrin
chamois
chiffon
cow-hide
crochet
delaine
doeskin
dornick
drabbet
drugget
ermelin
felting
flannel
foulard
fustian
galloon
genappe
gingham
grogram
guipure
hessian
holland
jaconet
leather
lockram
malines
matting
mechlin
minever
miniver
mockado
morocco
nacarat
nankeen
organza
orleans
orphrey
oil-silk
paisley
percale
pigskin
ratteen
sacking
scarlet

stammel
suiting
tabaret
tabinet
taffeta
taffety
tatting
ticking
tiffany
tussore
velours
vesting
worsted

8

barathea
barracan
baudekin
bayadere
bearskin
bobbinet
bonelace
brocatel
buckskin
Burberry
cashmere
chenille
corduroy
cordwain
cretonne
dagswain
deerskin
drabette
drilling
dungaree
florence
flox silk
gambroon
gossamer
homespun
jacquard
lambskin
moleskin
moquette
muslinet

musquash
nainsook
oilcloth
organdie
osnaburg
paduasoy
prunella
prunello
pure silk
sarcenet
sarsenet
sealskin
shagreen
shalloon
shantung
shot silk
spun silk
suedette
tabbinet
tapestry
tarlatan
Terylene
Thai silk
valentia
wool lace

9

astrakhan
baldachin
baldaquin
blond lace
bobbinnet
bombasine
bombazeen
bombazine
calamanco
camelhair
cassimere
cerecloth
Chantilly
Courtelle
crepoline
crinoline
floss silk
folk-weave

fur fabric
gaberdine
gabardine
georgette
grosgrain
haircloth
horsehair
huckaback
lambswool
levantine
moiré silk
organzine
paramatta
percaline
persienne
petersham
pina cloth
point lace
polyester
sackcloth
sailcloth
satinette
sharkskin
sheepskin
silk serge
snakeskin
spun rayon
tarpaulin
towelling
veloutine
velveteen

10

angora wool
Balbriggan
beaverteen
Berlin wool
blanketing
bobbin-lace
broadcloth
brocatelle
cassinette
chinchilla
corded silk
florentine

grass cloth
hodden-grey
hodden-gray
Irish linen
jersey silk
jersey wool
kerseymere
khaki drill
khaki serge
mackintosh
mock velvet
mousseline
needlecord
parramatta
pillow-lace
pilot cloth
rabbitskin
seersucker
thrown-silk
tussah silk
tusseh silk
tusser-silk
winceyette

11

cheesecloth
flannelette
Harris tweed
Honiton lace
Kendal cloth
leatherette
leopardskin
Mechlin lace
nettle-cloth
Persian lamb
stockinette
torchon lace
tussore silk
watered silk

12

cavalry twill
crêpe-de-chine
double jersey
gros de Naples
Indian cotton

Mechlin black
moire antique
moire taffeta
Welsh flannel

13

Chantilly lace
crocodile skin
linsey-woolsey
patent leather
Russia leather
uncut moquette

14

artificial silk
Morocco leather

15 +

broderie anglaise
mousseline-de-soie
mousseline-de-laine

Fairies, devils, ghosts, nymphs, etc.

3	jinn	Ariel	genie	troll	Egeria
	Loki	bogey	genii		faunus
elf	Moth	Bucca	ghost		goblin
fay	peri	demon	ghoul	**6**	hobbit
imp	pixy	devil	gnome		hyades
Mab	Puck	dryad	guelf	Acheri	ifreet
nix	Rahu	duppi	kelpy	Aegena	jinnee
Pan	soul	duppy	lutin	afreet	kelpie
	trow	dwarf	naiad	Azazel	kobold
		Eblis	nymph	Befana	Laurin
4		faery	oread	Calyce	Lilith
bogy	**5**	fairy	pisky	cherub	Merope
drow		fauni	pixie	Clytie	nereid
Echo	alfar	fetch	Satan	Cobweb	nicker
geni	afrit	fiend	spook	Cyrene	Oberon
	angel			Daphne	

Oenone
piskey
Rhodas
Scylla
shades
sprite
tangie
Thetis
Thoosa
wraith

7
Alastor
Asteria
banshee
brownie
Clymene
Coronis
Galatea
gremlin
Gytrash
knocker
lemures
Manitou
Morgana
Morgane
oceanid
Old Nick
phantom
sandman
Setebos
shedeem

spectre
Titania
Titivil

8
Alberich
Arethusa
Asmodeus
Barbason
bogeyman
Castalia
Cymodoce
Echenais
Eurydice
lubrican
mazikeen
Morgaine
Penelope
Periboca
phantasm
psammead
Queen Mab
Rübezahl
spriggan

9
adamastor
archangel
archfiend
Beelzebub
dockalfar

ectoplasm
hamadryad
hobgoblin
lubberkin
Mauthe Dog
nain rouge
oceanides
Parabanou
phantasma
pigwidgin
pigwiggen
white lady

10
apparition
archimagus
cacodaemon
cluricaune
demogorgon
ghibbeline
leprechaun
May Mollock
Morganetta
Tinkerbell
Tutivillus
tooth fairy
tylwyth teg

11
Fata Morgana
Morgan le Fay

Mustardseed
poltergeist

12
Jack o' the Bowl
La Dame Abonde
little people
Morgue la Fay
Phynnodderee
Peaseblossom
Wayland Smith

13
astral spirits
Cock Lane ghost
Lady of the Lake
Mother Shipton
Sampford ghost

14
La Dame d' Aprigny
Le Cheval Bayard
Mephistopheles
Stockwell ghost

15 +
Prince of Darkness
Robin Goodfellow
Rumplestiltskin
White lady of Avenel

Faiths and religions

3
Jew
Zen

4
Ainu

Babi
Copt
Jain
Sikh
Sufi
Yogi

5
Arian
Bahai
Deism
Deist
Druid
Fakir

Hadji
Hindu
Islam
Shiah
Sunni

6
Babism
Babist
Dipper
Dopper
Dunker
Essene

Hebrew
Jesuit
Jewess
Levite
Marist
Moonie
Mormon

Moslem
Muslim
Mystic
Papist
Parsee
Quaker
Ranter
Shaker
Shiite
Shinto
Taoism
Taoist
Theism
Theist
Voodoo
Wahabi
Zealot

7

Abelian
Abelite
Adamite
Ajivika
Amarite
Ascetic
Atheism
Atheist
Baalite
Bahaism
Bahaist
Baptist
Beghard
Brahman
Brahmin
Cluniac
Convert
Gentile
Gnostic
Heathen
Heretic
Infidel
Jacobin
Jainism
Judaism
Judaist

Lamaism
Lamaist
Lateran
Limiter
Lollard
Mahdism
Mahdist
Maurist
Mormons
Paulian
Puritan
Quakery
Saracen
Sceptic
Seceder
Shakers
Sikhism
Sivaite
Sunnite
Templar
Wahabis
Zionism
Zionist

8

Agnostic
Anglican
Apostasy
Apostate
Arianism
Armenian
Believer
Buddhism
Buddhist
Capuchin
Catholic
Disciple
Ditheism
Ditheist
Donatism
Donatist
Druidism
Druidess
Erastian
Essenism

Follower
Hinduism
Huguenot
Humanism
Humanist
Ignatian
Incenser
Islamite
Lutheran
Mahdiism
Mahdiist
Maronite
Minorite
Nazarene
Nazarite
Pharisee
Reformer
Sadducee
Salesian
Satanist
Shafiite
Talapoin
Totemism
Totemist
Trappist
Ursuline
Wahabite
Wesleyan

9

Abstinent
Adventist
Ambrosian
Augustine
Bacchanal
Balaamite
Buchanite
Calvinism
Calvinist
Carmelite
Christian
Dissenter
Dominican
Gospeller
Hebrewess

Jansenism
Jansenist
Lutherism
Lutherist
Methodism
Methodist
Mithraism
Mithraist
Mussalman
Mussulman
Mysticism
Occultism
Occultist
Orangeman
Oratorian
Pamtheism
Pantheist
Parseeism
Quakeress
Quakerism
Rabbinist
Rabbinite
Reformism
Reformist
Sectarian
Shamanism
Shamanist
Shintoism
Shintoist
Simeonite
Unitarian
Wyclifite

10

Abrahamite
Albigenses
Anabaptism
Anabaptist
Basilidean
Bernardine
Brahmanism
Brigittine
Carthusian
Church Army
Church-goer

Cistercian
Conformism
Conformist
Covenanter
Evangelism
Evangelist
Franciscan
Gilbertine
Gnosticism
Jeronymite
Limitarian
Lollardism
Mohammedan
Monotheism
Monotheist
Polytheism
Polytheist
Protestant
Puritanism
Revivalism
Revivalist
Schismatic
Secularism
Secularist
Unbeliever
Worshipper
Wycliffite

11

Abecedarian
Agnosticism
Albigensian
Anglicanism
Arminianism
Augustinian
Benedictine
Catabaptist
Catholicism
Devotionist
Disbeliever

Erastianism
Hospitaller
Lutheranism
Neo-Catholic
Old Catholic
Orthodox Jew
Plymouthism
Rastafarian
Rosicrucian
Sabbatarian
Tetratheism
Tetratheist
Theosophism
Theosophist
Trinitarian
Wesleyanism
Zen Buddhism
Zen Buddhist
Zoroastrian

12

Christianity
Confucianism
Confucianist
Episcopalian
Hot Gospeller
Neo-Christian
Paedobaptist
Presbyterian
Salvationism
Salvationist
Sectarianism
Unitarianism

13

Anglo-Catholic
Greek Orthodox
Mohammedanism
Nonconformism

Nonconformist
Protestantism
Redemptionist
Reform Judaism
Roman Catholic
Salvation Army
Scripturalist
Sun-worshipper
Zarathustrian

14

Congregational
Fire-worshipper
Fundamentalism
Fundamentalist
Latter-Day Saint
Sacramentalist
Uniformitarian

15 +

Anthroposophism
Anthroposophist
Antipaedobaptist
Christian Science
Christadelphian
Congregationalism
Conservative Judaism
Crypto-Christian
Devil-worshipper
Episcopalianism
Jehovah's Witness
Orthodox Judaism
Plymouth Brother
Plymouth Brethren
Presbyterianism
Roman Catholicism
Second-Adventist
Seventh-Day Adventist
Society of Friends

Famous pairings

Abraham and Isaac
Achemon and Basalas
Achilles and the Tortoise
Acis and Galatea
Adam and Eve
Sir John ALCOCK and Arthur Whitten BROWN
Ray ALLEN and LORD CHARLES
Alpheus and Arethusa
Amadis and Oriana
Amos and Andy
Ananias and Sapphira
Amis et Amiles
Amys and Amylion
Androcles and the Lion
Anthony and Cleopatra
Fred ASTAIRE and Ginger ROGERS
Lucille BALL and Desi ARNAZ
Daniel BARENBOIM and Jaqueline DU PRÉ
Barlaam and Josaphat
Phineas BARNUM and James BAILEY
Batman and Robin
Beauty and the Beast
BEERY, Noah and Wallace
Bennet and Williams
Bill and Ben
BONNIE Parker and CLYDE Barrow
Bernard BRADEN and Barbara KELLY
Brahma and Sarasvati
Peter BROUGH and Archie ANDREWS
Buddha and the Boar
Guy BURGESS and Donald MACLEAN
William BURKE and William HARE
George BURNS and Gracie ALLEN

Richard BURTON and Elizabeth TAYLOR
Butch Casssidy and the Sundance Kid
Cain and Abel
Calisto and Arcas
Leon CALMETTE and Camille GUERIN
Tommy CANNON and Bobby BALL
Castor and Pollux
Cephalus and Pocris
Dr Hawley Harvey CRIPPEN and Ethel LE NEVE
Bing CROSBY and Bob HOPE
Robinson CRUSOE and MAN FRIDAY
CURIE, Marie and Pierre
Gottlieb DAIMLER and Karl BENZ
Damon and Pythias
Dante and Beatrice
Daphnis and Chloe
Darby and Joan
David and Goliath
David and Jonathan
Diana and Artemis
Dido and Aeneas
EDWARD VIII and Mrs. Wallis SIMPSON
Esau and Jacob
EVERLEY BROTHERS, Don and Phil
Douglas FAIRBANKS and Mary PICKFORD
Ferrex and Porrex
Michael FLANDERS and Donald SWANN
Flotsam and Jetsam
Dawn FRENCH and Jennifer SAUNDERS
Gert and Daisy
Sir William GILBERT and Sir Arthur SULLIVAN

Famous pairings

Gog and Magog
Gareth HALE and Norman PACE
Hansel and Gretel
Harlequin and Columbine
Bill HARLEY and Walter DAV-
  IDSON
Tony HATCH and Jackie TRENT
Heathcliff and Catherine
Helen of Troy and Paris
Heloïse and Abelard
Hengist and Horsa
Hero and Leander
Hiawatha and Minnehaha
Sir Edmund HILLARY and
  Sherpa TENZING
Myra HINDLEY and Ian BRADY
Dame Evadne HINGE and Dr
  Hilda BRACKET
Adolf HITLER and Eva BRAUN
Sherlock HOLMES and Dr
  WATSON
Isis and Osiris
Jack and Jill
Dr JEKYLL and Mr HYDE
Jewell and Warriss
Teddy JOHNSON and Pearl CARR
KRAY TWINS, Ronald and
  Reginald
KROGER, Peter and Helen
Lady and the Tramp
Lancelot and Guinevere
Stanley LAUREL and Oliver
  HARDY
Layton and Johnson
John LENNON and Paul MCCA-
  RTNEY
Sid LITTLE and Eddie LARGE
Andrew LLOYD WEBBER and Tim
  RICE
LOUIS XVI and MARIE ANTOI-
  NETTE
Ben LYON and Bebe DANIELS
Victor MACLAGEN and Marie
  DRESSLER
Mary and Martha
Mary and Joseph

MARY Queen of Scots and
  Henry DARNLEY
Jessie MATTHEWS and Sonie
  HALE
Mickey and Minnie Mouse
Jim MOLLISON and Amy JOHNSON
MONTGOLFIER, Joseph and
  Jacques Etiene
Eric MORECAMBE and Ernie
  WISE
MURRAY, John and Nora
Napoleon and Joséphine
Naughton and Gold
Lord Horatio NELSON and Lady
  Emma HAMILTON
Nervo and Knox
Oberon and Titania
Orpheus and Eurydice
Owl and the Pussycat
PANKHURST, Emily and Sylvia
Paola and Francesca
Pat and Mick
PEARSON, Bob and Alf
Perseus and Andromeda
Peter and the Wolf
Peter Pan and Wendy
Peters and Lee
Philemon and Baucis
Pinky and Perky
Popeye and Olive Oyl
Punch and Judy
Pyramus and Thisbe
Quasimodo and Esmeralda
Don QUIXOTE and SANCHO PANZA
Rawicz and Landauer
Ethel REVNELL and Gracie
  WEST
Richard RODGERS and Oscar
  HAMMERSTEIN
Robin Hood and Maid Marian
ROMEO Montague and JULIET
  Capulet
Romulus and Remus
Charles ROLLS and Sir (Fred-
  erick) Henry ROYCE
Ruth and Naomi

St.George and the dragon
Samson and Delilah
Ira SANKEY and Dwight MOODY
Scylla and Charybdis
Shiva and Kali
Paul SIMON and Art GARFUNKEL
Mel SMITH and Griff Rhys JONES
Sooty and Sweep
Sir Henry STANLEY and David LIVINGSTONE
Tarzan and Jane
Tom and Jerry
Tortoise and the Hare
Jayne TORVILLE and Christopher DEAN
Tristan and Isolda
Troilus and Cressida
Tweedledum and Tweedledee
TWO RONNIES, Corbett and Barker
Vishnu and Lakshmi
Walrus and the Carpenter
WATERS, Elsie and Doris
WESLEY, John and Charles
WINTERS, Mike and Bernie
WRIGHT, Orville and Wilbur
Yin and Yang
Anne ZEIGLER and Webster BOOTH

First names

Female names

2
Di
Em
Jo
Vi

3

Ada	Flo	Nan	Aimé	Dido	Gert	Kate
Amy	Gay	Net	Alba	Dodo	Gill	Katy
Ann	Han	Pam	Alex	Doll	Gina	Kaye
Ava	Hat	Pat	Ally	Dora	Gola	Lala
Bab	Ida	Peg	Alma	Edie	Gwen	Leah
Bea	Ina	Pen	Alys	Edna	Gwyn	Lena
Bee	Isa	Pip	Anna	Edye	Hebe	Lila
Bel	Ivy	Pru	Anne	Ella	Hope	Lily
Bet	Iza	Ray	Anny	Elma	Ilse	Lina
Dol	Jan	Rio	Avis	Elsa	Ines	Lisa
Dot	Jem	Sal	Baba	Else	Inez	Lita
Deb	Jen	Sis	Babs	Emma	Iona	Liza
Eda	Joy	Sue	Bebe	Emmy	Ione	Lois
Ena	Kay	Tam	Beck	Enid	Iris	Lola
Eva	Kit	Toy	Bell	Erna	Irma	Lucy
Eve	Kim	Una	Bess	Esme	Isla	Lulu
Fay	Lea	Val	Beth	Etta	Isma	Lynn
	Lee	Viv	Cara	Etty	Ivey	Mags
	Liz	Win	Caré	Evie	Jade	Maie
	Lot	Yda	Cely	Fifi	Jane	Mana
	Lou	Zia	Ciss	Floy	Jean	Mary
	Lyn	Zoë	Clea	Beck	Jess	Maud
	Mae		Cleo	Gaby	Jill	Megs
	Mai	**4**	Cora	Gage	Joan	Meta
	May	Aggy	Cory	Gail	Judy	Mimi
	Meg		Dawn	Gene	June	Mima

125

First names

Mina	Zena	Carly	Emmie	Jilly	Marie
Moll	Zita	Carol	Erica	Joann	Matty
Mona	Zora	Carré	Essie	Josie	Maude
Muff		Caryl	Ethel	Joyce	Mavis
Muir		Casey	Ettie	Julia	Meave
Myra	**5**	Cathy	Faith	Julie	Megan
Nell	Abbey	Celia	Fanny	Karen	Mercy
Nena	Abbie	Chloe	Feona	Karin	Merle
Neva	Adela	Chris	Filia	Katey	Meryl
Niki	Adele	Chune	Fiona	Kathy	Merry
Nina	Aggie	Cilla	Fleur	Katie	Milly
Nino	Agnes	Circe	Flora	Kelly	Minna
Nita	Ailie	Cissy	Freda	Kerry	Mitzi
Noll	Ailsa	Clair	Gabie	Kitty	Moira
Nora	Aimée	Clara	Gemma	Laila	Molly
Olga	Alice	Clare	Gerda	Laura	Morag
Oona	Aline	Coral	Gerty	Leigh	Morna
Pola	Allie	Corin	Ginny	Leila	Moyra
Poll	Altha	Daisy	Gipsy	Letty	Myrle
Prue	Amata	Debby	Grace	Libby	Myrna
Puss	Angel	Delia	Greer	Lilia	Mysie
Rena	Anita	Della	Greta	Lilly	Nance
Rene	Annie	Denes	Gussy	Linda	Nancy
Rita	Annis	Diana	Hatty	Lindy	Nanny
Rosa	Annot	Diane	Hazel	Lizzy	Naomi
Rose	April	Dilys	Helen	Lolly	Nelly
Rosy	Arbel	Dinah	Helga	Lorna	Nessa
Ruby	Arden	Dodie	Henny	Lotta	Nesta
Ruth	Avice	Dolly	Hetty	Lotty	Netta
Sara	Avril	Donie	Hilda	Louie	Netty
Sita	Barbi	Donna	Honor	Lucia	Ninie
Spry	Barby	Dorah	Hulda	Lydia	Ninny
Suky	Becky	Doris	Hylda	Lynne	Ninon
Susy	Bella	Dreda	Idina	Lynda	Niobe
Syme	Belle	Dulce	Innes	Mabel	Nolly
Tess	Berta	Edith	Irene	Madge	Norah
Thea	Beryl	Effie	Isbel	Maeve	Norma
Tina	Bessy	Eilsa	Isold	Magda	Olive
Toni	Betsy	Elena	Janet	Maggy	Olwen
Trix	Betty	Elfie	Janey	Maida	Pansy
Vera	Biddy	Elise	Janie	Màiri	Patsy
Vida	Bobby	Eliza	Janny	Mamie	Patty
Viki	Budie	Ellen	Jayne	Manie	Paula
Vita	Buena	Ellie	Jenny	Manon	Pearl
Viva	Bunty	Elsie	Jesse	Marge	Peggy
Zara	Carla	Emily	Jessy	Maria	Penny

	6	Blaise	Eyleen	Jessie	Miriam
Phebe		Bobbie	Fannie	Joanna	Mollie
Pippa	Agatha	Brenda	Fatima	Joanne	Monica
Pixie	Aileen	Bridie	Felice	Judith	Morwen
Polly	Airlie	Brigid	Flavia	Juliet	Moulie
Poppy	Alexia	Bryony	Frieda	Kathie	Muriel
Queen	Alicia	Carmen	Galena	Kirsty	Murtle
Rahel	Alison	Carole	Gerrie	Kittie	Myrtle
Renée	Almond	Carrie	Gertie	Lalage	Nadine
Rhoda	Althea	Cathie	Gleana	Lallie	Nancie
Rhona	Amabel	Cecile	Gladys	Lassie	Nellie
Robin	Amanda	Cecily	Glenda	Leonie	Nelsie
Rosie	Amalia	Celina	Gloria	Lesley	Nessie
Sadie	Amelia	Charis	Godiva	Lettie	Nettie
Sally	Amélie	Cherry	Gracie	Levina	Nicola
Sandy	Anabel	Cicely	Greeba	Lilian	Nicole
Sarah	Andrea	Cissie	Gretel	Lilias	Noelle
Sasie	Angela	Claire	Gussie	Lillah	Noreen
Shona	Anthea	Connie	Gwenda	Lillie	Odette
Sonia	Armyne	Daphne	Gwynne	Lizzie	Olivia
Susan	Astrid	Davina	Hannah	Lolita	Oonagh
Susie	Athene	Debbie	Hattie	Lorina	Oriana
Sybil	Audrey	Denise	Hedwig	Lottie	Paddie
Tania	Aurora	Dianne	Helena	Louisa	Pamela
Tanya	Averil	Dorcas	Hester	Louise	Parnel
Tanis	Awdrey	Doreen	Hilary	Lucile	Pattie
Tatum	Azelle	Dorice	Honora	Maggie	Pegeen
Teify	Babbie	Dulcie	Honour	Maimie	Peggie
Terka	Barbie	Editha	Ianthe	Maisie	Pernel
Terri	Baubie	Edwina	Ileana	Marcia	Persis
Tessa	Beatie	Edythe	Imelda	Marcie	Petula
Thora	Beatty	Eileen	Imogen	Margie	Phoebe
Tilly	Benita	Eirene	Ingrid	Margot	Poppet
Tracy	Bertha	Elaine	Ioanna	Marian	Poppie
Trudy	Berthe	Elgiva	Isabel	Marion	Popsie
Urith	Bessie	Elinor	Ishbel	Marnie	Portia
Venis	Bettie	Eloisa	Isobel	Martha	Rachel
Venus	Bianca	Eloïse	Isolda	Mattie	Ramona
Vesta	Bibbie	Elspet	Isolde	Maxine	Raquel
Vicki	Biddie	Elvira	Jackie	Melita	Regina
Vicky	Billie	Emilia	Jacoba	Mercia	Renata
Viola	Binnie	Emilie	Janice	Merial	Renira
Vivie	Birdie	Esther	Jeanie	Mignon	Richie
Wanda	Blanca	Eunice	Jeanne	Millie	Robina
Wendy	Blanch	Evadne	Jemima	Mimosa	Rosana
Zeeta	Blanka	Evelyn	Jennie	Minnie	Rosina
Zelia					

Rowena	Yvonne	Clarice	Frances	Lisbeth	Queenie
Roxana		Claudia	Francie	Lizbeth	Rachael
Sabina		Colette	Frankie	Lorinda	Rachele
Sabine	**7**	Colleen	Georgia	Lucilla	Rebecca
Salome		Coralie	Georgie	Lucille	Rebekah
Sandra	Abigail	Corinne	Gertrud	Lucinda	Rhodena
Sappho	Adeline	Corinna	Gillian	Lucrece	Ricarda
Seabel	Adriana	Crystal	Giselle	Mabelle	Roberta
Selina	Alberta	Cynthia	Gladden	Mafalda	Rosabel
Seonad	Alethea	Damozel	Gwennie	Margery	Rosalie
Serena	Alfrida	Deborah	Gwyneth	Marilyn	Rosella
Sharon	Ameline	Deirdre	Gwynnie	Marjery	Rosetta
Sheena	Ankaret	Delysia	Harriet	Marjory	Rosette
Sheila	Annabel	Désirée	Heather	Marlene	Roxanne
Sicele	Annaple	Diamond	Hellena	Martina	Sabrina
Silvia	Annette	Dolores	Heloïse	Martine	Shambra
Simone	Anstice	Dorinda	Honoria	Matilda	Shelagh
Sophia	Antonia	Dorothe	Horatia	Maudlin	Shirley
Sophie	Antonie	Dorothy	Hypatia	Maureen	Sidonia
Stella	Ariadne	Dorrice	Isadora	Melanie	Siobhan
Sybell	Asenath	Dulcima	Isidora	Melissa	Susanna
Sylvia	Athenia	Eleanor	Janetta	Michele	Susanne
Tamsin	Augusta	Elfreda	Janette	Mildred	Suzanne
Teresa	Aurelia	Elfrida	Janitha	Minella	Sybilla
Terrie	Aveline	Ellenor	Jasmine	Minerva	Tabitha
Tertia	Babette	Ellinor	Jeannie	Mirabel	Tatania
Tessie	Barbara	Elspeth	Jenifer	Miralda	Theresa
Thalia	Barbary	Emerald	Jessica	Miranda	Therese
Thecla	Beatrix	Emiline	Jillian	Modesty	Titania
Thelma	Belinda	Estella	Jocelyn	Myfanwy	Tootles
Tootie	Bettina	Estelle	Johanna	Natalia	Valerie
Tracey	Beverly	Etienne	Juanita	Natalie	Valetta
Tricia	Blanche	Eudoxia	Juliana	Natasha	Vanessa
Trixie	Blodwen	Eugenia	Justine	Nigella	Venetia
Trudie	Blossom	Eugenie	Kathryn	Ninette	Winsome
Ulrica	Brigida	Eulalia	Katrina	Octavia	Yolande
Ursula	Bridget	Evaline	Katrine	Ophelia	Zirphie
Verity	Bronwen	Eveleen	Kirstie	Ottilia	
Verona	Camilla	Eveline	Lavinia	Ottilie	
Violet	Candida	Fayette	Leoline	Palmyra	**8**
Vivian	Carolyn	Felicia	Leonora	Pandora	Adelaide
Vivien	Cecilia	Fenella	Letitia	Paulina	Adrienne
Vyvyen	Celeste	Feodora	Lettice	Pauline	Albertha
Willow	Charity	Fidelia	Lillian	Perdita	Amabelle
Winnie	Cherrie	Florrie	Lillias	Phillis	Angelica
Yvette	Chrissy	Flossie	Linette	Phyllis	Angelina

Angeline
Angharad
Arabella
Araminta
Atalanta
Beatrice
Berenice
Beverley
Cammilla
Carlotta
Carolina
Carolina
Caroline
Catalina
Caterina
Cathleen
Catriona
Chrissie
Christie
Chrystal
Clemency
Claribel
Clarinda
Clarissa
Clotilde
Collette
Consuelo
Cordelia
Cornelia
Cressida
Danielle
Dominica
Dorothea
Dorothie
Drusilla
Dulcinia
Eleanora
Eleanore
Elfriede
Ellaline
Emmanuel
Emmeline
Ethelind
Euphemia
Evelinda
Everalda

Faustina
Faustine
Felicity
Filomena
Florence
Francine
Georgina
Germaine
Gertrude
Gretchen
Griselda
Grizelda
Grizelle
Gwynneth
Harriett
Hermione
Hortense
Hyacinth
Immanuel
Isabella
Jacobina
Jamesina
Jeanette
Jennifer
Jeromina
Joceline
Julianna
Julietta
Juliette
Katerina
Katharin
Kathleen
Kimberly
Kirsteen
Laburnum
Laetitia
Lauretta
Laurinda
Lavender
Lorraine
Lucretia
Madeline
Magdalen
Marcella
Marcelle
Margaret

Marianne
Marietta
Mariette
Marigold
Marjorie
Marvella
Mathilda
Meredith
Michelle
Mireille
Morwenna
Murielle
Nathalie
Nathanie
Patience
Patricia
Penelope
Petronel
Philippa
Primrose
Prudence
Prunella
Raymonde
Rebeccah
Reinagle
Reinelde
Rosalind
Rosaline
Rosamond
Rosamund
Roseanna
Roseanne
Rosemary
Samantha
Sapphire
Seabelle
Scarlett
Sheelagh
Susannah
Tallulah
Theodora
Theresia
Veronica
Victoria
Violetta
Virginia

Vivienne
Vourneen
Winifred

9

Albertine
Alexandra
Ambrosine
Anastasia
Annabelle
Annabella
Britannia
Cassandra
Catharine
Catherine
Celestine
Charlotte
Christian
Christina
Christine
Clarenora
Cleopatra
Clothilde
Columbine
Constance
Corisande
Desdemona
Eglantine
Elisabeth
Elizabeth
Ermengard
Ernestine
Esmeralda
Esperance
Ethelinda
Francesca
Françoise
Franziska
Frederica
Gabrielle
Georgiana
Georgette
Genevieve
Geraldine

Guglielma
Guinevere
Gwendolyn
Gwenllian
Harriette
Henrietta
Henriette
Hildegard
Hortensia
Hyacinthe
Iphigenia
Jacquetta
Jaqueline
Jessamine
Josephine
Kathailin
Katharina
Katharine
Katherine
Kimberley
Madeleine
Magdalena
Magdalene
Maraquita
Margarete
Margarita
Melisande
Millicent
Mirabelle
Nicolette
Pepronill
Pierrette
Priscilla
Rosabella
Rosabelle
Rosaritta
Rosemarie
Seraphina
Stephanie
Theodosia
Thomasina
Valentina
Veronique
Winefride

First names

10

Alessandra
Antoinette
Bernadette
Christabel
Christiana

Christobel
Cinderella
Clementina
Clementine
Constantia
Desiderata
Ermentrude

Ethelwynne
Evangelina
Evangeline
Fredericka
Gwendoline
Hildegarde
Irmentrude

Jacqueline
Margaretta
Margherita
Marguerite
Petronella
Philippina
Wilhelmina

11

Alexandrina

Male names

2

Ad
Al
Cy
Ed
Hu
Jo
Mo
Os
Si

3

Abe
Ade
Air
Alf
Ali
Arn
Art
Asa
Baz
Ben
Bob
Cec
Cis
Col
Con
Cyr
Dai
Dan
Del
Den
Des
Dob

Dod
Don
Dud
Eck
Edd
Eli
Ely
Ern
Emo
Gay
Gib
Gil
Gus
Guy
Hal
Ham
Hew
Hob
Huw
Ian
Ike
Ing
Ira
Ivo
Jan
Jay
Jem
Jim
Job
Joe
Jon
Jos
Kai
Kay
Ken
Kid

Kit
Lam
Lee
Len
Leo
Les
Lew
Lex
Lix
Lob
Lou
Luk
Lyn
Mac
Mat
Max
Nat
Ned
Nob
Nye
Pan
Pat
Pip
Rab
Rae
Ray
Red
Reg
Rex
Ric
Rob
Rog
Rod
Ron
Roy
Ruy

Sam
Sid
Sim
Sly
Stu
Syd
Ted
Tel
Tim
Tom
Val
Vic
Viv
Vin
Wat
Wal
Zac
Zak

4

Abel
Abie
Able
Adam
Adda
Agar
Alan
Albe
Aldo
Alec
Alex
Algy
Ally
Alon
Alun

Alva
Amos
Andy
Arch
Arne
Arno
Arny
Arty
Axel
Bald
Barn
Bart
Bate
Beau
Bede
Bedo
Bert
Bill
Boyd
Bram
Buck
Burt
Bury
Cain
Carl
Cary
Cass
Cedd
Ciro
Chad
Chas
Clem
Clim
Cole
Colm
Conn

Curt
Cyro
Dahl
Dave
Davy
Deio
Dewi
Dick
Diot
Dirk
Doug
Drew
Duda
Duff
Duke
Earl
Ecky
Eddy
Edie
Eden
Edom
Elie
Elis
Elmo
Elye
Elon
Emil
Enog
Eoin
Eral
Eric
Erie
Eros
Esau
Esme
Esra

Euan
Evan
Ewan
Ewen
Eyre
Ezra
Ferd
Finn
Fitz
Flem
Fran
Fred
Frey
Fulk
Gabe
Gary
Gene
Gide
Glen
Glyn
Goth
Greg
Gwyn
Hank
Hans
Herb
Hope
Hugh
Hugo
Hume
Hyam
Iago
Iain
Ifan
Ifor
Igor

Ikey	Mark	Rudy	Albyn	Basil	Clive	Drogo
Ioan	Matt	Ryan	Aldis	Basty	Clyde	Dusty
Iohn	Merv	Saul	Aldus	Batty	Colet	Eamon
Ivan	Mick	Sean	Aleck	Beaty	Colin	Earle
Ives	Mike	Seth	Alfie	Benet	Colum	Ebert
Ivor	Milo	Sion	Algie	Benji	Conal	Eckie
Jack	Mort	Sior	Alick	Benjy	Conan	Ector
Jake	Moss	Stan	Allan	Benny	Corny	Eddie
Jago	Muir	Stew	Allen	Beppo	Cosmo	Edgar
Jean	Neal	Tavy	Allin	Bermy	Count	Edred
Jeff	Neil	Theo	Almer	Berno	Craig	Edwin
Jess	Nero	Toby	Aloys	Berty	Cyril	Edwyn
Jock	Nial	Todd	Alred	Bevis	Cyrus	Eille
Joel	Nick	Tony	Alroy	Billy	Dacre	Eirik
Joey	Noah	Trev	Alves	Bjorn	Dadoo	Eldon
John	Noel	Vane	Alvin	Blake	Dakin	Eliab
José	Norm	Vere	Alwin	Bobby	Damon	Elias
Josh	Ogle	Walt	Alwyn	Booth	Dandy	Eliot
Juan	Olaf	Wilf	Amand	Boris	Danny	Ellis
Jude	Orme	Will	Ambie	Brian	Darby	Elmer
Jule	Ossy	Wing	Amias	Brien	Darch	Elsye
Karl	Otho	Winn	Amiot	Bruce	Darcy	Elvis
Kaye	Otis	Wray	Amyas	Bruno	D'arcy	Elwyn
Keir	Otto	Wynn	Andie	Bryan	Daryl	Emery
Kemp	Owen	Yule	André	Bunny	David	Emlyn
Kent	Ozzy	Yuri	Angus	Cadog	Davit	Emory
Kiki	Page	Yves	Anson	Cairn	Davie	Emrys
King	Paul	Yvon	Anton	Caius	Denis	Emile
Kuno	Pedr	Zack	Archy	Caleb	Denny	Eneas
Kunz	Penn	Zeke	Ariel	Candy	Denri	Enoch
Kurt	Pepe		Artie	Carew	Denys	Eneys
Kyle	Pery		Artur	Carlo	Derby	Ernie
Lamy	Pete	**5**	Askew	Carne	Derek	Ernst
Lars	Phil	Aaron	Athol	Carol	Deric	Errol
Lacy	Pung	Abdul	Aubyn	Cecil	Derry	Euric
Leon	Rafe	Abner	Augie	Ceese	Deryk	Evans
Leri	Raff	Abram	Aurel	Celyn	Dickë	Ewart
Lexy	René	Adolf	Avere	César	Dicky	Eyles
Liam	Rhys	Aesop	Avery	Chris	Diego	Felix
Llew	Rich	Ailin	Aymar	Chuck	Doddy	Floyd
Loel	Rick	Airay	Aymie	Clair	Dodge	Franc
Luke	Riou	Alain	Baden	Clare	Dolph	Frank
Lyle	Rolf	Alawn	Barny	Clark	Donal	Franz
Lynd	Roly	Alban	Barry	Claud	Donny	Frith
Lyon	Rory	Albat	Barty	Claus	Dylan	Fritz
Marc	Ross	Albin	Basie	Cliff	Drake	Gabay

First names

Gabby	Jacky	Lucan	Oriel	Royce	Wolfe	August
Gabey	Jacob	Lucas	Orpen	Rufus	Wyatt	Austen
Gaius	Jaime	Luigi	Orson	Rurik	Wylie	Austin
Garin	James	Lysle	Oscar	Ryder	Wynne	Averil
Garry	Jamie	Lynch	Osmon	Sammy	Wyvil	Awstin
Garth	Jared	Madoc	Osric	Sandy	Yorke	Aylmer
Gavin	Jason	Major	Oswin	Saxon		Aylwin
Gawen	Jemmy	Manny	Owain	Scott		Balbus
Geoff	Jerry	Manus	Ozzie	Serge	**6**	Baldie
Gerry	Jesse	Marco	Pablo	Shane	Adolph	Baliol
Gidie	Jesus	Marty	Paolo	Shaun	Adolfo	Barney
Giles	Jevan	Massy	Paddy	Shawn	Adrian	Baston
Glyde	Jewel	Matty	Paget	Silas	Aeneas	Baxter
Glynn	Jimmy	Mavor	Paton	Simon	Alaric	Bedwyr
Gowin	Johan	Mayor	Pedro	Speed	Albany	Benett
Govan	Jolin	Merry	Pelan	Speke	Albert	Benito
Grant	Jonah	Meyer	Perce	Spike	Albery	Benjie
Gregg	Jonas	Miall	Percy	Starr	Albion	Bennet
Guido	Jonaz	Micah	Perry	Steve	Aldous	Bennie
Gyles	Jonty	Micky	Peter	Storm	Aldred	Benoît
Hagen	Joyce	Miles	Phene	Tabor	Alexis	Berend
Harry	Jozef	Mitch	Piers	Taffy	Alfons	Berney
Haden	Judah	Monte	Power	Tandy	Alfred	Bernie
Hebel	Judas	Monty	Punch	Teddy	Alleyn	Bertie
Heinz	Jules	Moray	Ralph	Terry	Alston	Billee
Henri	Keith	Morty	Ramon	Titus	Amilek	Billie
Henry	Kenny	Moses	Randy	Timmy	Anders	Blosse
Herne	Kevin	Moshe	Raoul	Tobie	Andrea	Bobbie
Heron	Klaus	Moule	Remis	Tobin	Andrés	Bossil
Hiram	Kuros	Mungo	Renée	Tolly	Andrew	Braham
Hodge	Lance	Murdo	Ricky	Tommy	Angelo	Briton
Homer	Lanty	Myles	Rider	Trant	Anselm	Brodie
Humph	Larry	Myrie	Robin	Tubby	Anthin	Brutus
Hyman	Leigh	Nahum	Roddy	Tudor	Anthon	Bryden
Hymie	Lenny	Nanty	Roden	Ulick	Antony	Bulwer
Hyram	Lewie	Neddy	Rodge	Ulric	Archer	Caesar
Ianto	Lewin	Neill	Roger	Uriah	Archie	Calvin
Idris	Lewis	Niall	Ralph	Usher	Armand	Camile
Iltyd	Lexie	Nicky	Rollo	Vijay	Arnaud	Canice
Inigo	Lisle	Nicco	Rolly	Vince	Arnaut	Carlos
Innes	Llelo	Nicol	Rolph	Vinny	Arnold	Caspar
Isaac	Lloyd	Nigel	Romeo	Wahab	Arthur	Cedric
Ivone	Lluyd	Odden	Romer	Wally	Arturo	Cenred
Ivory	Loren	Olave	Ronny	Wayne	Ashley	Cenydd
Izaak	Louie	Ollie	Rowan	Willi	Aubert	Cerdic
Jabez	Louis	Oprin	Rowly	Willy	Aubrey	Cesare

Charly	Dougal	Gareth	Hector	Jessie	Macsen	Nicolo
Chilla	Dryden	Garnet	Hedley	Jeston	Magnus	Nicols
Chippy	Dudley	Garret	Heintz	Jethro	Maidoc	Ninian
Cicero	Dugald	Garvey	Helier	Jockey	Malise	Norman
Clarry	Duggie	Gaspar	Henric	Johann	Mansel	Norris
Clarus	Duncan	Gaston	Henryk	Johnny	Manuel	Norton
Claude	Dundus	Gawain	Henzel	Joseph	Marcel	Nowell
Clovis	Dunlop	George	Herbie	Joshua	Marcus	Oberon
Colley	Dustin	Georgy	Herman	Josiah	Marius	Olafur
Connie	Dwight	Gerald	Hervey	Julian	Marten	Oliver
Connor	Eamonn	Gerard	Hilary	Julien	Martel	Onslow
Conrad	Earley	Gerold	Hilton	Julius	Marten	Orazio
Conway	Eddard	Gerrie	Hinton	Jollan	Martin	Osbert
Corney	Edmond	Gervas	Hobart	Jolyon	Marvin	Osborn
Crease	Edmund	Gibbie	Hobbie	Julyan	Mattus	Osmond
Crusoe	Eduard	Gideon	Holman	Justin	Mauris	Oswald
Cuddie	Edward	Gilbee	Horace	Justus	Melvin	Padrig
Curran	Egbert	Girard	Howard	Kaspar	Melvyn	Pascoe
Dafydd	Eggert	Giulio	Howell	Kersey	Merlin	Pelham
Dallas	Eilian	Godric	Hubert	Kester	Merrik	Pepito
Damian	Eldred	Godwin	Hubard	Kirwan	Mervyn	Percie
Dandie	Elfrid	Gonvil	Huberd	Konrad	Meurig	Perkin
Daniel	Elijah	Gordon	Hughie	Kunzel	Mickie	Petros
Danill	Elisha	Graeme	Hunter	Laddie	Mickey	Philip
Danilo	Ellick	Graham	Hylton	Lamley	Miguel	Pierre
Donnie	Elliot	Gregan	Ignace	Larrie	Millis	Pietro
Dansil	Ernest	Gregor	Inglis	Launce	Milton	Poldie
Darren	Erroll	Grizel	Ingram	Lauren	Minden	Powell
Darryl	Ervine	Grogan	Irvine	Laurie	Montie	Prince
Deakin	Esmond	Gunner	Irving	Lawrie	Morgan	Rabbie
Decius	Eugene	Gunter	Isaiah	Lawley	Moritz	Rafael
Declan	Evelyn	Gussie	Isidor	Lemuel	Morris	Ramage
Dekker	Fabian	Gustof	Israel	Lennie	Morvyn	Ramsay
Demian	Fabius	Gustus	Jackey	Leslie	Mostyn	Ranald
Dennis	Felton	Gwilym	Jackie	Lester	Murphy	Randal
Denzil	Ferdie	Hallam	Jacomb	Linnel	Murray	Randle
Derick	Fergie	Hamish	Jacopo	Lionel	Nainby	Ranson
Dermot	Fergus	Hamlet	Jairus	Loftus	Nairne	Raphel
Derric	Fingal	Hamlyn	Janion	Lowrie	Napier	Rasmus
Deryck	Finlay	Harold	Japhet	Lucian	Nathan	Rastus
Dickey	Forbes	Harrel	Jaques	Lucien	Nelson	Ratsey
Dickie	Franck	Harris	Jarvis	Lucius	Neddie	Rawden
Dickon	Franco	Harrow	Jasper	Ludwig	Nevile	Rayner
Dobbin	Franko	Harvey	Jeremy	Lupton	Nevill	Reggie
Dominy	Freddy	Hayden	Jerome	Luther	Nikita	Rendle
Donald	Fyodor	Haydon	Jervis	Lyonel	Nickel	Reuben

First names

Rhodes	Stiven	Ainslie	Calvert	Diarmid	Gervase
Rhodri	Stuart	Aladdin	Cameron	Diarmit	Gilbert
Ricard	Sydney	Alberic	Caradoc	Diggory	Gilmour
Richie	Symkyn	Alberto	Carlton	Dillwyn	Giacomo
Ringan	Symond	Alexius	Carlyon	Domingo	Gladwyn
Rippin	Talbot	Alfonso	Carolus	Dominic	Gloster
Robbie	Teodor	Alister	Casimir	Dominyk	Godfrey
Robert	Thaddy	Alleyne	Catesby	Donovan	Goronwy
Roddie	Thomas	Almeric	Cedrych	Douglas	Grahame
Rodger	Tizard	Alphege	Cennydd	Downing	Gregory
Rodney	Tobias	Alsager	Charles	Drystan	Gunther
Roland	Trefor	Amadeus	Charley	Duerdin	Gustave
Ronald	Trevor	Ambrose	Charlie	Dunstan	Gwythyr
Ronnie	Vashon	Anatole	Charlot	Eardley	Gwillym
Rowley	Verney	Andries	Chawner	Edouard	Hadrian
Rowlie	Vernon	Andreas	Chester	Eleazar	Halbert
Royden	Vicary	Aneirin	Chewton	Elphege	Hartley
Rudolf	Victor	Aneurin	Chollie	Emanuel	Herbert
Rupert	Viktor	Anthony	Christy	Emilius	Hermann
Russel	Vinnie	Antoine	Claudie	Ephraim	Hewlett
Samson	Virgil	Antonio	Claudio	Erasmus	Hilaire
Samuel	Vivian	Arnauld	Clayton	Erastus	Hilarie
Sancho	Vyvian	Artemas	Clement	Etienne	Hildred
Sander	Wallis	Artemus	Clemmie	Eustace	Horatio
Sandro	Walter	Auberon	Clinton	Everard	Humbert
Saurin	Warner	Auguste	Coemgen	Ezekiel	Humphry
Sawnie	Warren	Auveray	Collwyn	Faraday	Iachimo
Seamas	Watkin	Baptist	Columba	Faulder	Ibrahim
Seamus	Wesley	Baldwin	Compton	Fielder	Ingleby
Sefton	Wilbur	Balfour	Connell	Fithian	Jackson
Selwyn	Willem	Barclay	Conrade	Fitzroy	Jacques
Seumas	Willie	Barnaby	Crispin	Francis	Jaffray
Shafto	Willis	Barnard	Crispus	Frankie	Jalland
Shamus	Wilmot	Bartley	Cuthred	Freddie	Jeffrey
Sholto	Winnie	Bartram	Cynebil	Fredric	Jerrard
Sidney	Wolsey	Beaufoi	Cyriack	Gabriel	Joachim
Sigurd	Xavier	Bennett	Cyprian	Galahad	Johnnie
Sigrid	Yehudi	Bernard	Dalison	Gaspard	Jocelyn
Simeon	Yorick	Bertram	Dalziel	Geoffry	Justice
Simons		Berwald	Dandini	Geordie	Kasimir
Sinbad		Boswell	Deiniol	Georgie	Kenneth
Square	**7**	Brandon	Delancy	Geraint	Knyvett
Squire		Brendan	Denison	Gerallt	Lachlan
Stepan	Abraham	Brennan	Denzill	Gerhard	Lambart
Steven	Absalom	Buckler	Derrick	Gerhold	Lambard
Stevyn	Ackroyd	Burnard	Desmond	Gervais	Lambert
	Adolphe				

Lazarus	Quentin	Tertius	Alphonso	Crawford
Leander	Quintin	Theodor	Annesley	Crispian
Lennard	Quintus	Thorold	Antonius	Cuthbert
Leonard	Randall	Timothy	Aristide	Dederick
Leopold	Ranulph	Trenham	Augustin	Diarmaid
Lindsay	Raphael	Tristan	Augustus	Diarmuid
Lindsey	Raymond	Ughtred	Aurelius	Diarmuit
Lorenzo	Raymund	Ulysses	Balliser	Diederik
Lorimer	Redvers	Umberto	Bancroft	Dietrich
Lucifer	Reynard	Vaughan	Banister	Dominick
Luciano	Reynold	Vauncey	Bardolph	Drustens
Ludovic	Rhicert	Vincent	Barnabas	Ebenezer
Madison	Ricardo	Vittore	Bartlemy	Eberhard
Malachi	Richard	Wallace	Baudouin	Emmanuel
Malcolm	Rinaldo	Walther	Beaumont	Ethelred
Matthew	Rodbert	Wariner	Bedivere	Faithful
Maurice	Roderic	Warwick	Belgrave	Farquhar
Maxwell	Rodolph	Westley	Benedick	Fernando
Maynard	Rodrigo	Wilfred	Benedict	Fitzhugh
Merrick	Romulus	Wilfrid	Benjamin	Florizel
Michael	Ronayne	Wilhelm	Bernardi	Fluellen
Mogador	Roussel	William	Bernardo	François
Montagu	Rowland	Wilkins	Bernhard	Franklin
Morcant	Rudolph	Winston	Bertrand	Frederic
Murdoch	Rudyard	Wyndham	Boudewyn	Gabriele
Neville	Russell	Ximenes	Brenainn	Geoffrey
Nicolas	Rutland	Ystffan	Campbell	Geoffroy
Niccolo	Sergius	Zachary	Carleton	Geronimo
Nicolai	Seymour	Zebedee	Champion	Giovanni
Obadiah	Shachel		Chauncey	Greville
Olivier	Sheldon		Charnock	Griffith
Orlando	Sigmund	**8**	Charlton	Guiseppe
Orpheus	Silvius	Achilles	Cheyenny	Gulliver
Orville	Sylvius	Adalbert	Chretien	Gustavus
Osborne	Solomon	Adolphus	Christie	Hamilton
Paladin	Spencer	Agostino	Clarence	Hannibal
Padraic	Spenser	Alasdair	Claudius	Harcourt
Patrick	Stanley	Alastair	Clementi	Harrison
Peredur	Steffan	Albrecht	Clements	Havelock
Perseus	Stephan	Aleister	Clifford	Heinrich
Pheroze	Stenson	Algernon	Clotaire	Herbrand
Phillip	Stephen	Alisdair	Conbelin	Hercules
Philpot	Steuart	Alistair	Conradin	Hereward
Phineas	Stewart	Allister	Constans	Hezekiah
Pierrot	Tebaldo	Aloysius	Constant	Horatius
Placido	Terence	Alphonse	Crauford	Humphrey

First names

Ignatius
Immanuel
Ingenuel
Ingelram
Jeremiah
Jonathan
Joscelin
Joscelyn
Josephus
Kingsley
Lancelot
Laurence
Lavallin
Lawrance
Lawrence
Leonardo
Leonhard
Leonidas
Llewelyn
Llywelyn
Lothario
Lutwyche
Maddison
Maitland
Marshall
Martival
Matthias
Melchior
Meredith
Meredydd
Montague
Morrison
Mortimer
Nehemiah
Nicholas
Nicolaus
Octavius
Odysseus
Oliphant
Ormiston
Oughtred
Parsifal
Parzifal
Paulinus
Perceval
Percival

Peterkin
Philemon
Philippe
Raffaelo
Randolph
Randulph
Reginald
Robinson
Roderick
Rhisiart
Ruaraidh
Sandford
Scoltock
Secundus
Septimus
Sherlock
Siegmund
Silvanus
Sinclair
Somerset
Spensley
Stafford
Stephano
Stiobhan
Sylvanus
Tearlach
Thaddeus
Theobald
Theodore
Trelawny
Tristram
Valdimar
Vladimir
Wolseley
Zedekiah

9

Abernethy
Abimeleck
Alaistair
Alejandro
Alexander
Alexandre
Alisander
Allardyce

Almosnino
Alphonsus
Alysandyr
Antoninus
Arbuthnot
Archibald
Arcibaldo
Aristotle
Armstrong
Athelstan
Augustine
Baldewyne
Balthasar
Balthazar
Bartimeus
Beauchamp
Benedetto
Caratacos
Christian
Christmas
Constable
Cornelius
Courtenay
Courteney
Crispinus
Cristobal
Creighton
Cymbeline
Demetrius
Dionysius
Donalbian
Elshender
Ethelbert
Ferdinand
Fortescue
Francesco
Francisco
Frederick
Friedrich
Gascoigne
Glanville
Gottfried
Granville
Grenville
Hazledine
Honoratus

Jefferson
Josceline
Juscelino
Llewellyn
Lucretius
Mackenzie
Marmaduke
Martineau
Nathaniel
Nicodemus
Outhwaite
Peregrine
Rodriguez
Rupprecht
Sackville
Sebastian
Sébastien
Siegfried
Sigismund
Silvester
Stephanos
Sylvester
Stanislas
Thaddaeus
Theodoric
Valentine
Valentino
Vincentio
Wenceslas
Wilbraham
Zachariah
Zacharias
Zechariah

10

Alessandro
Alaksandus
Alisaundre
Athanasius
Athelstane
Augustulus
Barrington
Barthelémy
Bartolomeu
Belshazzar

Caractacus
Carmichael
Cecilianus
Christiern
Crispinian
Cristoforo
Eustachius
Haliburton
Hildebrand
Llewhellin
Maximilian
Montgomery
Pierrepont
Sacheverel
Somerville
Stanislaus
Theodosius
Theophilus
Tyrrhenian
Washington
Willoughby

11

Bartholomew
Bartolommeo
Benedictine
Christopher
Charlemagne
Constantine
Constantius
Cruickshank
Fitzherbert
Fitzpatrick
Ravenscroft
Skeffington

12

Chesterfield

13

Cristopheros

Fish

3

bib
cod
dab
eel
gar
hag
ide
ray

4

bass
blay
brit
carp
char
chub
chum
coho
cusk
dace
dory
drum
goby
grig
hake
jack
kelt
ling
luce
moor
opah
orfe
parr
peal
pike
pogy
pope
pout
rudd
ruff
scad

scup
shad
sild
sole
tope
tuna

5

bleak
bream
brill
charr
cisco
cobia
coley
cuddy
danio
elver
fluke
grunt
gummy
guppy
lance
loach
manta
molly
moray
musky
perch
pogge
porgy
powan
roach
ruffe
saury
scrod
sepia
sewin
shark
skate
smelt
smolt

smout
smowt
snoek
snook
sprat
tench
tetra
toady
torsk
trout
tunny
witch

6

alevin
anabas
barbel
beluga
blenny
bonito
bowfin
burbot
callop
caplin
conger
cottus
darter
dentex
dorado
gadoid
ganoid
grilse
groper
gunnel
gurnet
kipper
launce
marlin
megrim
milter
minnow
mudcat

mud eel
mullet
muskie
plaice
pollan
puffer
red cod
redeye
redfin
remora
robalo
runner
saithe
salmon
sauger
saurel
sea bat
sea dog
sea fox
sea hog
sea pig
shanny
shiner
sucker
tailor
tarpon
tautog
turbot
weever
wirrah
wrasse
zander

7

alewife
anchovy
batfish
bloater
blue cod
bummalo
capelin
catfish

cavalla
cavally
cichlid
clupeid
codfish
codling
cowfish
croaker
crucian
dipnoan
dogfish
eelpout
escolar
fantail
finnock
garfish
garpike
gourami
grouper
grunion
grunter
gudgeon
gurnard
gwyniad
haddock
hagfish
halibut
herring
hogfish
houting
ice fish
jewfish
kahawai
kokanee
lampern
lamprey
mahseer
mooneye
morwong
mudfish
oarfish
oldwife
pandora
pigfish

pinfish
piranha
pollack
pollock
pomfret
pompano
quinnat
ratfish
rat-tail
redfish
rock cod
sand dab
sand eel
sardine
sawfish
sculpin
sea bass
sea pike
sea wolf
silurid
skipper
snapper
sockeye
sterlet
sunfish
teleost
tiddler
topknot
torpedo
vendace
walleye
whiting

8

albacore
billfish
boarfish
bullhead
blowfish
bluefish
bluegill
bonefish

Fish

brisling
bullhead
cave fish
characin
coalfish
dealfish
devil ray
dragonet
drumfish
eagle ray
filefish
flatfish
flathead
flounder
frogfish
gamefish
gilthead
goatfish
goldfish
grayling
jackfish
John Dory
kingfish
lemon fish
lionfish
lumpfish
lungfish
mackerel
manta ray
menhaden
monkfish
moonfish
moray eel
nannygai
numbfish
pickerel
pilchard
pipefish
red porgy
red tetra
rockfish
rockling
rosefish
sailfish
salmonid
sea bream

sea devil
sea-horse
sea purse
sea raven
sea perch
sea robin
sea trout
skipjack
sparling
stingray
sturgeon
suckfish
swamp eel
tarwhine
teraglin
toadfish
weakfish
wolf-fish

9

angelfish
barracuda
black bass
blackfish
black moor
blindfish
blue shark
bull trout
clingfish
conger eel
coral fish
devilfish
Dover sole
glassfish
globefish
goldfinny
goldsinny
goosefish
greenbone
greenling
grenadier
houndfish
killifish
latimeria
lemon sole

murray cod
pearlfish
pike perch
pilot fish
porbeagle
razor fish
red mullet
red salmon
scaldfish
schnapper
selachian
sheatfish
snipefish
solenette
spearfish
stargazer
stockfish
stone bass
stonefish
surfperch
surmullet
swordfish
swordtail
thornback
threadfin
topminnow
trunkfish
whitebait
whitefish
wobbegong
wreckfish
zebra fish

10

angel shark
angler fish
archer fish
bitterling
Bombay duck
brook trout
brown trout
candlefish
carpet shark
coelacanth
damselfish

dragonfish
fingerling
flame tetra
flying fish
ghost shark
great skate
grey mullet
groundling
guitar fish
lancet fish
lumpsucker
midshipman
mirror carp
mossbunker
mudskipper
needlefish
nurse shark
paddlefish
parrot fish
pink salmon
red grouper
red snapper
ribbonfish
rock salmon
rock turbot
sand launce
sea poacher
shovelhead
shovelnose
silverfish
silverside
squeteague
tiger shark
whale shark
white shark
yellowtail

11

bellows fish
Dolly Varden
electric eel
electric ray
golden perch
hippocampus
lake herring

138

lantern fish
leatherskin
lepidosiren
lophobranch
Moorish idol
muskellunge
plectognath
salmon trout
sea scorpion
stickleback
surgeonfish
swallowfish
triggerfish
whitingpout

fatherlasher
fighting fish
four-eyed fish
miller's thumb
mouthbrooder
paradise fish
rainbow trout
requiem shark
river lamprey
sea porcupine
scorpion fish
silver salmon
walleyed pike

flying gurnard
labyrinth fish
leatherjacket
mackerel shark
porcupine fish
snake mackerel
sockeye salmon
thresher shark

14 +

Australian salmon
great white shark
hammerhead shark
king of the herrings
shovelhead shark
Spanish mackerel
wheel animalcule

12

basking shark

13

climbing perch
horse mackerel
finnan haddock

Flowers

3 & 4

acer
aloe
arum
balm
bixa
flag
geum
ilex
iris
ivy
ixia
lily
ling
may
meum
musa
musk
olea
poa
pink
rapa
rhus

rosa
rose
ruta
sium
thea
ulex
whin
zea

5

abies
abrus
agave
algae
anona
areca
aspic
aster
avens
briza
butea
calla

camas
canna
carex
carya
chara
daisy
dwale
erica
glaux
gowan
hosta
larix
ledum
lemna
linum
lotus
lupin
malva
melia
morus
mucor
musci
naias

orris
oryza
ox-eye
oxlip
panax
pansy
peony
phlox
picea
pinus
piper
poker
poppy
pyrus
rheum
ribes
rubia
rubus
rumen
sabal
salix
sedum
stipa

stock
tansy
taxus
thuja
tilia
tsuga
tuber
tulip
typha
ulmas
urena
usnea
vetch
vinca
viola
vitex
vitis
xyris
yucca
yulan
zamia

6

abroma
acacia
acorus
alhagi
alisma
alpine
amomum
arabis
aralia
arnica
aucuba
betula
bryony
cactus
caltha
camass
carapa
carica
cassia
cedrus
celtis
cereus

Flowers

cicuta
cistus
clover
clusia
cnicus
cosmos
costus
crocus
croton
dahlia
daphne
datura
derris
elaeis
elodea
empusa
gnetum
hedera
henbit
hypnum
iberis
isatis
kalmia
kerria
laurus
lucuma
lupine
madder
mallow
mimosa
myrica
myrtus
nerine
nerium
nostoc
nuphar
orchid
orchis
oxalis
paigle
peziza
phleum
protea
pteris
punica
pyrola

raphia
reseda
rocket
riccia
ruscus
sagina
salvia
sapium
sapota
scilla
sesame
seseli
silene
smilax
squill
styrax
sundew
sylvia
thrift
tulipa
urtica
violet
viscum
yarrow
zinnia

7

aconite
althaea
alyssum
anchusa
anemone
arachis
arbutus
banksia
bartsia
begonia
boletus
bugloss
burdock
bursera
calluna
campion
catalpa
cat' s ear

cedrela
chelone
clarkia
corylus
corypha
cowslip
cudweed
curcuma
cyathea
cyperus
cytisus
day lily
deutzia
digynia
dioecia
dionaea
dog rose
drosera
epacris
ephedra
erodium
eugenia
figwort
filices
freesia
frogbit
fuchsia
fumaria
gazania
genista
gentian
gerbera
godetia
honesty
hordeum
ipomoea
isoetes
jacinth
jasmine
jonquil
juglans
kingcup
lactuca
lantana
lobelia
logania

lychnis
lythrum
manihot
maranta
may lily
melilot
melissa
milfoil
mimulus
monilia
moringa
mullein
musales
nelumbo
nemesia
nigella
nopalea
opuntia
osmunda
panicum
papaver
petunia
phallus
picotee
populus
primula
pythium
quercus
ragwort
rambler
rampion
rhamnus
ricinus
robinia
ruellia
saffron
salsola
scandix
scirpus
sea-pink
senecio
sequoia
skimmia
solanum
sonchus
sorghum

spiraea
statice
syringa
tagetes
tamarix
tea rose
thistle
trefoil
tritoma
verbena
vervain
xylopia
zizania
zostera

8

abutilon
acanthus
achillea
ageratum
amaranth
angelica
anthemis
arum lily
asphodel
aubretia
auricula
bedstraw
bignonia
bindweed
bird' s eye
bluebell
calamint
camellia
catchfly
centaury
clematis
corn lily
crowfoot
cyclamen
daffodil
dianthus
dicentra
dog-brier
dropwort

erigeron
fleabane
foxglove
gardenia
geranium
gladioli
gloriosa
gloxinia
harebell
hawkweed
helenium
hepatica
hibiscus
hyacinth
ice plant
japonica
knapweed
larkspur
lavatera
lent lily
marigold
martagon
milkwort
moss rose
musk rose
myosotis
phacelia
phormium
plumbago
pond lily
primrose
rockrose
sandwort
scabious
skullcap
snowdrop
soapwort
starwort
sweet pea
tigridia
toadflax
trillium
tuberose
valerian
veronica
viscaria

wild rose
wood sage
xanthium

9

Aaron's rod
achimenes
amaryllis
bear's foot
bee orchid
buttercup
calendula
candytuft
campanula
candytuft
carnation
celandine
chamomile
cherry-pie
chickweed
China rose
cineraria
clove pink
cockscomb
colchicum
colt's foot
columbine
coreopsis
corn poppy
cotyledon
dandelion
digitalis
dog violet
edelweiss
eglantine
gladiolus
golden rod
hellebore
hollyhock
impatiens
jessamine
kniphofia
mayflower
narcissus
nemophila

pimpernel
pyrethrum
saxifrage
sea rocket
snowflake
spearwort
speedwell
stonecrop
sunflower
tiger lily
twayblade
wake robin
waterlily
wolf's-bane

10

agapanthus
amaranthus
aspidistra
belladonna
bellflower
bluebottle
burnet rose
busy lizzie
China aster
cinquefoil
coquelicot
compositae
corn cockle
cornflower
cranesbill
cuckoopint
damask rose
deadnettle
delphinium
Dutch tulip
Easter lily
field poppy
fritillary
fox and cubs
gaillardia
goat's beard
goldilocks
gypsophila
heart's-ease

helianthus
heliotrope
immortelle
lady orchid
lady's smock
marguerite
mignonette
nasturtium
nightshade
opium poppy
oxeye daisy
passiflora
periwinkle
poached egg
poinsettia
polyanthus
potentilla
ranunculus
red campion
rose mallow
sarracenia
snake's head
snapdragon
stitchwort
storksbill
wallflower
Welsh poppy
willowherb
windflower
wood sorrel
yellow wort

11

antirrhinum
bell heather
bitter-cress
black medick
bouncing Bet
cabbage rose
calceolaria
convolvulus
cotoneaster
eschschozia
everlasting
fig marigold

forget-me-not
gentianella
gilliflower
gillyflower
globeflower
helichrysum
helleborine
honeysuckle
kidney vetch
love-in-a-mist
London pride
loosestrife
meadowsweet
Parma violet
pelargonium
ragged robin
rambler rose
red-hot poker
St. John's wort
schizanthus
stephanotis
sweet cicely
tiger flower
wood anemone

12

adder's tongue
alpine flower
apple blossom
autumn crocus
bacon and eggs
corn marigold
cuckoo flower
fool's parsley
huntsman's cup
Iceland poppy
Jacob's ladder

lady's slipper
monkey flower
monkey orchid
morning glory
old man's beard
pasque flower
pitcher plant
prickly poppy
salpiglossis
snow in summer
Solomon's seal
sweet william
Turk's cap lily
weasel's snout
venus flytrap
virgin's bower
wild hyacinth

13

African violet
bleeding heart
butter-and-eggs
cherry blossom
Christmas rose
chrysanthemum
creeping Jenny
grape hyacinth
huntsman's horn
Joseph and Mary
ladies' fingers
marsh marigold
meadow saffron
orange blossom
passion flower
soldier orchid
townhall clock
traveller's joy
trumpet flower

water hyacinth

14

bladder campion
Canterbury bell
cardinal flower
creeping Jennie
creeping Myrtle
jack-by-the-hedge
lords-and-ladies
love-in-idleness
military orchid
shepherd's purse

15 +

batchelor's buttons
bats-in-the-belfry
blood-drop emlets
bristly ox-tongue
butterfly orchid
creeping Charlie
deadly nightshade
Duke of Argyll's
  tea-plant
evening primrose
love-lies-bleeding
lily of the valley
Michaelmas daisy
mother-in-law's
  tongue
poor man's weather-
  glass
scarlet pimpernel
shepherd's weather-
  glass
star of Bethlehem
woody nightshade

Food and cooking

3

bap
bun
cru
dip
ear
egg
fat
fig
fry
ham
ice
jam
leg
nan
nut
oil
pie
rib
roe
soy
wok

4

anna
bake
bean
beef
blin
boil
bran
butt
cake
cate
chop
chow
clod
crab
crib
curd
dhal

dill
dine
dish
duck
duff
fare
fish
flan
fool
fowl
game
ghee
grub
hand
hare
hash
herb
hock
jowl
Kiev
junk
lamb
lard
lean
loaf
loin
lung
malt
mash
meal
meat
menu
milk
neck
olio
olla
pâté
peel
pork
puff
raan
rare
rice

rock
roll
roux
rump
rusk
sago
salt
shin
snow
sopa
soup
stew
suet
taco
tart
tuna
veal
whey
wing
yolk
zest

5

à demi
aspic
bacon
baste
belly
blade
blini
bombe
boned
brawn
bread
brose
broth
brulé
bully
candy
capon
cheek
chips

chuck
condé
cream
crêpe
crown
cruet
crumb
crust
curds
curry
diane
dough
dulse
fancy
feast
filet
flank
flour
fruit
fudge
gigot
glace
glaze
goose
gravy
grill
gruel
gumbo
halva
heart
honey
humus
icing
jelly
joint
juice
kebab
kofta
liver
lunch
manna
matzo
melba

mince
mocha
offal
pasta
pasty
patty
pecan
pilaf
pilau
pilaw
pirog
pizza
poach
prawn
prune
pulse
purée
quail
reine
roast
rojak
russe
salad
salmi
sauce
sauté
scone
scrag
shank
skirt
snack
spice
steak
steam
stock
sugar
sushi
sweet
syrup
taffy
T bone
toast
torte

tripe
verte
viand
vichy
wafer
yeast

6

alaska
alecha
almond
barder
banger
batter
biffin
blintz
brains
braise
breast
brunch
burger
buffet
butter
canapé
casein
catsup
caviar
cheese
cockle
coddle
collar
collop
comfit
congee
cookie
corner
cornet
creole
crisps
croute
crumbs

cutlet	omelet	tariff	chutney	knuckle
dainty	oxtail	tiffin	cobbler	lardoon
dinner	paella	tit-bit	cobloaf	lasagne
dragée	panada	toffee	compote	lichees
eclair	parkin	tongue	cookies	lobster
eggnog	passer	top rib	corn cob	lozenge
entrée	pastry	trifle	cracker	matzoon
etuver	perkin	turbot	crouton	matzoth
faggot	pickle	turkey	crumble	meat pie
fillet	picnic	umbles	crumpet	mustard
finnan	pilaff	viande	cuisine	niçoise
flambé	pillau	viands	cup cake	noodles
flitch	poeler	waffle	currant	oat cake
fodder	polony	yogurt	cushion	oatmeal
fondue	posset		custard	pabulum
frappé	potage	**7**	dariole	panache
fumado	potato		dartois	pancake
gammon	quiche	albumen	deep fry	parboil
gateau	rabbit	anchovy	dessert	parfait
gaufre	ragout	back rib	egg yolk	pavlova
grease	raisin	banbury	epicure	pickles
greens	rasher	bannock	essence	pigs fry
grouse	relish	banquet	fancies	pikelet
haggis	rolled	Bath bun	fig cake	pilaffe
haunch	romaño	beef tea	fig roll	pimento
hot dog	royale	best end	fondant	piquant
hot-pot	saddle	biltong	foo yung	plum jam
hummus	salami	biryani	fore end	plum pie
jujube	salmon	biscuit	fritter	poisson
jumble	samosa	blossom	galette	popcorn
junket	scouse	borscht	game pie	popover
kernel	sea-pie	bouilli	garnish	pork pie
kidney	shrimp	brioche	gelatin	potargo
kipper	simmer	brisket	giblets	pottage
leaven	simnel	broiler	glucose	poultry
lights	sorbet	brownie	gnocchi	praline
mornay	sowens	calipee	goulash	pretzel
mousse	sponge	candies	gourmet	pudding
muffin	spread	caramel	gratine	ramekin
mussel	spring	carvery	gristle	rarebit
mutton	sundae	catchup	high tea	ratafia
noodle	supper	caviare	hoummos	ravioli
nougat	sweets	chapati	houmous	rice bun
noyeau	tamale	charqui	jam roll	risotto
nut oil	tamara	chicken	jam tart	rissole
oliver	tamari	chowder	ketchup	rossini

roulade	amandine	ensalada	mince pie	soda cake
rum baba	ambrosia	escalope	molasses	soy sauce
sabayon	aperitif	escargot	moussaka	spare rib
samosas	apple jam	fish cake	mushroom	squab pie
sapsago	apple pie	fishmeal	noisette	steak pie
sardine	au gratin	flan case	olive oil	stockpot
sausage	barbeque	flapjack	omelette	stuffing
saveloy	barvadis	flamande	pastrami	syllabub
savoury	bath chap	fleorons	pemmican	tamarind
scallop	béchamel	flummery	pheasant	tipsy cod
seafood	beignets	foie gras	pilchard	tea break
sherbet	biscotin	fore hock	plum cake	tortilla
sirloin	bouchées	frosting	plum duff	trotters
soubise	bouillon	fruit pie	pope's eye	turnover
soufflé	bun fight	frumenty	poppadom	undercut
soupçon	chapatti	gazpacho	poppadum	viaticum
starter	chasseur	gelatine	porridge	victuals
stir-fry	chop suey	gourmand	pot au feu	vindaloo
strudel	chow mein	grand-duc	pot roast	water ice
succado	cinnamon	gratiner	preserve	wishbone
sucrose	clambake	hardbake	quenelle	white-pot
sultana	coleslaw	hardtack	racahout	yoghourt
supreme	concasse	hotchpot	raisiné	Zwieback
tapioca	confetti	hung beef	ravigote	
tartlet	conserve	ice cream	rice cake	
tatties	consommé	iced cake	rock cake	**9**
teacake	coq au vin	jambalay	rock salt	
terrine	couscous	jam butty	rollmops	aitchbone
top side	cracknel	Julienne	roly poly	a la turque
treacle	cream bun	kedgeree	rye bread	allumette
trotter	cross bun	licorice	salad oil	angel cake
truffle	croutons	loblolly	salpicon	antipasto
vanilla	crudités	loin chop	salt beef	appetizer
venison	dainties	lollipop	salt fish	apple tart
veloute	date roll	luncheon	salt junk	arrowroot
vinegar	dauphine	lyonaise	salt pork	bara brith
wing rib	déjeuner	macaroni	sandwich	barmbrack
yoghurt	delicacy	macaroon	scrag end	barquette
york ham	doughnut	marinade	scramble	bean feast
yule log	dressing	marinate	seedcake	bearnaise
	dripping	marzipan	semolina	beaugency
	duchesse	meatball	shoulder	beefsteak
8	duckling	meat loaf	side dish	blanching
	dumpling	meat roll	skim-milk	bolognese
aigrette	egg white	meringue	slapjack	boucherie
à la carte	en croûte	meunière	smorbrod	bratwurst
à la creme				breakfast

brochette
bridecake
bully beef
butter pat
canneloni
cassareep
casserole
cassonade
cassoulet
chantilly
charlotte
chatillon
cheese dip
chip butty
chipolata
chocolate
chump-chop
club steak
cochineal
colcannon
cornflour
comfiture
condiment
corn bread
corn salad
crackling
cream cake
cream horn
cream puff
croissant
croquette
croustade
dark bread
delmonico
drop scone
drumstick
Easter egg
enchilada
entremets
fish-paste
forcemeat
fricassee
fruit cake
fruit flan
fruit tart
galantine

Genoa cake
giblet pie
gravy soup
hamburger
hard sauce
hatelette
honeycomb
humble pie
Irish stew
italienne
layer cake
left-overs
lemon curd
liquorice
liver pâté
loafsugar
lobscouse
macedoine
madeleine
marchpane
margarine
marinière
marmalade
meat-paste
medallion
middle cut
mincemeat
mint sauce
mutton ham
mutton pie
onion soup
partridge
petit four
pigeon pie
pistachio
potato pie
pot pourri
pound cake
preserves
princesse
raised pie
ravigotte
rechauffe
red pepper
remoulade
rice paper

rump steak
sally lunn
schnitzel
scotch egg
seasoning
shellfish
shortcake
small hock
soda bread
soda scone
sour cream
sourdough
spaghetti
spare ribs
spit roast
spun sugar
stirabout
succotash
sugarloaf
sugar-lump
sugar-plum
sweet corn
sweetmeat
swiss roll
tipsy cake
tournedos
vegetable
vol-au-vent
Welsh cake
wet nellie
wheatgerm
white meat
wholemeal
wild honey

10

apple sauce
baked beans
Bath oliver
bill of fare
blanquette
beefburger
bêche-de-mer
beef olives
bercy sauce

blancmange
blanquette
blue cheese
boiled cake
bolognaise
Bombay duck
bonne femme
bosh butter
bourgeoise
brandy-snap
breadcrumb
bread sauce
bread stick
breadstuff
bridescake
brown bread
brown sugar
buttermilk
candy floss
cannelloni
caper sauce
capillaire
carrot cake
chaud-froid
cheesecake
Chelsea bun
comestible
confection
cooking fat
cooking oil
cordon bleu
corned beef
cornflakes
corroboree
cottage pie
cream slice
cromesquis
currant bun
curry sauce
custard pie
delicacies
dill pickle
double loin
Dundee cake
Eccles cake
eggs mornay

fig pudding
flank steak
florentine
frangipane
French cake
French loaf
fresh cream
fricandeau
fruit salad
garlic salt
gaufrettes
giblet soup
ginger cake
gingernuts
ginger-snap
girdle cake
grape sugar
green salad
ground rice
guava jelly
hickory nut
hodge-podge
honey crisp
hotch-potch
ice pudding
icing sugar
indian corn
jardinière
jelly cream
jugged hare
knackwurst
knockwurst
lamb cutlet
laver bread
liverwurst
maple syrup
marble cake
marrow bone
mayonnaise
Melba toast
middle neck
mimosa eggs
minced meat
minestrone
mixed grill
mock turtle

mutton chop
onion sauce
oxtail soup
panzanella
parisienne
parmentier
pastry case
pâtisserie
peach melba
pepper cake
peppermint
piccalilli
pickled egg
plat du jour
poached egg
potted fish
potted meat
printanier
provençale
pudding pie
puff pastry
raisin loaf
rhubarb pie
rolled oats
rotisserie
round steak
royal icing
saccharine
salmagundi
salt butter
sauerkraut
shallow fry
shirred egg
shish kebab
shortbread
shortcrust
silverside
simnel cake
smorrebrod
sour pickle
spatchcock
sponge cake
steak diane
stewed meat
stroganoff
stuffed egg

sucking pig
sugar candy
sugar mouse
sweetbread
tea biscuit
temse bread
tenderloin
tikka kebab
tinned food
tomato soup
turtle soup
vermicelli
Vienna loaf
Vienna roll
water gruel
water icing
white bread
white sauce
zabaglione

11

almond icing
almond paste
baked alaska
banana split
Banbury cake
barley sugar
bashed neeps
black butter
black pepper
bonne bouche
bourguignon
braised beef
brandy sauce
brandy snaps
breadcrumbs
bread sticks
bridge rolls
burnt almond
carbonnades
cassava cake
cassoulette
caster sugar
cheese board
cheese sauce

Chester cake
chiffon cake
chilli sauce
choux pastry
clam chowder
clove pepper
cock-a-leekie
corn fritter
cottage loaf
cream cheese
curry powder
custard tart
devilled egg
double cream
dressed crab
Eve's pudding
fillet steak
fish fingers
flank mutton
frankfurter
French bread
French toast
gammon steak
gingerbread
golden syrup
green pepper
green turtle
griddle cake
ground spice
Hollandaise
hors d'oeuvre
hot cross bun
iron rations
jam turnover
jellied eels
loaf of bread
madras curry
Madeira cake
marshmallow
meat biscuit
meat pudding
medlar jelly
milk pudding
minute steak
montpensier
napolitaine

Food and cooking

olla podrida
oyster patty
parson's nose
pig's trotter
plum pudding
porterhouse
potato crisp
potato salad
pressed beef
raisin bread
ratatouille
rice biscuit
rice pudding
roast potato
sago pudding
sauerbraten
sausage meat
sausage roll
scotch broth
ship biscuit
short pastry
side of bacon
singin' hinny
single cream
skimmed milk
sliced bread
smörgåsbord
spotted Dick
staff of life
stewed fruit
suet pudding
sweet almond
sweet pepper
sweet pickle
tagliatelle
toffee apple
tomato sauce
tossed salad
treacle tart
vichyssoise
Vienna steak
wedding cake
Welsh mutton
Welsh rabbit
wheaten loaf
white potato

wine biscuit
windsor soup
zabagilione

12

afternoon tea
apple fritter
apple strudel
bakewell tart
baking powder
birthday cake
bitter almond
black pudding
bouquet garni
bouquetierre
brandy butter
bread pudding
brewer's yeast
burnt almonds
butterscotch
caraway seeds
cheeseburger
cheese straws
chilli pepper
chip potatoes
chitterlings
cinnamon ball
clotted cream
club sandwich
cockieleekie
Cornish pasty
corn-on-the-cob
cream cracker
crème caramel
crêpe suzette
crust of bread
curds and whey
custard sauce
Danish pastry
duck a l' orange
dunmow flitch
fillet of sole
finnan haddie
flamenco eggs
French pastry

grated cheese
ground almond
ground ginger
ground pepper
guarana-bread
Hamburg steak
hasty pudding
haute cuisine
ice cream cone
jacket potato
Julienne soup
liver sausage
lobster patty
luncheon-meat
maid of honour
maitre d' hotel
millefueille
mulligatawny
nutmeg butter
parsley sauce
peanut butter
pease pudding
pickled onion
planked steak
plum porridge
profiteroles
pumpernickel
Russian salad
salted peanut
scampi fritti
scrambled egg
shepherd's pie
sherry trifle
ship's biscuit
sirloin steak
smoked salmon
sponge finger
steak pudding
streaky bacon
stuffed heart
sweet and sour
tabasco sauce
taramasalata
tartare sauce
tripe de roche
vegetable oil

vichy carrots
Waldorf salad
water biscuit
Welsh rarebit
whipped cream

13

apple dumpling
barbecue sauce
béchamel sauce
bouillabaisse
chateaubriand
cheese biscuit
chili con carne
Christmas cake
condensed milk
confectionery
custard-coffin
custard powder
devilled sauce
finnan haddock
flitch of bacon
French mustard
fruit cocktail
German sausage
gigot de mouton
ginger pudding
guard of honour
lemon meringue
lobster bisque
mess of potage
milk chocolate
millefeuilles
minced collops
Neopolitan ice
Oxford sausage
pease porridge
pickled walnut

prawn cocktail
rasher of bacon
salad dressing
scotch collops
scrambled eggs
sirloin of beef
smoked sausage
sole veronique
soused herring
sponge pudding
strawberry jam
summer pudding
toad in the hole
veal-and-ham pie

14

almond hardbake
apple charlotte
bearnaise sauce
beef stroganoff
bologna sausage
cabinet pudding
Canterbury lamb
caramel custard
charlotte russe
chilli con carne
college pudding
cranberry sauce
evaporated milk
French dressing
gooseberry fool
haunch of mutton
ice cream sundae
macaroni cheese
mashed potatoes
mock-turtle soup
paté de foie gras
pickled herring

plain chocolate
pontefract cake
quiche Lorraine
remoulade sauce
saddle of mutton
tapioca pudding
toasted teacake
treacle pudding
Turkish delight
upside-down cake
Victoria sponge
Worcester sauce
wholemeal bread

15
bakewell pudding
beef bourguignon
black-cap pudding
bubble and squeak
chicken Maryland
chilli con carne
chocolate eclair
devilled kidneys
haunch of venison
ploughman' s lunch
semi-skimmed milk
Spanish omelette
Wiener schnitzel

15 +

angels on horseback
christmas pudding
devils on horseback
duchesse potatoes
horseradish sauce
Lancashire hotpot
lobster thermidor
wedding breakfast
Yorkshire pudding

French Revolutionary Calendar

6
Nivôse - snow (Dec 22 - Jan 20)

7
Floréal - flowers (April 21 - May 20)
Ventôse - wind (Feb 20 - March 21)

8
Brumaire - mist (Oct 23 - Nov 21)
Fervidor - heat (July 20 - Aug 18)
Frimaire - frost (Nov 22 - Dec 21)

Germinal - buds (March 22 - April 20)
Messidor - harvest (June 20 - July 19)
Pluviôse - rain (Jan 21 - Feb 19)
Prairial - meadows (May 21 - June 19)

9
Fructidor - fruit (Aug 19 - Sept 22)
Thermidor - heat (July 20 - Aug 18)

11
Vendémiaire - vintage (Sept 23 - Oct 22)

Fruit, nuts and vegetables

3	cole	soya	Dancy	mooli	6	celery
ber	Czar	spud	drupe	morel		cherry
cob	date	taro	Dwarf	Navel	Alfred	chives
cos	eddo	ugli	eddoe	navew	almond	citron
fig	Gala		Galia	olive	ananas	cob nut
haw	Hass	5	grape	onion	Aromel	Comice
hip	kale	apple	guava	orach	babaco	cowpea
pea	kiwi	Ariel	habal	peach	Bogota	daikon
yam	leek	betel	Jaffa	pecan	Bolero	damson
	lime	Bobbi	Lavan	prune	Bounty	durian
	mung	carob	lemon	pulse	Breton	endive
4	Ogen	chard	lichi	Royal	banana	Elruge
bean	okra	chive	mâche	savoy	batata	feijoa
beet	neep	choko	maize	swede	bhindi	fennel
Beth	pear	colza	mango	Topaz	Brandt	frijol
chou	plum	cress	melon	tuber	carrot	Fuerte
					cashew	

garlic
greens
Italia
jicama
jujube
kiwano
kumera
kumara
lablab
legume
lentil
lichee
longan
loquat
lychee
manioc
marrow
medlar
murphy
Muscat
nettle
orange
papaya
pawpaw
peanut
pepper
pomelo
potato
quince
radish
raisin
rocket
Romano
runner
sorrel
sprout
squash
Temple
tomato
turnip
walnut

7

Almeria
apricot
Atemoya
avocado
Baldwin
Ben More
bok choy
bramble
Bramley
brinjal
Bullace
cabbage
cardoon
Cascade
cassava
celtuce
chayote
chicory
coconut
collard
costard
Crispin
cymling
currant
dasheen
Delight
Domanil
Edwards
filbert
gherkin
Iceberg
Gorella
Grandee
haricot
hubbard
kumquat
lettuce
limetta
Morello
Oak-leaf
Pandora
parsnip
pimento

pitanga
pumpkin
rampion
rhubarb
rose hip
salsify
satsuma
seakale
Seville
shallot
skirret
snow pea
soursop
Spartan
spinach
Sturmer
sultana
sweetie
tangelo
witloof
yam bean

8

Alicante
Alphonse
baby corn
beetroot
Ben Nevis
Ben Sarek
betel nut
bilberry
Bluecrop
borecole
brassica
broccoli
Burbanks
calabash
capsicum
Careless
celeriac
Champion
Cherokee
chestnut
chickpea
Cocktail

cole-wort
Concorde
cucumber
dewberry
eggplant
eschalot
Ettinger
Fava bean
Heritage
honeydew
hazelnut
ivory nut
jakfruit
java plum
Jonathon
kohlrabi
leaf beet
lima bean
Lord Derby
lima-bean
mandarin
McIntosh
may apple
minneola
mulberry
mung bean
mushroom
oleaster
patty pan
pearmain
pecan nut
Pentland
physalis
pimentos
Quetsche
rambutan
Red flame
rutabaga
scallion
shaddock
soya bean
split pea
Starking
sweetsop
tamarind

Valencia
Victoria
Williams
zucchini

9

actinidia
aduki bean
artichoke
Asian pear
asparagus
aubergine
beech mast
Ben Lomond
blaeberry
blueberry
Bobbi bean
Bountiful
brazil nut
breadroot
broad bean
Brunswick
butternut
calabrese
cantaloup
carambola
cashew nut
Charlotte
Chasselas
Cherimoya
coco de mer
corn salad
courgette
crab apple
cranberry
crookneck
curly kale
dandelion
Discovery
Durondeau
Dwarf bean
Dwarf corn
Earliblue
garden pea
green bean

Fruit, nuts and vegetables

greengage
Grenadier
groundnut
horse bean
Indian fig
jackfruit
kiwi fruit
kolocassi
Little gem
love apple
macedoine
mangetout
Maris bard
melanzane
Mirabelle
naseberry
nectarine
new potato
Ortanique
persimmon
petit pois
pigeon pea
pineapple
pistachio
plantains
radicchio
raspberry
red banana
red pepper
rock melon
Salad bowl
Santa Rosa
sapodilla
September
star apple
star fruit
sweetcorn
tamarillo
tangerine
winged pea

10

Alexandria
Amsden June
bean shoots

beansprout
Bellegarde
blackberry
black grape
Black satin
Black tokay
blueberry
breadfruit
butterball
butter bean
canteloupe
Charantais
Cherry plum
cider apple
clementine
cloudberry
Conference
cos lettuce
Duke of York
elderberry
French bean
Giant prune
gooseberry
grapefruit
Indian corn
Indian lime
Indian plum
Italian red
kidney bean
King Edward
Kirke's blue
lemon guava
loganberry
Lollo Rosso
mangosteen
Maris piper
plum tomato
red cabbage
red chicory
redcurrant
Roma tomato
runner bean
salad cress
scorzonera
strawberry

string bean
sugar apple
sweet lemon
Swiss chard
tree tomato
watercress
water melon
white grape

11

acorn squash
Ashton cross
Autumn bliss
bean sprouts
bitter gourd
black radish
Black reward
Black velvet
blood orange
Breton onion
boysenberry
Brown Turkey
cactus fruit
cauliflower
Charles Ross
Chinese leaf
curly endive
cup mushroom
Early laxton
Early rivers
Granny Smith
green pepper
haricot bean
haricor vert
horned melon
horseradish
huckleberry
Jaffa orange
Lady's finger
Lloyd George
navel orange
pomegranate
oyster plant
prickly pear
Pershore egg

Redgauntlet
scarlet-bean
seakale beet
Sharon fruit
spinach beet
spring onion
sweet fennel
sweet manioc
sweet pepper
sweet potato
Webb's wonder
white pepper
whortleberry
wild spinach
winter cress

12

Arthur Turner
asparagus pea
Bartlett pear
Beauty of Bath
Bedford giant
blackcurrant
black salsify
Boskoop giant
Bullock tomato
Chasselas d' Or
cherry tomato
Chestnut brown
chilli pepper
Chinese apple
Chinese chard
christophene
corn-on-the-
    cob
cooking apple
custard apple
dessert apple
Early sulphur
flat mushroom
French sorrel
green shallot
ground cherry
Hottentot fig
Japanese plum
lady's fingers

lamb's lettuce
mangel-wurzel
marrowfat pea
marrow squash
Newton wonder
Pantagruella
passion fruit
pea aubergine
savoy cabbage
Red delicious
Savoy cabbage
Scotch bonnet
Spanish onion
spider endive
spring greens
sugar snap pea
summer squash
Victoria plum
white cabbage
white currant
whortleberry
winter squash
yellow pepper

13

asparagus tips
blackeyed bean
Black Hamburgh
black mulberry
Bullock's heart
Byrnes apricot
Cambridge gage
Caribbean lime
celery cabbage
Compact Stella
cooking banana
custard marrow
dessert banana
double coconut
Early Victoria
Golden Everest
Good King Henry
ladies' fingers
Morello cherry

pe-tsai cabbage
pickling onion
prairie-turnip
ridge cucumber
Ross de Treviso
Rossa di Verona
sapodilla plum
scarlet runner
Spanish radish
spring cabbage
Surinam cherry
Swedish turnip
Thai aubergine
turnip cabbage
Tydeman's early
water chestnut

14

American mother
Annie Elizabeth
Batavian endive
Beurre superfin
Blenheim orange
Brusells sprout
button mushroom
cabbage lettuce
Cape gooseberry
chicorée frisée
Chinese lantern
Conference pear
Egremont russet
English spinach
Florence fennel
French Imperial
globe artichoke
iceberg lettuce
Jamaican banana
Japanese medlar
Laxton's superb
Madagascar bean
Malling promise
mercury spinach
oyster mushroom
pineapple guava
pink grapefruit

Royal sovereign
sprue asparagus
stinging nettle
stringless bean

15 +

Alpine strawberry
American watercress
Ashmead's kernel
asparagus lettuce
Baron Solemacher
beafsteak tomato
Belle de Fontenay
Beurre d'Amanlis
Bigarreau Napoleon
Bourjasotte grise
Bramley's seedling
Buckland sweetwater
Californian seedless
Cambridge favourite
Cambridge vigour
Chinese artichoke
Chinese gooseberry
Cox's orange pippin
Denniston's superb
Doyenne du Comice
Ellison's orange
Feuille de Chêne
Florentine fennel
forced radicchio
Golden delicious
Italian broccoli
Jerusalem artichoke
Marjorie's seedling
Miller's seedling
miniature red cabbage
New Zealand spinach
Oak-leaf lettuce
Packham's triumph
perpetual spinach
purple granadilla
spaghetti squash
spaghetti marrow
strawberry guava
strawberry tomato

summer cauliflower
sweet granadilla
turnip-rooted celery
vegetable marrow
vegetable oyster

Whinham's industry
William's Bon Chretien
winter cauliflower
Worcester pearmain
Yellow pear tomato

Gardening (general)

3

bed
bud
eye
hoe
pip
pot
pot
sap
sow

4

acid
axil
bole
bulb
burr
bush
cane
cone
corm
crop
curd
cyme
damp
fern
fork
gall
haft
herb
hose
keel
lawn

leaf
lime
loam
lobe
mist
moss
node
peat
pest
posy
rake
ring
root
sand
seed
slug
soil
spur
stem
tray
tree
trug
twig
vine
weed
wilt
wood

5

acute
algae
aphid
berry
besom

bloom
bough
bract
calyx
clamp
clone
crest
crock
crown
drawn
drupe
flora
frame
frond
fruit
genus
graft
grass
haulm
hardy
humus
light
mould
mulch
ovary
ovate
ovule
petal
plant
pulse
sandy
scent
scion
scree
sepal

shade
shoot
shrub
snail
spade
spike
spray
sprig
stalk
stool
style
tepal
tilth
tuber
tunic
trunk
truss
umbel
virus
whorl

6

alpine
annual
anther
blanch
branch
bulbil
calcar
callus
canopy
catkin
cloche
column

cordon
corona
corymb
dibble
dibber
flower
floret
fungus
gravel
heel in
hybrid
in leaf
leader
leaves
legume
linear
maiden
manure
mildew
mutant
nectar
nodule
oblong
obtuse
offset
pedate
pistil
pollen
potash
pruner
raceme
raffia
roller
rugate
rugose

rugous
runner
shears
shovel
spadix
spathe
stamen
stigma
stolon
strain
strike
sucker
throat
timber
trowel
wreath

7

baccate
bearded
blossom
bolting
bouquet
budding
bulb fly
bulb rot
cambium
capsule
climber
compost
conifer
cordate
corolla
corm rot
creeper
crenate
damp off
dentate
die back
disease
dormant
dry area
epicarp
exposed

falcate
fertile
foliage
forcing
friable
full sun
genetic
globose
habitat
harvest
hirsute
incided
leaflet
obovate
palmate
panicle
pedicel
pedicle
peltate
perfume
petiole
picotee
pinnate
plicate
potting
pyramid
radical
radicle
rhizome
rockery
root rot
root run
rosette
runners
sapwood
seed box
seed pod
sessile
spatula
species
staking
stem rot
sterile
storing
taproot

tendril
topiary
variety
weeping

8

acid soil
aeration
alkaline
axillary
biennial
bleeding
blooming
bone meal
botanist
botryose
botrytis
brassica
bud burst
bulb mite
club root
cropping
crucifer
cultivar
diaspore
digitate
Dutch hoe
earthing
elliptic
endocarp
espalier
filament
florigen
follicle
fragrant
fumigate
glabrate
glabrous
glaucous
greenery
greenfly
grafting
humidity
leaf fall

leaf spot
moisture
mutation
notching
parasite
peduncle
perianth
pericarp
petaloid
pinch out
planting
poor soil
pot group
rainfall
reniform
rich soil
scandent
scree bed
seedling
serrated
standard
stellate
systemic
terminal
thinning
tomentum
truncate
tuber rot
whitefly
windfall

9

acid-lover
acuminate
arboretum
bipinnate
biternate
bulb aphid
calcicole
calcifuge
catch-crop
chlorosis
cold frame
columella

cotyledon
cultivate
deciduous
decompose
decumbent
digitated
evergreen
feathered
fimbriate
flowerage
flowering
flowerpot
fragrance
fungicide
grey mould
half-hardy
half shade
harden off
herbarium
inorganic
intercrop
internode
involucre
landscape
lawn mower
leaf mould
leafy gall
lime-hater
orbucular
perennial
pollinate
pot pourri
pubescent
remontant
repellant
rock plant
rootstock
saggitate
secateurs
sheltered
shrubbery
spatulate
sprinkler
sprouting
strobilus

succulent
temperate
terrarium
tomentose
tulip fire
unisexual
varieties
variegated
weedkiller
wind-borne
window box

10

basal shoot
botryoidal
common name
fan-trained
calcareous
calceiform
chlorophyl
compositae
coriaceous
damping off
decomposed
greenhouse
fasciation
flore pleno
floribunda
flower head
foliar feed
herbacious
involucrum
jardinière
lanceolate
leguminous
lignotuber
monocarpic
monoecious
ornamental
pebble tray
perfoliate
pinnatifid
procumbent
propagated

reticulate
rhizome rot
sooty mould
spathulate
springtime
sub-shrubby
summertime
trifoliate
tripartite
viviparous
wild flower

11

aerial root
air humidity
campanulate
caterpillar
chlorophyll
contractile
dead-heading
dense growth
everlasting
family group
flowerheads
frost pocket
germination
ground cover
ground flora
infestation
inflorescent
insecticide
leaf-climber
leaf-cutting
leaf-sweeper
neutral soil
performance
pinching out
pollination
propagation
scale insect
self-fertile
self-sterile
severe frost
shade-loving

stem-cutting
tip layering
top dressing
ventilation
waterlogged

12

aquatic plant
black root rot
bottle garden
clematis wilt
garden centre
half-standard
hardening off
horticulture
indoor garden
oblanceolate
walled garden

13

country flower
dormant period
fertilization
growing pwriod
hanging basket
hedge trimming
lateral branch
monocotyledon
night-blooming
peach leaf curl
powdery mildew
resting period
shade tolerant
specimen plant
transpiration
transplanting

14

aquarium plants
classification
direct sunlight
floral envelope

fructification
mild conditions
photosynthesis
potting compost
rooting compound

15 +
botanical gardens
cross pollination
exposed position
ground-cover plant

low-growing plant
seasonal changes
sheltered position
soil composition
water frequently

Gemstones

3 & 4
jade
jet
onyx
opal
ruby
sard
YAG

5
agate
amber
balas
beryl
copal
coral
lapis
nacre
pearl
topaz

6
garnet
iolite
jasper
quartz
sphene
spinel
zircon

7
abalone
axinite
cat's eye
citrine

diamond
emerald
epidote
euclase
howlite
jadeite
kunzite
peridot
sardine
syenite
violane

8
amethyst
blue john
bowenite
dioptase
fire opal
heliodor
nephrite
obsidian
porphyry
sapphire
sardonyx
sodalite
sunstone
wood opal
wurtzite

9
alabaster
amazonite
balas ruby
benitoite
cairngorm
carnelian

cymophane
enstatite
fire agate
hessonite
lace agate
malachite
marcasite
moldavite
morganite
moonstone
moss agate
pectolite
scapolite
spodumene
tanzanite
tiger's eye
turquoise
unakite
zoisite

10
andalusite
aquamarine
aventurine
bloodstone
blue quartz
brazilianite
chalcedony
chrysolite
cordierite
false topaz
heliotrope
hyalophane
iris quartz
piemontite
rose quartz

ruby spinel
serpentine
tourmaline

11
alexandrite
amblygonite
carborundum
chrysoberyl
chrysocolla
chrysoprase
labradorite
lapis lazuli
smoky quartz

12
granodiorite

13
black sapphire
citrine quartz
cubic zirconia
mother of pearl
oriental topaz
rhodochrosite

14
pink chalcedony

15
rutilated quartz

15+
snowflake obsidian

Geological times

Archaean (period)
Cambrian (period)
Carboniferous (period)
Cenozoic (era)
Cretaceous (period)
Devonian (period)
Eocene (epoch)
Jurassic (period)
Mesozoic (era)
Miocene (epoch)
Oligocene (epoch)

Ordovician (period)
Palaeocene (epoch)
Palaeozoic (era)
Permian (period)
Pleistocene (epoch)
Precambrian (era)
Proterozoic (period)
Quaternary (period)
Silurian (period)
Tertiary (period)
Triassic (period)

Giants

3 & 4
Gog
Irus
ogre
Otus
Rhea
Ymir

6
Cottus
Cronus
ogress
Pallas
Phoebe
Tethys
Themis

8
behemoth
Bellerus
Briareus
colossus
Cormoran
Ferragus
giantess
Hyperion
Orgoglio
Steropes
Titaness
Typhoeus

Mnemosyne

10
Alifafaron
Pantagruel
Polyphemus
Ysbadadden

5
Agres
Argus
Atlas
Balan
Cacus
Coeus
Crius
Hydra
Magog
Orion
Theia
Titan

7
Antaeus
Brontes
Cyclops
Despair
Goliath
Iapetos
Oceanus

9
Colbronde
Enceladus
Ephialtes
Fierabras
Gargantua
leviathan

11
Blunderbore

15 +
giants of Brobdingnag
Harbin of the Mountain
Morgante Maggiore

Gods and goddesses

2 & 3

Aah
Anu
Ate
Bel
Bes
Dis
Don
Ea
Eir
Eos
Ge
Geb
Hel
Hor
Io
Jok
lar
Lug
Mut
Nox
Nut
Nyx
Ops
Oro
Pan
Pax
Ra
Re
Seb
Set
Shu
Sol
Tiu
Tyr

4

Agni
Amor
Amun
Apis

Ares
Aten
Atua
Ba' al
Brag
deva
Diva
Enyo
Eris
Eros
Frey
Gaea
Hari
Hebe
Hera
Here
Iris
Isis
Jove
Juno
Kali
Kama
Kami
Leza
Loki
Luba
Luna
Maat
Maia
Mars
Mont
Mors
Nabu
Nebo
Nike
Odin
Papa
Ptah
Rama
Rhea
Seth
Shay

Sita
Siva
Tane
Thor
Upis
Yama
Zeus

5

Aegir
Aesir
Ammon
Atlas
Belus
Bragi
Ceres
Chaos
Comus
Cupid
Dagda
Dagon
Diana
disir
Donar
durga
Euros
Fates
Flora
Freya
Freyr
Frigg
Hodur
Horus
Hymen
Imana
Indra
Irene
Iruva
Janus
lares
Momus

Mwari
Nanna
Neheh
Njord
Norns
Orcus
Pluto
Rangi
Shiva
Theoi
Thoth
Tyche
Vanir
Venus
Vesta
Vidar
Wodan
Wotan

6

Aeolus
Amen-Ra
Anubis
Apollo
Aquilo
Athene
Auster
Aurora
Balder
Boreas
Brahma
Brigit
Caurus
Cronos
Cronus
Cybele
Daimon
Faunus
Freyja
Frigga
Furies

Graces
Hathor
Hecate
Helios
Hermes
Heroes
Hestia
Hother
Hygeia
Hypnos
Ishtar
Kaikas
Kronos
Lucina
Marduk
Mexitl
Mextli
Mithra
Modimo
Moloch
Moirai
Nereus
Njorth
Nzambi
Orisha
Osiris
Pallas
Parcae
Phenix
Pluton
Plutus
Renpet
Saturn
Selene
Shaiva
Shakti
Skiron
Somnus
Tlaloc
Tellus
Tefnut
Typhon

Upuaut
Vishnu
Vulcan
Vishnu
Zephyr

7

Abraxas
Africus
Alastor
Apollon
Artemis
Bacchus
Bellona
Berchta
Demeter
Forseti
Fortuna
Heimdal
Ishvara
Jupiter
Katonda
Kon-Tiki
Krishna
Lakshmi
Masalai
Mercury
Minerva
Mithras
Mulunga
Nemesis
Neptune
Oceanus
Parvata
penates
Pheobus
Priapus
Proteus
Ruhanga
Sekhmet
Shamash

Greek alphabet

Silenus
Victory

Ometeotl
Poseidon
Quirinus
Silvanus
Tangaroa
Terminus
Thanatos
Zephyrus
Victoria
Zephyrus

Asclepius
Cernunnos
Dipankara
Discordia
Tetoinnan

Prometheus
Proserpine

8
Amitabha
Bubastis
Charites
Dionysos
Dionysus
Favonius
Ganymede
Juventas
Mahadevi
Morpheus

9
Apeliotes
Aphrodite

10
Akal Purakh
Dii Majores
Dii Minores
Hephaestus
Hephaistos
Juggernaut
Persephone

11 +
Agathodaemon
Aesculapius
Bodhisattva
Eileithyia
Huitzilopochtli
Pallas Athene
Phoebus Apollo
Quetzalcoatl
Scamandius
Tezcatlipoca
Tuatha de Danaan

Greek alphabet

2
mu
nu
pi
xi

3
chi
eta
phi
psi

rho
tau

iota
zeta

delta
gamma
kappa
omega
sigma
theta

6
lambda

omicron
upsilon

4
beta

5
alpha

7
epsilon

Heavenly bodies

2 & 3
Io
Sun

4
belt
coma
Faye
halo
Juno
Leda
limb
Moon
nova

pole
Rhea
Ross
star
Vega
Wolf

5
Algol
Ariel
Biela
Carme
Ceres
comet

Cygni
Deneb
Dione
Elara
Encke
epact
epoch
flare
giant
Hamal
Hyads
Janus
Kopff
lunar
Metis

Mimas
nadir
orbit
phase
Rigel
Sirus
solar
space
Spica
Thebe
Titan
umbra
Vesta

6
Adhara
albedo
Altair
Ananke
apogee
astral
aurora
binary
bolide
Castor
Charon
colure
corona
crater

Crucis
Europa
Deimos
galaxy
Halley
Huyten
Hyades
Icarus
lunary
Lyrids
meteor
nebula
Nereid
Oberon
Olbers
parsec
Phobos
Phoebe
planet
Plough
Pollux
pulsar
quasar
Shaula
Sinope
Sirius
sphere
sundog
syzygy
Tethys
Triton
Tuttle
Ursids
zenith
zodiac

7

Antares
apogean
auroral
azimuth
Bennett
Canopus
Capella
cluster

cometic
Cygnids
D′ Arrest
Dog Star
eclipse
equator
equinox
gibbous
Iapetus
Lalande
Leonids
metonic
Milalia
Miranda
mock sun
nebulae
new moon
perigee
Polaris
Procyon
radiant
Regulus
sextile
spectra
sputnik
stellar
sunspot
synodic
Tau Ceti
Taurids
transit
Titania
Umbriel
Vaisala

8

Achernar
Adrastea
aerolite
almagest
Alpherat
Amalthea
aphelion
Arcturus
asterism

asteroid
Barnard′s
Borrelly
Callisto
Centauri
Cepheids
cometary
daylight
ecliptic
epicycle
evection
fireball
full moon
Ganymede
Geminids
Hale-Bopp
Hyperion
Kapteyn′s
Kohoutek
latitude
Lodestar
lunarium
lunation
Lysithea
meridian
meteoric
Milky Way
nutation
parallax
Pasiphae
penumbra
perigeal
perigeon
Orionids
Perseids
Pleiades
Pole Star
quartile
quintile
red giant
red shift
sidereal
solstice
spectrum
spheroid
stardust

stellary
sublunar
universe
variable
Westphal
zodiacal

9

aerolitic
Aldebaran
astrology
astronomy
Ballatrix
black hole
canicular
celestial
Comas Sola
cosmogony
cosmology
Crommelin
elevation
Enceladus
epicyclic
firmament
Fomalhaut
giant star
hour angle
Ikeya-Seki
light-year
longitude
lunar year
magnitude
meteorite
meteoroid
moonquake
moonshine
parhelion
planetary
planetoid
Red Planet
reflector
refractor
satellite
solar wind
star-gazer

starlight
starshine
sublunary
supernova
synodical
telescope

10

abberation
altazimuth
asteroidal
astrologer
astrometry
astronomer
astronomic
Australids
Betelgeuse
binary star
cosmic dust
cosmic rays
Crab nebula
depression
double star
earthshine
elongation
evectional
hour circle
lunar month
lunar probe
meteoritic
Ophiuchids
opposition
outer space
perihelion
Phoenicids
precession
prominence
quadrature
refraction
retrograde
selenology
siderolite
solar flare
solar month

supergiant
terminator
trajectory
white dwarf

11

conjunction
declination
Epsilon Indi
falling star
Gegenschein
giant planet
last quarter
minor planet
neutron star
occultation
photosphere
observatory
planetarium
Quadrantids
solar system
stratopause
terrestrial
uranography

12

astrogeology
astronomical
astrophysics
Capricornids
chromosphere
eccentricity
Halley's comet
interstellar
lunar eclipse
lunar rainbow
meteor shower
perturbation
selenography
shooting star
sidereal time
solar eclipse
spiral galaxy

stratosphere
synodic month
total eclipse
Van Allen belt
variable star

13

Alpha Centauri
celestial body
celestial pole
constellation
polar zenithal
sidereal month
zodiacal light

14

annular eclipse
astronavigation
celestial globe
interplanetary
partial eclipse
radio astronomy
radio telescope
right ascension
summer solstice
supergiant star
vertical circle
winter solstice

15

armillary sphere
celestial bodies
celestial sphere
eclipsing binary
equinoctial year
Fraunhoffer lines
oblique zenithal
Proxima Centauri

16 +

astronomical unit

astronomical year
azimuthal projection
Cassegrainian telescope
celestial guidance
celestial latitude
celestial longitude

celestial mechanics
equatorial telescope
equatorial zenithal
Newtonian telescope
zenithal projection
zodiacal constellation

Henry VIII's wives

Anne Boleyn (or Bullen)
Jane Seymour
Anne of Cleves

Catherine Parr
Catherine Howard
Katherine of Aragon

*Note: The spelling of Katherine seems to be in dispute.
Katharine and Catharine are suggested alternatives to the
ones above.*

Herbs and spices

3 & 4
balm
bay
dill
mace
mint
race
rue
sage

5
agave
anise
basil
caper
chive
clove
cumin
curry
senna
tansy

thyme

6
bennet
borage
burnet
chilli
cicely
fennel
garlic
ginger
hyssop
lovage
nutmeg
pepper
savory
sesame
sorrel

7
aniseed

bay leaf
caraway
cayenne
chervil
comfrey
mustard
oregano
paprika
parsley
pimento
saffron
Tabasco
vanilla

8
allspice
angelica
bergamot
camomile
capsicum
cinnamon
costmary

marjoram
rosemary
tarragon
turmeric
woodruff

9
chamomile
coriander
fenugreek
spearmint

10
mixed spice
pennyroyal
peppermint
rubbed sage

11
black pepper
curry powder
fines herbes
garam masala
herb of grace
pot marigold
salad burnet
sweet cicely
white pepper

12
bouquet garni
chilli powder

13
cayenne powder
sweet woodruff

Hobbies and pastimes

(including handicrafts)

3

ace
art
bed
bet
bid
box
cup
cut
die
DIY
leg
loo
man
nap
oxo
peg
pig
pip
pit
rob
run
see

4

ball
bank
bone
brag
card
chip
club
coup
crib
deal
deck
dice
draw
faro

game
hand
home
jack
jink
king
ludo
mace
mate
move
noir
pack
pair
paix
pass
pawn
play
pool
pope
rook
skat
snap
solo
spin
stud
suit
trio
vint

5

après
banco
bango
batik
bingo
block
bluff
bower
capot
carré

check
chess
clubs
demon
deuce
divan
dummy
flush
grand
halma
heart
injun
inlay
joker
kitty
knave
knock
mitre
monte
motif
mould
nappa
passe
pay me
picot
plait
point
poker
print
punch
queen
quint
resin
rouge
royal
rules
rummy
score
scram
sheaf
skive

spade
stake
stamp
stick
stock
stops
straw
talon
taper
tarot
teeth
thong
trace
trade
trick
trump
twist
wager
weave
wheel
whist
widow

6

attack
banker
barter
basket
batten
bergen
bishop
bobbin
bonsai
boodle
boston
bridge
candle
canvas
casino
castle

cat-hop
cement
cinema
cotton
crowns
dabber
design
donkey
double
écarté
euchre
fan tan
figure
firing
floral
flower
frieze
fumage
fusing
gambit
gamble
go-bang
go boom
honour
impair
kaolin
knaves
knight
manque
marble
marker
milieu
milton
minoru
misère
misery
mobile
mosaic
needle
oil ink

paroli
pebble
piquet
plaque
punter
quinto
quinze
raffia
reading
red dog
refait
renege
revoke
ribbon
roller
rubber
rushes
scraps
screen
sewing
silica
sphere
sponge
spiral
staple
stitch
strand
stuzka
sultan
tallow
tassel
thread
treble
veneer
waxing
yablon

7

à cheval
alumina

aquaria
art deco
auction
beeswax
bézique
binding
blucher
bouquet
brisque
brulage
burnish
canasta
carding
cassino
casting
collage
colonel
conkers
conleur
counter
crochet
cookery
defence
diamond
discard
doublet
encarte
end-game
engrave
en plein
en prise
etching
feather
flat bar
forfeit
hessian
imprint
impress
inverse
j' adoube
jackpot
lacquer
leather
lozenge
keep fit

macramé
marbles
misdeal
old maid
order up
origami
partner
pattern
peep nap
penalty
picture
plaster
pontoon
pottery
propose
pysanky
red suit
reversi
rolling
sandown
scorper
sequins
seven up
shuffle
sleeper
spinado
stencil
tarocco
tatting
topiary
treadle
twining
varnish
vingt-un
weaving
whister
wood cut

8

aerobics
all fours
all fives
antiqued
appliqué

assemble
baccarat
bead work
bevelled
blown egg
cachette
cane work
castling
charcoal
commerce
cribbage
croupier
dead ball
decolage
decorate
dernière
dominoes
douzaine
draughts
dry point
embossed
flat knot
fretwork
full hand
fuse wire
gin rummy
gouge nib
heraldry
imperial
intrigue
knitting
knotting
Irish loo
linoleum
matadore
material
merelles
Michigan
Napoleon
no-trumps
open slam
painting
partager
patience
penuchle

picot bar
pinch pot
pinochle
polignac
Pope Joan
première
puppetry
pyramids
quilting
quatorze
roll-call
roulette
saw frame
scissors
Scrabble
sequence
shanghai
shell-out
skinball
spinning
staining
straight
smocking
spray-gun
tailleur
tapestry
template
tourneur
transfer
tweezers
vignette
windmill
woodwork
vinamold

9

abondance
arabesque
astrology
astronomy
bagatelle
balsa wood
berry knot
black jack

black suit
burnisher
cardboard
champleve
checkmate
cloisonné
coiled pot
court card
curl grain
découpage
double run
dowelling
draw poker
dummy hand
engraving
en passant
forty-five
gardening
genealogy
grand coup
grand slam
gum-arabic
half-hitch
hardboard
hem stitch
horse race
index card
indian ink
jewellery
lampshade
left bower
marquetry
matrimony
modelling
monte bank
newmarket
old sledge
overtrick
pair-royal
palmistry
patch work
pelmanism
philately
photogram
planisher

poker work
rug making
sculpture
shell work
solitaire
solo whist
spoil five
sprigging
stalemate
stud poker
stoneware
straw work
thirty-one
thrown pot
top stitch
vingt-et-un
wavy grain
web stitch
wood block
ziginette
zinc plate

10

arabic cage
backgammon
back stitch
basketwork
bearing off
bee-keeping
beer-making
black maria
bone folder
cat-showing
chess board
cotton wool
craft knife
crêpe paper
crosswords
decoration
dog-showing
double paix
drawing pin
embroidery
enamelling

fly-fishing
Genoese bar
heartsette
kalabriasz
kite flying
kite making
lace making
lansquenet
little slam
long stitch
metal frame
needlework
open misère
paintbrush
paix-paroli
plasticine
preference
pyrography
quint royal
rice stitch
right bower
sebastopol
spot hearts
spread slam
stop the bus
sweepstake
tent stitch
travellers
treble paix
turpentine
undertrick
upholstery
Wellington
whip stitch
willow reed
wine making

11

archaeology
arrangement
bark rubbing
basse taille
bell ringing
blind hookey

book binding
butt veneers
calligraphy
campanology
carbon paper
card-playing
catch the ten
chain stitch
chemin-de-fer
Chinese knot
confederacy
copper plate
coral stitch
cross stitch
crochet hook
crotch grain
dressmaking
earthenware
five hundred
five card loo
gutta-percha
German whist
grand spread
Greek hearts
jeux de règle
joker hearts
knotted lace
leather work
lepidoptery
lino cutting
my ship sails
papier colle
papier mâché
parrafin wax
photography
picture card
plique-a-jour
poster paint
purchase nap
quilt-making
racing demon
red and black
rubber mould
sand carving
sand picture

satin stitch
Scotch whist
short stitch
slippery Sam
speculation
stencilling
tamping tool
tissue paper
twill stitch
vintage cars

12

auction pitch
beach combing
bird watching
branch stitch
brass rubbing
calabrasella
candle making
card dominoes
carte blanche
chef-de-partie
corkscrew bar
cutting board
diamond point
domino hearts
faggot stitch
florist's wire
flower garden
flower making
French boston
glass etching
gouache paint
hoggenheimer
Japanese knot
Josephine knot
ladder stitch
little spread
Miss Milligan
mosaic stitch
parallel bars
parish stitch
petit chevaux
piccolissimo

rouge-et-noir
royal cassino
sand bottling
sand pictures
seven card nap
shadow stitch
shove-ha' penny
slip trailing
slobberhannes
spade cassino
stanley knife
three card loo
tie-and-dyeing
tracing paper
transversale
tropical fish
ventriloquism
well dressing
zig-zag stitch

13

auction bridge
basket weaving
blanket stitch
bulls and bears
call ace euchre
Chinese fan tan
clock patience
cribbage board
double bézique
egg decorating
feather stitch
giant patience
happy families
highest bidder
jigsaw puzzles
Kentucky derby
knockout whist
lattice stitch
misère ouverte
modelling clay
model railways
old man's bundle
outline stitch

poker patience
ranter-go-round
rawhide hammer
rolling stones
royal marriage
round the clock
single bézique
spray adhesive
straight flush
straight grain
the cannon game
three card brag
train spotting
Turkish stitch
water divining

14

Austrian tarock
baccarat banque
ball on the watch
cake decorating
California Jack
card put and take
coin collecting
common marriage
contract bridge
diagonal stitch
egg decorating
enamel painting
flower pressing
French knitting
hairpin crochet
metal detecting
nine men's morris
paper sculpture
pebble painting
pigeon fancying
plaster of Paris
railroad euchre
rubicon bézique
six deck bézique
snip snap snorem
three-stake brag
Trivial Pursuit

15 +

abondance declarée
amateur dramatics
auction forty-five
auction pinochle
autograph hunting
ballroom dancing
beggar my neighbour
butterfly collecting
corn-dolly making
double pair-royal
ducks and drakes
duplicate bridge
eight deck bézique
florentine stitch
flower arranging
foundation leader
hand-bell ringing
herringbone stitch
hurricane candle
interlocking grain
Japanese bézique
Japanese flower cards
jewellery making
lampshade making
lazy daisy stitch
pin and thread work
pressing flowers
quadruple bézique
royal draw cassino
Scottish dancing
serpent poker patience
shell collecting
single-stake brag
snakes and ladders
stamp collecting
traction engines
trente-et-quarante

Horses and ponies

3

Cob
Don
Jaf

4

Arab
Barb
Fell
Polo

5

Alter
Batak
Dales
Fjord
Haiti
Huzul

Jomud
Konik
Lokai
Minho
Orlov
Pinto
Shire
Timor
Toric
Waler
Welsh

6

Albino
Basuto
Breton
Brumby
Dülmen
Exmoor
Fulani

Morgan
Nonius
Peneia
Pindos
Poznan
Skyros
Tarpan
Viatka

7

Comtois
Costeno
Criollo
Crioulo
Furioso
Gotland
Hackney
Jutland
Kirghiz
Llanero

Marwari
Masuren
Mustang
Noriker
Pechora
Sokólsk
Sorraia
Trotter

8

Ardennes
Budjonny
Camargue
Dartmoor
Galiceño
Highland
Holstein
Kabardin
Karabair
Karabakh

Lusitano
Palomino
Polo pony
Shetland
Turkmene
Turkoman

9

Achal-Teké
Anglo-Arab
Appaloosa
Calabrese
Campolino
Connemara
Groningen
Haflinger
Haiti pony
Kladruber
Knabstrup
Kustanair

Morochuco
New Forest
Oldenburg
Percheron
Pinzgauer
Poitevine
Schleswig
Trakehner

Lipizzaner
Mangalarga
Peneia pony
Pindos pony
Sandalwood
Skyros pony
Shagya Arab
Tchenarani

Spotted Horse
Strelets Arab
Suffolk Punch
thoroughbred

13
Frederiksborg
Welsh mountain

10
Andalusian
Assateague
Avelignese
Carthusian
Clydesdale
Darashoori
Einsiedler
Frieberger
Gelderland
Hanoverian
Kathiawari

11
Anglo-Norman
Chicoteague
Chinese pony
Sable Island
Trait du Nord
Wurttemberg

15 +
Canadian Cutting Horse
Döle-Gudsbrandsdal
Kentucky Sadsler
Missouri Fox Trotting Horse
Pony of the Americas
Seine Inférieure
Tennessee Walking Horse

12
Cleveland Bay
Quarter Horse

Insects, arachnids, worms and snails

3
ant
bee
bot
bug
dor
fly
nit
pug

4
cleg
flea
frit

gnat
goat
grub
hawk
lice
mite
moth
pupa
puss
tick
wasp

5
aphid
aphis

borer
cimex
comma
culex
drone
egger
emmet
flies
fluke
imago
larva
louse
midge
nymph
sedge
tiger

6
acarid
ant cow
bedbug
bee fly
beetle
botfly
breeze
burnet
caddis
chafer
chegre
chigoe
chinch
cicada

cicala
cimbex
coccid
coccus
cocoon
copper
dayfly
dobson
earwig
elater
ermine
gadfly
herald
hopper
hornet
jigger

lackey
lappet
larvae
locust
looper
maggot
magpie
mantid
mantis
maybug
mayfly
midget
nereis
palolo
red ant
redbug

Insects, arachnids, worms and snails

sawfly
scarab
slater
sow bug
sphinx
spider
Thrips
tineid
tsetse
vespid
weevil
worker

7

annelid
ant lion
araneae
army ant
bagworm
bee moth
blowfly
carabid
cestoid
chalcid
chigger
cricket
culicid
cutworm
daphnia
drinker
dung fly
emerald
epizoon
firefly
fire ant
frit fly
frogfly
gallfly
goldbug
grannon
hexapod
June bug
katydid
lace bug

monarch
peacock
phasmid
pill bug
pinworm
pismire
pug moth
pyralid
ragworm
ringlet
rotifer
sandfly
skipper
spinner
syrphid
termite
trumpet
vespine
wax moth
wood ant

8

acaridan
alder fly
apterous
arachnid
army worm
black ant
blackfly
bollworm
caseworm
Colorado
cranefly
curculio
December
dipteran
ephemera
firebrat
flatworm
flesh fly
fruit fly
gall mite
gall wasp
glow-worm

goat moth
greenfly
hairworm
hawk moth
helminth
honey bee
hookworm
horntail
horsefly
housefly
inchworm
itch mite
lacewing
ladybird
longhorn
meal moth
mealy bug
mealworm
milkweed
milliped
mosquito
muckworm
multiped
myriapod
oak egger
parasite
puss moth
queen bee
ramshorn
sand flea
sand wasp
scorpion
sheep ked
silkworm
slave ant
slow worm
stonefly
subimago
tapeworm
tubeworm
water-bug
wheel bug
white ant
whitefly
wireworm

woodlice
wood mite
wood moth
wood wasp
woodworm

9

amazon ant
anopheles
arachnoid
bee beetle
blindworm
brandling
brimstone
bumble bee
butterfly
caddis fly
capsid bug
carpet bug
centipede
chaetopod
chinch bug
chrysalis
clavicorn
cochineal
cockroach
cornborer
crab louse
damselfly
dermestid
dragonfly
driver ant
egger moth
ephemerid
flour mite
flour moth
flower bug
flying ant
funnel-web
gall midge
ghost moth
gipsy moth
ground bug
holly blue

hornet fly
ichneumon
lac insect
leaf miner
longicorn
millipede
multipede
orange-tip
red spider
pea weevil
peripatus
plume moth
pond snail
robber fly
roundworm
saltatory
saucer bug
sheep tick
squash bug
swift moth
tarantula
thysanura
tiger moth
trematode
tsetse fly
tzetze fly
wall brown
warble fly
water flea
wax insect
whirligig
willowfly
woodborer
woodlouse
worker ant
worker bee
xylophaga

10

antler moth
antlion fly
bark beetle
bean weevil
bird spider

black widow
bluebottle
boll weevil
bombardier
burnet moth
cabbage bug
cabbage fly
canker worm
carpet moth
chalcid fly
cheese mite
chironomid
cluster fly
cockchafer
codlin moth
coleoptera
death's head
death watch
digger wasp
drosophila
dung beetle
flea beetle
fritillary
frog hopper
gatekeeper
gold beetle
grey dagger
grove snail
Guinea worm
hairstreak
harvestman
hemipteran
hessian fly
jigger flea
June beetle
kitten moth
lackey moth
lantern fly
lappet moth
leaf beetle
leaf hopper
leaf roller
looper moth
neuroptera
orthoptera

palmer worm
phylloxera
plant louse
pond skater
pond sponge
pupiparous
red admiral
ribbonworm
Roman snail
rosechafer
rose beetle
rove beetle
saltigrade
sand hopper
scarabaeus
silverfish
soldier ant
Spanish fly
spider mite
springtail
stag beetle
thysanuran
tree hopper
turnip moth
vinegar fly
vine weevil
water louse
winter moth
wolf spider
woolly bear
xylophagan

11

angle shades
apple maggot
assassin bug
August thorn
bacon beetle
bagworm moth
black arches
black beetle
bristletail
buffalo gnat
cabbage moth

cabbage worm
canatharides
caterpillar
clothes moth
codling moth
coleopteran
corn-ear worm
drinker moth
emperor moth
flour weavil
garden tiger
grasshopper
greenbottle
harvest mite
harvest tick
hymenoptera
Lepidoptera
meadow brown
mole cricket
money spider
painted lady
pharoah's ant
scale insect
scorpion fly
Scotch argus
snout beetle
stick insect
swallowtail
tetrapteran
tiger beetle
trichoptera
tussock moth
water skater
water spider
woolly aphid
zebra spider

12

book scorpion
cabbage white
carpenter bee
carpet beetle
cecropia moth
chafer beetle

cinnabar moth
diadem spider
diving beetle
feather louse
goldtail moth
ground beetle
harlequin bug
heart and dart
hellgrammite
ichneumon fly
lightning bug
marbled white
museum beetle
peach blossom
pirate spider
poplar kitten
rhynchophore
scarab beetle
speckled wood
trumpet snail
vapourer moth
walking stick
water boatman
water strider
white admiral

13

blister beetle
browntail moth

carpenter moth
cheese skipper
daddy-longlegs
false scorpion
goliath beetle
honeycomb moth
ichneumon wasp
jumping-spider
leafcutter ant
leafcutter bee
leatherjacket
measuring worm
mother-of-pearl
pied shieldbug
pill millipede
praying mantis
purple emperor
ramshorn snail
redback spider
red spider mite
tortoiseshell
water measurer
water scorpion

14

cabbage-root fly
Colorado beetle
comma butterfly
death's head moth

Hercules beetle
purse-web spider
trap-door spider

15

furniture beetle
grizzled skipper
heath potter wasp
hummingbird hawk
whirligig beetle
yellow longicorn

16 +

bloody-nosed beetle
bombardier beetle
cabbage white but-
  terfly
Camberwell beauty
churchyard beetle
deathwatch beetle
devil's coach-horse
funnel-web spider
giant peacock moth
Jenkin's spire shell
jumping plant louse
long-horned beetle
oriental cockroach
robin's pincushion
spider-hunting wasp
water stick insect

International car codes

Aden	ADN	Bahrain	BRN	Burma	BUR
Afghanistan	AGF	Bangladesh	BD	Burundi	RU
Albania	AL	Barbados	BDS	Cameroon	RFC
Alderney	GBA	Belgium	B	Canada	CDN
Algeria	DY	Belize	BH	Central African	
Andorra	AND	Benin	DY	Republic	RCA
Argentina	RA	Botswana	RB	Chile	RCH
Australia	AUS	Brazil	BR	China	TJ
Austria	A	Brunei	BRU	Colombia	CO
Bahamas	BS	Bulgaria	BG	Congo	RCB

Costa Rica	CR	Kenya	EAK	Rwanda	RWA
Côte d' Ivoire	CI	Kampuchea	K	St. Lucia	WL
Cuba	C	Kuwait	KWT	St. Vincent and	
Cyprus	CY	Laos	LAO	the Grenadines	WV
Czech Republic	CS	Lebanon	RL	Samoa	WS
Denmark	D	Lesotho	LS	San Marino	RSM
Dominica	WD	Liberia	LB	Senegal	SN
Dominican Rep.	DOM	Libya	LAR	Seychelles	SY
East Germany	DDR	Liechtenstein	FL	Sierra Leone	WAL
Egypt	ET	Luxembourg	L	Singapore	SGP
El Salvador	ES	Madagascar	RM	South Africa	ZA
Ethiopia	ETH	Malawi	MW	South Korea	ROK
Faroe Islands	FR	Malaysia	MAL	Spain	E
Fiji	FDI	Mali	RMM	Sri Lanka	CL
Finland	SF	Malta	M	Suriname	SME
France	F	Mauritania	RIM	Sweden	S
Gambia	WAG	Mauritius	MS	Swaziland	SD
Ghana	GH	Mexico	MEX	Switzerland	CH
Gibraltar	GBZ	Monaco	MC	Syria	SYR
Granada	WG	Morocco	MA	Tanzania	EAT
Great Britain	GB	Myanmar	BUR	Taiwan	RC
Greece	GR	Namibia	SWA	Thailand	T
Guatemala	GCA	Netherlands	NL	Togo	TG
Guernsey	GBG	Netherlands		Trinidad and	
Guyana	GUY	Antilles	NA	Tobago	TT
Haiti	RH	New Zealand	NZ	Tunisia	TN
Hongkong	HK	Nicaragua	NIC	Turkey	TR
Hungary	H	Niger	RN	Uganda	EAU
Iceland	IS	Nigeria	WAN	Uruguay	ROU
India	IND	Norway	N	USA	USA
Indonesia	RI	Pakistan	PAK	USSR	SU
Iran	IR	Panama	PA	Vatican City	V
Iraq	IRQ	Papua New Guinea		Vietnam	VN
Ireland	IRL	PNG		West Germany	D
Isle of Man	GBM	Paraguay	PY	Yemen	ADN
Israel	IL	Peru	PE	Yugoslavia	YU
Italy	I	Philippines	RP	Venezuela	YV
Jamaica	JA	Poland	PL	Zaïre	ZRE
Japan	J	Portugal	P	Zambia	Z
Jersey	GBJ	Qatar	QA	Zimbabwe	ZW
Jordan	HKJ	Romania	RO		

Islands

(Where Island, Islands, Isles or Isle of is a normal part of the name, it is usually indicated in brackets as I., Is., or I. of)

2 & 3

Adi
Bay (Is.)
Bua
Ely (I. of)
Eve
Ewe
Hoy
Kei (Is.)
Man (I. of)
May (I. of)
Neb
Rat (Is.)
Ré
Red
Roa
Rum
Yap
Zea

4

Adam
Amoy
Aran (I. of)
Arru (Is.)
Bali
Bear (I.)
Bere
Bird (I.)
Buru
Bute
Calf (I.)
Cebu
Ceos
Coll
Cook (Is.)
Cuba

Dago
Dogs (I. of)
Eday
Edge
Eigg
Elba
Farn (Is.)
Faro
Fiji
Fohr
Goat (I.)
Gozo
Guam
Gugh
Hall (Is.)
Herm
High (I.)
Holy (I.)
Idra
Iona
Java
Jura
Long (I.)
Milo
Moen
Mona
Muck
Mull (I. of)
Noss
Oahu
Omey
Osea (I.)
Rhum
Rona
Saba
Sark
Scio

Skye
Sulu (Is.)
Sylt
Syra
Swan (I.)
Tory
Uist
Ulva
Unst
Yell
Yezo
Zebu

5

Abaco
Aland (Is.)
Albay
Arran
Banca
Banda
Banks
Barra
Barry
Bonin (Is.)
Caldy
Canna
Capri
Ceram
Chios
Clare
Cocos (Is.)
Corfu
Corvo
Crete
Dabaz
Delos
Devon
Disco

Disko
Eagle (I.)
Ellis
Farne (Is.)
Fayal
Ferro
Foula
Funen
Goree
Gozzo
Grain (I. of)
Haiti
Hart's (I.)
Hatia
Hondo
Hydra
Ibiza
Inyak
Islay
Ivica
Lewis
Leyte
Lissa
Lobos (Is.)
Lundy (I.)
Luzon
Malta
Matsu
Melos
Milos
Nauru
Naxos
Nevis
Ormuz
Panay
Papua
Paros
Parry (Is.)
Paxoi

Pearl (Is.)
Pelew (Is.)
Pemba
Perim
Pines (I. of)
Pinos
Rhode (I.)
Rugen
Sable (I.)
Samar
Samoa
Samos
Skyro
Spice (Is.)
Sunda (Is.)
Texel
Timor
Tiree
Tonga
Turk's (I.)
Voorn
Whale (I.)
Wight (I. of)
Zante

6

Achill
Aegina
Albany
Anamba (Is.)
Andros
Azores
Baffin (I.)
Banana (Is.)
Bissao
Borkum
Borneo
Bounty (Is.)
Brazza
Bryher
Burray
Caicos (Is.)
Calamo

Candia
Canary (Is.)
Canvey (I.)
Cayman (Is.)
Ceylon
Cerigo
Cherso
Chiloe
Chusan
Comoro (Is.)
Crozet (Is.)
Cyprus
Dursey
Easter (I.)
Ellice (Is.)
Euboea
Flores
Gilolo
Gomera
Hainan
Harris
Hawaii
Honshu
Imbros
Inagua
Ionian (Is.)
Ischia
Ithaca
Iturup
Jaluit
Jersey
Jethou
Kishni
Kodiak
Kurile (Is.)
Kyushu
Labuan
Lambay
Lemnos
Lerins (Is.)
Lesbos
Limmos
Lipari (Is.)
Lombok
Madura

Marajo
Marken
Negros
Oleron
Orkney (Is.)
Patmos
Penang
Philae
Pomona
Puffin (I.)
Quemoy
Ramsey
Rhodes
Robben
Rottum
St. John
St. Paul
Samsoe
Sangir (Is.)
Savage (I.)
Scarba
Scilly (Is.)
Sicily
Staffa
Staten (I.)
Stroma
Tahiti
Taiwan
Thanet (I. of)
Tholen
Tobago
Tresco
Trömso
Tubuai (Is.)
Tuvalu
Ushant
Vaigen
Virgin (Is.)
Walney

7

Aegades (Is.)
Aeolian (Is.)
Amboina

Ameland
Andaman (Is.)
Antigua
Bahamas
Bahrain
Balleny (Is.)
Bardsey
Barents
Behring (Is.)
Bermuda
Bernera
British (Is.)
Bourbon
Cabrera
Capraja
Caprera
Celebes
Channel (Is.)
Chatham (Is.)
Chincha (Is.)
Corisco
Corsica
Cumbrae
Curaçao
Curzola
Dampier (Is.)
Dinding (Is.)
Diomede (Is.)
Domingo
Faeroes
Falster
Fanning
Fehmeru
Flannan (Is.)
Formosa
Frisian (Is.)
Gambier (Is.)
Gilbert (Is.)
Gotland
Grenada
Hayling (I.)
Iceland
Ireland
Jamaica
Johanna

Kamaran
Kandava
Keeling (Is.)
Kolonev
Laaland
Leeward (Is.)
Liakhov (Is.)
Lofoten (Is.)
Loyalty (Is.)
Madeira
Mageroe
Majorca
Maldive (Is.)
Massowa
Mayotte
Menorca
Mindoro
Minicoy
Minorca
Molokai
Molucca (Is.)
Mombasa
Mykonos
Nicobar (Is.)
Norfolk (I.)
Nossi Be
Okinawa
Orkneys
Palawan
Phoenix (I.)
Portsea (I.)
Princes (Is.)
Purbeck (I. of)
Rathlin
Reunion
Roanoke
Rockall
Rotumah
St. Agnes
St. Kilda
St. Kitts
St. Lucia
St. Marie
Salamis
Sao Tomé

Sheppy (I. of)
Sherbro
Shikoku
Society (Is.)
Socotra
Solomon (Is.)
Stewart (I.)
Sumatra
Sumbawa
Tenedos
Ternate
Tokelau (Is.)
Tortola
Tortuga
Tuamotu
Watling (I.)
Whalsay
Wrangel

8

Alderney
Aleutian (Is.)
Amirante (Is.)
Andamans
Anglesey
Antilles
Auklands (Is.)
Balearic (Is.)
Barbados
Berneray
Billiton
Bissagos (Is.)
Bornholm
Brownsea
Campbell
Canaries
Caribbee (Is.)
Caroline (Is.)
Colonsay
Copeland (Is.)
Cyclades (Is.)
Desertas
Desirade
Dominica
Fair Isle

Falkland (Is.)
Flat Holm
Flinders
Foulness
Friendly (Is.)
Furneaux (Is.)
Guernsey
Hebrides
Hokkaido
Hong Kong
Inchcolm
Jan Mayen
Kangaroo (Is.)
Kermadec (Is.)
Kiribati
Krakatoa
Ladrones
Leucadia
Lord Howe (Is.)
Magdalen (Is.)
Malagasy
Maldives
Malicolo
Mallorca
Manihiki (Is.)
Marianne (Is.)
Marshall (Is.)
Melville
Mindanao
Miquelon
Mitylene
Moluccas
Otaheite
Pitcairn (Is.)
Portland (I. of)
Pribilov (Is.)
Quelpart
Rothesay
St. Helena
St. Martin
St. Thomas
Sakhalin
Salsette
Sandwich (Is.)
Sardinia

Scillies
Somerset
Sri Lanka
Shetland (Is.)
Starbuck
Sulawesi
Sverdrup
Tasmania
Tenerife
Thousand (Is.)
Thursday (I.)
Tortugas (Is.)
Trinidad
Unalaska
Valancia
Valentia
Victoria
Viti-Levu
Vlieland
Windward (Is.)
Zanzibar

9

Admiralty (Is.)
Aleutians
Anticosti
Arranmore
Ascension
Australia
Belle Isle
Beverland
Calf of Man
Cape Verde (Is.)
Cerigotto
Christmas (I.)
Dordrecht
Elephanta
Eleuthera
Ellesmere
Erromanga
Falklands
Galapagos (Is.)
Greenland
Halmahera
Inchkeith

Inishturk
Isle of Man
Isle of May
Lampedusa
Langeland
Manhattan (I.)
Margarita
Marquesas (Is.)
Marshalls
Mauritius
Nantucket
Negropont
New Guinea
Norderney
North Uist
Porto Rico
Raratonga
Rodrigues
Saghalien
Saint John
St. Martin's
St. Michael
St. Nicholas
Saint Paul
St. Vincent
Santa Cruz
Santorini
Scarpanto
Shetlands
Singapore
South Uist
Steep Holm
Stromboli
Teneriffe
Timor Laut (Is.)
Vancouver
Vanua Levu
Walcheren
Wellesley (Is.)

10

Ailsa Craig
Bay Islands
Calamianes

Cape Barren (I.)
Cape Breton (I.)
Cephalonia
Dirk Hartog (I.)
Fernando Po
Formentara
Fortune Bay (I.)
Friendlies
Grenadines
Guadeloupe
Heligoland
Hispaniola
Inchgarvie
Isle of Dogs
Isle of Skye
Isle of Mull
Kuria Muria (Is.)
Laccadives
Long Island
Madagascar
Manitoulin
Martinique
Montserrat
New Britain
New Ireland
New Siberia
New Zealand
North Devon
Nova Zembla
Philippine (Is.)
Puerto Rico
Ronaldshay
Saint Agnes
Saint Kilda
Saint Kitts
Saint Lucia
Saint Marie
Sandalwood (I.)
Seychelles
Skerryvore
West Indies

11

Axel Heiberg

Dirk Hartogs
Grand Canary
Guadalcanal
Isle of Pines
Isle of Wight
Isola Grossa
Lindisfarne
Mascarenene (Is.)
Monte Cristo
New Hebrides
North Island
Pantellaria
Philippines
Rhode Island
Saint Helena
Saint Martin
Saint Thomas
Scilly Isles
Southampton
South Island
Spitsbergen

Easter Island
Great Britain
Great Cumbrae
Inaccessible (I.)
Isle of Thanet
Mariagalante
Melville Land
New Caledonia
Newfoundland
Novaya Zemlya
Prince Albert
Prince Edward (I.)
Puffin Island
Saint Michael
Saint Martin's
Saint Nicolas
Saint Vincent
South Georgia
Staten (I.)

Norfolk Island
North East Land
Prince Charles
Prince of Wales
 (I.)
Prince Patrick
St. Bartholomew
St. Christopher
Santa Catalina
Stewart Island

14

Isle of Portland
Queen Elizabeth
South Shetlands
Tierra del Fuego
Tristan da Cunha

15 +

Martha's Vineyard
Prince Edward
 Island
Van Dieman's Land
West Spitsbergen

12

Baffin Island
Bougainville
British Isles

13

Isle of Purpeck
Isle of Sheppey
Juan Fernandez
Kerguelen Land
Little Cumbrae

Labours of Hercules

Slay the Nemean lion.
Kill the Lernean hydra.
Catch and retain the Arcadian stag.
Destroy the Erymanthian boar.
Cleanse the Augean stables.
Drive off the cannibal birds of Lake Stymphalis.
Capture the Cretan bull.
Catch the mares of the Thracian Diomedes.
Get possession of the girdle of Hippolyta, Queen of the Amazons.
Capture the oxen of the monster Geryon.
Obtain the golden apples of the Hesperides.
Bring Cerberus from the infernal regions.

Lakes, lochs, loughs and waterfalls

Lakes, lochs and loughs

3
Ard
Awe
Eil
Ewe
Key
Ree
Tay
Tuz
Van
Zug

4
Aral
Chad
Bala
Como
Conn
Derg
Earn
Erie
Erne
Eyre
Fyne
Holy
Kivu
Long
Mask
Nemi
Ness
Ryan
Tana
Utah

5
Abaya
Allen
Baker
Broom
Etive
Foyle
Frome
Garda
Garry
Great
Huron
Kasba
Kyoga
Leane
Leman
Leven
Lochy
Loyne
Maree
Minto
Mjosa
Moore
Mweru
Neagh
Nyasa
Onega
Poopo
Rainy
Rayne
Sevan
Shiel
Taupo
Trout
Urmia
Volta

6
Albert
Arkaig
Assynt
Austin
Baykal
Chilka
Chilko
Corrib
Edward
Geneva
George
Kariba
Ladoga
Khanka
Linnhe
Lomond
Lop Nor
Lugano
Mackay
Malawi
Mobutu
Nasser
Natron
Oneida
Peipus
Poyang
Rudolf
St. Jean
Saimaa
Shasta
Simcoe
Te Anu
Vanern
Viedma
Vyrnwy

Wanaka
Zaysan

7
Abitibi
Balaton
Blanch
Chapela
Dead Sea
Derwent
Dubawnt
Egridir
Fannich
Galilee
Idi Amin
Katrine
Koko Nor
Leopold
Lucerne
Managua
Nipigon
Nonacho
Nu Jiang
Ontario
Qinghai
Quesnel
Rannoch
St. Clair
Sheelin
Swilley
Torrens
Turkana
Wannsee

8
Balkhash
Beysehir
Chiemsee
Colville
Coniston
Dongting
Gairdner
Grasmere
Issyk Kul
Maggiore
Manitoba
Mazurian
Menindee
Michigan
Neusiedl
Reindeer
Salt Lake
Stefanie
Superior
Titicaca
Tonle Sap
Tung-T' ing
Victoria
Wakatipu
Winnipeg

9
Argentino
Athabasca
Bangweulu
Champlain
Chudskoye
Constance
Ennerdale

Faguibine
Great Bear
Great Salt
Mai Ndombe
Maracaibo
Neuchâtel
Nicaragua
Nipissing
Thirlmere
Trasimene

Ullswater
Wastwater
Wollaston

10 +

Buttermere
Coniston Water
Connewarre
Cabora Bassa

Derwent Water
Great Slave
Haogoundou
Ijsselmeer
Lake of the Woods
Okeechobee
Rydal water
Serpentine
Tanganyika
Windermere
Winnipegosis

Waterfalls and cataracts

5
Angel
Cedar
Della
Glass
Sioux

6
Boyoma
Foyers
Guayra
Iguaca
Ribbon
Rogart
Tugela

7
Glomach
Measach
Niagara
Roraima
Stanley
Swallow
Utigard

8
Cuquenan
Gavarnie
Hamilton
Iroquois
Kabalega

Kukenaam
Takkakaw
Victoria
Yosemite

9
Angrabies
Churchill
Invershin
Linn of Dee

10
Salto Angel
Skjeggedal
Sutherland
Wollomombi

11
Mardalsfoss
Mongefossen
Powerscourt

12 +
Caldron Snout
Eas Coul Aulin
Great Kamarang
Khone Cataracts
Pistyll Rhaeadr
Tyssestrengane

Land transport

2 & 3	BSA	gig	rod	Benz	drag
AA	bus	hub	van	bike	dray
AC	cab	JAP	VW	body	Fiat
AJS	cam	jet		boot	Ford
cc	car	key		bush	frog
bhp	fan	pas	**4**	cart	gear
BMW	fly	RAC	auto	coil	hack
BMX	FWD	rev	axle	dome	halt

horn	knock	dickey	snocat	chassis
hump	lorry	diesel	stroke	Citroën
jeep	Metro	dodgem	Subaru	cutting
lock	moped	doolie	surrey	Daimler
loco	motor	driver	Suzuki	dog-cart
mini	palki	drosky	tandem	Douglas
pram	pulka	dynamo	tanker	droshky
Saab	sedan	engine	tappet	ejector
shay	servo	fiacre	tender	exhaust
skis	shaft	filter	torque	express
sled	spike	flange	tourer	fan belt
sump	sulky	funnel	Toyota	Ferrari
tank	tonga	ganger	tricar	firebox
taxi	track	gasket	troika	fireman
tram	train	go-cart	Trojan	flivver
trap	trike	go-kart	tuning	flyover
tube	truck	Hansom	tunnel	foreman
tyre	turbo	hearse	waggon	gearbox
wain	valve	Hiundi	weasel	growler
	Volvo	hot-rod	whisky	hackney
	wagon	hub cap		hard-top
	wheel	Humber		hay wain
		hurdle		Hillman
5		Indian	**7**	learner
Alvis	**6**	Jaguar	Amilcar	licence
araba		jalopy	amtrack	Lincoln
Ariel	Austin	jaunty	autobus	log book
block	banger	jitnry	autocar	mail van
bogie	Bantam	kit car	ballast	minibus
brake	Beetle	Lancia	battery	minicab
buggy	Berlin	landau	bearing	Mustang
brake	big end	limber	Bentley	omnibus
Buick	boiler	litter	bicycle	Packard
chain	bonnet	maglev	bob-sled	pannier
chair	bowser	Model T	britska	Peugeot
choke	bridge	Morris	britzka	phaeton
coach	Brough	Norton	browser	pillion
coupé	buffer	pedals	Bugatti	Porsche
crank	buffet	piston	caboose	Pullman
crate	bumper	points	caleche	Raleigh
cycle	calash	porter	caravan	road map
dandy	chaise	Proton	cariole	road tax
Essex	clutch	saloon	caroche	scooter
float	damper	sledge	cat's eye	shunter
grate	Datsun	sleigh	chariot	sidecar
guard	dennet			
Honda				

skidpan
sleeper
station
taxi cab
tilbury
tonneau
Trabant
trailer
tractor
trailer
tramcar
Transit
Triumph
trolley
tumbril
two-door
viaduct
voiture
whiskey
whistle

8

autobahn
barouche
bearings
brake pad
brake van
britzska
Brougham
bulkhead
cable car
cabriole
Cadillac
calliper
camshaft
carriage
carriole
catenary
clarence
corridor
coupling
crank pin
curricle
cylinder

dipstick
dustcart
flywheel
footrest
four-door
fuel pump
goods van
handcart
high ride
horse bus
horse cab
ice-yacht
ignition
injector
junction
Kawasaki
kick-down
knocking
live axle
manifold
Mercedes
monorail
motor car
motorist
motor van
motorway
old crock
open road
overtake
pavement
platform
pony cart
push-bike
radiator
reverser
rickshaw
roadster
rotor arm
runabout
selector
silencer
small end
smokebox
sociable
staff car

stanhope
steam car
steering
stock car
terminus
throttle
track rod
toboggan
tricycle
unicycle
Vauxhaul
victoria

9

air filter
ambulance
Alfa Romeo
bandwagon
bath chair
blast pipe
boat train
bobsleigh
brake shoe
britschka
bubblecar
buckboard
buffet car
cabriolet
charabanc
composite
condenser
conductor
crosshead
crossover
diligence
dining car
dipswitch
disc brake
Dormobile
drum brake
estate car
foot brake
footplate
funicular

gear lever
gear stick
generator
goods shed
goods yard
guards van
half shaft
hand brake
hatchback
landaulet
Land Rover
limousine
mail coach
milk float
monocycle
motorbike
overdrive
palanquin
piston rod
police car
prop shaft
racing car
regulator
saddlebag
saloon car
sand yacht
side valve
signal box
signalman
spark plug
sports car
street car
Tin Lizzie
T-junction
trunk road
turntable
two-seater
two-stroke
underseal
Velocette
wagonette
wheelbase
wheelspin

10

access road
alternator
Austin mini
automobile
Black Maria
boneshaker
brake fluid
buffer beam
buffer stop
broad gauge
cattle dock
conveyance
crankshaft
donkey cart
drive shaft
embankment
engine shed
fire engine
footbridge
four-in-hand
four-seater
four-stroke
glass coach
goods train
hackney cab
handlebars
hobby horse
horsepower
jinricksha
Lamborgini
Lanchester
Land Rover
locomotive
lubricator
mobile home
motor coach
motorcycle
Oldsmobile
paddywagon
pedal cycle
piston ring
post chaise
private car

rattletrap
removal van
rev counter
Rolls Royce
roundabout
roundhouse
safety belt
sedan chair
snowplough
spare wheel
speed limit
stagecoach
state coach
Studebaker
suspension
tachograph
tachometer
thermostat
tip-up lorry
trolleybus
trolley-car
two-wheeler
understeer
valve chest
velocipede
Volkswagen
wheelbrace
wheelchair
windscreen
wing mirror

11

accelerator
anti-roll bar
Aston Martin
Austin Rover
bullock cart
caravanette
carburettor
caterpillar
compression
convertible
delivery van
diesel train

distributor
driving test
four-wheeler
ground frame
gun carriage
jaunting car
jinrickshaw
landaulette
luggage rack
oil pressure
petrol gauge
quadricycle
racing cycle
safety valve
sleeping car
steam engine
steam roller
superheater
synchromesh
three-in-hand
tipper lorry
transporter
vacuum gauge
waiting room
water column
water trough
wheeltapper

12

booking clerk
coach and four
covered wagon
cylinder head
diesel engine
differential
double-decker
driving wheel
express train
freight train
furniture van
gypsy caravan
horse and cart
loading gauge
motorcyclist

motor scooter
motor vehicle
mountain bike
pantechnicon
perambulator
petrol engine
Puffing Billy
railway train
registration
single-decker
sparking plug
station wagon
supercharger
three-wheeler
ticket office
transmission
turbocharger

penny-farthing
power steering
rack-and-pinion
restaurant car
shock absorber
shooting brake
slave cylinder
spark ignition
station master

14 +

automatic transmission
compression ignition
crown wheel and pinion
four-wheel drive
Hackney carriage
Harley Davidson
horseless carriage
independent suspension
marshalling yard
off-road vehicle
passenger train
petrol ignition
power-assisted steering
prairie schooner
revolution counter
traction engine
underground train

13

connecting rod
cooling system
electric train
fuel injection
governess cart
level crossing
overhead valve

Languages and nationalities/ races

2 & 3	Giz	Kru	Shi	4	Bali
Bat	Gur	Kui	Suk	Agni	Balt
Edo	Hun	Kwa	Tiv	Ainu	Bant
Ewe	Ibo	Lao	Twi	Akan	Beja
Fon	Ido	Luo	Vai	Ambo	Bena
Fur	Ijo	Min	Wa	Arab	Bete
Ga	Ila	Mon	Wu	Avar	Bini
Gin	Iru	Neo	Yao	Baga	Bisa
	Jew	Rom			Bodo

Boer	Manx	Acoli	Gauls	Lunda	Sioux
Brit	Maya	Adeni	Gbari	Malay	Sotho
Bubi	Mede	Afars	Gipsy	Mande	Sudra
Celt	Meru	Aleut	Gissi	Maori	Suomi
Chad	Moor	Angle	Gondi	Masai	Swazi
Copt	Moxu	Anuak	Grebo	Mende	Swede
Cree	Naga	Arabs	Greek	Metis	Swiss
dago	Nama	Aryan	Griff	Mogul	Tamil
Dane	Norn	Asian	Gujar	Mossi	Tatar
Dyak	Nuba	Attic	Gumbo	Munda	Temne
Ebon	Nuer	Aztec	gypsy	Myall	Tigré
Efik	Nupe	Bamum	Hadza	Nandi	Tonga
Erse	Nyao	Bantu	Hausa	Naron	Turki
Fang	Pali	Bassa	Hindi	Negro	Tussi
Finn	Pedi	Batak	Hindu	Ngala	Tutsi
Fula	Pict	Baule	Husky	Ngoni	Uzbeg
Gael	Pole	Bemba	idiom	Nguni	Uzbek
Garo	Riff	Benga	Idoma	Nguru	Vedda
Gaul	Russ	Berta	Indic	Nisei	Venda
Ge'ez	Sard	Bhili	Inuit	Nkore	Vlach
Gogo	Scot	Black	Ionic	Norse	Welsh
Gond	Sena	Bulom	Iraqi	Nyong	Wolof
Goth	Serb	Bussi	Iraqu	Nyoro	Xhosa
Grig	Shan	Carib	Irish	Omani	Yakut
Guro	Sikh	Chaga	Kadai	Oriya	Yupik
Haya	Slav	Chewa	Kafir	Osage	Zande
Hima	Sobo	Chopi	Kamla	Oscan	
Hova	Sorb	Creek	Karen	Punic	
Hutu	Susu	Croat	Kazak	Pygmy	**6**
Igbo	Teso	Cuban	Khasi	rayah	Acholi
Impi	Thai	Cymry	Khmer	Roman	Aeolic
Inca	Tswa	Czech	Kissi	Romic	Afghan
Jute	Tupi	Dayak	Koine	Ronga	Almain
Kelt	Turk	Dinka	Kongo	Rundi	Alpine
Kroo	Urdu	Dogon	Kuo-Yu	Sabra	Altaic
Kurd	Wend	Doric	Ladin	Sakai	Amazon
Lala	Yako	Druse	Lamba	Sango	Andean
Lapp	Yank	Dutch	Lango	Saudi	Angoni
Lari	Zend	Dyold	Latin	Saxon	Apache
Lett	Zulu	Dyula	Lenge	Scots	Arabic
Loma	Zuni	Fante	limey	Shilh	Arawak
Lozi		Fanti	lingo	Shona	Argive
Luba		Frank	Lomwe	Sican	Ascian
Mali	**5**	Galla	lubra	Sikel	Aussie
Mano	Abuna	Ganda	Lulua	Sinic	Aymara

Bakota	Hamite	Nordic	Sindhi	Angevin
Balega	Hebrew	Norman	Slavic	Angolan
Baltic	Herero	Novial	Slovak	Arabian
Baoule	Ibibio	Nsenga	Somali	Aramaic
Basque	Indian	Nubian	Soviet	Aramean
Basuto	Inupik	Nyanja	Sukuma	Armoric
Bateke	Ionian	Ojibwa	Syriac	Ashanti
Bayaka	Italic	Ostman	Syrian	Asiatic
Belgae	Jewess	Ostyak	Telegu	Avestan
Berber	Jewish	Paduan	Telugu	Avestic
Bihari	Judaic	Pahari	Teuton	Baganda
Bokmal	Kabyle	Pakeha	Theban	Bagirmi
Brahui	Kaffir	Papuan	Thonga	Bakweii
Breton	Kanuri	Pariah	Tlokwa	Balanta
Briton	Kenyan	Parian	Tongan	Balochi
Bulgar	Kikuyu	Parsee	tongue	Bambara
Cantii	Korean	Pathan	Trojan	Bangala
Canuck	Kpelle	patois	Tsonga	Bapende
Celtic	Kpessi	Pawnee	Tswana	Barotse
Chagga	Kpwesi	Persic	Tuareg	Barundi
Chokwe	Kurukh	pidgin	Tungus	Basonge
Coptic	Ladino	Pueblo	Turkic	Batonka
Creole	Levite	Polish	Tuscan	Batutsi
Cretan	Libyan	Pushto	Tyrian	Bedouin
Cymric	Lumbwa	Pushtu	Ugrian	Belgian
Danish	Luvale	Rajput	Vaisya	Bengali
Dorian	Lydian	Rolong	Vandal	Berbers
Eskimo	Magyar	Romaic	Veddah	Bisayan
Fijian	Manchu	Romany	Viking	British
Franks	Median	Rwanda	Votyak	Brython
French	Mestee	Ryukyu	Warega	Bunduka
Fulani	Micmac	Sabine	Yankee	Burmese
Gadhel	Minoan	Salian	Yemeni	Bushman
Gaelic	Mohawk	Salsa	Yoruba	Cairene
Gallic	Mongol	Sambaa	Zenaga	Catalan
Gascon	Murozi	Samian	Zouave	Chaldee
Gentoo	native	Samiot		Chechen
German	Navaho	Samoan		Chilean
Gitana	Navajo	Saxons	**7**	Chinese
Gitano	Ndonga	Scotch	Acadian	Chinook
Gothic	Nepali	Semite	Achaean	Choctaw
Grikwa	Nesiot	Seneca	Aeolian	Cockney
Griqua	Ngbaka	Senufo	African	Cornish
Gullah	Ngombe	Sérère	Amerind	Cypriot
Gurkha	Ngwato	Sherpa	Amharic	Dagomba

Dalicad	Lugbara	Ruthene	Zantiot	Deerfoot
dialect	Maduran	Rwandan	zingaro	Delphian
Dorians	Malayan	Samburu		Devonian
English	Malinke	Samiote		dog Latin
Finnish	Maltese	Samnite	**8**	Dutchman
Fleming	Mandyak	Samoyed	Abderite	Egyptian
Flemish	Mantuan	Sandawe	Akkadian	Ephesian
Frisian	Manxman	Santali	Albanian	Estonian
Gambian	Marathi	Saracen	Algerian	Ethiopic
Gaulish	Mashona	Semitic	Algerine	Etruscan
Genoese	Mestizo	Senussi	Alsatian	Eurasian
Grecian	Mexican	Serbian	American	European
Griquas	Moabite	Shawnee	Andorran	Fanariot
Guarani	Mohican	Shilluk	Antiguan	Filipino
Haitian	Mongols	Siamese	Armenian	Frankish
Harijan	Moorish	Sienese	Assamese	Gadhelic
Hamitic	Mordvin	Slovene	Assyrian	Galilean
Hebraic	Morisco	Songhai	Athenian	Gallican
Hellene	Mozareb	Sorbian	Austrian	Georgian
Hessian	Mulatto	Spanish	Balinese	Germanic
Hittite	Nahuatl	Spartan	Batavian	Ghanaian
Iberian	Namaqua	Swahili	Bavarian	Guernsey
Ilocano	Nauruan	Swedish	Bergdama	Gujariti
Iranian	Ndebele	Switzer	Bermudan	Guyanese
Ishmael	Negress	Tagalog	Biscayan	Hawaiian
Ismaili	Ngbandi	Tartars	Boeotian	Hellenic
Israeli	Nilotes	Tibetan	Bohemian	Helvetic
Italian	Nilotic	Tigrina	Bolivian	Hittites
Judaean	Nynorsk	Tsigane	Bulgaric	Honduran
Kalmuck	Osmanli	Turkana	Bushongo	Illyrian
Kannada	Ottoman	Turkish	Cambrian	indigene
Karanga	Pahlavi	Ugandan	Canadian	Irishman
Kennick	Palaung	Umbrian	Cathayan	Iroquois
Khoisan	Paphian	Umbubdu	Chaldaic	islander
Kirghiz	Pehlevi	Valapuk	Chaldean	Jamaican
Kurdish	Persian	Vandals	Chamarro	Japanese
Kuwaiti	Prakrit	Vaudois	Cherokee	Javanese
Laotian	Punjabi	Veddoid	clansman	Jugoslav
Laotien	Pythian	Venetic	Congoese	Kanarese
Lappish	Quashee	Walloon	Corsican	Kashmiri
Latvian	Quechua	Watutsi	Cossacks	Kimbundu
Lettish	redskin	Wendish	Cumbrian	Kingwana
Lingala	Riffian	Yiddish	Cushitic	Kipsigis
Llanero	Romance	Zaïrese	Cyreniac	Kolarian
Lombard	Russian	Zambian	Dalesman	Kuki-Chin

Kukuruku
Kwanyama
language
Lebanese
Levanter
Liberian
Londoner
Low Latin
Maeonian
Mahratta
Makassar
Malagash
Malagasy
Malawian
Mameluco
Mamprusi
Mandaean
Mandarin
Mandingo
Mandinka
Matabele
Memphian
Milesian
Moravian
Moroccan
Moru-Madi
national
Nazarene
Neo-Latin
Nepalese
Nigerian
Norseman
Nuba-Fula
Nyamwesi
Old Norse
Old Saxon
Orcadian
Oriental
paleface
Parisian
Parthian
Pekinese
Pelasgic
Peruvian
Phrygian

Polabian
Polonian
Prussian
Pyrenean
Rabbinic
Romanian
Romansch
Rumanian
Sanskrit
Savoyard
Scandian
Scotsman
Scottish
Scythian
Seminole
shagroon
Sicilian
Silesian
Slavonic
Spaniard
Spartans
Sudanese
Sumerian
Sybarite
Tahitian
Tallensi
Teucrian
Teutonic
Tunisian
Turanian
Turkoman
Tyrolean
Tyrolese
Tyrrhene
Ukranian
Vandalic
Venetian
Viennese
Visigoth
Volscian
Warragal
Welshman
Yugoslav

9

Abkhasian
aborigine
Afrikaans
Afrikaner
Afro-Asian
Algonquin
Anatolian
Argentine
Armorican
Atrebates
Barbadian
Bengalese
Bratoslav
Barbadian
Bergamask
Blackfoot
Brazilian
Brigantes
Britisher
Bulgarian
Byzantine
Cambodian
Cantonese
Caribbean
Castilian
Caucasian
Ceylonese
Char-Nile
Cheremiss
Cimmerian
Colombian
Congolese
Damascene
Dravidian
Easterner
Englander
Esperanto
Esquimaux
Ethiopian
Finlander
Frenchman
Galwegian
Grenadian

Hanseatic
Hebridian
Hesperian
Hibernian
High Dutch
Himyarite
Hollander
Hottentot
Hungarian
Icelander
Icelandic
Israelite
Jordanian
Kabardian
Kannarese
Kgalagedi
Landsmaal
langue d' oc
Laplander
Late Latin
Longobard
Low German
lowlander
Malayalam
Malaysian
Manxwoman
Mauritian
Mongolian
Mongoloid
Muscovite
Nabataean
Nepaulese
New Yorker
Norwegian
Ostrogoth
Pakistani
Parthians
Pekingese
Periscian
plainsman
Provencal
Red Indian
Rhodesian
Roumanian
Ruthenian

Sabellian
Samaritan
Sardinian
Sassenach
Scotchman
Sere Mundu
Sinhalese
Slavonian
Slovenian
Springbok
Sri Lankan
Stagirite
Sundanese
Taiwanese
Tangerine
Tanzanian
Tasmanian
Tocharian
tribesman
Ukrainian
Ulotrichi
Ulsterman
Uruguayan
Varangian
Westerner
West Saxon
Zanzibari

10
aboriginal
Abyssinian
Afrikander
Algonquian
Amerindian
Andalusian
Anglo-Saxon
Australian
Autochthon
Babylonian
Bathlaping
Caledonian
Circassian
clanswoman
Cornishman

Costa Rican
countryman
Devanagari
East Indian
Ecuadorian
Englishman
Eurafrican
Finno-Ugric
Florentine
Glaswegian
Guatemalan
Hanoverian
High German
Highlander
Hindustani
Hottentots
Indonesian
Irishwoman
Ishmaelite
Israelitic
journalese
Karamojong
langue d' oil
Lithuanian
mainlander
Melanesian
Mingrelian
Monegasque
Neapolitan
Nicaraguan
Nicobarese
Niger-Congo
Northerner
Occidental
Old English
Ostrogoths
Panamanian
Paraguayan
Parisienne
Patagonian
Philippine
Philistine
Phillipian
Phoenician
Polynesian

Pomeranian
Portuguese
Rajasthani
Scillonian
Scotswoman
Senegalese
Serbo-Croat
Shetlander
Singhalese
Southerner
Thailander
townswoman
tramontane
Tridentine
Tyrrhenian
Venezuelan
vernacular
Vietnamese
Welshwoman
West Indian
woodlander
Zimbabwean

11
Afro-Asiatic
Anglo-Indian
Argentinian
Azerbaijani
Bangarwanda
Bangladeshi
Belorussian
continental
Frenchwoman
Greenlander
Indo-Hittite
Indo-Iranian
Lancastrian
marshlander
Mauretanian
Micronesian
Middle Latin
Modern Latin
Old Prussian
pakeha Maori

Palestinian
Scots Gaelic
Sino-Tibetan
transmontane
tribeswoman
Trinidadian
Ulsterwoman
Westphalian
Yugoslavian

12
Afro-American
Australasian
basic English
Byelorussian
Cornishwoman
countrywoman
Czechoslovak
dead language
Englishwoman
Eiro-American
frontiersman
Gibraltarian
Indo-European
King' s English
lingua franca
Lunda-Bajokwe
Moru-Mangbetu
mother tongue
Netherlander
New Englander
New Zealander
Norman French
Northumbrian
Plattdeutsch
Pre-Dravidian
Saudi-Arabian
Scandinavian
Tibeto-Burman
Yorkshireman

13
Anglo-American

Knickerbocker
Oxford English
Peloponnesian
Philadelphian
pidgin English
Queen's English

Rhaeto-Romanic
Serbo-Croatian

14
American Indian
French Canadian

15
Czechoslovakian
North Countryman
received English
standard English

Male and female animals

Male animals

3

cob (swan)
dog (coyote, dog, wolf)
fox (fox)
ram (impala, sheep)
tom (bobcat, cat, cougar)
tup (sheep)

4

boar (badger, bear, pig, weasel)
buck (antelope, hare, kangaroo, rabbit, rat)
bull (buffalo, camel, cattle, eland, elephant, giraffe, hartebeest, moose, oxen, rhinoceros, seal, walrus, whale)
cock (birds, crab, fish, lobster)
jack (ass, donkey, ferret)
lion (lion)
sire (dog, horse)
stag (caribou, deer, turkey)

5

billy (goat)
drake (duck)
steer (cattle, oxen)
tiger (tiger)

6
gander (goose)

7
bullock (cattle, oxen)
jackass (ass, donkey)
leopard (leopard)
peacock (peafowl)

8
stallion (horse, zebra)

9
billygoat (goat)

Female animals

3
dam (dog, horse)

doe (antelope, caribou, deer, ferret, hare, kangaroo, rabbit, rat)

cow (buffalo, camel, cattle,
 eland, elephant, giraffe,
 hartebeest, moose, oxen,
 rhinoceros, seal, walrus,
 weasel, whale)
ewe (impala, sheep)
hen (birds, crab, fish, lobster)
pen (swan)
sow (badger, bear, pig)

4
duck (duck)
gill (ferret)
hind (deer)
jill (ferret)

5
bitch (coyote, dog, wolf)
brach (hunting dog)

goose (goose)
jenny (ass, donkey)
nanny (goat)
queen (cat)
reeve (ruff, sandpiper)
vixen (fox)

6
peahen (peafowl)

7
lioness (bobcat, cougar,
 lion)
tigress (tiger)

9
nannygoat (goat)

10
leopardess (leopard)

Mammals

(including whales, sealions, etc.)

2 & 3	ox	hart	puma	5	fossa
ape	pig	hind	saki	addax	gayal
ai	rat	ibex	seal	bison	genet
bat	tod	joey	stag	bongo	goral
cat	yak	kudu	tahr	camel	hippo
doe		lion	tehr	civet	horse
dog	**4**	lynx	thar	coati	hyena
elk		mink	titi	coney	hyrax
fox	bear	mole	unua	coypu	izard
gam	boar	mona	ursa	daman	kiang
gnu	buck	musk	vole	dhole	koala
hob	bull	oont	wolf	dingo	kulan
hog	cony	oryx	zebu	drill	lemur
kob	deer	paca		eland	liger
orc	gaur	pard		fitch	llama
	hare	pika			loris

Mammals

moose
mouse
okapi
orang
otter
ounce
panda
pi-dog
pongo
potto
rasse
ratel
rhino
sable
saiga
sasin
serow
shrew
skunk
sloth
stoat
takin
tapir
tiger
whale
zebra
zibet

6

agouti
alpaca
angora
aoudad
argali
aye-aye
baboon
badger
baleen
beaver
beluga
bharal
burhel
bobcat
chacma

coluga
cougar
coyote
cuscus
dassie
desman
dik-dik
dog fox
du gong
duiker
duyker
ermine
feline
fennec
ferret
fox bat
gibbon
gopher
grison
grivet
guenon
howler
hyaena
impala
jackal
jaguar
jerboa
kit fox
koodoo
langur
lupine
margay
marmot
marten
monkey
musk ox
nilgai
numbat
ocelot
possum
pie-dog
pye-dog
quagga
rabbit
racoon

red fox
reebok
rhesus
rodent
sambar
sambur
sea cow
serval
simian
tarpan
teledu
tenrec
ursine
vermin
vervet
vicuna
walrus
wapiti
weasel
wild ox
wombat

7

ant bear
bear cat
blaubok
blesbol
blue fox
brocket
buffalo
bushpig
caracal
caribou
cervine
cetacea
chamois
cheetah
colobus
dolphin
echidna
finback
fitchet
fitchen
foumart

fur seal
gazelle
gemsbok
giraffe
glutton
gorilla
grampus
grey fox
grysbok
guanaco
guereza
hunuman
keitloa
lemming
leonine
leopard
leveret
linsang
lioness
macaque
manatee
markhor
meerkat
mole rat
mouflon
muntjac
muskrat
mustang
narwhal
opossum
pack rat
panther
peccary
polecat
primate
pricket
raccoon
red deer
roebuck
roe deer
rorqual
sapajou
sea calf
sea-lion
siamang

sirenia
sun bear
tamarin
tarsier
tigress
vampire
vulpine
wallaby
warthog
water ox
wild ass
wild cat
wood rat

8

aardvark
aardwolf
anteater
antelope
babirusa
bactrian
black rat
blue buck
brown rat
bushbaby
bush buck
bontebok
boschbok
burramys
cachalot
capuchin
capybara
carcajou
chigetai
chipmunk
civet cat
dormouse
duckbill
edentate
elephant
fin whale
fruit bat
grey wolf
harp seal

hedgehog
hedgepig
humpback
Irish elk
kangaroo
kinkajou
kolinsky
leoparine
mandrill
mangabey
markhoor
marmoset
mongoose
monk seal
moufflon
mule deer
musquash
omnivore
pangolin
pinniped
platypus
porpoise
predator
reindeer
sea otter
sei whale
serotine
squirrel
steinbok
swift fox
tamandua
ungulate
viscacha
wanderoo
water rat
wharf rat
whistler
white fox
wild boar
wild goat

9

arctic fox
armadillo

bandicoot
binturong
black bear
black buck
blacktail
blue whale
brown bear
carnivore
catamount
chickaree
deer mouse
desert rat
dromedary
dziggetai
flying fox
groundhog
herbivore
hog badger
honey bear
ichneumon
koala bear
March hare
marsupial
menagerie
monotreme
mouldwarp
mouse deer
orang-utan
pachyderm
palm civet
pariah dog
phalanger
polar bear
porcupine
pronghorn
quadruped
razorback
scavenger
shrew mole
silver fox
sloth bear
swamp hare
springbok
tree shrew
waterbuck

water vole
white bear
wolverine
woodchuck
youngling

10

angwantibo
Barbary ape
black whale
bottlenose
camelopard
chevrotain
chimpanzee
cottontail
desert lynx
fallow deer
field mouse
giant panda
hartebeest
honey mouse
hooded seal
jackrabbit
jaguarundi
Kodiak bear
leopardess
mona monkey
native bear
ottershrew
pantheress
pine marten
pouched rat
prairie dog
raccoon dog
rhinoceros
right whale
river horse
saki monkey
shrewmouse
sperm whale
spring buck
spring hare
timber wolf
vampire bat

vertebrate
white whale
wildebeest

11

Cape buffalo
barking deer
douroucouli
flying lemur
grizzly bear
ground sloth
honey badger
honey sucker
horned horse
kangaroo rat
killer whale
mountain cat
orang-outang
pipistrelle
plantigrade
pocket mouse
prairie wolf
red squirrel
sea elephant
snow leopard
stone marten
swamp rabbit
white ermine
wishtonwish

12

bonnet monkey
Cashmere goat
cinnamon bear
elephant seal
ferret badger
goat antelope
grampus whale
grey squirrel
harvest mouse
hippopotamus
horse-shoe bat
howler monkey

jumping mouse
klipspringer
mountain goat
mountain lion
pocket gopher
rhesus monkey
snowshoe hare
spider monkey
tree kangaroo
ursine monkey
Virginia deer
water buffalo
woolly monkey

13
Chapman's zebra

giant anteater
man of the woods
rogue elephant
scaly anteater
spiny anteater
star-nosed mole
Tasmanian wolf

14
banded anteater
flying squirrel
ground squirrel
Indian elephant
New World monkey
Old World monkey
Père David's deer

snowshoe rabbit
spectacled bear
Tasmanian devil

15 +
African elephant
Chinese water deer
duck-billed platypus
mountain viscacha
mountain chinchilla
prairie squirrel
Przewalski's horse
proboscis monkey
pygmy hippopotamus
Thomson's gazelle
white rhinoceros

Measurements and units

2					
cg	nm	rad	hide	yard	lumen
cm	ns	rod	hour		*metre
dl	oz	ton	inch		minim
dm	yd	tun	kilo	**5**	neper
dr			knot	cable	ounce
el			link	carat	perch
em	**3**	**4**	mile	chain	point
en	amp	acre	mole	cubit	poise
ft	are	bale	nail	curie	pound
gr	bit	barn	peck	cusec	quart
hl	BTU	bolt	phon	farad	quire
in	cal	byte	phot	fermi	stere
kg	cwt	cord	pica	gerah	stone
km	dal	cran	pint	guage	tesla
lb	dam	dram	pole	grain	therm
mg	dwt	dyne	ream	gross	tithe
mi.	ell	feet	rood	gauss	tonne
mm	erg	foot	slug	grain	weber
mt	lux	gill	span	henry	
MV	mho	gram	torr	hertz	**6**
MW	mil	gray	troy	joule	ampère
	nit	hand	volt	karat	bushel
	ohm	hank	watt	*litre	

candle
cental
cupful
decare
degree
denier
drachm
fathom
firkin
gallon
gramme
kelvin
league
megohm
micron
minute
net ton
newton
octane
parsec
pascal
radian
second
shekel
stokes

gilbert
hectare
kiloton
lambert
long ton
maxwell
megabit
megaton
oersted
poundal
quarter
quintal
röntgen
scruple
sea mile
siemens
sievert
tonnage

7

Calorie
calorie
candela
coulomb
decibel
dioptre
diopter
faraday
furlong

8

angstrom
chaldron
imperial
kilobyte
kilogram
kilovolt
kilowatt
megabyte
megavolt
megawatt
millibar
roentgen
short ton
spoonful
watt-hour

9

becquerel
board foot
centigram
cubic foot
cubic inch
cubic yard
decalitre
decimetre
foot-pound
hectogram
kilocycle
kilohertz
light-year
megacycle
metric ton
microgram
milligram
nanometre
ounce troy
pound troy
steradium
troy ounce
troy pound

10

barleycorn
centilitre
centimetre
cubic metre
fluid ounce
freight ton
hectolitre
hectometre
horsepower

kilogramme
microfarad
millilitre
millimetre
nanosecond
rutherford
square acre
square foot
square inch
square mile
square yard

11

avoirdupois
gram calorie
hectogramme
kilocalorie
metric tonne
microsecond
milligramme
millimicron
millisecond
pennyweight
register ton
shipping ton

12 +

displacement ton
hundredweight
kilogramme calorie
kilowatt-hour
measurement ton
nautical mile
ounce apothecaries
short hundred-
  weight
square kilometre

*(*The spelling of litre and metre is liter and meter in America and should be taken into consideration when using a word with these elements.)*

Medical terms

2

id
IQ
ME
MS
TB
VD

3

AID
AIH
ALS
bug
cap
CAT
CPR
ECT
ECG
EEG
ego
ENT
ESP
fit
flu
FSH
HRT
ion
IUD
NMR
NSU
PKU
PMS
PMT
pox
pus
REM
sex
STD
tic

TPR
TSH
wax
wen

4

ache
acid
acne
agar
ague
AIDS
aura
bile
bite
boil
bubo
burn
cast
case
clot
coil
cold
coma
corn
cure
cyst
diet
dose
drip
drug
duct
dumb
germ
gout
heal
host
iron
lint
mole

oral
otic
ovum
pain
pica
pill
pulp
rest
rash
scab
scar
sore
stye
swab
weal
wind
X-ray
yaws

5

acute
angst
assay
ataxy
atopy
aural
bends
birth
blood
brace
bulla
bursa
chill
chyle
chyme
clone
colic
cough
cramp
croup

D and C
death
donor
enema
ether
faint
fever
fibre
fluke
flush
focus
fugue
graft
gripe
hives
ileus
laser
leech
locum
lupus
mania
moron
mucus
mumps
myope
nurse
opium
palsy
phial
piles
polio
polyp
pulse
renal
rheum
rigor
scald
scurf
sebum
serum
shock

shunt
sleep
sling
spasm
spore
sprue
stoma
stone
stria
swoon
sweat
taste
taxis
tests
tinea
tonic
tonus
toxin
truss
twins
ulcer
urine
venom
virus
worms
wound

6

albino
alexia
alkali
amnion
amoeba
angina
anoxia
anuria
apathy
apnoea
asthma
asylum

ataxia
autism
barium
bedpan
benign
biopsy
bougie
bruise
bunion
by-pass
callus
cancer
caries
chorea
climax
clinic
coccus
coitus
comedo
condom
coryza
costal
cowpox
crisis
crutch
dengue
distal
doctor
dorsal
douche
dropsy
eczema
elixir
emesis
emetic
enamel
energy
eunuch
fascia
favism
fester

fibrin
flatus
fungus
fusion
gargle
gluten
goitre
grippe
growth
healer
health
hernia
heroin
herpes
hiccup
hunger
incest
infirm
injury
intern
iodine
iritis
jet lag
kaolin
labour
lanugo
laxity
lesion
libido
lipoma
lochia
lumbar
lunacy
malady
matron
medium
megrim
memory
murmur
mutism
myopia
naevus
nausea
oedema
opiate

otitis
oxygen
period
phenol
phlegm
phobia
physic
pimple
plague
plaque
poison
pollen
potion
powder
psyche
Q fever
quinsy
rabies
radium
reflex
remedy
saline
saliva
scurvy
senses
sepsis
sheath
sister
splint
sprain
sputum
squint
stapes
stitch
strain
stress
stroke
stupor
tablet
tetany
thrush
tissue
torpor
toxoid
trance

trauma
tremor
trepan
tumour
typhus
unwell
vector
zygote

7

abscess
acetone
acidity
adenoma
adipose
agnosia
ailment
allergy
amalgam
amentia
anatomy
ammonia
amnesia
anaemia
angioma
anodyne
anosmia
antacid
anthrax
antigen
anxiety
aphasia
aphonia
asepsis
aspirin
atrophy
autopsy
balance
bandage
bedsore
blister
booster
boracic
bow legs

bubonic
bulimia
cadaver
caesium
caliper
cannula
capsule
cardiac
carrier
CAT scan
catarrh
cautery
chancre
chiasma
choking
cholera
choline
chorion
chronic
cocaine
colitis
colloid
complex
coroner
culture
cupping
curette
dentine
dentist
dietary
dioptre
disease
embolus
emotion
empyema
endemic
ethanol
eupepsy
exudate
fatigue
fibroid
filling
fissure
fistula
flexion

flutter
forceps
glasses
gumboil
grommet
hare lip
healing
healthy
hearing
hormone
hospice
hygeine
icterus
inquest
insulin
invalid
in vitro
itching
keratin
lanolin
lozenge
leprosy
linctus
lockjaw
lumbago
malaise
malaria
massage
measles
meiosis
melaena
melasma
microbe
midwife
mitosis
mixture
morphia
myalgia
mycosis
neonate
nostrum
obesity
oculist
oestrus
operate

organic	symptom	apoplexy	cyanosis	flooding
osmosis	syncope	Asian flu	cystitis	fluoride
panacea	syringe	asphyxia	dandruff	focusing
Pap test	systole	atheroma	deaf-mute	formalin
paresis	talipes	atropine	deafness	fracture
patient	tension	bacillus	debility	freckles
peptide	tetanus	backache	deformed	furuncle
persona	theatre	bacteria	delirium	ganglion
pessary	the Pill	baldness	delivery	gangrene
pink eye	torsion	beriberi	delusion	genetics
placebo	toxemia	bifocals	dementia	genotype
plaster	typhoid	bioassay	dentures	glaucoma
posture	urology	black eye	diabetes	grand mal
potency	vaccine	blackout	diagnose	handicap
puberty	variola	bleeding	dialysis	hangnail
purpura	ventral	blue baby	diastole	hangover
pustule	verruca	blushing	diplopia	hay fever
pyrexia	vertigo	botulism	diuretic	headache
quinine	vesicle	bursitis	dreaming	heat bump
recover	viscera	caduceus	dressing	heat rash
regimen	vitamin	caffeine	drowning	heredity
relapse	wasting	calamine	dwarfism	hospital
rickets	weaning	calculus	dyslexia	hot flush
rosacea	whitlow	calliper	dyspnoea	hygienic
roseola	wry neck	carotene	efferent	hypnosis
rubella	yawning	cataract	effusion	hysteria
rubeola		catheter	embolism	illusion
rupture		cephalic	epidemic	immunity
sarcoma	**8**	chloasma	epidural	impacted
scabies		chlorine	epilepsy	impetigo
section	ablation	cicatrix	erection	incision
seizure	abortion	claw foot	ergotism	inflamed
sibling	abrasion	claw hand	eruption	infusion
sick bay	acidosis	clinical	erythema	inhalant
snoring	adenitis	clotting	etiology	insanity
spastic	adhesion	clubbing	eugenics	insomnia
sterile	alkaloid	club foot	euphoria	instinct
styptic	allergen	coenzyme	exanthem	intersex
stutter	alopecia	cold sore	excision	irritant
stammer	analysis	collapse	face lift	jaundice
suicide	androgen	coloboma	fainting	kala-azar
sunburn	aneurysm	compound	filament	knee-jerk
surgeon	anorexia	cortisol	first aid	kyphosis
surgery	antibody	crepitus	fixation	lameness
sutures	antidote	cross-eye	flat foot	laudanum
	aperient			

laxative
lecithin
lethargy
ligature
liniment
lobotomy
lordosis
marasmus
mastitis
medicine
melanoma
menarche
methanol
migraine
moribund
morphine
mutation
myelitis
narcotic
necrosis
neoplasm
neuritis
neurosis
nicotine
nocturia
occlusal
ointment
oncology
optician
orchitis
osteitis
otoscope
pandemic
paranoia
parasite
parietal
paroxysm
pathogen
pellagra
petit mal
phimosis
pleurisy
polyuria
poultice
priapism

prolapse
proximal
pruritus
reaction
recovery
relaxant
rest-cure
rhinitis
ringworm
sanitary
scanning
schizoid
sciatica
sedation
sedative
senility
shingles
sickness
skin test
smallpox
sneezing
speculum
stenosis
steroids
stitches
superego
surgical
swelling
syndrome
syphilis
systemic
tapeworm
teething
terminal
test meal
thrombin
thrombus
tincture
tinnitus
toxaemia
traction
vagotomy
virilism
virology
virulent

vitiligo
vomiting
vulvitis
wheezing
xanthoma
zoonosis

9

achalasia
acidaemia
addiction
adrenalin
aetiology
alkalosis
alleviate
allopathy
amino acid
anabolism
anaerobic
analgesia
analgesic
anamnesis
androgyny
angiogram
angiology
ankylosis
anorectic
antenatal
antiserum
antitoxin
antivenin
antivenom
arthritis
aspirator
autoclave
autograft
autolysis
bacterium
bad breath
bedridden
birth rate
birthmark
blackhead
bland diet

blindness
blind spot
blood bank
blood clot
blood test
body odour
bone graft
breathing
Caesarean
carbuncle
carcinoma
catalepsy
catharsis
cathartic
causalgia
cauterise
chalazion
chancroid
chilblain
chiropody
Chlamydia
cirrhosis
cognition
colostomy
colostrum
commensal
contagion
contusion
cordotomy
cortisone
crab louse
cretinism
curvature
cytopenia
deformity
dentition
diagnosis
diaphragm
diarrhoea
diathermy
dietician
dietetics
digestion
digitalis
disinfect

dislocate
dizziness
drug abuse
dysentery
dyspepsia
dystrophy
echovirus
eclampsia
ectomorph
emollient
emphysema
endomorph
endoscope
enteritis
epileptic
epistaxis
excretion
extension
extrovert
eyestrain
fatty acid
fertility
fetishism
fever sore
focussing
folic acid
frigidity
frost bite
fulminant
gallstone
gastritis
germicide
gestation
gigantism
glossitis
haematoma
halitosis
hammertoe
heartbeat
heartburn
heart rate
hepatitis
herbalism
hirsutism
histamine

histology	occipital	roundworm	antisepsis
hunchback	occlusion	sclerosis	Apgar score
hydrocele	olfactory	scoliosis	apoplectic
hypnotism	open-heart	screening	apothecary
ileostomy	operation	serotonin	arrhythmia
impotence	osteology	sex change	asbestosis
incidence	osteopath	shivering	ascariasis
incubator	ovulation	silicosis	aspiration
induction	pacemaker	sinusitis	astringent
infection	palpation	skin graft	automatism
infirmary	papilloma	smear test	barium meal
influenza	paralysis	sterility	barotrauma
injection	paramedic	stimulant	BCG vaccine
inoculate	parotitis	stretcher	bed wetting
intellect	patch test	stricture	Bell's palsy
introvert	pathology	sunstroke	bionic limb
ischaemia	pemphigus	surrogate	Black Death
isolation	perfusion	symbiosis	blood cells
keratitis	perinatal	synergism	blood count
knock knee	pertussis	synovitis	blood donor
lactation	phenotype	teratogen	blood group
lassitude	phlebitis	toothache	brain death
leukaemia	physician	treatment	brainwaves
lithotomy	pneumonia	umbilicus	bronchiole
magnesium	poisoning	urine test	bronchitis
malignant	polygraph	urticaria	canker sore
masochism	pompholyx	vaginitis	carcinogen
medicinal	porphyria	varicella	cardiogram
menopause	precocity	vasectomy	cardiology
mesomorph	pregnancy	wrist drop	castration
metophase	prodromal	xeroderma	catabolism
methadone	prognosis		cellulitis
microtome	protazoan		chickenpox
mongolism	psoriasis	**10**	childbirth
myxoedema	psychosis		chloroform
myxovirus	psychotic	abreaction	colposcopy
nephritis	pulmonary	acromegaly	common cold
nephrosis	purgative	adenovirus	compulsion
neuralgia	pyelogram	afterbirth	conception
neurology	radiology	alcoholism	concretion
nosebleed	reduction	alkalaemia	concussion
novocaine	rejection	amoebiasis	congenital
nutrition	remission	amputation	congestion
nystagmus	retractor	antibiotic	consultant
obsession	rheumatic	antiseptic	contrecoup
		antiemetic	

conversion
convulsion
coprolalia
cystic duct
dependence
depilatory
depressant
depression
dermatitis
diphtheria
dipsomania
dispensary
dissection
DPT vaccine
ecchymosis
emaciation
embryology
episiotomy
euthanasia
exhaustion
extradural
eyeglasses
fallen arch
false teeth
fibrositis
filariasis
filtration
flatulence
geriatrics
gingivitis
glomerulus
gonorrhoea
grey matter
haematuria
haemolysis
hearing aid
heart block
heatstroke
hemiplegia
hypodermic
hypophysis
idiopathic
imbecility
immunology
inbreeding

infarction
inhalation
inhibition
insanitary
interferon
irrigation
kiss of life
lactic acid
laparotomy
laryngitis
Lassa fever
leucopenia
lightening
lung cancer
masectomy
meditation
meningitis
metabolism
microscope
moniliasis
mouth ulcer
narcissism
narcolepsy
nephrology
nerve block
nerve fibre
nettle rash
nucleotide
nyctalopia
obstetrics
ophthalmia
ornithosis
osteopathy
palliative
paraplegia
penicillin
perception
percussion
pharmacist
phrenology
physiology
post mortem
presbyopia
proctology
prokaryote

prostheses
prosthesis
psychiatry
psychology
peurperium
quarantine
quickening
relaxation
renal colic
repression
respirator
rheumatism
safe period
Salmonella
sanatorium
sanitation
scar tissue
seborrhoea
shell shock
sonography
spectacles
staff nurse
stomatitis
strabismus
subliminal
suggestion
swallowing
threadworm
thrombosis
tissue bank
tomography
tooth decay
tourniquet
toxicology
tracheitis
transplant
trench foot
trepanning
tryptophan
ulceration
ultrasound
urethritis
varicocele
withdrawal
xenophobia

11

acupuncture
adolescence
agoraphobia
air embolism
air sickness
albuminuria
amenorrhoea
amphetamine
anaesthesia
anaesthetic
anaphylaxis
anastomosis
anencephaly
anthracosis
antipyretic
antitussive
arteriogram
arthrodesis
astigmatism
ausculation
bacteraemia
barbiturate
barium enema
beta-blocker
biofeedback
bisexuality
blepharitis
borborygmus
bradycardia
breech birth
brucellosis
candidiasis
car sickness
carminative
cauterizing
charge nurse
cholesterol
choroiditis
chylomicron
circulation
cleft palate
climacteric
coagulation

coarctation
cold abscess
consumption
contact lens
contracture
corn plaster
crepitation
cryosurgery
cryotherapy
day hospital
dehydration
denervation
dental brace
dermatology
dislocation
drunkenness
dysfunction
ejaculation
electrolyte
embrocation
equilibrium
expectorant
farmer's lung
fibre-optics
fluoroscope
fomentation
food allergy
fulguration
gall bladder
genetic code
gerontology
gynaecology
habituation
haemophilia
haemorrhage
heart attack
heart murmur
homeostasis
homoeopathy
hydatid cyst
hydrophobia
hyperemesis
hyperplasia
hypertrophy
hypotension

hypothermia
indigestion
infantilism
infestation
infertility
inheritance
inkblot test
inoculation
intravenous
irradiation
kidney stone
kleptomania
kwashiorkor
lacrimation
laparoscopy
laughing gas
litholapaxy
locum tenens
malingering
malpractice
mammography
mammoplasty
mastication
melancholia
meningocele
menorrhagia
micturation
miscarriage
mustard bath
myelography
naturopathy
ovarian cyst
oxygenation
palpitation
paracetamol
paratyphoid
parturition
pediculosis
peptic ulcer
perforation
peristalsis
peritonitis
phantom limb
pharyngitis
photophobia

plantar wart
polypeptide
potentation
prickly heat
prosthetics
proteinuria
psittacosis
psychopathy
radiography
respiration
retardation
rhinoplasty
salpingitis
sea sickness
septicaemia
side-effects
slipped disc
spina bifida
spirochaete
spondylitis
spondylosis
stethoscope
stomach pump
sublimation
suffocation
sulpha drugs
suppository
suppression
suppuration
tachycardia
temperature
tennis elbow
thermometer
tonsillitis
torticollis
tracheotomy
transfusion
trans-sexual
trench fever
trichinosis
unconscious
vaccination
vasodilator
venereology
ventilation
visual field

X-chromosome
Y-chromosome
yellow fever

12

abortus fever
accouchement
acrocyanosis
anthelmintic
anthropology
antinauseant
antipruritic
aphrodisiacs
appendectomy
appendicitis
apperception
arthroplasty
articulation
athlete's
  foot
autoantibody
bacteriology
behaviourism
bilharziasis
biliary colic
biochemistry
biomechanics
birth control
blood alcohol
breast cancer
bromhidrosis
bronchoscopy
carbolic acid
cardiac cycle
chemotherapy
chiropractic
circumcision
claudication
colour vision
complication
conditioning
constipation
constitution
convalescent
corneal graft

decongestant
degeneration
dental caries
dental clinic
desalination
disinfectant
dissociation
diverticulum
double vision
electrolysis
emasculation
encephalitis
endocarditis
enteric fever
epidemiology
excitability
exophthalmos
extrasystole
faith healing
family doctor
feminization
fibrillation
folk medicine
friar's balsam
gamma gobulin
gastric juice
gastric ulcer
generic drugs
group therapy
haematemesis
haemorrhoids
hallucinogen
hallux valgus
heart disease
heart failure
heliotherapy
hiatus hernia
hydrotherapy
hyperkinesia
hypertension
hypnotic drug
hypochondria
hysterectomy
idiosyncrasy
immune system

immunization
implantation
incompetence
incontinence
inflammation
insemination
intelligence
intoxication
irritability
laryngectomy
malformation
malnutrition
manipulation
MAO inhibitor
menstruation
microbiology
microsurgery
neurosurgery
nematode worm
night terrors
nitrous oxide
oophorectomy
opisthotonos
orthopaedics
ossification
osteoporosis
otosclerosis
pancreatitis
paraesthesia
Parkinsonism
pericarditis
perspiration
pharmacology
pigmentation
pneumothorax
prescription
presentation
pressure sore
primigravida
progesterone
prophylactic
pulled muscle
quadriplegic
quartan fever
radiotherapy

referred pain
Rhesus factor
rheumatology
scarlet fever
sense of smell
Siamese twins
sleeping pill
sleepwalking
solvent abuse
somnambulism
somnambulist
St Vitus dance
steatorrhoea
subarachnoid
subconscious
subcutaneous
surgical boot
tertian fever
test-tube baby
thalassaemia
thermography
thoracic duct
tranquillizer
sense of touch
stroke volume
surgeon's knot
trephination
trichuriasis
tuberculosis
tunnel vision
typhoid fever
vasodilation
writer's cramp

13

accommodation
acetylcholine
agglutination
amniocentesis
anthropometry
anticoagulant
antihistamine
antirheumatic
antispasmodic

aphthous ulcer
atrial flutter
bacteriophage
battle fatigue
blastomycosis
blood pressure
bottle feeding
breast feeding
bubonic plague
calcification
callisthenics
carbon dioxide
cardiac arrest
cardiac output
cerebral palsy
certification
cholangiogram
cholecystitis
choriod plexus
clinical trial
compatability
consanguinity
consciousness
contraception
contraceptive
convalescence
Crohn's disease
defibrillator
dental surgery
district nurse
Down's syndrome
drug addiction
duodenal ulcer
elephantiasis
endocrinology
erogenous zone
exhibitionism
fertility drug
fertilization
food poisoning
genetic traits
German measles
Graves' disease
gynaecomastia
haemodialysis

hallucination
health visitor
helminthiasis
hermaphrodite
hydrocephalus
hypermetropia
hypoglycaemia
hyperactivity
intensive care
intramuscular
Ishihara tests
lead poisoning
leishmaniasis
materia medica
medical record
mental illness
metabolic rate
micro-organism
mononucleosis
neuromuscular
noradrenaline
ophthalmology
osteomyelitis
oxygen therapy
paternity test
periodontitis
pharmacopoeia
physiotherapy
plantar reflex
poliomyelitis
polyarteritis
portwine stain
Pott's fracture
pregnancy test
premedication
prostate gland
prostatectomy
psychosomatic
psychosurgery
psychotherapy
regurgitation
reinforcement
renal dialysis
resuscitation
Rorschach test

schizophrenia
sebaceous cyst
sensitization
serum sickness
smelling salts
speech therapy
sterilization
Streptococcus
tenosynovitis
tissue culture
toxoplasmosis
trace elements
tranquillizer
varicose ulcer
varicose veins
vital capacity
whooping cough
xerophthalmia
zygomatic arch

14

achondroplasia
adrenocortical
angina pectoris
anticonvulsant
antidepressant
aortic stenosis
appendicectomy
autosuggestion
Babinski reflex
barefoot doctor
benzodiazepine
blood poisoning
breathlessness
Bright's disease
bronchodilator
carbon monoxide
cardiac massage
cardiomyopathy
cardiovascular
cathode-ray tube
cervical collar
chelating agent
cholelithiasis

chromatography
claustrophobia
coeliac disease
Colles' fracture
community nurse
conjunctivitis
coronary by-pass
cross-infection
cryptorchidism
cystic fibrosis
cytotoxic drugs
dacryocystitis
defibrillation
detached retina
detoxification
disorientation
diverticulitis
electrotherapy
family planning
fringe medicine
frozen shoulder
fraternal twins
glandular fever
Hansen's disease
heat exhaustion
hip replacement
histoplasmosis
housemaid's knee
house physician
hydrocortisone
hyperglycaemia
hypothyroidism
identical twins
immune response
inguinal hernia
menstrual cycle
mental disorder
motion sickness
muscle relaxant
night blindness
nitroglycerine
nodes of Ranvier
Oedipus complex
ophthalmoscope
osteoarthritis

parapsychology
pasteurization
patent medicine
pharmaceutical
plasmapheresis
plaster of Paris
plastic surgery
pneumoconiosis
premature birth
psychoanalysis
puerperal fever
pyelonephritis
rehabilitation
relapsing fever
rheumatic fever
sexual medicine
speech disorder
spinal puncture
Staphylococcus
surgical spirit
tolerance level
tranquillizers
travel sickness
trichomoniasis
tuberculin test
whiplash injury

15

Addison's disease
adhesive plaster
adverse reaction
anabolic steriod
anorexia nervosa
aplastic anaemia
artificial heart
blackwater fever
body temperature
Bornholm disease
cat-scratch fever
circadian rhythm
colour blindness
cosmetic surgery
cottage hospital
delirium tremens

dental hygienist
general medicine
heart transplant
heterosexuality
Hodgkin's disease
intussusception
locomotor ataxia
manic depressive
Ménière's disease
Minimata disease
morning sickness
nuclear medicine
organ transplant
pyloric stenosis
sticking plaster
Sydenham's chorea
trypanosomiasis
venereal disease
X-linked disorder

16 +

alternative medicine
altitude sickness
aluminium hydroxide
Alzheimer's disease
ankylosing spondylitis
anti-inflammatory
aortic incompetence
artificial
    insemination
artificial kidney
artificial respiration
atrial fibrillation
autonomic nervous
  system
basal metabolic rate
behaviour therapy
biomedical engineering
blood transfusion
Caesarean section
cardiac pacemaker
carpal tunnel syndrome
cerebral haemorrhage
cerebral thrombosis
cervical vertebrae

Medical terms

Cheyne-Stokes breathing
chromatic aberration
coitus interruptus
colonic irrigation
comminuted fracture
communicable disease
community medicine
compound fracture
compressed air sickness
conditioned reflex
congenital disorder
contraceptive drug
coronary heart disease
coronary thrombosis
Coxsackie viruses
decompression sickness
deficiency disorders
dental technician
dilatation and curettage
Dupuytren's contracture
ectopic pregnancy
electron microscope
Epstein-Barr virus
extrasensory perception
Fallot's tetralogy
feedback mechanism
follicle-stimulating hormone
forensic medicine
functional disorder
general practioner
genetic counselling
genetic engineering
genetic fingerprints
glucose tolerance test
glyceryl trinitrate
granulation tissue
greenstick fracture
Hashimoto's disease
heart-lung machine
high blood pressure
holistic medicine
hormone replacement therapy
Huntingdon's chorea
incubation period
infectious disease

inferiority complex
ingrowing toenail
intelligence quotient
intelligence test
intermittent claudication
intrauterine device
intravenous pyelogram
in vitro fertilization
Jacksonian epilepsy
kidney transplant
Legionaire's disease
life-support machine
maintenance therapy
maternal deprivation
mental deficiency
mental retardation
mercury poisoning
monoclonal antibody
motor neurone disease
mountain sickness
multiple sclerosis
muscular dystrophy
myocardial infarction
natural childbirth
nephrotic syndrome
nervous breakdown
neuromuscular disorder
non-specific urethritis
obstructive lung disease
occupational therapy
open-heart surgery
opportunistic infection
painkilling drugs
paramedical services
Parkinson's disease
peritoneal dialysis
pernicious anaemia
premenstrual syndrome
prepatellar bursitis
presenile dementia
preventative medicine
psychosexual development
psychotropic drugs
radiation sickness
rapid eye movement

replacement surgery	spinal anaesthesia
respiratory arrest	Stokes-Adams syndrome
respiratory disorders	strawberry birthmark
respiratory failure	toxaemia of pregnancy
rheumatoid arthritis	transplant surgery
sex-linked disorders	tropical medicine
sexually transmitted disease	ventricular fibrillation
sickle-cell anaemia	ventricular flutter
sleeping sickness	vitamin deficiency
spare-parts surgery	withdrawal method

(Note: haemo- compounds may appear hemo-, especially in American spelling.)

Military ranks, titles, etc.

2 & 3
AB
AC1
AC2
ADC
AOC
CO
Col.
CSM
FO
GI
LAC
Lt.
MP
NCO
OC
OS
PO
RSM
RTO

4
Capt.
C in C
cook
mate

peon
ulan
WAAF
Wren
WRNS

5
bosun
cadet
diver
fifer
Lieut.
major
middy
pilot
piper
scout
sepoy
spahi
subah
Tommy
uhlan

6
airman
ataman

batman
bomber
bowman
bow oar
bugler
cooper
cornet
driver
ensign
fitter
Ghurka
gunner
hetman
hussar
lancer
lascar
marine
master
purser
ranger
rating
reefer
rigger
sapper
seaman
sentry
snotty
spahee

stoker
yeoman
Zouave

7
admiral
ancient
armorer
aviator
captain
cavalry
colonel
Cossack
dragoon
drummer
general
hoplite
jemadar
marshal
matelot
militia
officer
orderly
pikeman
pioneer
private
provost

recruit
redcoat
regular
reserve
shipman
soldier
skipper
steward
subadar
surgeon
Terrier
trooper
vedette
veteran
warrior

8
adjutant
armourer
bandsman
cabin boy
cavalier
chaplain
chasseur
commando
corporal
coxswain

decurion
deserter
doughboy
engineer
fencible
flag rank
fugelman
fusilier
guerilla
havildar
helmsman
infantry
leadsman
janizary
Landwehr
marksman
messmate
mutineer
mechanic
observer
partisan
rifleman
sentinel
sergeant
ship's
  boy
spearman
subahdar

turncoat
winchman

9

air gunner
artificer
artillary
beefeater
berserker
boatswain
brigadier
cannoneer
carbineer
centurion
combatant
commander
commodore
conscript
cook's mate
field army
field rank
drum-major
fife-major
grenadier
guardsman
guerrilla
Home Guard
irregular
janissary
mercenary
musketeer
navigator
paymaster
pipe-major
press gang
sailmaker
ship's cook
signaller
signalman
subaltern
tugmaster
volunteer

10

able seaman
aide-de-camp
air marshal
apprentice
bandmaster
bombardier
campaigner
carabineer
carabinier
cavalryman
coastguard
commandant
cuirassier
drummer-boy
halbardier
Life Guards
lansquenet
lieutenant
militiaman
midshipman
paratroops
rear gunner
shipmaster
shipwright

11

aircraftman
air mechanic
bashibazook
bersaglieri
chief stoker
condottière
crack troops
crossbowman
field cornet
flag captain
flag officer
foot soldier
gunner's mate
Horse Guards
horse marine
infantryman

landsknecht
master pilot
naval rating
paratrooper
rear-admiral
second pilot
Tommy Atkins
vice-admiral

12

air commodore
armour-bearer
artillaryman
cabin steward
camp-follower
chief officer
chief steward
ensign-bearer
field marshal
field officer
first officer
group captain
horse soldier
junior seaman
major-general
master-at-arms
master gunner
officer cadet
petty officer
pilot officer
powder monkey
second master
senior purser
ship's surgeon
staff officer
storm-trooper
telegraphist
third officer

13

armourer's mate
army commander
barrack master

captain's clerk
chief armourer
chief engineer
dispatch rider
drill sergeant
flying officer
fourth officer
generalissimo
harbourmaster
lance corporal
leading seaman
leading stoker
light infantry
machine-gunner
master aircrew
prisoner of war
quartermaster
radio operator
sergeant major
second officer
signal officer
staff sergeant
sub-lieutenant
third engineer
torpedo-gunner
wing commander

14

air vice-marshal
colonel-in-chief
colour sergeant
flag lieutenant
flight engineer
flight mechanic
flight sergeant
leading steward
liaison officer
master corporal
master engineer
master sergeant
medical officer
ordinary seaman

provost marshal
second corporal
second engineer
ship's carpenter
signals officer
squadron leader
standard bearer
warrant officer

15 +

adjutant-general
air chief marshal
Chelsea Pensioner
chief technician
corporal of horse
first lieutenant
gentleman-at-arms
household troops
master navigator
master signaller
officer's steward
ordnance officer
second lieutenant
soldier of fortune

16 +

admiral of the fleet
chief petty officer
flight lieutenant
junior technician
lieutenant colonel
lieutenant commander
lieutenant general
marshal of the Royal Air Force
master air electronic operator
master air loadmaster
military policeman
officer of the day
officer of the guard
second-leutenant
senior aircraftman
quartermaster-sergeant

Monday's child rhyme

Monday's child is fair of face
Tuesday's child is full of grace
Wednesday's child is full of woe
Thursday's child has far to go
Friday's child is loving and giving
Saturday's child works hard for a living
But a child that's born on the Sabbath day
Is bonny and blythe and good and gay.

Money

1

c (cent)
d (penny, pence)
f (farthing)
l (lira, pound, £)
p (penny, pence)
q (quadrans = far-
   thing)
R (rand)
s (shilling)
$ (dollar)
Y (Yen, ¥)

2

as
at
DM (Deutschmark)
fl (florin/guilder)
xu

3

ban
bit
bob
écu
fen
fil

fin
hào
IOU
jon
kip
lek
lei
leu
lev
lsd
mil
öre
ore
pay
pie
pul
pya
sen
sol
sou
tin
won
yen

4

anna
ante
avos

baht
bani
bean
bill
birr
bits
buck
cash
cedi
cent
chon
coin
dime
doit
dong
euro
fare
fils
gelt
gold
inti
jiao
jeon
kina
kobo
kyat
lira
lire
loot

loti
lwei
mark
mill
mint
mite
note
obol
para
pelf
peso
pice
pony
pula
puli
pund
punt
quid
rand
real
reis
rial
riel
ryal
sene
slug
syli
taka
tala

toea
vatu
yuan

5

agora
angel
asper
aurar
baiza
belga
booty
brass
bread
butut
colón
conto
crown
daric
dinar
dobra
dough
ducat
eagle
fiver
franc
funds
grand
groat

ingot
khoum
kitty
kopek
krona
krone
kurus
leone
lepta
livre
lolly
louis
lucre
manna
means
mohur
möngö
naira
ngwee
noble
oncer
paisa
paise
paper
pence
penni
penny
perks
piece
pound
prize
purse
qursh
riyal
rupee
scudi
scudo
senik
soldo
sucre
taler
thebe
tical
toman
wages

zaïre
zloty

6

agorot
assets
aureus
balboa
bawbee
boodle
cauris
change
cheque
copeck
copper
credit
dalasi
denier
dirham
doblón
dollar
drachm
ekuele
escudo
filler
florin
forint
gourde
groszy
guinea
gulden
haléru
kopeck
koruna
kwacha
kwanza
leptae
lepton
likuta
living
makata
makuta
markka
mazuma

monkey
moolah
nickel
obolus
pa' anga
pataca
payout
pennia
peseta
pesewa
poisha
qindar
qintar
ransom
Rappen
riches
rouble
rupiah
salary
satang
seniti
sequin
shekel
siglos
silver
solidi
specie
spoils
stater
stiver
tanner
tariff
tenner
tester
teston
thaler
tugrik
wampum
wealth

7

Afghani
Austral
bolívar

bullion
capital
carfare
centavo
centime
céntimo
chetrum
córdoba
crusado
cruzado
denarii
drachma
ekpwele
guarani
guilder
halalah
ha' penny
hellers
lempira
lisente
lump sum
metical
milreis
moidore
nest egg
östmark
ouguiya
peanuts
pfennig
piastre
quarter
quetzal
readies
red cent
ringgit
rufiyaa
savings
sawbuck
smacker
solidus
stipend
tambala
testoon
two bits

8

banknote
bankroll
cruzeiro
currency
denarius
doubloon
farthing
finances
finnmark
groschen
hard cash
louis d' or
millième
napoleon
new pence
new penny
ngultrum
picayune
pin money
round sum
sesterce
shilling
sixpence
smackers
sterling
stotinki
tikchung
tuppence
two pence
windfall
winnings
zecchino

9

boliviano
centesimi
centesimo
dupondius
easy money
emolument
fourpence
fourpenny

gold piece
half-crown
half-eagle
half-noble
halfpenny
hush money
greenback
lilangeni
petty cash
pistareen
schilling
sovereign
spondulix

10

angel-noble
blood money
credit card
half-a-crown
money order
paper money
ready money
reichsmark
sestertium
threepence

11

bank account
bank balance
chickenfeed
danger money
decimal coin
deutschmark
double eagle
legal tender
Maundy Money
money for jam
pocket money
postal order
premium bond
sixpenny bit
small change
spondulicks
wherewithal

12

banker's draft
banker's order
hard currency
liquid assets
piece of eight
quarter-noble
remuneration
silver dollars

soft currency

13

brass farthing
caboverdianos
half-sovereign
pieces of eight
spending money
threepenny bit

14

certified check
coin of the realm
current account
letter of credit
peseta Guineana
promissory note

15+

checking account
conscience money
East Caribbean
   dollar
escudo
   caboverdianos
money for old rope
traveller's cheque

Mountain ranges, mountains, hills and volcanoes

2 & 3	4			
Abu	Alps	Fuji (v.)	Rosa	Altai
Aso	Blue	Harz	Rigi	Andes
Ida	Caha	Iron	Ural	Asama (v.)
K2	Cook	Jaya		Athos
Kea (v.)	Ebal	Jura		Atlas
	Etna (v.)	Kibo	**5**	Baker (v.)
		Meru	Adams	
		Ossa		

Black
Cenis
Coast
Cuzco
Eiger
Elgon
Galty
Ghats
Hecla (v.)
Huica
Kamet
Kenya
Hekla
Lenin (Peak)
Logan
Naipo
Misti
Ozark
Pelée
Rocky
Sayan
Sinai
Snowy
Table
Tatra
Weald (hills)
White

6

Ararat
Azufre
Balkan
Bonete
Brooks
Carmel
Darwin
Dumuyo
Egmont
Elbert
Elbrus
Elburz
Erebus (v.)
Hermon
Hoggar

Katmai
Kazbek
Koryak
Kunlun
Ladakh (range)
Lenina
Levick
Lhotse
Makula
Matopo (hills)
Mourne
Muztag
Nephin
Ochils (hills)
Olives (Mt of)
Pamirs
Pindus
Pissis
Pobedy
Purace (v.)
Sajama
Sangay (v.)
Scafel
Shasta
Sidlaw (hills)
Slioch
Taurus
Terror
Tunari
Vosges
Zagros

7

Ahaggar
Ben More
Bernina
Brocken
Cascade (range)
Cayambe
Chianti
Chillan (v.)
Copiapu
Errigal
Everest

Helicon
Illampu
Jorullo (v.)
Kilauea (v.)
Lliamna (v.)
Malvern (hills)
Mam Soul
Markham
Mendips (hills)
Muckish
Nan Ling
Nan Shan
Ollague
Olympus
Palomar
Peteroa
Rainier
Rockies
Roraima
Ruapehu (v.)
St. Elias
Samford
Scafell
Skiddaw
Snowdon
Socompa
The Peak
Tibesti
Tolimar
Triglav
Vulcano (v.)
Whitney

8

Anapurna
Ansuhuma
Antisana
Ardennes
Auvergne
Ben Attow
Ben Dearg
Ben Nevis
Ben Wyvis
Cambrian

Mountain ranges, mountains, hills and volcanoes

Cameroon (v.)
Caucasus
Cevennes
Chachani
Cheviots
Chirripo
Coropuna
Cotopaxi (v.)
Cuillins
Demavend
Flinders (range)
Fujiyama
Goat Fell
Humphrey
Hymettus
Jungfrau
Hualalai (v.)
Kaikoura (ranges)
Kinabalu
Krakatoa (v.)
Knockboy
Mauna Loa (v.)
McKinley
Mitchell
Musgrave (ranges)
Palumani
Pennines
Pentland (hills)
Pyrenees
Quantock (hills)
St. Helens (v.)
Sgurr Nor
Stanovoi (range)
Sulaiman (range)
Tian Shan
Tien Shan
Vesuvius (v.)
Wrangell (v.)
Yerupaja
Yucamani

9

Aconcagua
Allegheny
Annapurna

Antofalla
Appenines
Beenoskee
Ben Lawers
Ben Lomond
Ben Macdui
Braeriach
Cairn Toul
Chilterns
Cotswolds
Cross Fell
Co del Toro
Dolomites
Dunsinane
Galtymore
Grampians
Hamersley (range)
Helvellyn (range)
Himalayas
Hindu Kush
Huascaran
Karakoram (range)
Kosciusko
Lochnager
Mangerton
Mont Blanc
Muztagata
Nanda Devi
Ngauruhoe (v.)
Pacaraima
Parnassus
Pikes Peak
Puy de Dome
Ras Dashan
Ruwenzori
Pen-y-Ghent
Pichincha
Rakaposhi
Sillajhua
Slieve Car
Sonequera
Stromboli (v.)
Tirich Mir
Tocorpuri
Tongariro (v.)

Villarica (v.)
Weisshorn
Whernside
Zugspitze

10

Adirondack
An Teallach
Arakam Yoma
Cader Idris
Cairngorms
Cantabrian
Carpathian
Chimborazo
Chomolhati
Col del Putro
Companario
Dent du Midi
Dhaulagiri
Erzgebirge
Gasherbrum
Kebnekaise
King George
Kommunisma
Konger Shan
Lammermuir
Lassen Peak
Macdonnell (rang-
  es)
Majuba Hill
Matterhorn
Middleback (range)
Montserrat
Mount Lofty
  (ranges)
North Downs
  (hills)
Nyiragongo (v.)
St. Gotthard
South Downs
  (hills)
Torcurpure
Twelve Pins
Wetterhorn

11

Anti-Lebanon
Appalachian
Ben Cruachan
Drakensburg
Fairweather
Jotunheimen
Kangrinboqe
Kilimanjaro
Mendip Hills
Monadhliath
Namcha Barwa
Nanga Parbat
Nyamoragira (v.)
Scafell Pike
Sierra Madre

12

Appalachians

Cheviot Hills
Citlaltepetl
Godwin Austen
Golan Heights
Gran Paradiso
Ingleborough
Kanchenjunga
Kluchevskaya
Peak District
Popocatepetl
Schiehallion
Siding Spring
Sierra Morena
Sierra Nevada
Tinguiririca
Warrumbungle

13

Carrantuohill
Chiltern Hills

Co del Olivares
Communism Peak
Cotswold Hills
Grossglockner
Gurla Mandhata
Kangchenjunga
Kommunizma Pik
Ojas del Salado
Riesengebirge
Sierra Maestra

14 +

Bernese Oberland
Cleveland Hills
Fichtelgebirge
Finsteraahorn
Nevsojos del Salado
MacGillicuddy's Reeks
Shire Highlands
Xixabangma Feng

Muses

4
Clio - history

5
Erato - love songs

6
Thalia - comedy and pastoral
  poetry
Urania - astronomy

7
Euterpe - lyric poetry

8
Calliope - epic poetry
Polymnia - sacred song

9
Melpomene - tragedy

10
Polyhymnia - sacred song

11
Terpsichore - choral song
  and dance

Musical instruments

3
kit
lur
oud
oat
sax
saz
tar
uti

4
band
bass
bata
bell
biwa
drum
fife
gong
harp
horn
kena
khen
koto
lira
lute
lyra
lyre
mu yu
oboe
outi
pean
pipe
rote
ruan
sona
tuba
urua
vina

viol
whip

5
anvil
aulos
banjo
bells
block
bones
brass
bugle
bumpa
buzuq
cello
chang
cheng
ching
chime
cobza
corno
cornu
crwth
dauli
dhola
dobro
drone
fidla
flute
gaita
gajdy
gamba
hi-hat
huruk
kakko
kazoo
kerar
mbila
naker
nebel

okedo
organ
piano
rebab
rebec
reeds
regal
saron
shalm
shawm
shell
sheng
sitar
snare
strad
tabla
tabor
taiko
tibia
tudum
tupan
vibes
viola
zinke
zurla
zurna

6
alboka
arghul
atabal
bagana
bonang
bongos
buglet
carynx
chimes
citole
claves
corona

cornet
cymbal
darbuk
dehors
dulcet
fandur
fiddle
flugel
guitar
kettle
kissar
koboro
lirica
lirone
nakers
racket
rattle
rebeck
sacbut
sancho
santir
shaker
shofar
sopile
spinet
spoons
syrinx
tabour
tabret
tam-tam
timbal
tom-tom
trigon
tromba
tucket
tymbal
ventil
vielle
violin
yangum
zambra

zither

7
alp-horn
althorn
alto sax
atumpan
bagpipe
bandora
bandore
baryton
bassoon
bazooka
big band
bodhran
bow harp
box lyre
celesta
celeste
cembalo
chanter
chikara
cithara
cithern
cittern
clapper
clarion
clavier
cornett
cowbell
crotalo
cymbalo
cymbals
dichord
fagotto
fistula
fithele
flutina
gadulka
gamelan

gittern
harpist
hautboy
hornlet
kalungu
kithara
mandola
mandora
maracas
marimba
murumbu
musette
ocarina
octavin
orphica
pandora
pandura
pan-pipe
phonica
pianino
pianola
piccolo
posaune
sackbut
salpinx
sambuca
sambuke
samisen
santoor
sarangi
sarinda
saxhorn
saxtuba
serpent
sistrum
sithara
spinnet
taboret
tam am la
tambour
tambura
terbang
testudo
theorbo
tibicen

tiktiri
timbrel
timpani
timpano
trumpet
tubicen
ukulele
upright
vihuela
violone
warbler
whistle
zithern
zummara

8

alto-horn
arch-lute
autoharp
bagpipes
bandoura
bass drum
bass-horn
bass tuba
bass viol
bell harp
bombarde
bouzouki
calliope
carillon
castanet
chime bar
cimbalon
clappers
clarinet
clavecin
clavicor
continuo
cornpipe
crumhorn
ding-dong
dulcimer
gemshorn
handbell

harp lute
hornpipe
Jew's harp
keyboard
key-bugle
knackers
langspel
mandolin
melodeon
melodica
mirliton
pan pipes
pianette
pochette
polyphon
post horn
psaltery
recorder
reed pipe
side drum
slit drum
spinette
sringara
sticcado
surbahar
talambas
tamboura
tarabuka
tenor sax
timbales
triangle
trombone
tympanon
tympanum
violetta
virginal
vocalion
waldhorn
woodwind
zambomba

9

accordion
alpenhorn

alto-viola
angle harp
archilute
baby grand
balalaika
bandurria
banjolele
banjoline
bass-flute
bombardon
bongo drum
brass band
bugle-horn
castanets
celestina
chalumeau
chime bars
clarionet
claviharp
coach horn
cog rattle
componium
cornemuse
cornopean
crook horn
darabukke
decachord
drone-pipe
dulcitone
elbow-pipe
euphonium
flageolet
flexatone
flute-a-bec
gong ageng
hackbrett
hand organ
harmonica
harmonium
hydraulis
kelontong
könighorn
krummhorn
langspiel
mandoline

mandolone
mandolute
monochord
mouth harp
nose-flute
octachord
orchestra
orpharion
pantaleon
picco pipe
pipe organ
pitch-pipe
portative
reed organ
saxophone
semi-grand
seraphine
snare-drum
steel band
tabourine
tallharpa
tambourin
tenor horn
tenor tuba
tenor viol
tubophone
vibraharp
viola alto
washboard
wood block
Wurlitzer
xylophone
xylorimba

10

barrel drum
basset horn
bass fiddle
bass guitar
bird scarer
bongo drums
bull fiddle
bull-roarer
chittarone

choir-organ
clavichord
claviorgan
concertina
contrabass
cor anglais
didgeridoo
double bass
Eolian harp
Eolian lyre
euphonicon
flugelhorn
fortepiano
French harp
French horn
gong chimes
gramophone
grand piano
harmonicon
heptachord
hurdy-gurdy
instrument
kettle drum
lithophone
mandocello
mellophone
mouth-organ
oboe d' amore
ophicleide
pentachord
percussion
phonograph
pianoforte
piano-organ
saxotromba
sleighbell
soprano sax
sousaphone
spitzharpe
squeeze-box
Stradivari
string band
symphonion
symphonium
tamboureen

tambourine
thumb piano
tin whistle
tuning fork
vibraphone

11

Aeolian harp
Aeolian lyre
angel chimes
baritone sax
barrel organ
bell cittern
bladder pipe
cinema organ
fipple flute
German flute
graphophone
guitar-banjo
harmoniphon
harpsichord
heckelphone
hunting horn
hydraulicon
nickelodeon
orchestrina
orchestrion
piano-violin
player-piano
sleighbells
steel guitar
talking drum
viola d' amore
viol da gamba
violoncello
wobble-board

12

alto clarinet
alto trombone
bass recorder
cembal d' ambre
chamber organ

Chinese block
clavicembalo
concert grand
gansa gambang
gansa jongkok
glockenspiel
Hammond organ
hi-hat cymbals
kanteleharpe
mandolinetto
metallophone
military band
pandean pipes
penny whistle
rhythm guitar
sarrusophone
shoulder harp
Stradivarius
theatre organ
tromba marina
tubular bells
ukulele-banjo
upright piano
viola da gamba
whistle flute

13
alto saxophone
American organ
banjo-mandolin
contrabassoon
contrafagotto
cornet--piston
double bassoon
electric organ
hammerklavier
heckelclarina
marine trumpet
panharmonicon
positive organ
slide trombone
Swanee whistle
tenor recorder
tintinnabulum
valve trombone
viola bastarda

14
banjo-mandoline

brass instrument
clarinet d' amore
clavicytherium
electric guitar
flute-flageolet
piano accordion
regimental band
tenor saxophone
treble recorder
wind instrument

15 +
baritone saxophone
classical guitar
descant recorder
instrumentalist
Moog synthesizer
percussion instru-
  ment
soprano recorder
soprano saxophone
string instrument
string quartette
woodwind instru-
  ment

Musical terms

1
A
B
C
D
E
F
f
G
p

2
al
CD
DC
do
fa
EP
ff
fz
Hz
la
LP
me

mf
mi
mp
pp
re
sf
si
te
ud
ut

3
aak

air
alt
bar
bis
bop
bow
cue
dim
doh
duo
fah
gig
hum
jig

key
lah
lay
nut
ped
peg
pin
piu
piz
pop
rag
ray
rib
rit

run
sfz
ska
soh
sol
ten
tie
vox

4
alla
alto
arco

aria
arja
ayre
band
base
bass
beat
book
brio
buka
capo
clef
coda
desk

Musical terms

disc	riff	belly	kyrie	segno	valve
disk	ring	blare	largo	segue	vocal
duet	rock	blues	lento	senza	voice
echo	roll	break	lyric	shake	volta
fine	root	breve	major	sharp	volti
flat	rote	buffa	march	shift	waist
flue	scat	buffo	meter	sixth	waltz
form	sign	canon	mezzo	slide	wrest
fret	sing	canto	minim	soave	yodel
frog	sino	carol	minor	sol-fa	zoppa
glee	slur	catch	molto	sound	
heel	solo	cento	mosso	staff	
hi-fi	song	chant	motet	stave	**6**
high	soul	chime	motif	stick	
hold	stop	choir	music	stomp	accent
hymn	tail	chord	Muzak	strum	accord
jack	tape	clang	ninth	suite	action
jazz	time	clank	nodal	swell	adagio
jive	toll	comma	nonet	swing	al fine
lead	tone	conga	octet	table	answer
Lied	trad	Credo	opera	tacet	anthem
lilt	trio	croma	paean	tango	arioso
mass	tune	crook	pause	tanto	atonal
mese	turn	croon	pavan	tardo	attack
mode	vamp	dance	pedal	tempo	attune
mono	vivo	dirge	piano	tenor	aubade
mood	voce	ditty	piece	tenth	ballad
mort	voix	dolce	pieno	theme	ballet
moto	wind	drone	piper	third	beebop
mute	wood	dumka	pitch	thrum	beemol
neck	work	duple	polka	tiple	bolero
node		elegy	primo	title	boogie
note		etude	psalm	tonic	bourée
opus	**5**	f-hole	quasi	tonus	bridge
part		fifth	quill	touch	bugler
peal	acuta	forte	quint	triad	burden
play	ad lib	fugal	reply	trill	cadent
poco	album	fugue	resin	trite	can-can
port	arsis	galop	rondo	trope	cantor
punk	assai	gamut	round	tuner	cantus
raga	atone	gigue	samba	tutti	catgut
rall	barré	grace	sansa	twang	chaunt
reed	basso	grave	scale	up-bow	chiuso
reel	basta	hertz	scena	valse	choral
rest	baton	knell	score	value	choric
	bebop				chorus

contra	minuet	tenuto	big nabd	down-bow
crooks	monody	tercet	bitonal	drummer
da capo	morris	tierce	bravura	epicede
damper	motive	timbre	buccina	episode
design	niente	treble	cadence	estinto
diesis	nobile	tongue	cadency	euphony
ditone	oboist	treble	cadenza	eutonia
divisi	octave	triple	calando	fanfare
divoto	off-key	tune up	calypso	fermata
Dorian	ottava	tuning	cantata	fiddler
duetto	pavane	unison	canzona	flatten
eighth	peg-box	up-beat	canzone	flutist
encore	phrase	vamper	caprice	fuguist
entrée	piston	veloce	carioca	furioso
euphon	plagal	vivace	casette	gavotte
facile	plaint	volata	celeste	giocoso
fading	player	volume	cellist	gravita
figure	presto	warble	chamade	gravity
finale	quaver		chanson	G-string
fipple	record		chorale	harmony
follia	reggae	**7**	clapper	harpist
fourth	repeat		codetta	juke-box
fugato	revert	Aeolian	comique	keynote
fujara	retenu	aeolist	compass	lullaby
gallop	rhythm	agitato	con brio	machine
giusto	rubato	allegro	concert	maestro
ground	scales	al segno	conduct	marcato
hammer	second	amoroso	console	mazurka
hummel	sempre	andante	coranto	measure
intone	sennet	angelot	counter	mediant
Ionian	septet	animato	coupler	melisma
jingle	serial	apotome	courant	melodic
lament	sestet	apotomy	cremona	middle C
leader	sextet	arietta	crooner	mistune
legato	shanty	ariette	csardas	morbido
Lieder	singer	ars nova	czardas	mordent
litany	sketch	art-song	descant	morendo
lutist	snatch	attacca	descend	musette
Lydian	sonata	attuned	descent	musical
lyrics	stanza	backing	diagram	natural
lyrist	stereo	balance	dichord	nonette
manual	strain	ballade	diplice	octette
marcia	string	Baroque	discord	offbeat
medley	subito	bassist	distune	organum
melody	tattoo	battery	dolente	partita
		bellows		

Musical terms

pesante	sospiro	canticle	fandango	musicale
pianist	spagane	canzonet	fantasia	musician
pibcorn	stopped	castrato	fantasie	nocturne
pibroch	stretto	cavatina	festival	nonuplet
piffaro	strings	chaconne	flamenco	notation
piffero	strophe	chevalet	flautist	notturno
playing	sub-bass	cheville	flourish	obligato
plectre	subject	col canto	folk song	octuplet
pomposo	syncope	composer	folk tune	open note
pop song	taborer	composto	forzando	operatic
posaune	taboret	con amore	fughetta	operetta
prelude	tambura	con anima	galement	oratorio
quartet	tipping	concerto	galliard	organist
quintet	toccata	con fuoco	grazioso	ostinato
quinton	tone-row	conjusto	half-note	overtone
ragtime	tremolo	con mosso	harmonic	overture
rastrum	triplet	continuo	high note	part-song
recital	tuneful	courante	hornpipe	pastiche
refrain	twelfth	cromorna	infinito	pastoral
reprise	vamping	crotchet	interval	phantasy
requiem	vespers	dal segno	intonate	phrasing
ripieno	vibrato	demi-tone	isotonic	Phrygian
romance	violist	diapason	jongleur	plectrum
rondeau	voicing	diatonic	keyboard	pop music
rondino		diminish	langspil	portando
rosalia		doloroso	lentando	position
roulade	**8**	dominant	libretto	practice
Sanctus	a battuta	down beat	ligature	practise
scherzo	absonant	doxology	love-song	preludio
schisma	Agnus Dei	drumbeat	lutanist	putorino
sciolto	alto clef	drum-head	lutenist	register
scoring	animando	duettino	madrigal	resonant
secondo	antiphon	duettist	maestoso	response
septole	arpeggio	dulciana	major key	rhapsody
setting	backbeat	eleventh	melodics	rigadoon
settino	baritone	energico	melodist	rigaudon
seventh	barytone	ensemble	melodize	ritenuto
singing	bassetto	entr' acte	minor key	saraband
skiffle	bass note	euphonic	minstrel	semitone
slurred	bel canto	euphonon	miserere	septette
soloist	berceuse	evensong	moderato	sequence
song hit	blue note	exercise	modulate	serenade
soprano	boat song	faburden	monotone	serenata
sordino	brillant	falderal	monotony	sestetto
sordone	cake-walk	falsetto	movement	sextette

sforzato	allemande	flute-stop	monochord
sinfonia	andamento	folk music	monophony
sing-song	andantino	full organ	monotonic
smorzato	antiphony	full score	music book
sonajero	arabesque	frequency	obbligato
sonatina	arpanetta	furibondo	octachord
song form	atonality	gallopade	orchestra
songster	augmented	generator	organ-pipe
sound-bar	bacchanal	glissando	part music
sound-box	bagatelle	grace-note	paso doble
sourdine	bandstand	gradation	pastorale
spiccato	barcarole	grandioso	pianolist
staccato	barn dance	Gregorian	pizzicato
sticcado	bassonore	guitarist	plainsong
stopping	bow-string	half-close	polonaise
subtonic	brass band	half-shift	polyphony
symmetry	brillante	harmonics	polytonal
symphony	bugle call	harmonize	pressando
syntonic	cacophony	hexachord	principal
tabourer	cantabile	high pitch	quadrille
tabouret	cantilena	high-toned	quartette
tarogato	capriccio	homophony	quintette
terzetto	cassation	honky-tonk	quodlibet
threnody	charivari	imbroglio	recording
timoroso	chromatic	imitation	rehearsal
tonalist	conductor	impromptu	rendering
tonality	consonate	improvise	rendition
tone down	contralto	in harmony	resonance
tone poem	crescendo	inner part	resonator
trad jazz	dance tune	interlude	rhythmics
tremando	dead march	intonation	ricercare
trichord	death-bell	invention	rock' n' roll
vigoroso	decachord	inversion	roundelay
virtuoso	deep-toned	irregular	selection
vocalism	dissonant	lagrimoso	semibreve
vocalist	dithyramb	languente	semitonic
voce colo	Dixieland	larghetto	septimole
warbling	double bar	leger-line	seraphine
woodwind	drumstick	leitmotif	septuplet
	elevation	leitmotiv	sextuplet
	euphonism	melodious	sforzando
9	euphonize	meno mosso	siciliana
	extempore	metronome	siciliano
accompany	farandole	mezzo voce	signature
acoustics	fingering	modulator	slow march
adagietto			

soft pedal
solfeggio
sollecito
song cycle
sopranist
sostenuto
sotto voce
sound-hole
sound-post
spiritosa
spiritual
steel band
strascino
strumming
succentor
symphonic
syncopate
tablature
tail-piece
tenor bass
tenor clef
tessitura
theme song
theorbist
timpanist
toccatina
torch-song
trillando
troubador
trumpeter
tuning-key
tuning-peg
twelve-row
tympanist
unmusical
untunable
variation
violinist
voluntary
vox humana
whistling
wind chest

10

accidental
adaptation
added sixth
affettuoso
allargando
allegretto
appoggiato
background
bandmaster
barcarolle
bassanello
bassoonist
binary form
binotonous
bitonality
cantatrice
cantillate
canto fermo
canzonetta
chiroplast
colascione
coloratura
comic opera
common time
complement
concertino
consonance
consonancy
con spirito
continuato
cornettist
corroboree
dance music
demi-ditone
diastaltic
diminished
diminuendo
discordant
disharmony
dissonance
dissonancy
dolcemente
Dorian mode

dotted note
double-flat
double time
eisteddfod
embouchure
enharmonic
escapement
euphonious
exposition
expression
finger-hole
folk singer
fortissimo
gramophone
grand opera
ground bass
heavy metal
homophonic
humoresque
incidental
instrument
intermezzo
intonation
jam session
lentamente
light music
light opera
Lydian mode
mainstream
major chord
major scale
major third
meditation
mezzoforte
minor chord
minor scale
minor third
minstrelsy
Mixolydian
modern jazz
modulation
monotonous
mouth music
mouthpiece
musicality

musica viva
music-drama
musicology
music-stand
music-stool
nobilmente
opera buffa
opera music
opera seria
orchestral
organ-point
patter-song
pedal-board
pedal organ
pedal point
pentachord
percussion
phonograph
pianissimo
piano stool
piped music
plainchant
polyphonic
portamento
prima donna
quadruplet
quintuplet
recitative
recitativo
rehearsing
repertoire
repetition
resolution
ritardando
ritornello
rockabilly
scherzando
semiquaver
sonata form
sound-board
sourdeline
staphyline
strathspey
strepitoso
string band

stringendo
submediant
supertonic
suspension
symphonist
syncopated
syncopator
swing music
tarantella
tetrachord
theme music
tonic chord
tonic major
tonic minor
tonic sol-fa
triple time
transition
treble clef
triple time
trombonist
tuning fork
twelve-note
twelve-tone
undulation
variamento
virtuosity
vistomente
vocal music
water music

11

accelerando
Aeolian mode
affrettando
alla capella
alto-ripieno
arrangement
ballad opera
bene-placito
bothy ballad
broken chord
canned music
capriccioso
chansonette

church music
clairschach
clarion note
common chord
composition
concertante
contra-basso
contrapunto
contra-tenor
counterpart
decrescendo
demi-cadence
development
diatessaron
discordance
discordancy
double-sharp
equisonance
extemporize
fiddlestick
figured bass
fingerboard
first violin
fundamental
gospel music
harmonizing
high-pitched
hunting song
incantation
leading note
madrigalist

12

mandolinist
minnesinger
music master
natural note
nickelodeon
open cadence
open harmony
opera bouffe
orchestrate
partial note
passacaglia
passing note
performance
polyphonism

prestissimo
progression
quarter-note
quarter-tone
rallentando
rock and roll
recessional
sacred music
saxophonist
schottische
senza rigore
square dance
stereophony
string music
subdominant
subsemitone
symphonious
syncopation
temperament
torch singer
transposing
transposing
tridiapason
unaccordant
vivacissimo
voce-di-petto
voce-di-testa
volti-subito

12

acciaccatura
accordionist
acoustic bass
alla cappella
allegrissimo
anticipation
appassionata
appoggiatura
assai allegro
audio casette
augmentation
backing group
bass baritone
boogie-woogie

cantus firmus
chamber music
chromaticism
clarinettist
close harmony
comedy ballet
compound time
concert pitch
concert waltz
contrapuntal
counterpoint
counter-tenor
divertimento
double-octave
extravaganza
false cadence
funeral march
high fidelity
inharmonious
instrumental
introduction
key signature
leggeramente
melodic minoe
mezzo-relievo
mezzo-soprano
military band
moto perpetuo
musical drama
musicologist
natural scale
opera comique
orchestrator
organ grinder
organ recital
passion music
perfect fifth
perfect pitch
philharmonic
philomusical
Phrygian mode
polytonality
quadraphonic
quadrophonic
registration

repercussion
sight-reading
sounding post
spheremelody
stereophonic
thorough-bass
vocalization
wedding march

13

absolute pitch
accompaniment
basso profondo
choral singing
closed cadence
common measure
concrete music
concertmaster
conservatoire
disharmonious
false relation
gospel singing
Gregorian mode
harmonic chord
harmonic minor
improvisation
musical comedy
music festival
operatic music

orchestration
plagal cadence
ranz-des-vaches
serialization
signature tune
sol-fa notation
staff notation
string octette
string quartet
superdominant
tetradiapason
time signature
transcription
transposition
violoncellist

14

Ambrosian chant
chromatic scale
contrary motion
demi-semi-quaver
direct interval
double-stopping
Gregorian chant
interpretation
mainstream jazz
Mixolydian mode
national anthem
perfect cadence

programme music
recapitulation
reed instrument
regimental band
wind instrument

15 +

augmented seventh
barber-shop quartet
barber-shop singing
brass instrument
diminished seventh
double-tongueing
electronic music
incidental music
instrumentalist
instrumentation
musical director
musique concrete
percussion instru-
    ment
perfect interval
serial technique
string instrument
string quartette
symphony concert
traditional jazz
triple-tongueing
woodwind instrument

Mythology

Mythology

2 & 3
Ate
Eos
Ge
Hel
Io
Ino
Nox
Nyx

Ops
Orc
Roc
Tiu
Tyr

4
Ajax
Ares

Argo
Dido
Echo
Eden
Eris
faun
Gaea
Garm
Hebe
Hera

Iris
Isis
Juno
Leda
Leto
Loki
Maia
Mara
Ogam
Rhea

Styx
Troy
Tyro

5
Aegle
Aegus
Aello
Aeson

Arcas
Arges
Argus
Arion
Asura
Atlas
Balor
Belus
Cernu
Chaos

Chloë	Wotan	Neleus	Coronis	Zagreus
Circe		nymphs	Cyanean	
Creon		Osiris	Cyclops	
Ceryx	**6**	Orthos	Cyzicus	**8**
Danae	Adonis	Pelion	Daphnis	Absyrtus
Delos	Aeacus	Pelias	Demeter	Achilles
dryad	Aeetes	Phoebe	Diomede	Aglaucus
Fates	Aegeus	Pollux	Echidna	Alcestis
Hades	Aegina	Psyche	Eleusis	Alcimede
Harpy	Agenor	Scylla	Elysium	ambrosia
Helen	Alecto	Semele	Erinyes	Anacreon
Helle	Amazon	Selene	Euryale	Antigone
Herse	Amycus	Sirens	Gorgons	Apollyon
Hydra	Apollo	Sphinx	Glaucus	Atalanta
ichor	Areion	Stheno	Goeteia	Arethusa
Ilium	Athene	Teucer	griffin	basilisk
Irene	Athens	Tiphys	griffon	Bebryces
Ixion	Boreas	Titans	gryphon	Bithynia
Jason	Cadmus	Triton	Harpies	Brunhild
Kakon	Castor	Typhon	Jocasta	Brynhild
Ladon	Chione	Uranus	Megaera	Caduceus
Laius	Chiron	Zethus	Minoans	Callisto
Lethe	Charon		Nemesis	Caucasus
Medea	Clotho		Nephele	Cephalus
Medus	Cybele	**7**	Ocypete	Cerberus
Metis	Europa	Achates	Oedipus	Chimaera
Midas	Fenrir	Actaeon	Olympus	Daedalus
Minos	Furies	Alcides	Orestes	Damocles
Muses	fylgja	Alcmene	Orpheus	Dardanus
naiad	Geryon	Amphion	Orthrus	Dionysus
Niobe	Gorgon	Ancaeus	Pandora	Doliones
Nisus	Hector	Antaeus	Pegasus	Endymion
Orion	Helios	Antenor	Perseus	Erytheia
Paris	Hermes	Antiope	Phineus	Eumolpus
Perse	Hyades	Artemis	Phoenix	Euphemus
Phebe	Hygeia	Astarte	Phrixus	Eurydice
Priam	Icarus	Athamas	Pyrrhus	Eurynome
Remus	Ithaca	Atropos	Pyramus	Ganymede
Runes	Kronos	Brontes	Podarge	Hamingja
satyr	Mageia	Busiris	Romulus	Heracles
Sibyl	Matres	Celaeno	Stentor	Hercules
Siren	Medusa	centaur	Telamon	Hesperus
Talos	Megara	Chimera	Theseus	Hyperion
Tegea	Mopsus	Chloris	Ulysses	Lachesis
Woden	nectar	Colchis	Xanthus	Lapithae

Menelaus
Minotaur
Nauplius
Nausicaa
Odysseus
Olympian
Pleiades
Poseidon
Ragnarok
Sarpedon
Sleipnir
Steropes
Tantalus
Tartarus
Thessaly
Thyestes
Tiresias
Typhoeus
Valhalla
Windingo

9

Agememnon
Archelous
Argonauts
Asclepius
Autolycus
Bosphorus
Charybdis
Deianoira
Eumenides
Gilgamesh
Iphigenia
Narcissus
Parnassus
Parthenon
Philomela
Polynices
Pygmalion
Scamander
Thersites
Tisiphone

Valkyries
Yggdrasil

10

Amphimarus
Amphitrite
Amphitryon
Brünnhilde
Bucephalus
Dii majores
Dii minores
Fenriswolf
Hephaestus
Hesperides
Hippodamia
Orchomenus
Persephone
Polyphemus
Polydeuces
Procrustes
Prometheus

Proserpina
Proserpine
Telemachus

11

Aesculapios
Amphilocous
Bellerophon
Euphrostyne
Helen of Troy
Lyssianassa
Philoctetes

12 +

Castor and Pollux
Cyanean Rocks
Golden Fleece
Golden Apples
Hecatoncheires
Hesperethusa
Rhadamanthus
Romulus and Remus

Numbers 1 to 10 in various languages

English	French	German	Greek	Italian
one	un	ein	heis	uno
two	deux	zwei	duo	due
three	trois	drei	treis	tre
four	quatre	vier	tessares	quattro
five	cinq	funf	pente	cinque
six	six	sechs	hex	sei
seven	sept	sieben	hepta	sette
eight	huit	acht	okto	otto
nine	neuf	neun	ennea	nove
ten	dix	zehn	deka	dieci

English	Latin	Portugese	Spanish
(one)	unus/unum	um/uma	uno
(two)	duus/duum	dois	dos
(three)	tres/tria	tres	tres
(four)	quatuor	quatro	cuatro
(five)	quinque	cinco	cinco
(six)	sex	seis	seis
(seven)	septem	sete	siete
(eight)	octo	oito	ocho
(nine)	novem	nove	nueve
(ten)	decem	dez	diez

Operas and their characters

Operas

4 & 5
Aida
Aleko
Calaf
Faen
Faust
Halka
Iris
Lakme
Manon
Manru
Mavra
Medée
Mlada
Norma
Sapho
Sarka
Teseo
Thais
Tosca
Uthal
Zaide
Zaza

6
Alcina
Almira
Alzira
Amadis
Aniara
Attila
Carmen
Hamlet
Joseph
Julian
Mignon
Nerone
Oberon
Otello
Salomé
Sigurd
Tarare
Ulisse

7
Aladdin
Alceste
Arianna

Arminio
Bank Ban
Dalibor
Guntraw
Irmelin
Isabeau
Ivanhoe
L' Aiglon
La Juive
La Wally
Lowland
Macbeth
Mazeppa
Nabucco
Nose, The
Olympia
Orlando
Ormindo
Rusalka
Savitri
Wozzeck
Yolande

Berenice
Deidamia
Ebn-Hakia
Fevernot
Giustino
Gloriana
Goyescas
Guiditta
Ice Break
Jessonda
John Hary
La Boheme
Le Roi d' Ys
Loddiska
Maritana
Masks, The
May Night
Mona Lisa
Parisina
Polituto
Scipione
Tiefland
Turandot

8
Ariodant

9

Abu Hassan
Africaine
Agrippina
Angelique
Belisario
Billy Budd
Campiello
Capriccio
Cardillac
Consul, The
Der Vampyr
Dybbuk, The
Hary Janos
Herodiade
Il Tabarro
I Puritani
Joan of Arc
King Priam
King Roger
La Calisto
La Rondine
L' Erismena
Lodoletta
Löhengrin
Maskarade
Mother, The
Pagliacci
Perichole
Rigoletto
Rodelinda
Secret, The
Stiffelio

10

Alessandro
Anna Bolena
Archers, The
Artaxerxes
Danton' s Tod
Der Revisor
Devil' s Walk
Die Abreise

Donna Diana
Don Rodrigo
Fra Diavolo
Fra Gherado
Griselidis
Gwendoline
Intermezzo
Jacobin, The
Kazakhstan
L' Arlesiana
L' Atlantide
La Traviata
Le Comte Ory
Le Maschere
Le Prophete
Les Martyrs
Les Troyens
Masnadieri
Monna Vanna
Semiramide
Swallow, The
Tannhauser
Trojans, The
Uzbekistan

11

Dead City, The
Die Soldaten
Doktor Faust
Don Giovanni
Don Pasquale
I Due Foscari
Il Duca D' Alba
Il Trovatore
Jean de Paris
John of Paris
King of Ys, The
L' Amico Fritz
La Nazaraise
La Straniera
La Vida Breve
Mefistofele
Night Flight
Noyes Fludde

Peter Grimes
Prisoner, The
Si j' etais Roi
Volo di Notte
War and Peace
William Tell

12

Ban of Love, The
Bassarids, The
Boris Godunov
Cosi Fan Tutte
Danton' s Death
Debora Jaele
Die Tote Stadt
Foreigner, The
Giulio Cesare
Kath Kabanova
Konigskinder
La Somnabula
Le Domino Noir
Les Huguenots
L' Oca del Cairo
Manon Lescaut
Maria di Rohan
Maria Stuarda
Moses und Aron
Olympians, The
Owen Wingrave
Porgy and Bess

13

Albert Herring
Andrea Chenier
Death in Venice
Der Corregidor
Der Freischutz
Die Drei Pintos
Fairy Queen, The
Giovanna d' Arco
Guillaume Tell
Hugh the Drover
Hunyadi Laszlo

Il Prigioniero
Khovanshchina
King's Henchmen
Knot Garden, The
La Cenerentola
La Reine de Saba
La Scala di Seta
L' Elisir d' amor
Marino Fallero
Merrie England
Mother of Us All
Peter Ibbetson
Poor Sailor, The
Sir John in Love
Snow Maiden, The
Tenderland, The
Torquato Tasso
Tsar' s Bride, The

14

A Night in Venice
Castor et Pollux
Decembrists, The
Der Dorfbarbier
Devils of London
Die Berglnappen
Henry the Eighth
Il Piccolo Marat
Irische Legende
Jonny Soielt Auf
La Donna del Lago
L' Amore del Tre Re
Le Pré aux Clercs
Lucrezia Borgia
Madame Sans Gene
Perfect Fool, The
Riders to the Sea
Robert le Diable
Robert the Devil
Samson et Dalila
Silent Woman, The
Sleepwalker, The
Spanish Hour, The

15

A Life for the Tsar
Beatrice di Tenda
Beggars Opera, The
Bohemian Girl, The
Das Liebesverbot
Devil and Kate, The
Down in the Valley
Fair Maid of Perth
Goose of Cairo, The
Hansel and Gretel
Immortal Hour, The
Le Nozze di Figaro
Le Pauvre Matelôt
L' Heure Espagnole
Madame Butterfly
Orphée aux Enfers
Pearl Fishers, The
Poisoned Kiss, The
Queen of Sheba, The
Riders to the Sea
Romeo et Juliette
Simon Boccanegra
Tale of Two Cities

16

Benvenuto Cellini
La Buona Figliuola
L' Attaque de Moulin
Linda di Chamounix
Queen of Spades, The
Rakes Progress, The
Royal Children, The
Samson and Delilah
Tristan und Isolda

17

Adriana Lecouvreur
Barber of Bagdad, The
Boatswain' s Mate, The
Boulevard Solitude
Die Königin von Saba

Operas and their characters

Flying Dutchman, The
Force of Destiny, The
Francesca da Rimini
Gentle Shepherd, The
Guglielmo Ratcliff
Iphigenie en Aulide
I Puritan di Scozia
La Campana Sommersa
La Forza del Destino
La Muette de Portici
L' Italiana in Algeri
Lucia di Lammermoor
Madonna' s Jewels, The
Makropoulos Affair
Midsummer Marriage
Mozart and Salliers
Rape of Lucretia, The
Re di Creta Idomenso
Ruslan and Lyudmila
Turn of the Screw, The

18

Beatrice et Benedict
Die Schweigsame Frau
Eine Nacht in Venedig
Il Filosolo di Campagna
Il Crociato in Egitto
Iphigenie en Tauride
La Finta Giardiniera
Le Austuzie Femminili
Le Maître de Chapelle
Les Contes d' Hoffmann
Les Malheurs d' Orphée
Richard Coeur de Lion
Story of a Real Man, The

19

Admento re di Tessaglia
Allesa ndro Stradella
Cavelleria Rusticana
Der Barbier von Bagdad
Die Agyptische Helena
Die Frau Öhne Schatten
Elegy for Young Lovers
Il Campanello di Notte
Il Matrimonio Segreto
La Jolie fille de Perth
Les Pêcheurs de Perles
Marriage of Figaro, The
Much Ado About Nothing
Pilgrim' s Progress, The
Secret of Marriage, The
Sorrows of Orpheus, The

20 +

Besuch der Alten Dame Der
Coronation of Poppea, The
Cunning Little Vixen, The
Der Fliegende Hollander
Dialogues des Carmelites
Duke Bluebeard' s Castle
Dumb Girl of Portici, The
Gioielli della Madonna
Girl of the Golden West, The
I Capuleti e I Montecchi
Italian Girl in Algiers
La Cambiale di Matrimonio
Les Cloches de Cornville
L' Incoronazione di Poppea
Merry Wives of Windsor, The
Midsummer Night' s Dream, A
Orpheus in the Underworld
Travelling Companion, The

Operatic characters

3	Asa	Eva	Liu	Meg	Ugo	4
Ada	Cas	Lel	Mab	Mel		Aron
	Dov	Lev	Max	Pan		

Bess
Cuno
Duke
Elsa
Emmy
Ezio
Finn
Hero
Hugh
Iago
Ilia
Iris
Inez
Jack
Joan
Jove
Juno
Kate
Kath
Leah
Lina
Lola
Lucy
Luke
Manz
Mark
Mary
Mimi
Mino
Moth
Nero
Nils
Nora
Olga
Omar
Owen
Oros
Paco
Paul
Pisa
Puck
Rose
Sali
Snug
Thea

Tita
Toni
Ursa
Wurm
Yuri
Zaza

5

Adele
Adina
Agnes
Alain
Aleen
Aleko
Alfio
Alice
Amina
Anita
Armel
Assad
Assur
Aubry
Avito
Barak
Bassi
Bella
Benda
Benes
Beppe
Bobyl
Canio
Carlo
Chloe
Crown
Dalva
Danae
Diana
Edgar
Etain
Faber
Fanny
Faust
Fides
Flora

Flute
Folco
Frank
Fritz
Gayle
Gilda
Gomez
Grant
Groma
Guido
Hanna
Helen
Henry
Herod
Jacob
Julia
Kyoto
Lapak
Laura
Levko
Leila
Lilla
Linda
Luigi
Luisa
Luise
Lykov
Mamon
Manru
Maria
Magda
Marti
Mauri
Melot
Midas
Midir
Moses
Mylio
Nadir
Naina
Nancy
Nardo
Nedda
Norma
Orest

Osaka
Osmin
Paolo
Paris
Pasha
Pedro
Pimen
Polly
Porgy
Priam
Rajah
Ralph
Ramon
Reiza
Romeo
Salvo
Sapho
Senta
Silva
Simon
Snook
Snout
Suzel
Tasso
Thais
Tisbe
Tonio
Tosca
Trott
Ulana
Venus
Zaide

6

Adolar
Agatha
Agnese
Alaide
Alfred
Alexey
Alvise
Amalia
Amelia
Aminta

Amazil
Andres
Andrea
Andrey
Annina
Armida
Arnold
Arsace
Arturo
Astron
Balkis
Becket
Bertha
Blonde
Bottom
Castor
Chanon
Claire
Cobweb
Ctirad
Cyrano
Daland
Daphne
Daudon
Denise
Dmitry
Dorvil
Eadgar
Egmont
Elvino
Elvira
Enrico
Ernani
Fabien
Fanuel
Farlaf
Fatima
Fatime
Fiesco
Figaro
Gerald
Gerard
Giulia
Gomatz
Gilfen

Hannah
Hecuba
Hector
Hermes
Hermio
Janthe
Janusz
Judith
Julien
Kaspar
Kunrad
Kupava
Lensky
Libuse
Lionel
Lockit
Louise
Lubino
Luther
Lycoan
Mangus
Martha
Maurya
Mignon
Milada
Miller
Minnie
Mizgir
Mozart
Nadori
Nerone
Noriva
Oberon
Ortrud
Otello
Ottone
Pollux
Pompeo
Poppea
Phoebe
Premys
Quince
Ramiro
Rachel
Robert

Operas and their characters

Roxane
Rozenn
Ruslan
Salomé
Samiel
Samson
Selika
Seneca
Silvio
Shadow
Sophie
Spring
Stella
Suzuki
Taddeo
Thisbe
Tichon
Timida
Vasily
Zamord
Zdenek

7

Adriano
Aegisth
Aladino
Aleskey
Alidono
Alfonso
Allazim
Amneris
Antinea
Antonia
Araquil
Armanro
Arminda
Asteria
Atlanta
Baculus
Barbara
Barnaba
Bartley
Bartolo
Basilio

Bellina
Belmont
Berlioz
Bertram
Calisto
Cellini
Charles
Charlot
Chemier
Chrudos
Claudia
Corrado
Dandini
Delaqua
Delilah
Despina
Die Feen
Douglas
Edoardo
Eleazar
Elektra
Ernesto
Eugenia
Ferrano
Fidelia
Foresto
Gellner
Gennaro
Germont
Geronte
Giacomo
Grigory
Guntran
Harasta
Hermann
Hoffman
Irmelin
Isolier
Jacobin
Jenifer
Juliett
Jupiter
Koanger
Krasava
Kudrjas

La Cieca
Leander
Leonora
Lesbina
Lescaut
Licinio
Lindoro
Lorenzo
Lysiart
Macbeth
MacDuff
Malcolm
Mariola
Masetto
May King
Mazeppa
Mercury
Metifio
Micaela
Michele
Missail
Musetta
Nabucco
Natasha
Nelusko
Octavia
Olympia
Ottavio
Orpheus
Palmide
Palmyra
Paolino
Parasha
Pauline
Paquiro
Piquillo
Pope Leo
Poliuto
Radames
Rambaud
Rinaldo
Rivière
Rodolfo
Romanov
Rosario

Rossane
Ruggero
Rusalka
Salieri
Shuisky
Slender
Sobinin
Sperata
Stahlay
Stankar
Statire
Susanin
Tatyana
Telaira
Terynka
Tigrana
Titzkan
Tristan
Trouble
Turiddu
Tytania
Variaam
Varvara
Vincent
Vivette
Wolfram
Wozzeck
Zempira
Zerlina

8

Achilles
Adalgisa
Adrienne
Aennchem
Alphonso
Almansor
Amonasro
Ambrosio
Angelina
Antonida
Aristeau
Beatrice
Blondell

Boniface
Brangane
Carolina
Cathleen
Claggart
Clarrisa
Cleophas
Clorinda
Comte Ory
Die Kluge
Don Pinto
Drusilla
Dufresne
Elmireno
Elisetta
Eochaida
Eutripio
Euridice
Eurydice
Fernando
Filandro
Floreski
Freihild
Geronimo
Giampolo
Giocondo
Giovanni
Gonsalve
Gretchen
Gryaznoy
Heinrich
Huguette
I Damante
Isabella
Isoletae
Jezibaba
Juliette
King Mark
King René
Kochubey
Kutwenal
Lefebvre
Lodoiska
Lothario
Lucrezia

Lysander	Aphrodite	Justinian	Don Alfonso
Lyubasha	Bluebeard	Kabanicha	Don Lisargo
Lyudmila	Bobylikha	Katherine	Don Pttavio
MacHeath	Butterfly	King Priam	Dourlinski
Maliella	Caramello	King Roger	Duke of Alba
Manfredo	Cassandra	Loddletta	Duke Robert
Marcello	Christian	Löhengrin	Fieramosca
Margiana	Christine	Leicester	Fransquita
Margared	Cherubino	Leporello	Fra Daviolo
Marietta	Chevreuse	MacGregor	Gianciotto
Mathilde	Ciboletta	Maddalena	Gwendoline
Meleager	Colombine	Militrisa	Henry Smith
Mercedes	Constanze	Nerodiade	Khlestakov
Mercutto	Coppelius	Orombello	King Fisher
Mrs. Grose	Cio-Cio-San	Pannochka	King Harald
Mireille	Demetrius	Poppacoda	Lady Pamela
Nemorino	Desdemona	Patroclus	Lord Walton
Niclause	Des Grieux	Pinkerton	Lucy Ashton
Nourabad	Dominique	Povarikha	Marcellina
Nureddin	Donabella	Richelieu	Margherita
Odabella	Don Andres	Rigoletto	Marguerite
Olympian	Don Alvaro	Rosalinde	Mary Stuart
Pedrillo	Don Gaston	Schaunard	Miss Jessel
Pollione	Donna Anna	Sharpless	Nick Shadow
Raffaele	Dulcamara	Sherasmin	Nilakantha
Raimbaud	Eglantine	Skradella	Peter Quint
Sandrina	Elisabeth	Simon Mago	Saxon Armel
Santuzza	Euryanthe	Sosostris	Sebastiano
Serafina	Escamillo	Stiffelio	Simon Perez
Serpetia	Faramondo	Sula Smith	Sir Morosus
Serverus	Françoise	Svyetozar	Spalanzini
Somarone	Francesco	Telramund	Starveling
Stolzius	Frau Fluth	Tkachikha	Tannhauser
Tio Lucas	Frau Reich	Tsar Peter	Torquemade
Titzikan	Frederica	Valentine	Tsar Sultan
Toreador	Friedhold	Venusberg	Valdeburgo
Turandot	Giorgetta		
	Guadalett		
	Gottfried	**10**	**11**
9	Guilielmo	Aethewold	Anne Trulove
Abigaille	Hagenbach	Ann Boleyn	Baba the Turk
Adonigram	Harlequin	Boccanegra	Captain Vere
Amaryllus	Hilda Mack	Bourlinski	Chrysothems
Angelotti	I Damanteo	De Bretigny	Count of Moor
Angelique	Jack Rançe	Doctor Falke	Count Walter

Operas and their characters

Charlemagne
Dick Johnson
Doge of Genoa
Don Ruy Gomez
Duke Ferrara
Earl of Essex
Emir of Tunis
Fata Morgana
Friedenstag
George Brown
Jane Seymour
Jean Gaussin
King of Spain
King Solomon
Lady Billows
Lady Harriet
Lady Macbeth
La Perichole
Lord Ruthven
Malatestino
Massimician
Princivalle
Prince Calaf
Queen Roxane
Roderick Dhu
Snegurochka
Sparafucile
Tom Bakewell
Tormentilla
Vasca de Gama
Vasco de Saxe
William Tell

12

Baron de Mercy
Baron Douphol
Baron Soarpia
Count Douglas
Count Rodolfo
Don Magnifico
Don Triternio
Duke of Mantua
Duke of Norway
Duke of Venice

Duke of Urbino
Enzo Grimaldo
Fanny Legrand
Flora Bervoix
Hunyadi Lazlo
Madame Larina
Iola Gioconda
John of Leydon
Lord Cockburn
Miss Wingrave
Pease-blossom
Piccolo Marat
Prince Gremin
Prince Guidon
Prince Ramiro
Prince Ratmir
Quenn of Sheba
Rautendelein
Robert Storch
Spencer Coyle
Thomas Bouche
Tsar Berendey

13

Andrew Jackson
Byronic Onegin
Captain Zunica
Countess Adele
Count Robinson
Daniel Webster
Der Freischutz
Doctor Miracle
Don Inigo Gomez
Duke of Norfolk
Duke of Rothsay
Federico Manton
Friar Laurence
Il Mlle Blanche
Jacopo Foscari
Jennie Parsons
King of Castile
La Dame Blanche
L' Etoile du Nord
Major Kovalyon

Monsieur Emile
Peter Ibbetson
Prince Arindal
Queen of Spades
Sultan Aladino
Susan B. Anthony
Ulysses S. Grant

14

Alfredo Germont
Baron Desportes
Cardinal Brogni
Count Belifiore
Count of Chalais
Doctor Romaulda
Duke of Burgundy
John the Baptist
King Archibaldo
Prince Oriofsky
Queen Elizabeth
Queen Henrietta
Sir Tobias Mills
Tristan d' Acunha
William Meister

15

Catherine Glover
Colonel Ibbetson
Count of Eberbagh
Das Liebesverbot
Doctor Malatesta
Don Jose Martinez
Don Juan de Aragon
Duchess of Danzig
Duchess of Towers
Edgar Ravenswood
Der Evangelimann
Isabelle de Bearn
King Henry Eighth
Monsieur Triquet
Princess Irmelin
Princess Isabeau
Sergeant Belcore

Stella de Tolomel
William Ratcliff

16
Cardinal Salviati
Countess Cathleen
Councillor Kalina
Henry of Brunswick
Landgrave Hermann
Lord Arthur Talbot
Princess Bouillon
Princess Turandot
Princess of Navare
Sir Walter Raleigh

17
Alexander the Great

High Priest of Dagon
Katerina Izmaylova
Lord Arthur Bucklow
Marchese Attavanti
Marquis of San Marco
Parisina Malatesta

18 +
Bessie Throckmorton
Countess Violanta Onesti
Crown Prince of France
Eleandra di Scandiano
Filippo, Duke of Milan
Marguerite of Flanders
Marquis of Calatrava
Percy, Earl of Northumberland

Paper and board

2, 3 & 4
demy
ISO
leaf
MF
MG
post
pot
pott
ream
SG

5
atlas
brief
crown
folio
royal

6
bag cap
casing
metric
octavo
quarto
tissue

7
airmail
emperor
imperial
kent cap

8
artboard
art paper

elephant
foolscap
haven cap
imperial
quad demy

9
cartridge
cardboard
chipboard
colombier
large post
music demy
newsprint
onionskin
pulp board
quad crown
quad sheet

10
bible paper
double demy
double post
grand eagle
India paper
pasteboard
small royal
strawboard
super royal

11
antiquarian
crown quarto
double crown
imperial cap
pinched post
ticket board

12
drawing board
imitation art
quad foolscap

14
double elephant
double foolscap
double imperial
lined chipboard

15
double large post
double quad crown
double four pound

13
mounting board

Parts of the body

2 & 3	gene	ankle	organ	**6**	genome
ADP	gums	aorta	ovary		gullet
arm	hair	atlas	penis	airway	humour
ATP	hand	blood	pinna	areola	kidney
CNS	head	bowel	pubis	armpit	lanugo
DNA	heel	brain	pulse	artery	larynx
ear	iris	bursa	pupil	atrium	lobule
egg	knee	chord	renin	axilla	lumbar
eye	lens	cilia	semen	biceps	marrow
fat	lips	colon	serum	breast	muscle
gut	lobe	cones	sinus	caecum	myelin
hip	lung	elbow	skull	canine	myosin
jaw	nail	femur	sperm	carpal	neuron
leg	node	gland	spine	carpus	nipple
LH	nose	gonad	talus	cervix	nodule
RNA	ovum	groin	tears	coccyx	palate
rib	pore	heart	teeth	corium	pelvis
rod	ribs	hymen	thumb	cornea	pepsin
toe	rods	ileum	tibia	cortex	plasma
	skin	ilium	tinea	dermis	pleura
	ulna	incus	tooth	earwax	plexus
4	urea	joint	tract	embryo	radius
	wart	labia	trunk	enzyme	rectum
ACTH	womb	liver	urine	eyelid	rennin
anus	ulna	lymph	uvula	faeces	retina
axis	vein	molar	valve	fascia	sacrum
axon		mucus	vulva	fibula	saliva
bile		navel	wrist	flexor	sclera
bone	**5**	nerve		foetus	septum
disc		nares		fundus	smegma
cell	actin	orbit		gamete	socket
foot					

spleen
tarsal
tarsus
tendon
testis
thorax
thymus
tissue
tongue
ureter
uterus
vagina
venule
villus

7

abdomen
agonist
albumin
auricle
bladder
calcium
capsule
cardiac
carotid
choroid
cochlea
condyle
cranium
cuticle
eardrum
ethmoid
eyelash
femoral
fimbria
glottis
gristle
heparin
hormone
humerus
incisor
insulin
ischium
jejunum

malleus
mastoid
maxilla
medulla
melanin
neurone
nucleus
ossicle
papilla
patella
phallus
pharynx
prepuce
protein
pudenda
pylorus
scapula
scrotum
sternum
stomach
tonsils
trachea
urethra
vacuole
viscera

8

adenoids
alveolus
androgen
backbone
bile duct
bronchus
cerebrum
chlorine
clitoris
clavicle
collagen
cortisol
dendrite
duodenum
extensor
filament
follicle

foreskin
ganglion
globulin
glucagon
incisors
inner ear
ligament
mandible
masseter
mast cell
membrane
meninges
mesoderm
midbrain
monocyte
oxytocin
pancreas
pectoral
peduncle
perineum
pia mater
placenta
platelet
premolar
receptor
ribosome
secretin
shinbone
skeleton
steroids
thalamus
tympanum
tyrosine
uric acid
vena cava
vertebra
windpipe
xanthoma

9

arteriole
bilirubin
brainstem
calcaneus

capillary
cartilage
corpuscle
cortisone
diaphragm
dura mater
epidermis
forebrain
funny bone
genitalia
hamstring
hindbrain
hyoid bone
labyrinth
leukocyte
lymph node
mesentery
middle ear
milk teeth
nerve cell
oestrogen
olecranon
organelle
phagocyte
phalanges
prolactin
reflex arc
rhodopsin
serotonin
sphincter
thyroxine
ventricle
vestibule
vocal cord

10

acetabulum
Adam's apple
adrenaline
antagonist
birth canal
blood cells
blastocyst
blood sugar

bone marrow
breastbone
calcitonin
cerebellum
chromosome
collar bone
endorphins
epididymis
epiglottis
epithelium
fibrinogen
fontanelle
glomerulus
grey matter
heart valve
integument
intestines
lymphocyte
macrophage
metacarpal
metacarpus
metatarsal
metatarsus
myocardium
oesophagus
optic nerve
periosteum
peritoneum
pineal body
portal vein
protoplasm
spinal cord
vagus nerve

11

agglutinins
aldosterone
blood vessel
cauda equina
conjunctiva
endocardium
endometrium
erythrocyte
facial nerve

floating rib
granulocyte
haemoglobin
hippocampus
jugular vein
lipoprotein
loop of Henle
median nerve
mitral valve
motor cortex
nasal cavity
nasal septum
nasopharynx
nucleic acid
pericardium
sex hormones
solar plexus
vas deferens
vasopressin
white matter
wisdom teeth

12

adrenal gland
barorecepter
basal ganglia
dominant gene
eccrine gland
gonadotropin
hair follicle
hypothalamus
Langer's lines
limbic system
mammary gland
optic chiasma
organ of Corti
parathormone
phrenic nerve
red blood cell
sciatic nerve
smooth muscle
spermatozoon
spinal nerves
testosterone

thoracic duct
thyroid gland
urinary tract

13

deltoid muscle
ductless gland
exocrine gland
Fallopian tube
femoral artery
gamma globulin
gastric juices
gonadotropins
growth hormone
lacrimal gland
mitochondrion
nervous system
noradrenaline
parotid glands
recessive gene
salivary gland
shoulder blade
umbilical cord
zygomatic arch
zygomatic bone

14

Achilles tendon
Bowman's capsule
cerebral cortex
circle of Willis
coronary artery
corticosteroid
deciduous teeth
digestive tract
endocrine gland
Eustachian tube
exteroreceptor
Golgi apparatus
mucous membrane
olfactory nerve
oxyhaemaglobin
paranasal sinus

pituitary gland
proprioceptors
prostaglandins
sebaceous gland
semilunar valve
seminal vesicle
sinoatrial node
skeletal muscle
striated muscle
thoracic cavity
tricuspid valve
vitreous humour
white blood cell

15

alimentary canal
Haversian system
lumbar vertebrae
oculomotor nerve
ovarian follicle
ribonucleic acid
sacroiliac joint
trigeminal nerve
vertebral column

16 +

antidiuretic hormone

arachnoid membrane
basement membrane
cardiovascular system
cerebral hemispheres
cervical vertebrae
central nervous system
cerebrospinal fluid
connective tissue
extracellular fluid
glossopharyngeal nerve
glucocorticoid hormone
hepatic portal vein
hydrochloric acid
intervertebral disc
islets of Langerhans
luteinizing hormone
medulla oblongata
parathyroid glands
parathyroid hormone
peripheral nervous system
respiratory centre
reticular activating system
semicircular canals
seminiferous tubules
sympathetic nervous system
synovial membrane
thoracic vertebrae
thyroid-stimulating hormone
urogenital system

Patron saints

3 & 4

Anne - Canada; housewives
Elmo - sailors
Eloi - jewellers;
 metalworkers
Eric - Sweden
Ivo - lawyers
Jude - afflicted; hopeless
 causes
Luke - artists; brewers;
 physicians; surgeons
Olaf - Norway

Zita - domestic servants

5

Amand - inkeepers; wine
 merchants
Asgar - Denmark
David - poets; Wales
Denys - France
Giles - beggers; black-
 smiths; cripples
James - Spain

Menas - merchants
Vitus - epilepsy; nervous
  diseases

6

Adrian - soldiers
Agatha - bell founders;
  nurses
Albert - scientists
Andrew - Greece; Russia;
  Scotland
Antony - lost property; poor
Blaise - woolcombers
Canute - Denmark
Claude - sculptors
Dympna - insane
Dysmas - funeral directors
Fiacre - drivers; gardeners
George - England; farmers;
  scouts; soldiers
Hubert - huntsmen
Jerome - librarians
Joseph - Belgium; Canada;
  carpenters; workers
Julian - boatmen; inkeepers;
  travellers
Martha - cooks; housewives
Monica - Christian mothers
Teresa - foreign missions;
  Spain
Ursula - schools

7

Adelard - gardeners
Alexius - nurses
Barbara - architects;
  gunners; miners
Brendan - sailors
Bridget - Ireland; Sweden
Casimir - Poland
Cassian - secretaries
Cecilia - church music;
  musicians; poets

Crispin - shoemakers;
  leatherworkers
Dunstan - blacksmiths; gold-
  smiths; jewellers; lock-
  smiths; musicians; singers
Eligius - metalworkers
Erasmus - sailors
Eulalia - sailors
Eustace - huntsmen
Florian - firemen
Gabriel - post;
  telecommunications
Isidore - farmers
Leonard - prisoners
Matthew - accountants;
  bankers; book-keepers; tax-
  collectors
Maurice - infantrymen
Michael - Germany; grocers;
  paratroopers; police
  officers
Patrick - Ireland
Raphael - nurses; physicians
Stephen - bricklayers;
  Hungary
Therese - florists

8

Boniface - Germany
Camillus - nurses
Cuthbert - sailors
Dorothea - florists;
  gardeners
Genesius - actors; lawyers;
  secretaries
Gertrude - West Indies
Ignatius - soldiers
Lawrence - cooks
Nicholas - apothecaries;
  bakers; children; Greece;
  merchants; pawnbrokers;
  perfumiers; Russia;
  sailors; unmarried girls
Venerius - lighthouse-
  keepers

9

Apollonia   - dentists
Catherine   - attorneys;
  scholars; teachers;
  wheelwrights
Joan of Arc - France;
  soldiers
John of God   - booksellers;
  hospitals; nurses; printers
Pantaleon   - physicians
Procopius   - Czechoslovakia
Sebastian   - archers;
  athletes; soldiers
Valentine   - lovers
Wenceslas   - Bohemia;
  Czechoslovakia

10

Crispinian - leatherworkers
Frideswide - Oxford
Thomas More - lawyers
Willibrord - Holland

11

Christopher - motorists;
  sailors; wayfarers

12

Peter Nolasco - midwives

13

Frances of Rome - motorists
Francis Xavier - foreign
  missions
John of Nepomuk -
  Czechoslovakia
Thomas Aquinas - scholars
Vincent Ferrer - builders

14

Francis de Sales   -
  writers; journalists
Jerome Emiliani - orphans
  and abandoned children
Our Lady of Grace   -
  motorcyclists

15 +

Bernadine of Siena -
  advertising
Bernard of Mount Joux -
  mountaineers
Camillus of Lellis - nurses
Catherine of Siena - Italy
Elizabeth of Hungary -
  bakers
Francis of Assisi - animals;
  Italy
Francis of Cabrini -
  emigrants
Gregory the Great -
  musicians; singers;
  teachers
Joseph Cupertino - airmen
Joseph of Arimathea   -
  funeral directors
Katherine of Alexandria
  - scholars; philosophers;
  craftsmen
Our Lady Help of Christians
  - Australia; New Zealand
Our Lady of Loreto - airmen
Our Lady of the Assumption
  - India; South Africa
Therese of Lisieux - airmen;
  Russia

Phobias

9

apiphobia - bees
atephobia - being ruined
neophobia - change; anything new
zoophobia - animals

10

acrophobia - heights
aerophobia - air; aircraft
algophobia - pain
autophobia - being alone; oneself
cenophobia - empty spaces
cibophobia - food
cynophobia - dogs
demophobia - crowds
eosophobia - dawn
gynophobia - women
hemophobia - blood
hodophobia - travel
hylophobia - woods
kenophobia - empty spaces
monophobia - being alone
musophobia - mice
nosophobia - disease
panophobia - everything
polyphobia - many things
pyrophobia - fire
sitophobia - food
theophobia - God
xenophobia - strangers

11

acarophobia - insects
agoraphobia - open spaces
androphobia - men
anemophobia - wind

astraphobia - thunder and lightning
chionphobia - snow
dromophobia - crossing roads
gymnophobia - nakedness
haemophobia - blood
haphephobia - being touched
heliophobia - sunlight
hierophobia - sacred things
hippophobia - horses
hormephobia - shocks
hydrophobia - water
hygrophobia - moisture
hypnophobia - sleep
laliophobia - speaking
maniaphobia - insanity
microphobia - small objects
necrophobia - dead bodies
noctiphobia - night
nyctophobia - darkness; night
ochlophobia - crowds
ombrophobia - rain
pathophobia - disease
phobophobia - fear
phonophobia - speaking aloud
photophobia - light
scopophobia - being watched
scotophobia - darkness
stasiphobia - standing

12

ailurophobia - cats
anginophobia - choking, suffocation
brontophobia - thunder
chronophobia - time
entomophobia - insects
hedonophobia - pleasure
hyposophobia - heights
icthyophobia - fish

kinesophobia - motion
kleptophobia - stealing
megalophobia - large objects
odontophobia - dentistry
phasmophobia - ghosts
potamophobia - rivers
satanophobia - the Devil
stygiophobia - hell
thermophobia - heat
toxicophobia - poison
trichophobia - hair

13

arachnophobia - spiders
asthenophobia - weakness
erythrophobia - blushing;
  red
climacophobia - stairs
harpaxophobia - thieves
melissophobia - bees
ophidiophobia - snakes

ornithophobia - birds
peccatiphobia - corruption
psychrophobia - cold
pteronophobia - feathers
scelerophobia - burglars
sidereophobia - stars
thanatophobia - death
tridekaphobia - the number 13

14

anthropophobia - people
ballistophobia - missiles
batrachophobia - frogs
chrematophobia - money
chromatophobia - colour
claustrophobia - being shut
  in
maieutiophobia - childbirth
parthenophobia - young women
pharmacophobia - medicine
thalassophobia - sea
traumatophobia - injury

Places in London

3	Euston	Clapton	The Oval	Highbury
Bow	Fulham	Croydon	Tooting	Holloway
	Harrow	Dulwich	Wapping	Hounslow
	Hendon	East End	Wembley	Hyde Park
4	Ilford	East Ham	West End	Kingston
Soho	Newham	Enfield	West Ham	Lewisham
	Putney	Edgware		Mill Hill
	Sutton	Hackney		Richmond
5		Holborn	**8**	Southall
Acton		Kilburn	Barbican	Surbiton
Brent	**7**	Lambeth	Chiswick	Victoria
	Aldgate	Mayfair	Deptford	Vauxhall
	Barking	Mile End	Edmonton	Wanstead
6	Brixton	Mitcham	Finchley	Waterloo
Barnet	Bromley	Peckham	Finsbury	Woodford
Camden	Catford	Pimlico	Grays Inn	Woolwich
Ealing	Chelsea	Stepney	Haringey	
	Clapham	The Mall	Highgate	

Places in London

9

Battersea
Bayswater
Brentford
Docklands
Greenwich
Guildhall
Hampstead
Islington
Old Bailey
Redbridge
Rotten Row
Royal Mint
Southgate
Southwark
Stockwell
Stratford
Streatham
The Temple
Tottenham
Tower Hill
Tulse Hill
White City
Whitehall
Willesden
Wimbledon
Wood Green

10

Albert Hall
Bermondsey
Bloomsbury
Camberwell
Camden Town
County Hall
Earls Court
Hillingdon
Kennington
Kensington
Marble Arch
Marylebone
Paddington

Piccadilly
Serpentine
Shoreditch
Teddington
The Strand
Twickenham
Wandsworth

11

Bishopsgate
Blackfriars
Bond Street
Fleet Street
Hammersmith
Hither Green
Holland Park
Kentish Town
Notting Hill
Regents Park
Sloane Square
St. Johns Wood
Tate Gallery
Tower Bridge
Walthamstow
Westminster
Whitechapel

12

Bethnal Green
Billingsgate
Charing Cross
Covent Garden
Golders Green
Harley Street
Lavender Hill
London Bridge
Oxford Circus
Oxford Street
Primrose Hill
Regent Street
Royal Academy
Swiss Cottage

Tower Hamlets

13

Admiralty Arch
British Museum
Bank of England
Berkley Square
Crystal Palace
Downing Street
Knightsbridge
Lambeth Palace
Nelson's column
Shepherds Bush
Somerset House
Stock Exchange
Tower of London
Waltham Forest

14

Madame Tussaud's
Parliament Hill
St. James's Palace
Stoke Newington
The Planetarium
Wembley Stadium

15

Chelsea Hospital
Leicester Square
Liverpool Street
National Gallery
National Theatre
New Scotland Yard
Post Office Tower
Royal Opera House
Trafalgar Square

16 +

Buckingham Palace
Covent Garden Market

Elephant and Castle
Horse Guards Parade
Houses of Parliament
Imperial War Museum
Kensington Gardens
Kingston-upon-Thames
Lord's Cricket Ground
Natural History Museum

Royal College of Music
Royal Geographical Society
Royal Festival Hall
St. Paul's Cathedral
Threadneedle Street
Victoria and Albert Museum
Westminster Abbey
Westminster Cathedral

Planets and asteroids

4	5	6	7	8
Amor	Earth	Adonis	Astreae	Achilles
Eros	Ceres	Apollo	Eunomia	
Hebe	Flora	Chiron	Hidalgo	
Iris	Metis	Hermes	Mercury	**10**
Juno	Pluto	Hygeia	Jupiter	Euphrosyne
Mars	Vesta	Icarus		
	Venus	Pallas		
		Uranus		
		Saturn		

Reptiles and amphibians

3 & 4		6	7	8
asp	agama	caiman	axolotl	anaconda
boa	cobra	cayman	gharial	basilisk
eft	draco	garial	ghavial	bullfrog
frog	gecko	gavial	hognose	cerastes
gila	guana	goanna	monitor	colubrid
newt	krait	iguana	paddock	Congo eel
pipa	mamba	lizard	rattler	moccasin
toad	siren	muggar	saurian	mud puppy
	skink	mugger	serpent	
	snake	muggur	snapper	
5	swift	python	tadpole	
adder	tokay	taipan	tuatara	
	viper	turtle	urodele	

ophidian
pit viper
polliwog
rat snake
rhingals
sea snake
slow worm
terrapin
tortoise
tree frog
stinkpot
rat snake
water boa

9

alligator
blindworm
blue racer
boomslang
bull snake
box turtle
caecilion
chameleon
chelonian
crocodile
frog spawn
galliwasp
hairy frog
hamadryad
hoop snake
iguanodon
jew lizard
king cobra
king snake
milk snake
mud turtle
puff adder
ring snake

rock snake
sea turtle
tiger snake
tree snake
whip snake

10

batrachian
black snake
bushmaster
chuckwalla
congo snake
copperhead
coral snake
fer-de-lance
flying frog
glass snake
grass snake
green snake
hellbender
horned toad
loggerhead
natterjack
rock python
salamander
sand lizard
sidewinder
tiger snake
wall lizard
water snake

11

amphisbaena
carpet snake
constrictor
cottonmouth
diamond back

draco lizard
fence lizard
flying snake
garter snake
gila monster
goliath frog
gopher snake
green turtle
horned viper
midwife toad
rattlesnake
smooth snake
Surinam toad

12

carpet python
dragon lizard
flying lizard
hognose snake
Komodo dragon
Komodo lizard
horned lizard

13

bearded lizard
frilled lizard
giant tortoise
monitor lizard
water moccasin

14 +

boa constrictor
leatherback turtle
marsh crocodile
painted terrapin
soft-shelled turtle

Rivers

1

E
Y

2

Aa
Ii
Ob
Po
Si

3

Aar
Ahi
Ain
Aln
Alt
Axe
Ayr
Bug
Cam
Can
Chu
Dal
Dee
Dja
Don
Dua
Ely
Ems
Esk
Exe
Fal
Fly
Han
Hay
Hex
Hsi

Hue
Ili
Ill
Inn
Jiu
Ket
Kur
Kwa
Lea
Lee
Lek
Lim
Lot
Lys
Moy
Nar
Nen
Obi
Oka
Ord
Pic
Pur
Red
Rib
Roe
Rur
Rye
Sid
Sir
Sow
Syr
Taw
Tay
Tom
Tye
Ure
Usa
Usk
Var
Ver
Wey

Wye
Yeo
Zab

4

Aare
Adda
Adur
Agra
Agri
Aire
Alma
Alph
Alta
Amoo
Amur
Anio
Arno
Arun
Aube
Aude
Avon
Back
Bann
Beas
Beni
Brue
Bure
Bush
Cart
Cary
Cher
Chew
Chir
Cole
Coln
Cree
Dart
Doon
Dora

Dove
Duna
Earn
Ebro
Eden
Elan
Elbe
Elwy
Enns
Erne
Eure
Fall
Finn
Geba
Gila
Glan
Glen
Gota
Grey
Ha Ha
Hase
Hull
Irin
Isar
Isis
Isla
Juba
Kama
Kura
Kusi
Lahn
Leaf
Lech
Lena
Lima
Loir
Lune
Lynd
Lyon
Maas
Main

Meon
Meta
Milk
Mole
Mooi
Moth
Naze
Nene
Neva
Nida
Nile
Nith
Nore
Oder
Ohio
Oise
Orne
Ouse
Oxus
Para
Peel
Pina
Plym
Prah
Prut
Qena
Ravi
Rede
Reno
Rock
Roer
Ruhr
Saar
Salt
Save
Seal
Spey
Styr
Suir
Swan
Taff

Tana
Tara
Tarn
Tawe
Tees
Teme
Test
Thur
Tons
Towy
Tyne
Tywi
Ugie
Umea
Ural
Vaal
Vire
Waag
Waal
Wear
Yaln
Yana
Yare
York
Yser
Zorn

5

Abana
Adige
Adour
Aeron
Agano
Agout
Aisne
Aldan
Alice
Allen
Aller
Annan

Apure	Gumti	Neuse	Tamar	Albert	Granta
Argun	Habra	Niger	Tapti	Allier	Hamble
Avoca	Havel	Oglio	Tarim	Almond	Hawash
Benue	Hondo	Onega	Teffe	Amazon	Hudson
Black	Huang	Osage	Teifi	Angara	Huelva
Blood	Hugli	Otter	Teign	Aragon	Humber
Bober	Hunza	Oykel	Teith	Arinos	Hwan-Ho
Bogie	Ikopa	Payne	Temes	Atbara	Iguacu
Boyne	Indre	Peace	Tiber	Bandon	Ijssel
Brent	Indus	Pearl	Tisza	Barcoo	Irtysh
Bride	Isère	Pecos	Torne	Barrow	Irwell
Brora	Ishim	Pei Ho	Traun	Barwon	Itchen
Cairn	Jelum	Pelly	Trent	Beauly	Japura
Camel	Jumna	Perak	Tweed	Bio-Bio	Javari
Cedar	Jurva	Piave	Usuri	Bolsas	Jhelum
Clare	Kabul	Plate	Vitim	Bourne	Jordan
Clwyd	Kafue	Pruth	Volga	Brazos	Kagera
Clyde	Karun	Purus	Volta	Buchan	Kaveri
Colne	Kasai	Rance	Wahgi	Buller	Kennet
Congo	Katun	Reuss	Warta	Bulloo	Kikori
Conwy	Kings	Rhine	Welle	Calder	Kolyma
Cothi	Koros	Rhone	Werra	Canton	Komati
Deben	Kowie	Roper	Weser	Caroni	Konkib
Derry	Kuram	Saale	Whale	Carron	Kwanza
Desna	Lagan	Saöne	Whion	Chenab	Lehigh
Devon	Lenea	Sarre	White	Conway	Leitha
Douro	Lethe	Seine	Xingu	Coquet	Liddel
Dovey	Leven	Shari	Xiugo	Crouch	Liffey
Drina	Liard	Sheaf	Yanda	Cuanza	Loddon
Dvina	Lippe	Shiel	Yaqui	Cuiaba	Lomami
Eider	Loire	Shire	Yarty	Danube	Mamore
Ellen	Lotta	Siang	Yonne	Dihong	Medina
Etive	Marne	Siont	Yssel	Donets	Medway
Feale	Maroo	Slave	Ythan	Draava	Mekong
Fleet	Memel	Snake	Yukon	Elster	Mersey
Flint	Menam	Snowy	Zaïre	Escaut	Mincio
Forth	Meuse	Somme	Zenta	Farrar	Mobile
Fowey	Miami	Spree		Foyers	Modder
Foyle	Minho	Stolp		Fraser	Mohawk
Frome	Mosel	Stour	**6**	French	Moisie
Gabon	Moose	Swale	Abdiel	Gambia	Moldau
Garry	Nairn	Sugar	Agogno	Gandak	Monnow
Gogra	Neath	Sulir	Aguada	Ganges	Morava
Grand	Negro	Swale	Alagon	Glomma	Moskva
Green	Neman	Tagus	Albany	Grande	Murray

Neckar	Sutluj	Analong	Limpopo	Surinam
Neisse	Swakop	Annalee	Lualaba	Suwanee
Nelson	Swilly	Berbice	Luangwa	Tampico
Neutra	Tamega	Bermejo	Lugendi	Tapajos
Niemen	Tanana	Big Blue	Madeira	Thomson
Noatak	Tanaro	Big Horn	Marañón	Tobique
Ogowai	Teviot	Buffalo	Maritsa	Trinity
Oneida	Thames	Calabar	Maritza	Tsangpo
Orange	Theiss	Catawba	Mattawa	Ucayali
Orwell	Thurso	Cauvery	Mayenne	Uruguay
Ottawa	Ticino	Chambal	Meander	Vistula
Paraná	Tigris	Chelmer	Meklong	Waikato
Parima	Tormes	Chumbal	Meranon	Waitaki
Parret	Tornio	Cleddau	Moselle	Warrego
Platte	Tugela	Darling	Muluvar	Washita
Porali	Tummel	Derwent	Murghab	Waveney
Pripet	Turkey	Deveron	Narbuda	Welland
Pungwe	Ubangi	Dneiper	Niagara	Wichita
Quoile	Umpqua	Douglas	Olifant	Xanthus
Racket	Ussuri	Dubawnt	Orinoco	Yangtse
Ribble	Viatka	Dunajec	Orontes	Yarkand
Roding	Vienne	Durance	Owenboy	Yenesei
Rother	Vilyny	Ettrick	Parsnip	Ystwyth
Rovuma	Vilyui	Feather	Passaic	Yuruari
Rufiji	Vlatva	Fitzroy	Pechora	Zambezi
Rupert	Wabash	Gamtoos	Potomac	
Sabine	Waihou	Garonne	Red Deer	
St. Paul	Wandle	Gauritz	Roanoke	**8**
Salado	Warthe	Genesee	Rubicon	Amu Darya
Salmon	Weaver	Gilbert	Salween	Araguaia
Sambre	Wensum	Gironde	San Juan	Arkansas
Sarthe	Wharfe	Glenelg	Sankuru	Beaulieu
Salwin	Wipper	Glommen	St. Johns	Beresina
Sambre	Witham	Guapore	Salween	Big Black
Santee	Yamuna	Helmand	Schelde	Blue Nile
Scheld	Yarrow	Heri Rud	Scheldt	Brisbane
Scioto	Yavari	Huang He	Selenga	Campaspe
Seiont	Yellow	Hooghli	Semliki	Cape Fear
Seneca	Zarang	Hwangho	Senegal	Chambezi
Sereth	Zontag	Juniata	Shannon	Cherwell
Severn		Kanawha	Shibeli	Cheyenne
Slaney		Krishna	Si Kiang	Chindwin
Stroma	**7**	Kubango	Spokane	Clarence
Sunday	Abitibi	Lachlan	Sundays	Colorado
Sutlej	Alabama	La Plata	Sungari	Columbia

Rivers

Delaware
Demerara
Dneister
Dordogne
Eastmain
Evenlode
Findhorn
Flinders
Gallinas
Gascoyne
Gatineau
Georgina
Godavari
Goulburn
Great Kei
Guadiana
Guiviari
Hamilton
Hankiang
Huallaga
Humboldt
Illinois
Irtysh Ob
Itimbiri
Kankakee
Kelantan
Kennebec
Klondyke
Kootenay
Mahanadi
Mazaruni
Merrimac
Missouri
Mitchell
Nebraska
Ob Irtish
Paraguay
Paracuta
Parnaíba
Putumayo
Red River
Richmond
Rimouski
Rio Negro
Rio Tinto

Saguenay
St. Claire
Santiago
Savannah
Stinchor
Suwannee
Syr Daria
Torridge
Tunguska
Umvolosi
Victoria
Wanganui
Wansbeck
Windrush
Winnipeg

9

Abbitibee
Athabaska
Churchill
Crocodile
East River
Esmeralda
Essequibo
Euphrates
Gala Water
Great Fish
Great Ouse
Guadelete
Helmsdale
Indigirka
Irrawaddy
Kalamazoo
Kizil Uzen
Mackenzie
Magdalena
Mallagami
Miramichi
Murchison
Nipisquit
Paranaíba
Penobscot
Pilcomayo
Porcupine

Qu' Appelle
Rede River
Richelieu
Rio Branco
Rio Grande
Roosevelt
Saint John
Saint Paul
Salt River
Tennessee
Tocantins
Toombudra
Trombetas
White Nile
Wisconsin
Zarafshan

10

Allenwater
Black River
Blackwater
Blood River
Great Slave
Green River
Hackensack
Hawkesbury
Kizil Irmak
Lackawanna
Manzanares
Paranahiba
Parramatta
Republican
Sacramento
San Joaquin
Saint John's
St. Lawrence
Shat-el-Arab
Shenandoah
Snake River
White River
Yarra Yarra

11

Bonaventure

Brahmaptura
Chiang Jiang
Desaguadero
Madre de Dois
Mississippi
Modder River
Monongahela
Restigouche
Rio del Norte
Saint Claire
Susquehanna
Upper Paraná

Yarrowwater
Yellow River
Yellowstone

12

Big Blue River
Big Horn River
Ettrickwater
Great Kanawka
Guadalquivir
Murrumbidgee

Rappahannock
Sao Franciso
Saskatchewan
Shubenacadia
Yangtse Kiang

13

Big Black River
Big Sandy River
Big Sioux River
Saint Lawrence

Rocks and minerals

3 & 4
alum
clay
coal
jet
marl
mica
oil
onyx
peat
sand
talc
till
tufa
tuff

5
beryl
borax
chalk
chert
emery
flint
karst
loess

ochre
prase
pyrite
shale
scree
skarn
slate
trona

6
albite
aplite
arkose
augite
baryte
basalt
dacite
gabbro
galena
gneiss
gravel
gypsum
halite
hauyne
humite

latite
marble
norite
pumice
rutile
schist
schorl
silica

7
adamite
alunite
anatase
apatite
arsenic
asphalt
auxinite
azurite
bauxite
biotite
bismuth
bitumen
boleite
bornite
breccia

brucite
calcite
cuprite
diorite
duftite
felsite
granite
ilvaite
jadeite
kernite
kyanite
langite
leucite
lignite
moraine
okenite
sulphur
sylvine
thulite
unakite
verdite
zeolite
zincite

8
aegirine
allanite
analcime
ancylite
andesine
ankerite
artinite
asbestos
asbolane
autunite
basanite
bentonite
boehmite
boracite
bowenite
brookite
chromite
cinnabar
corundum
creedite
cryolite
danalite
datolite
diaspore
diopside

dioptase	sanidine	china clay	rubellite
dolerite	selenite	cobaltite	scheelite
dolomite	siderite	columbite	scholzite
eclogite	smaltite	copiapite	scolecite
enargite	steatite	cornetite	scorodite
epsomite	stibnite	covellite	siltstone
essexite	stilbite	cuspidine	soapstone
feldspar	tenorite	danburite	sphalerite
fluorite	tephrite	dawsonite	stellerite
fossaite	tilasite	dufrenite	stichtite
fuchsite	trachyte	dundasite	strunzite
gibbsite	tyrolite	erythrite	tantalite
goethite	xenolith	eudialyte	tephroite
graphite	xenotime	foshagite	tremolite
gyrolite	zeolite	gehlenite	tridymite
hematite		granulite	uraninite
hornfels		greensand	uvarovite
ilmenite	**9**	greywacke	variscite
jarosite		haematite	vonsenite
laterite	acanthite	hubnerite	willemite
limonite	alabaster	ironstone	wulfenite
linarite	allophane	jordanite	zeunerite
litharge	aluminite	kaolinite	zinkenite
luzonite	amazonite	laccolith	
massicot	andradite	larvikite	
melilite	anglesite	leucitite	**10**
mesolite	anhydrite	limestone	actinolite
mimetite	aragonite	ludlamite	adamellite
monazite	argentite	ludwigite	antigorite
mudstone	argillite	magnetite	baddleyite
mylonite	arthurite	marcasite	bayldonite
nadorite	atacamite	migmatite	beudanite
obsidian	azovskite	millerite	bournonite
oligoclase	barrerite	moldavite	brochantite
orpiment	batholith	natrolite	cacoxenite
pahoehoe	beaverite	nepheline	calc-schist
petalite	bismutite	neptunite	caledonite
phyllite	bustamite	niccolite	cancrinite
pisolite	carminite	olivenite	cannel coal
prehenite	carnotite	phonolite	carnallite
pyroxine	cavansite	proustite	chalcedony
rhyolite	celestine	quartzite	chalcocite
rock salt	ceruleite	red jasper	chrysotile
rosasite	cerussite	rhodizite	clinoclase
roselite	chabazite	rodingite	colemanite
	chamosite		

connellite
coquimbite
cordierite
coronadite
cumengeite
cylindrite
desert rose
diaboleite
embrechite
Epsom salts
ettringite
gadolinite
garnierite
glauberite
glauconite
granophyre
heulandite
hornblende
indicolite
kimberlite
mottramite
natural gas
norbergite
paragonite
peridotite
phlogopite
phosgenite
pillow lava
plancheite
potash alum
pyroaurite
pyrolusite
pyrrhotine
riebeckite
samarskite
staurolite
sturmanite
tennantite
thenardite
thomsonite
torbernite
touchstone
travertine
troctolite
tsumcorite

uranophane
vanadinite
vishnevite
wolframite

11

agglomerate
amphibolite
annabergite
anorthosite
apophyllite
bindheimite
boulder clay
brewsterite
brochantite
carbonatite
carborumdum
cassiterite
childrenite
chrysoberyl
clinochlore
crocidolite
dachiardite
descloizite
franklinite
glaucophane
greenockite
hausmannite
hornblende
Iceland spar
kammererite
kutnohorite
leadhillite
leopard skin
libenthite
liskeardite
meneghinite
molybdenite
nephelinite
pentlandite
pitchblende
plattnerite
phillipsite
pyrargyrite

sillimanite
stibiconite
svanbergite
taramellite
tetrahedite
zinnwaldite

12

anorthoclase
arfvedsonite
arsenopyrite
aurochalcite
bismuthinite
botallackite
boulangerite
callaghanite
chalcanthite
chalcopyrite
clinozoisite
conglomerate
conichalcite
cristobalite
cuproadamite
fuller's earth
granodiorite
hedenbergite
hemimorphite
hornblendite
hydrozincite
johanssenite
luxullianite
palygorskite
pickeringite
pudding stone
pyromorphite
pyrophyllite
silver glance
skutterudite
strontianite
varlamoffite

13

anthophyllite

astrophyllite
barytocalcite
chloroxiphite
hydroboracite
lepidocrocite
lithiophilite
nuees ardentes
orthopyroxine
plumbogummite
porphyroblast
red sandstone
stilpnomelane

14

chalcophyllite
chalcosiderite
plaster of Paris

15

pseudomalachite

15+

manganese nodule
oolitic limestone
pharmacosiderite
schlossmacherite
sphaerocobaltite

Roman emperors

3

Leo (I&II)

4

Geta
Nero
Otho

5

Carus
Galba
Nerva
Titus

6

Avitus
Decius
Gallus
Jovian
Julian
Julius
Philip
Probus
Trajan

Valens

7

Carinus
Gordian (I-
III)
Gratian
Hadrian
Marcian
Maximin
Maximus
Severus
Tacitus

8

Arcadius
Augustus
Aurelian
Balbinus
Caligula
Claudius
(I&II)
Commodus
Constans
Domitian
Eugenius

Galerius
Honorius
Lucinius
Macrinus
Majorian
Maximian
Olybrius
Pertinax
Tiberius
Valerian

9

Anthemius
Caracalla
Florianus
Gallienus
Glycerius
Maxentius
Vespasian
Vitellius

10

Aemilianus
Diocletian
Magnentius

Numerianus
Theodosius (I&II)

11

Constantine
(I&II)
Constantius (I-
III)
Hostilianus
Julius Nepos
Lucius Verus
Valentinian (I-
III)

12

Heliogabalus

13

Antoninus Pius
Libius Severus

14

Didius Julianus
Marcus Aurelius

15
Pupienus Maximus

16 +
Alexander Severus
Julian the Apostate

Petronius Maximus
Philip the Arabian
Romulus Augustulus
Theodosius the Great

Roman numerals

1 = I	6 = VI	11 = XI	91 = XC	600 = DC
4 = IV	9 = IX	50 = L	100 = C	900 = CM
5 = V	10 = X	51 = LI	200 = CC	1000 = M
			500 = D	2000 = MM

(This list only includes letters that might be useful in a crossword solution.)

Rulers of Britain and Royal Houses

Royal Houses

4
York

Tudor

7
Hanover
Windsor

8
Normandy

10
Saxe-Coburg

6
Stuart

5
Blois

9
Lancaster

11
Plantagenet

Rulers of England and Britain

4
Anne
Edwy
John
Mary (I & II)

5
David (I & II)
Edgar
Edred
Henry (I-VIII)
James (I & II Eng; I-VI Scot)

6
Alfred
Canute
Dafydd
Duncan
Edmund
Edward (I-VIII)
Egbert

George (I-VI)
Harold (II)
Robert (I-III)

7
Charles (I & II)
Macbeth

Malcolm (III)
Richard (I-III)
Stephen
William (I-IV)

8

LLewelyn
Margaret
Victoria

9

Aethelred
Alexander (II &
 III)
Athelstan
Elizabeth (I & II)
Rhodn Mawr

10

Aethelbald

Aethelbert
Aethelwulf

11

John Balliol

12

Harthacanute
William Rufus

13

David the Saint
Owen Glendower

14

Alfred the Great
Council of State
Edmund Ironside

Edward the Elder
Harold Harefoot
Malcolm Canmore
Oliver Cromwell
Robert the Bruce
William the Lion

15 +

Aethelred the Unready
Edward the Confessor
Edward the Martyr
LLewelyn ap Gruffydd
LLewelyn the Great
Margaret of Norway
Richard Coeur de Lion
Richard Cromwell
Richard the Lionheart
William the Conqueror

Russian rulers

4

Anna
Ivan (III-VI)
Paul (I)

5

Peter (I-III)

6

Alexis
Dmitri
Feodor (I-III)

Vasily (III-IV)

7

Michael

8

Nicholas (I&II)

9

Alexander (I-III)
Elizabeth
Catherine (I&II)

12

Boris Godunov
Ivan the Great

13

Peter the Great

15 +

Catherine the
 Great
Ivan the Terrible

Scientific terms

2

aa
a.c.
AM
AU
d.c.
FM
pH

3

air
AMU
arc
bar
bel
bit
BTU
CCD
CFC
CRO
day
DDT
dip
DNA
erg
gas
gel
GeV
ion
jet
keV
LCD
LED
lux
lye
MHD
mho
mil
NMR
TNT

NTP
OCR
ohm
PVA
PVC
rad
RAM
r.a.m.
rem
RNA
ROM
sol
STP
SHM
VDU
VHF

4

acid
agar
alum
atom
barn
base
beam
bond
byte
cell
clay
coal
coke
core
data
deme
disk
dyne
echo
flex
flux
foci
fold

fuse
gain
gall
gate
germ
gill
gram
gray
haem
heat
host
hypo
lava
lens
mass
mica
Moho
mole
muon
node
onyx
opal
palp
peat
phon
pole
pome
pupa
ruby
seif
sere
sial
sima
slag
soda
talc
till
tone
torr
tufa
unit
volt

watt
X-ray
yoke
zeta

5

adder
agate
ALGOL
alloy
amber
amide
amine
anion
anode
ascus
atoll
auxin
basic
beats
beryl
biome
borax
boson
brine
carat
chalk
chert
choke
clone
COBOL
coral
curie
cycle
daraf
debug
decay
diazo
dimer
diode
donor

earth
emery
epoxy
ester
ether
facet
farad
fault
field
flame
flint
fluid
focus
force
Freon
gauss
genus
gluon
gonad
graph
henry
hertz
hypha
image
imago
index
inert
joule
larva
laser
latex
lever
light
lipid
litre
lumen
lysis
magma
maser
meson
metre
modem

molar
nacre
nadir
niche
nitre
nymph
ochre
optic
orbit
order
organ
oxide
ozone
petal
phase
polyp
power
prism
quark
radar
radio
redox
relay
scion
serac
shale
shunt
solum
sonar
spark
spore
steam
stele
stoke
stoma
style
taiga
taxis
tesla
testa
tilth
titre

tonne	charge	ice age	phloem	tetrad
topaz	chitin	instar	photon	theory
toxin	cilium	in vivo	phylum	thorax
tribe	cirque	iodide	pileus	thrust
weber	convex	isomer	plasma	tincal
xeric	corona	kaolin	potash	tissue
xylem	couple	kelvin	proton	torque
zooid	cresol	ketone	pulsar	toxoid
	cupric	labile	pumice	trimer
6	cyclic	labium	quanta	triode
	dalton	labrum	quartz	triton
achene	decant	lamina	quasar	tropic
action	defect	lepton	qwerty	tundra
adduct	dilute	ligand	radian	turgor
aerial	dipole	lignin	radome	vacuum
aerobe	domain	lipase	radula	vapour
agonic	dorsal	litmus	raster	venule
air sac	dry ice	maglev	ratite	vernal
albedo	dynamo	magnet	relict	volvox
albite	eluate	marble	retort	zenith
alkali	eluent	mascon	retrix	zygote
alkane	embryo	matrix	reflex	
alkene	energy	matter	reflux	
allele	enzyme	micron	saline	**7**
ampere	factor	mirror	samara	
anther	farina	moment	scaler	abyssal
antrum	ferric	mosaic	sensor	acetate
apical	filter	motile	silica	acetone
apogee	fossil	mutant	siphon	actinic
atomic	fusion	nastic	slurry	acyclic
aurora	gabbro	natron	solder	adapter
azo dye	galena	nectar	solute	adaptor
baleen	gamete	nekton	spinel	address
baryon	garnet	newton	stator	aerobic
basalt	genera	nodule	sterol	aerosol
binary	genome	on-line	stigma	agonist
bionic	gimbal	oocyte	stolon	airlock
bleach	glycol	oogamy	strain	airpump
bolide	gneiss	opaque	strata	alchemy
botany	gramme	operon	stress	alcohol
buffer	gypsum	optics	stroma	alumina
carpel	hadron	parsec	syphon	amalgam
casein	halide	pascal	syrinx	ammeter
cation	halite	pectin	telson	ammonia
cermet	hybrid	phenol	tephra	aneroid
				aniline

annulus	crystal	gilbert	nitrite	species
antenna	cuprite	glacial	nucleon	spectra
antigen	cuprous	granite	nucleus	spindle
apatite	current	gravity	ocellus	stannic
aqueous	cuticle	habitat	oersted	statics
aquifer	cyanide	halogen	ohmeter	steroid
asexual	dash-pot	haploid	Ohm's law	stomata
azimuth	decibel	hormone	olivine	stratum
back emf	degauss	hydrate	oospore	strigil
balance	dendron	hydride	ootecha	styrene
bar code	density	hydrous	orbital	sucrose
battery	dibasic	hyperon	osmosis	synapse
bauxite	digital	igneous	panicle	synergy
bearing	diluent	impulse	phellem	tektite
benthos	dioptre	inertia	physics	tensile
benzene	diploid	in vitro	pipette	ternate
beta ray	diurnal	isogamy	plastid	thermal
Big Bang	dry cell	isotone	plumule	thallus
bipolar	ductile	isotope	polymer	titrant
biology	ecdysis	kainite	polypus	tokamak
biomass	ecology	keratin	program	torsion
bitumen	elastic	kinesis	propane	transit
bromide	element	labiate	protein	tritium
burette	elution	lamella	quantum	trophic
calcite	emerald	lanolin	quinine	tropism
calomel	entropy	lattice	radiant	turbine
calorie	epigeal	lignite	radical	ungular
camphor	equinox	linkage	radicle	valence
candela	ethanol	magneto	rare gas	valency
carbide	exogamy	maxwell	reagent	variety
cathode	fall-out	methane	reactor	velamen
caustic	faraday	microbe	reflect	ventral
Celsius	fatigue	mimicry	refract	venturi
ceramic	felspar	mitosis	rhizoid	vernier
chelate	ferrite	monomer	rhizome	vesicle
chloral	ferrous	monitor	rontgen	vitriol
circuit	fissile	mordant	rostrum	voltage
coal gas	fission	mutagen	sagitta	wolfram
coal-tar	food web	naphtha	scanner	yardang
colloid	formula	neoteny	sessile	zeolite
complex	FORTRAN	neritic	siemens	zincite
concave	fuel rod	network	sievert	zoology
coolant	funicle	neutral	soluble	zymogen
coulomb	geodesy	neutron	solvent	
counter	geology	nitrate	somatic	

8

ablation	catalyst	emission	hydrated	nucellus
acid rain	centroid	emulsion	hypogeal	nucleate
acrosome	ceramics	endoderm	ignition	nutation
actinide	charcoal	enthalpy	impeller	oestrous
addition	chimaera	epiblast	inductor	oil shale
adhesion	chlorate	epigamic	inert gas	omnivore
aerostat	chloride	epiphyte	infra-red	ontogeny
affinity	chlorite	eutectic	iriscope	overload
agronomy	chromite	fascicle	isostasy	overtone
aldehyde	cinnabar	feedback	isotherm	paraffin
alkaline	cleavage	feldspar	isotonic	parallax
alkaloid	cohesion	filtrate	kerosene	parasite
allogamy	compiler	filament	kinetics	paradigm
alluvial	compound	fireclay	klystron	particle
alpha ray	computer	firedamp	laser gun	peak load
altitude	constant	fixation	laterite	pendulum
amethyst	corundum	flip-flop	latitude	peroxide
ammonium	coupling	fluidics	leaching	phosphor
anaerobe	covalent	fluidity	lecithin	plankton
analysis	cracking	fluoride	lenticel	polarity
anaphase	cryolite	fluorite	light pen	porosity
anechoic	cytology	follicle	limonite	positive
angstrom	data bank	free fall	liposome	positron
anterior	data base	friction	lysosome	predator
antibody	delta ray	fuel cell	lysozome	pressure
antinode	dendrite	galvanic	magneton	print-out
aperture	deuteron	gamma ray	meniscus	promoter
aphelion	dew point	gas laser	meridian	prophase
apoplast	dialysis	genetics	mesoderm	radiance
armature	diapause	geodesic	mesoglea	radiator
artesian	diastema	geotaxis	methanol	reactant
asbestos	diatomic	glove box	miscible	reaction
atomizer	dilution	glycerol	molality	receiver
autogamy	diskette	gradient	molarity	receptor
autosome	divalent	graphite	molecule	red shift
biconvex	dolomite	graviton	momentum	refining
bioassay	dominant	half-life	momocyte	resistor
biometry	dormancy	hard disk	mucilage	rheostat
bistable	dynamics	hardware	mutation	rock salt
bivalent	ecliptic	harmonic	mycelium	roentgen
buoyancy	ectoderm	heat sink	mycology	ruminant
calamine	effectoe	heredity	narcotic	sapphire
carboxyl	efferent	hologram	neotenin	scissile
	effusion	holozoic	neutrino	sediment
	electron	humidity	noble gas	serology

silicate	adsorbent	beta decay	dioecious	histology
silicone	advection	biconcave	discharge	homologue
sine wave	afterglow	biorhythm	dosimeter	hydration
smelting	air pocket	biosphere	ductility	hydraulic
software	alabaster	black body	ecosphere	hydrology
solenoid	algorithm	black hole	ecosystem	hydrostat
solution	alicyclic	bolometer	ectoplasm	hydroxide
spectrum	aliphatic	Boyle's	elastomer	hygrostat
spiracle	allotrope	law	electrode	hypotonic
stannous	allotropy	capacitor	empirical	ilmentite
steatite	altimeter	capillary	endoplasm	imbricate
stimulus	ambergris	carbonate	endosperm	impedance
sub-imago	amino acid	cataltsis	endospore	implosion
subsonic	amorphous	cellulose	ephemeral	indicator
sulphate	amphibole	character	eukaryote	induction
sulphide	amplifier	chemistry	eutrophic	inelastic
sulphite	amplitude	chirality	evolution	inorganic
symplast	anabolism	chromatid	exogenous	insoluble
syncline	anaerobic	chromatin	exosphere	insulator
tartrate	analogous	clathrate	explosion	intensity
taxonomy	anhydride	clinostat	factorial	interface
tetrapod	anhydrite	community	field coil	inversion
thrombin	anhydrous	component	filoplume	isomerism
tracheid	anisogamy	composite	flagellum	isotropic
ungulate	annealing	condenser	flame test	jet stream
ungulate	anodizing	conductor	flotation	koalinite
upthrust	anticline	converter	fluorspar	laser beam
vagility	aperiodic	copolymer	fluxmeter	Leyden jar
vascular	aqua regia	corrosion	food chain	light wave
velocity	aragonite	cosmic ray	foot-pound	light year
venation	aspirator	cosmogony	frequency	limestone
vesicant	astrolabe	cosmology	fungicide	lime water
volatile	atomicity	countdown	galvanize	limnology
water gas	autoclave	cyclotron	gamma rays	lodestone
watt-hour	autolysis	cytoplasm	generator	longitude
waveform	autotroph	Darwinism	gestation	lubricant
xenolith	azeotrope	deflector	glycerine	luciferin
zoetrope	bandwidth	deionizer	guard cell	luminance
	barograph	desiccant	gynaecium	lyophilic
9	barometer	detonator	gyroscope	lyophobic
	baroscope	deuterium	haematite	magnesite
acellular	base metal	diaphragm	halophyte	magnetism
acetylene	batholith	diatomite	heliostat	magnetite
acoustics	becquerel	dichroism	herbicide	magnetron
adiabatic	bentonite	diffusion	histogram	magnifier

magnitude	proton gun	tectonism	adsorption
malleable	pyrolysis	telemeter	air bladder
manometer	pyrometer	telemetry	alternator
mechanics	pyrometry	telephony	amphoteric
megascope	quicklime	telescope	androecium
metalloid	radiation	telophase	anemometer
mesophyte	radiology	telotaxis	angiosperm
metaphase	rare earth	teratogen	antagonist
micropyle	reactance	thelytoky	anthracite
microtome	recessive	thyratron	antimatter
microtron	rectifier	thyristor	antiproton
microwave	reduction	time clock	aposematic
moderator	reflector	titration	aqua fortis
molecular	refractor	transient	aquamarine
monatomic	resonance	triatomic	arenaceous
multipole	reticulum	trilobite	atmosphere
mutualism	rotoscope	trivalent	atomic mass
Newtonian	saccharin	turquoise	auriferous
nitration	saltpetre	unisexual	ballistics
objective	sandstone	univalent	bimetallic
occlusion	saprolite	uraninite	binary code
oogenesis	serotinal	variation	biogenesis
operculum	shock wave	verdigris	biophysics
oviparity	short-wave	vernation	bituminous
oxidation	silica gel	vestigial	bond energy
pachytene	sintering	vibration	Böhr theory
passivity	soapstone	viscosity	carboxylic
pearl spar	soft water	voltmeter	carnallite
periscope	solar cell	wattmeter	catabolism
permeable	solvation	waveguide	cathode ray
petroleum	sonometer	wire gauge	centigrade
petrology	sound wave	xerophyte	centrifuge
phenotype	statocyst		centromere
pheromone	steradian		chalcedony
phosphate	stopclock	**10**	chemotaxis
photocell	striation	aberration	chloroform
phylogeny	strobilus	abscission	chromosome
pitot tube	subatomic	absorption	citric acid
pneumatic	sublimate	access time	collimator
pollution	substrate	acetic acid	combustion
polyester	succulent	achromatic	commutator
posterior	symbiosis	activation	conduction
potential	synthesis	active mass	convection
precursor	synthetic	adaptation	cryogenics
proboscis	tachytely	admittance	degaussing

derivative	hydrolysis	nematocyst	seismograph
desiccator	hydrometer	nephridium	senescence
desorption	hydrophone	nitric acid	slaked lime
Dewar flask	hydrophyte	noble metal	solubility
diakinesis	hygrometer	nucleonics	solvolysis
dielectric	hygroscope	nucleotide	spallation
dimorphism	hypodermis	nyctinasty	spartalite
dispersion	hypothesis	ommatidium	sporangium
distillate	hysteresis	orgamology	sporophyll
distortion	imprinting	orogenesis	sporophyte
elasticity	incubation	oscillator	sputtering
embryology	inductance	ovipositor	stalactite
endodermis	infrasound	oxalic acid	stalagmite
endogenous	insulation	ozone layer	subspecies
etiolation	integument	parasitism	succession
eukaryotic	interferon	pentatomic	superfluid
excitation	interphase	photometer	supersonic
exothermic	ionization	photometry	surfactant
experiment	ionosphere	phototaxis	suspension
Fahrenheit	isonuclear	physiology	synchroton
filtration	isothermal	plasticity	tachograph
flash point	kieselguhr	polyploidy	tachometer
floppy disk	kinematics	precession	technology
fossil fuel	laboratory	primordium	telegraphy
free energy	lactic acid	propellant	television
geocentric	lanthanide	propulsion	tetratomic
geophysics	latent heat	prothallus	tetraploid
geothermal	luminosity	protoplasm	thanatosis
geotropism	Mach number	pseudocarp	theodolite
glaciation	macroprism	radiograph	thermionic
glycolysis	mass defect	radioscope	thermistor
goniometer	mass number	reactivity	thermopile
gravimeter	meerschaum	receptacle	thermostat
gymnosperm	mesomerism	reflection	thixotropy
halophilic	mesosphere	refraction	tourmaline
heat shield	metabolism	refractory	trajectory
heavy water	metallurgy	regelation	transducer
helioscope	micrometer	relativity	transistor
holography	micrometre	reluctance	trinoscope
holophytic	microphone	resilience	triple bond
homologous	microscope	resistance	trochotron
homozygous	modulation	saprophyte	turbulence
hornblende	monoclinic	saturation	ultrasonic
horsepower	morphology	schizogony	vacuum tube
hydraulics	multimeter	sciaphilic	vicariance

viscometer
viviparous
voltameter
water glass
wavelength
wave number
white light
white noise
winchester
wind tunnel
xerography
Zener diode
zwerschaum

11

abiogenesis
absorptance
accelerator
accumulator
achromatism
actinometer
aestivation
agamospermy
agglomerate
air pressure
anisotropic
antheridium
antherozoid
anticathode
antineutron
anticyclone
antioxidant
archegonium
aromaticity
atomic clock
attenuation
Auger effect
avoirdupois
Baily's beads
barycentric
bathyscaphe
bathysphere
boulder clay
bulk modulus

calcination
calibration
calorimeter
candle power
capacitance
capillarity
carbon black
carbon cycle
carborundum
Carnot cycle
carrier wave
cassiterite
caustic soda
chlorophyll
chloroplast
cholesterol
chronometer
colorimeter
conductance
conjugation
crystalline
crystalloid
cybernetics
Daniell cell
deamination
declination
degradation
dehydration
dicotyledon
diffraction
dislocation
dynamometer
eddy current
electricity
electrolyte
electron gun
electronics
endothermic
environment
epidiascope
equilibrium
evaporation
exoskeleton
expansivity
fibre optics

fissionable
fluorescein
fluorescent
fluoroscope
focal length
free radical
galvanizing
gametangium
gametophyte
gas exchange
Gegenschein
genetic code
germination
gibberellin
gravimetric
gravitation
ground state
habituation
heterolytic
hibernation
homeostasis
homogametic
homogeneous
hydrocarbon
hydrography
hydrophilic
hydrophobic
hydroponics
hydrosphere
hygroscopic
Iceland spar
ignus fatuus
impermeable
indehiscent
insecticide
interaction
ion exchange
iridescence
irradiation
isoelectric
isomorphism
lapis lazuli
linear motor
line printer
lithosphere

macroscopic
mensuration
metamorphic
meteorology
naphthalene
nucleophile
occultation
open circuit
outbreeding
periodicity
photosphere
pitchblende
plasticizer
polarimeter
polarimetry
polystyrene
precipitate
primary cell
producer gas
prussic acid
qualitative
quantum leap
radiant heat
radioactive
radio opaque
Raman effect
refrigerant
reluctivity
respiration
restitution
röntgen rays
sal volatile
sedimentary
seismograph
silicon chip
slickenside
Solar System
spherometer
spirochaete
stereophony
stereoscope
stratopause
stroboscope
sublimation
substituent

supercooled
supernatant
synchrotron
tau-particle
tautomerism
temperature
thermionics
thermograph
thermometer
thrombocyte
transformer
translation
translucent
transmitter
transparent
triple point
troposphere
tunnel diode
ultrasonics
ultraviolet
unicellular
unsaturated
vacuum flask
vermiculite
voltaic cell
xylophagous
zooplankton

12

absolute zero
absorptivity
acceleration
acetaldehyde
actinic glass
adventitious
aerodynamics
alphanumeric
angstrom unit
annihilation
anthropology
antineutrino
antiparticle
argillaceous
assimilation

astrophysics
atomic energy
atomic number
atomic theory
atomic weight
autotrophism
backing store
beta particle
biochemistry
biosynthesis
blast furnace
boiling point
borosilicate
Bourdon gauge
Bunsen burner
calcium oxide
carbohydrate
carbolic acid
centre of mass
chemotropism
chlorination
chromosphere
cloud chamber
commensalism
condensation
conductivity
conformation
conglomerate
critical mass
cytogenetics
daughter cell
deceleration
deionization
deliquescent
demodulation
desalination
diamagnetism
dipole moment
displacement
dissociation
distillation
echolocation
ectoparasite
elastic limit
electric cell

electrolysis
electrolytic
electrophile
electroscope
endoparasite
endoskeleton
experimental
extranuclear
fermentation
flocculation
fluidization
fluorescence
fluoridation
fluorination
fluorocarbon
fullers earth
galvanometer
Geissler tube
geochemistry
geomagnetism
halogenation
heat capacity
heliocentric
heterozygous
hydrostatics
hydrotropism
hyperphysics
implantation
inclinometer
iatrophysics
interference
intermediate
interstitial
irratibility
Kelvin effect
liquefaction
low frequency
luminescence
macrophysics
magnetic flux
magnetometer
mean free path
microammeter
microbalance
microbiology

Moire pattern
neo-Darwinism
Newton's rings
nuclear power
nuclear waste
oceanography
oligotrophic
optical laser
orthotropism
oscilloscope
output device
paedogenesis
palaeolithic
permeability
permittivity
pharmacology
phototropism
polarization
polarography
polyethylene
polymorphism
polyurethane
pteridophyte
putrefaction
pyrotechnics
quantitative
racemization
radiobiology
radio compass
radio-isotope
regeneration
reproduction
short circuit
solar battery
solar physics
specific heat
spectrometer
spectrometry
spectroscope
spectroscopy
stasigenesis
stereoisomer
stereoscopic
stratigraphy
stratosphere

stridulation
substitution
sulphonation
supercooling
sup
tartaric acid
thermocouple
thermography
thermosphere
thiosulphate
trace element
translusence
transmission
visible light
Wankel engine
zone refining

13

accelerometer
aerogenerator
alpha particle
amplification
Appleton layer
argentiferous
asthenosphere
autocatalysis
beta radiation
binding energy
bioenergetics
biotechnology
bubble chamber
camera obscura
carbon dioxide
caustic potash
chain reaction
chemoreceptor
chromatograph
compressed air
concentration
configuration
decomposition
decompression
decrepitation
deliquescence

direct current
discharge tube
Doppler effect
effervescence
efflorescence
electromagnet
electrophilic
electrophorus
electrostatic
electrovalent
extracellular
ferromagnetic
fertilization
fractionation
freezing point
Geiger counter
geomorphology
geostationary
graticulation
heat exchanger
hermaphrodite
heterogeneous
high frequency
homoiothermic
hybridization
hydrodynamics
hydroelectric
hydrogenation
incandescence
induction coil
inflorescence
intercellular
intracellular
kinetic energy
kinetic theory
magnetic field
magnetization
magnetosphere
magnification
metamorphosis
microcomputer
micro-organism
monochromatic
monocotyledon
morphogenesis

multicellular
nitrification
nitrogen cycle
nuclear fusion
ovoviviparity
palaeontology
paramagnetism
Periodic Table
perissodactyl
petrochemical
photochromism
photoelectric
phytoplankton
piezoelectric
polypropylene
potentiometer
precipitation
pressure gauge
primary colour
quantum theory
radioactivity
recombination
rectification
reducing agent
scintillation
sedimentation
self-induction
semiconductor
spring balance
splanchnology
sterilization
stoichiometry
sulphuric acid
supercritical
thermonuclear
thermoplastic
thigmotropism
transcription
translocation
transmittance
transpiration
triploblastic
word processor
zodiacal light

14

alpha radiation
atomic mass unit
audio frequency
Aurora Borealis
binary notation
biodegradation
bioengineering
breeder reactor
carbon monoxide
cathode-ray tube
chromatography
circuit breaker
counter-current
depolarization
differentiator
electrostatics
eutrophication
ferromagnetism
gamma radiation
harmonic motion
harmonic series
Heaviside layer
heterotrophism
image converter
induction motor
interferometer
intermolecular
keratinization
magnetic moment
microprocessor
neutralization
nitrocellulose
nitroglycerine
nuclear fission
nuclear reactor
organometallic
osmoregulation
oxidizing agent
pasteurization
photochemistry
photogrammetry
photosynthesis
plate tectonics

poikilothermic
polarized light
polymerization
radio astronomy
radiochemistry
radio frequency
radio telescope
saponification
servomechanism
sodium chloride
sulphur dioxide
superconductor
supersaturated
surface tension
susceptibility
thermodynamics
transformation
transverse wave
trickle charger
vapour pressure
weightlessness

15

acclimatization
activated carbon
angular momentum
bioluminescence
bleaching powder
bomb calorimeter
centre of gravity
cosmic radiation
crystallization
crystallography
daughter element
demagnetization
denitrification
devitrification
electroanalysis
electrodialysis
electrodynamics
electrokinetics
electronegative
electrophoresis
electropositive

freezing mixture
horseshoe magnet
incompatability
Lissajou' s figure
molecular weight
montmorillonite
nuclear reaction
palaeomagnetism
packing fraction
parthenogenesis
partial pressure
phosphorescence
photomicrograph
photomultiplier
Planck' s constant
potential energy
refractive index
relative density
ribonucleic acid
rotary converter
sodium carbonate
sodium hydroxide
specific gravity
stereochemistry
sulphur trioxide
superheterodyne
thermobarograph
ultramicroscope

16

astronomical unit
calcium carbonate
calcium hydroxide
centrifugal force
centripetal force
continental drift
continental shelf
data transmission
central processor
greenhouse effect
mass spectrograph
mass spectrometer
molecular biology
natural selection

negative feedback
organic chemistry
polyvinyl acetate
positive feedback
relative humidity
Wheatstone bridge

17 +

absolute temperature
absorption spectrum
adaptive radiation
alternating current
background radiation
Bessemer converter
catalytic converter
celestial mechanics
centre of curvature
charge-coupled device
diffraction grating
electrometic force
electron microscope
elementary particle

frequency modulation
gas chromatography
genetic engineering
glyceryl trinitrate
information retrieval
integrated circuit
light-emitting diode
linear accelerator
liquid-crystal display
mechanical advantage
photoelectric cell
polyvinyl chloride
potential difference
simple harmonic motion
sodium bicarbonate
solid-state physics
solvent extraction
spontaneous combustion
spontaneous generation
statistical mechanics
transition element
vacuum distillation
vegetative propagation

(Note: metre is preferred to meter in British English.)

Scientists, engineers and inventors

3	Ader	Born	Gahn	Ives	Otis
Dam	Airy	Bose	Gall	King	Otto
Ged	Babo	Cohn	Gold	Koch	Rabi
Kay	Baer	Coke	Gray	Kuhn	Reid
Lee	Ball	Colt	Hahn	Land	Rose
Ohm	Bell	Cort	Hale	Lanz	Ryle
Ray	Benz	Davy	Hero	Lenz	Salk
	Berg	Dean	Hess	Laue	Swan
	Best	Dorn	Holt	Loeb	Todd
4	Biro	Eads	Hope	Mach	Tull
Abel	Bode	Ford	Howe	Mayo	Urey
	Bohr	Fust	Hunt	Mohs	Urie

Watt	Cooke	Lawes	Weber	Darwin	Isaacs
Webb	Creed	Libby	White	Dawson	Jansky
Wren	Crick	Lodge	Young	de Bary	Jenner
Yale	Cross	Loewi		de Duve	Jenson
Yang	Curie	Lowry		Diesel	Joliot
Zinn	Debye	Lyell	**6**	Dreyer	Judson
	Dewar	Magee	Achard	Duggar	Karrer
	Diels	Marsh	Adrian	du Mont	Kelvin
5	Dirac	Maxim	Agnesi	Dulong	Kepler
Adams	Elton	Mayer	Aitkin	Dunlop	Kinsey
Aiken	Euler	Monge	Alfven	Eckert	Koller
Amici	Evans	Milne	Ampère	Edison	Kotter
Arago	Ewing	Monod	Appert	Elster	Landau
Aston	Ewins	Morse	Archer	Enders	Lartet
Auger	Fabre	Nobel	Aselli	Engler	Lawler
Avery	Fabry	Papin	Baeyer	Euclid	Leakey
Bacon	Fermi	Pasch	Balmer	Fermat	Lenoir
Baade	Frege	Pauli	Beadle	Finsen	Liebig
Baily	Freud	Petit	Berger	Fizeau	Lister
Baird	Gabor	Petri	Bodoni	Fokker	Lorenz
Baker	Galen	Popov	Bolyai	Franck	Lovell
Banks	Galle	Prout	Bottet	Frisch	Lowell
Bates	Gauss	Raman	Bordet	Frasch	Manson
Beebe	Geber	Raven	Boveri	Froude	Markov
Bethe	Gibbs	Reber	Bramah	Fulton	Martin
Bevan	Godel	Rhine	Brandt	Galois	Martin
Black	Haber	Ritty	Briggs	Galton	McAdam
Bloch	Hardy	Romer	Brunel	Geiger	Mendel
Bondi	Henry	Rosse	Buffon	Geitel	Morgan
Boole	Hertz	Sabin	Bunsen	Gesner	Morley
Booth	Hills	Saint	Calvin	Glaser	Morris
Bosch	Hirst	Salva	Cantor	Graham	Morton
Bothe	Hooke	Segré	Carnot	Gregor	Muller
Bovet	Hoyle	Smith	Carrel	Grosse	Napier
Bowen	Hyatt	Soddy	Carver	Hadley	Nernst
Bower	Ivatt	Stahl	Cauchy	Halley	Newton
Boyle	Jacob	Tatum	Caxton	Harvey	Niepce
Bragg	Jeans	Tesla	Cayley	Hevesy	Norman
Brahe	Jones	Tsvet	Cayley	Hewish	Olbers
Brand	Joule	Volta	Chappé	Holden	Parkes
Braun	Kilbe	Weber	Cierva	Hooker	Pascal
Brown	Kolff	Wells	Claude	Hubble	Pavlov
Burge	Konig	Whale	Cugnot	Hughes	Penney
Carre	Krebs	White	Cuvier	Hutton	Perkin
Chain	Kühne	Young	Dalton	Huxley	Perrin

Scientists, engineers and inventors

Planck	Audubon	Fresnel	Macleod	Siemens
Powell	Babbage	Gadolin	Malthus	Simpson
Proust	Banting	Gagarin	Marconi	Sobrero
Raoult	Bardeen	Galileo	Mauchly	Spenser
Ramsay	Barnard	Galvani	Maxwell	Stanley
Rennie	Bateson	Gatling	Medawar	Steptoe
Ritter	Battani	Gilbert	Meitner	Swinton
Roscoe	Beattie	Glidden	Messier	Szilard
Sanger	Bergius	Goddard	Michaux	Telford
Savery	Borlaug	Gossage	Midgley	Tennant
Schick	Bradley	Gregory	Moseley	Thenard
Sholes	Braille	Gresley	Nasmyth	Thomson
Singer	Brouwer	Haeckel	Neumann	Travers
Sloane	Burbank	Harteck	Nielson	Tupolev
Solvay	Candela	Hawking	Oersted	Tyndall
Sperry	Cardano	Haworth	Onsager	van Laue
Stokes	Carlson	Helmont	Ostwald	Vavilov
Struve	Cassini	Hermite	Parsons	Veksler
Sutton	Charles	Hilbert	Pasteur	Vernier
Talbot	Chladni	Hodgkin	Pauling	Virchow
Taylor	Collett	Holland	Peligot	Waksman
Teller	Compton	Hopkins	Philips	Wallace
Thales	Correns	Huggins	Piccard	Wegener
Tilden	Coulomb	Huygens	Poisson	Whitney
Townes	Crookes	Janssen	Pollitt	Whittle
Urbain	Curtiss	Johnson	Poulsen	Wilkins
Vauban	d' Abbans	Jussieu	Prandtl	Ziegler
Wallis	Daimler	Kapitza	Ptolemy	
Walter	Daniell	Kendall	Purcell	
Walton	Da Vinci	Kendrew	Reaumur	**8**
Watson	de Graaf	Khorana	Richter	Agricola
Wiener	de la Rue	Kidinnu	Riddles	Amontons
Wigner	Deville	Kozirev	Riemann	Anderson
Wilson	de Vries	Lalande	Röntgen	Angström
Wohler	Doppler	Lamarck	Rumford	Appleton
Wright	Driesch	Lambert	Russell	Aspinall
Yukawa	Eastman	Langley	Ruzicka	Avogrado
Zeeman	Edwards	Laplace	Rydberg	Bakewell
	Eichler	Leavitt	Sandage	Beaufort
	Ekeberg	Leibniz	Scheele	Berliner
7	Faraday	Lesseps	Scholes	Bessemer
Agassiz	Feynman	Lockyer	Schwann	Birdseye
Allbutt	Fischer	Lorentz	Seaborg	Birkhoff
Alvarez	Fleming	Lumiere	Seyfert	Bjerknes
Andrews	Fourier	Lysenko	Shepard	Blackett

Brattain
Brewster
Bridgman
Brindley
Bronsted
Browning
Bushnell
Calmette
Caventou
Chadwick
Clausius
Cockroft
Coriolis
Courtois
Cousteau
Crampton
Crompton
Culpeper
Daguerre
Dedekind
de Fermat
De Forest
De Morgan
Drummond
Edgerton
Einstein
Ericsson
Foucault
Franklin
Gassendi
Gauthier
Gell-Mann
Gillette
Goldmark
Goodyear
Guericke
Hamilton
Harrison
Herschel
Hisinger
Humboldt
Ilyushin
Ipatieff
Jacquard
Kennelly

Klaproth
Kornberg
Koroliov
Lagrange
Langmuir
Lawrence
Legendre
Lemaître
Leuckart
Linnaeus
Lipscomb
Lonsdale
Malpighi
Maudslay
Maunsell
McMillan
Mercator
Meyerhof
Millikan
Milstein
Mitchell
Mosander
Mulliken
Newcomen
Oliphant
Ortelius
Oughtred
Poincare
Rayleigh
Rheticus
Robinson
Roebling
Roentgen
Sabatier
Sakharov
Saussure
Schaefer
Sefstrom
Servetus
Shockley
Shrapnel
Sidgwick
Sikorsky
Stenning
Stirling

Sturgeon
Sturrock
Thompson
Tombaugh
Van Allen
Van' t Hoff
Vesalius
von Mayer
Waterman
Weismann
Woodward
Worsdell
Zeppelin
Zernicke
Zworykin

9

Abu Al-Wafa
Aristotle
Arkwright
Armstrong
Arrhenius
Baekeland
Bartholin
Becquerel
Bernoulli
Berthelot
Berzelius
Boltzmann
Bronowski
Butenandt
Cailletet
Carothers
Cavendish
Chebishev
Cherenkov
Cockcroft
Cockerell
Cornforth
Cronstedt
d' Alembert
Daubenton
Davenport
de Broglie

de Elhuyar
Descartes
Dutrochet
Eddington
Einthoven
Endlicher
Eustachio
Fabricius
Fairbairn
Falloppio
Fessenden
Fibonacci
Flamsteed
Fox Talbot
Friedmann
Gascoigne
Gay-Lussac
Goodricke
Gutenberg
Heaviside
Helmholtz
Heyrovsky
Hopkinson
Johannsen
Josephson
Kirchhoff
Kurchatov
Lankester
Lavoisier
Lederberg
Lenormand
Leverrier
Liouville
McCormick
Macintosh
Macmillan
Michelson
Mottelson
Nicholson
Nirenberg
Pelletier
Pettigrew
Priestley
Remington
Schleiden

Schonbein
Serturner
Steinmetz
Stroudley
Tartaglia
Tinbergen
Vauquelin
Whitelegg
Wilkinson
Withering
Wollaston
Zsigmondy
Zuckerman

10

Archimedes
Arrowsmith
Barkhausen
Berthollet
Blenkinsop
Bowen-Cooke
Cannizzaro
Cartwright
Cassegrain
Chardonnet
Churchward
Copernicus
Dobereiner
Dobzhansky
du Vigneaud
Fahrenheit
Fitzgerald
Fourneyron
Fracastoro
Fraunhofer
Hargreaves
Hawksworth
Heisenberg
Hipparchus
Hofmiester
Hounsfield
Ingen-Hausz
Kolmogorov
Lilienthal

Lindenmann
Lippershey
Lord Kelvin
Maupertuis
Mendeleyev
Metchnikov
Paracelsus
Richardson
Rutherford
Sanctorius
Schweigger
Senefelder
Sommerfeld
Staudinger
Stephenson
Swammerdam
Torricelli
Tournefort
Trevithick
van de Graaf
van Drebbel
von Purbach
Wainwright
Watson-Watt
Wheatstone

11

Al-Khwarizmi
Baskerville
Chamberlain
Goldschmidt
Hertzsprung
Hinshelwood
Joliot-Curie
Landsteiner
Le Chatelier
Leeuwenhoek
Lobachevski
Montgolfier
Nostradamus
Oppenheimer
Pickersgill
Schrodinger
Sherrington

Spallanzani
Szent-Györgi
Tsiolkovski
van der Waals
von Guericke
von Welsbach

12

Ambartsumian
Boussingault
Lord Rayleigh
Mergenthaler
Szent-Györgyi

13

Arago Francois
Brandenberger
Chandrasekhar
von Sauerbronn

14

Galileo Galilei
Eudoxus of Cnidus

15 +

Apollonius of Perga
Aristarchus of Samos
Boyd-Orr of Brechin Mearns
Cagniard de la Tour
Diophantus of Alexandria
Dioscorides Pedanius
Eratosthenes of Cyrence
Geoffroy Saint-Hilaire
Hero of Alexandria
Kamerlingh-Onnes
Kekule von Stradonitz
Lecoq de Boisbaudran
Pappus of Alexandria
Sosigenes of Alexandria

Sea creatures

4

clam
crab
cray

5

conch
coral
gaper
hydra
monad
murex
ormer
polyp
prawn
razor
salpa
squid
whelk

6

cockle
cowrie
cultch
cuttle
limpet
medusa
mussel
oyster
partan
quahog
scampi
sea-ear
sea fan
sea fir
sea pen
shrimp

sponge
squill
urchin
winkle
wampum

7

abalone
acaleph
actinia
bivalve
copepod
cyclops
dog-crab
fiddler
hydroid
lobster
man-o'-war
medusan
mollusc
octopod
octopus
pandora
pea crab
rotifer
scallop
sea hare
sea lily
sea slug
sea wasp
sea worm
toheroa
trepang

8

argonaut
ark shell
barnacle
crawfish

crayfish
ear shell
escallop
king crab
land crab
man-of-war
medusoid
nauplius
nautilus
pteropod
sea jelly
sea mouse
sea onion
sea snake
starfish
top shell
univalve

9

acorn worm
comb jelly
cone shell
date shell
ear cockle
fish louse
gastropod
ghost crab
giant clam
harp shell
horsefoot
jellyfish
lamp shell
langouste
moon jelly
razor clam
round clam
sea flower
sea squirt
sea urchin
sea walnut

shellfish
shore crab
tusk shell
wing shell

10

acorn shell
auger shell
bêche-de-mer
coelacanth
crustacean
cuttlefish
heart shell
hermit crab
lion's mane
mitre shell
oyster crab
periwinkle
palolo worm
quahog clam
razor shell
robber crab
sand dollar
sea anemone
seed oyster
spider crab
swan mussel
tooth shell
tulip shell
velvet crab
venus shell
xyphosuran

11

brine shrimp
bubble shell
calling crab
fiddler crab
heart cockle

heart urchin
helmet shell
horse mussel
mussel shell
pearl mussel
pearl oyster
sea cucumber
soldier crab
spectre crab
trough shell
venus' girdle

12

box jellyfish
coelanterate

mantis shrimp
pelican's foot
sea butterfly
sentinel crab
spectre shrimp
spindle shell
spiny lobster
trumpet shell
unicorn shell

13

acorn barnacle
goose barnacle
horseshoe crab
keyhole limpet

pilgrim's shell
sea gooseberry
slipper limpet
soft-shell crab
soft-shell clam

14 +

chamber nautilus
lion's mane jellyfish
opossum shrimp
paper nautilus
pearly nautilus
Portugese man-of-war
skeleton shrimp
wheel animalcule

Seas and Oceans

3 & 4

Aral
Azov
Bali
Dead
Java
Kara
Red
Ross
Sawu
Sulu

5

Banda
Black
Ceram
China
Coral
Crete
Davis
Irish

Japan
North
Timor
White

6

Aegean
Arctic (O.)
Baltic
Bering
Celtic
Flores
Indian (O.)
Inland
Ionian
Laptev
Scotia
Tasman
Yellow

7

Andaman

Arabian
Arafura
Barents
Caspian
Celebes
Chukchi
Galilee
Lincoln
Marmara
Molucca
Okhotsk
Pacific (O.)
Wandels
Weddell

8

Adriatic
Amundsen
Atlantic (O.)
Beaufort
Labrador
Ligurian
Sargasso

9

Antarctic (O.)
Caribbean
East China
Greenland
Hudson Bay
Norwegian

10

Sea of Japan
South China
Tyrrhenian

12 +

Bellinghausen
Dumont d'
   Urville
East Siberian
Mediterranean
Sea of Galilee
Sea of Okhotsk
Sea of Marmora

Sevens

Seven Deadly Sins

4
envy
lust

5
pride
sloth
wrath

7
avarice

8
gluttony

Seven Hills of Rome

7
Caelian
Colline (or
  Quirinal)
Viminal

8
Aventine
Palatine
Quirinal (or
  Colline)

9
Esquiline

10
Capitoline

Seven Sages (or Wise Men of Greece)

Bias of Priene - 'Most men are bad'
Chilo of Sparta - 'Consider the end'
Cleobulus of Lindos - 'Avoid extremes'
Periander of Corinth - 'Nothing is impossible to industry'
Pittacus of Mitylene - 'Seize time by the forelock'
Solon of Athens - 'Know thyself'
Thales of Miletus - 'Who hateth suretyship is sure'

Seven Seas

6
Arctic

11
Indian Ocean

South Pacific
Indian Ocean

9
Antarctic

13
North Pacific

14
North Atlantic
South Atlantic

Seven Virtues

4
hope

7
charity
justice

9
fortitude

5
faith

8
prudence

10
temperance

Seven Wonders of the Ancient World

(The) Tomb of Mausolus
(The) Pyramids of Egypt
(The) Colossus of Rhodes
(The) Pharos of Alexandria
(The) Hanging Gardens of Babylon
(The) Temple of Diana at Ephesus
(The) Statue of Jupiter by Phidias

Shakespeare

Plays by Shakespeare

6
Hamlet (Prince of Denmark)
Henry V

7
Henry IV (Parts 1&2)
Henry VI (Parts 1-3)
Macbeth
Othello (The Moor of Venice)

8
King John
King Lear

Pericles (Prince of Tyre)

9
Cymbeline
Henry VIII
Richard II

10
Coriolanus
King Henry V
Richard III
Tempest, The

11
As You Like It
King Henry IV (Parts 1&2)
King Henry VI (Parts 1-3)

12
Julius Caesar
Twelfth Night
What You Will

13
King Henry VIII
King Richard II
Timon of Athens

14
King Richard III
Romeo and Juliet

Winter's Tale, The

15
Comedy of Errors, A
Titus Andronicus

15 +
All's Well that Ends Well
Antony and Cleopatra
Hamlet, Prince of Denmark
Love's Labour's Lost
Measure for Measure
Merchant of Venice, The
Merry Wives of Windsor
Midsummer Night's Dream, A
Much Ado About Nothing
Othello, The Moor of Venice
Pericles, Prince of Tyre
Taming of the Shrew, The
Troilus and Cressida
Two Gentlemen of Verona

Shakespearean Characters

3 & 4
Adam
Ajax
Anne (Lady)
Bona
Cade
Cato
Davy
Dick
Dion
Dull
Eros
Fang
Ford
Ford (Mrs.)

Grey
Grey (Lady; Lord)
Hero
Hume
Iago
Iden
Iris
Jamy
John
John (Don; King;
  Prince)
Juno
Kent (Earl of)
Lear (King)
Lion
Luce

Lucy
Moth
Nym
Page
Page (Mrs.)
Peto
Puck
Ross
Ross (Lord)
Say (Lord)
Snug
Time
Vaux
Wall
Wart

York (Archbishop of;
  Duchess of; Duke
  of)

5

Aaron
Abram
Alice
Angus
Ariel
Bagot
Bates
Belch
Bigot
Biron
Blunt
Boult
Boyet
Bushy
Butts
Caius
Casca
Celia
Ceres
Cinna
Cleon
Clown
Corin
Court
Curan
Curio
Denny
Diana
Edgar
Egeus
Elbow
Essex
Evans
Feste
Flute
Froth
Ghost
Gobbo
Gower
Green

Helen
Henry
Henry (King;
  Prince)
Julia
Lafeu
Lewis (Dauphin)
Louis (Dauphin;
  King; Lord)
Lucio
March (Earl of)
Maria
Melun
Menas
Milan (Duke of)
Mopsa
Osric
Paris
Pedro (Don)
Percy
Percy (Lady)
Peter
Phebe
Philo
Pinch
Poins
Priam
Regan
Robin
Romeo
Rugby
Sands (Lord)
Smith
Snare
Snout
Speed
Timon
Titus
Tubal
Varro
Viola
Wales (Prince of)

6

Adrian
Aegeon
Aeneas
Albany (Duke of)
Alexas
Alonso
Amiens
Angelo
Antony
Armado
Arthur
Audrey
Banquo
Basset
Bianca
Blanch
Blount
Bottom
Brutus
Bullen
Cadwal
Caesar
Caphis
Cassio
Chiron
Cicero
Clitus
Cloten
Cobweb
Curtis
Dennis
Dorcas
Dorset (Marquis of)
Dromio
Dumain
Duncan (King)
Edmund
Edward
Edward (Earl; King;
  Prince of Wales)
Elinor (Queen)
Emilia
Exeter (Duke of)

Fabian
Feeble
Fenton
France (King of;
  Princess of)
Gallus
George
Gremio
Grumio
Gurney
Hamlet
Hecate
Hector
Helena
Henry V (King)
Hermia
Horner
Imogen
Isobel (Queen)
Jaques
Juliet
Launce
Le Beau
Lennox
Lovell
Lucius
Marina
Morgan
Morton
Mouldy
Mr. Ford
Mr. Page
Mutius
Nestor
Oberon
Oliver
Olivia
Orsino
Oscric
Oswald
Oxford (Duke of;
  Earl of)
Pedant
Philip (King)
Pierce

Pistol
Pompey
Porter
Portia
Scarus
Quince
Rivers (Earl; Lord)
Rogero
Rumour
Scales (Lord)
Scroop
Scroop (Lord)
Seyton
Shadow
Silius
Silvia
Simple
Siward
Strato
Surrey (Duke of;
  Earl of)
Talbot
Talbot (Lord)
Tamora
Taurus
Thiasa
Thisbe
Thomas
Thurio
Tranio
Tybalt
Tyrrel
Ursula
Venice (Duke of)
Verges
Vernon
Wolsey (Lord)

7
Abraham
Adriana
Aemilia
Agrippa
Alarbus

Alencon (Duke of)
Antenor
Antonio
Arragon
Aumerle (Duke of)
Bedford (Duke of)
Berkley (Earl)
Berowne
Bertram
Bourbon (Duke of)
Brandon
Calchas
Caliban
Camillo
Capulet
Capulet (Lady)
Cassius
Catesby
Cerimon
Charles
Charles (Dauphin;
  King)
Claudio
Conrade
Costard
Cranmer (Archbishop)
Dauphin, The
Dionyza
Don John
Douglas (Earl of)
Dr. Butts
Eleanor
Escalus
Escanes
Flavius
Fleance
Francis
Gloster (Duchess of;
  Duke of; Earl of;
  Prince of)
Goneril
Gonzalo
Gregory
Helenus
Henry IV (King)

Henry VI (King)
Herbert
Horatio
Hostess
Hotspur
Iachimo
Jessica
Laertes
Lavache
Lavinia
Leonato
Leonine
Leontes
Lepidus
Lincoln (Bishop of)
Lord Say
Lorenzo
Lucetta
Luciana
Macbeth
Macbeth (Lady)
Macduff
Macduff (Lady)
Malcolm
Marcade
Marcius
Mardian
Mariana
Martext
Martius
Mercade
Messala
Michael
Michael (Sir)
Miranda
Montano
Morocco (Prince of)
Mowbray
Mowbray (Lord)
Mrs. Ford
Mrs. Page
Nerissa
Nicanor
Norfolk (Duke of)
Octavia

Ophelia
Orlando
Orleans (Duke of)
Othello
Paulina
Perdita
Phrynia
Pisanio
Proteus
Publius
Pucelle
Pyramus
Quickly (Mrs.)
Quintus
Richard
Richard (Duke;
King)
Salanio
Salerio
Sampson
Setebos
Shallow
Shylock
Silence
Silvius
Simpcox
Slender
Solinus
Stanley
Stanley (Lord)
Steward
Suffolk (Duke;
Earl)
Theseus
Thyreus
Titania
Travers
Tressel
Troilus
Ulysses
Urswick
Valeria
Varrius
Vaughan
Velutus

Warwick (Earl of)
William

8

Abhorson
Achilles
Aemilius
Aufidius
Auvergne (Countess
of)
Baptista
Bardolph
Bardolph (Lord)
Bassanio
Beatrice
Beaufort
Beaufort (Cardinal)
Belarius
Benedick
Benvolio
Berkeley
Bernardo
Borachio
Bullcalf
Burgundy (Duke of)
Campeius (Cardinal)
Canidius
Capucius
Charmian
Clarence (Duke of)
Claudius
Claudius (King)
Clifford
Clifford (Lord)
Colville
Cominius
Cordelia
Cornwall (Duke of)
Cressida
Cromwell
Dercetas
Diomedes
Dogberry
Don Pedro

Edward VI (King)
Eglamour
Falstaff
Fastolfe
Florence
Florizel
Fluellen
Gadshill
Gardiner
Gargrave
Gertrude (Queen)
Grandpre
Gratiano
Griffith
Harcourt
Hastings (Lord)
Hermione
Humphrey
Isabella
Jack Cade
John Hume
Jourdain
King John
King Lear
Lady Anne
Lady Grey
Lawrence
Leonardo
Leonatus
Ligarius
Lodovico
Lord Grey
Lord Ross
Lucentio
Lucilius
Lucullus
Lysander
Malvolio
Margaret
Margaret (Queen)
Maecenas
Menelaus
Menteith
Mercutio
Montague

Montague (Lady)
Montague (Marquis of)
Mortimer
Mortimer (Lady)
Mountjoy
Old Gobbo
Overdone (Mrs.)
Pandarus
Pandulph (Cardinal)
Panthino
Parolles
Patience
Pembroke (Earl of)
Pericles
Philario
Philemon
Philotus
Pindarus
Polonius
Polydore
Prospero
Rambures
Ratcliff
Reignier
Reynaldo
Richmond (Earl of)
Roderigo
Rosalind
Rosaline
Rotheram
Salarino
Seleucus
Somerset (Duke of)
Stafford
Stafford (Lord)
Stephano
Thaliard
Timandra
Titinius
Trinculo
Vicentio
Violenta
Virgilia
Volumnia
Whitmore

Williams

9

Agamemnon
Aguecheek
Alexander
Antigonus
Antiochus
Apemantus
Archibald
Arviragus
Autolycus
Balthazar
Bassianus
Biondello
Bourchier (Cardinal)
Brabantio
Caithness
Cambridge (Earl of)
Cassandra
Chatillon
Cleomenes
Cleopatra
Constance
Cornelius
Cymbeline
Dardanius
Deiphobus
Demetrius
Desdemona
Dolabella
Donalbain
Elizabeth
Enobarbus
Erpingham
Ferdinand
Ferdinand (King)
Fitz-Peter
Fitzwater (Lord)
Flaminius
Francisca
Francisco
Frederick
Friar John

Glansdale
Glendower
Grandpree
Guiderius
Guildford
Helicanus
Henry VIII (King)
Hippolyta
Hortensio
Katharina
Katherine
Katharine (Princess)
King Henry (IV; V;
  VI & VIII)
King Louis
Lady Percy
Lancaster (Duke of)
Lancaster (Prince
  of)
Longsword
Lord Bigot
Lord Lewis
Lord Lovel
Lord Sands
Lychorida
Macmorris
Mamillius
Marcellus
Mareshall
Moonshine
Nathaniel
Patroclus
Petruchio
Polixenes
Richard II (King)
Rousillon (Count of)
Rousillon
  (Countess of)
Salisbury (Earl of)
Sebastian
Servilius
Simonides
Southwell
Tearsheet
Thersites
Trebonius

Valentine
Ventidius
Vincentio
Voltimand
Volumnius
Woodville
Worcester (Earl of)
Young Cato

10

Alcibiades
Andromache
Andronicus
Anne Bullen
Antipholus
Archidamus
Barnardine
Brakenbury
Buckingham (Duke
  of)
Calphurnia
Canterbury
  (Archbishop of)
Coriolanus
Duke of York
Earl of Kent
Earl Rivers
Euphronius
Fortinbras
Henry Percy
Holofernes
Hortensius
Jaquenetta
John Talbot
John Morton
King Duncan
King Edward
King Henry V
King Philip
Longaville
Lord Rivers
Lord Sandys
Lord Scales
Lord Scroop
Lord Talbot

Lord Wolsey
Lysimachus
Mark Antony
Margarelon
Menacrates
Montgomery
Mrs. Quickly
Prince John
Proculeius
Richard III (King)
Saturninus
Sempronius
Sir Michael
Somerville
Starveling
The Dauphin
Thomas Wart
Touchstone
Willoughby (Lord)
Winchester (Bishop
  of)

11

Abergavenny (Lord)
Artimidorus
Bishop of Ely
Bolingbroke
Caius Lucius
Dame Quickly
Doctor Butts
Doctor Caius
Duke of Anjou
Duke of Milan
Earl Berkely
Earl of Derby
Earl of Essex
Earl of March
Edward Poins
George Bevis
James Gurney
John Holland
John of Gaunt
King Charles
King Henry IV
King Henry VI

King Richard (II & III)
Lady Capulet
Lady Macbeth
Lady Macduff
Lord Mowbray
Lord Stanley
Mayor of York
Mrs. Anne Page
Mrs. Overdone
Mustardseed
Peasblossom
Philostrate
Plantagenet
Prince Henry
Queen Elinor
Queen Isobel
Ralph Mouldy
Robert Bigot
Rosencrantz
Simon Shadow
Thomas Percy
Westminster (Archbishop of)
William Page
Young Lucius
Young Siward

King of France
Lady Montague
Lady Mortimer
Lord Bardolph
Lord Clifford
Lord Hastings
Lord Stafford
Marcus Brutus
Matthew Goffe
Mistress Ford
Mistress Page
Peaseblossom
Popilius Lena
Sir Hugh Evans
Sir Nathaniel
Sir Toby Belch
Thomas Horner
Three Witches
Titus Lartius
Westmoreland (Earl of)
Young Marcius

12

Caius Marcus
Decius Brutus
Duke of Albany
Duke of Exeter
Duke of Oxford
Duke of Surrey
Duke of Venice
Earl Berkeley
Earl of Oxford
Earl of Surrey
Friar Francis
Guildenstern
John Beaufort (Earl)
Julius Caesar
Junius Brutus
King Claudius
King Edward VI

13

Alexander Iden
Doll Tearsheet
Duchess of York
Duke of Alençon
Duke of Aumerle
Duke of Bedford
Duke of Bourbon
Duke of Gloster
Duke of Norfolk
Duke of Orleans
Duke of Suffolk
Earl Mortimer
Earl of Douglas
Earl of Gloster
Earl of Suffolk
Earl of Warwick
Faulconbridge
Faulconbridge (Lady)
Francis Feeble
Friar Lawrence
Henry Beaufort (Bishop)

Henry Gildford (Sir)
Hubert de Burgh
Joan la Pucelle
John Southwell
King Ferdinand
King Henry VIII
King Richard II
Lord Fitzwater
Mayor of London
Owen Glendower
Peter Bullcalf
Pierce of Exton (Sir)
Prince of Wales
Richard Vernon (Sir)
Robert Shallow
Stephen Scroop (Sir)
Queen Gertrude
Queen Margaret
Sir Thomas Grey
Thomas Mowbray
Thomas Vaughan (Sir)
Walter Herbert (Sir)
William Brando (Sir)
Young Clifford

Marcus Antonius
Metellus Cimber
Northumberland (Earl of)
Northumberland (Lady of)
Octavius Caesar
Peter of Pomfret
Pompeius Sextus
Prince Humphrey
Queen Elizabeth
Queen Katharine
Saunder Simpcox
Sextus Pompeius
Sir James Blount
Sir James Tyrrel
Sir John Stanley
Sir Walter Blunt
Sir William Lucy
Smith the Weaver
Thomas Beaufort (Duke)
Thomas Gargrave (Sir)
Tullus Aufidius
Walter Whilmore

15

Aemilius Lepidus
Bishop of Lincoln
Dromio of Ephesus
Duke of Lancaster
Earl of Cambridge
Earl of Salisbury
Earl of Worcester
Edmund of Langley
Governer of Paris
Lord Abergavenny
Margery Jourdain
Marquis of Dorset
Mayor of St. Albans
Menenius Agrippa
Mistress Quickly
Prince of Arragon
Prince of Morocco
Robin Goodfellow
Sicinius Volutus
Sir Anthony Denny
Sir Hugh Mortimer

14

Baptista Minola
Cardinal Wolsey
Christopher Sly
Clerk of Chatham
Duke of Burgundy
Duke of Clarence
Duke of Cornwall
Duke of Florence
Duke of Somerset
Earl of Pembroke
Earl of Richmond
Edmund Mortimer (Earl)
Hostess Quickly
John Somerville (Sir)
Justice Shallow
King Richard III
Launcelot Gobbo
Lord Willoughby

Sir John Colville
Sir John Falstaff
Sir John Fastolfe
Sir John Mortimer
Sir Nicholas Vaux
Sir Thomas Lovell
Titus Andronicus
William Stafford

16 +

Abbot of Westminster
Archbishop of Canterbury
Archbishop Cranmer
Archbishop of York
Bastard of Orleans
Bishop of Carlisle
Cardinal Beaufort
Cardinal Bourchier
Cardinal Campeius
Cardinal Pandulph
Countess of Auvergne
Countess of Rousillon
Count of Rousillon
Domitius Enobarbus
Don Adriano de Armado
Dromio of Syracuse
Duchess of Gloster
Duke of Buckingham
Duke of Gloucester
Earl of Northumberland

Earl of Westmoreland
Governor of Harfleur
Henry Bolingbroke
Henry Percy Hotspur
King Philip of France
Lady Falconbridge
Lady of Northumberland
Margaret Plantagenet
Marquis of Montague
Mistress Anne Page
Mistress Overdone
Philip the Bastard
Posthumus Leonatus
Prince of Lancaster
Princess Katherine
Princess of France
Richard Plantagenet
Robert Falconbridge
Roger Bolingbroke
Sir Andrew Aguecheek
Sir Humphrey Stafford
Sir Pierce of Exton
Sir Richard Ratcliff
Sir Richard Vernon
Sir Robert Glansdale
Sir Stephen Scroop
Sir Thomas Vaughan
Sir Thomas Erpingham
Sir William Glansdale
Sheriff of Wiltshire

Shipping forecast areas and stations

4	5	Wight	Fisher	7
Sole	Dover		Humber	Faeroes
Tyne	Forth		Jersey	Fastnet
	Lundy	**6**	Thames	Forties
	Malin	Bailey	Viking	Rockall
	Tiree	Biscay		Shannon
		Dogger		

8
Cromarty
Fair Isle
Hebrides
Irish Sea
Land' s End
Plymouth
Portland
Sumburgh
Valentia

9
Malin Head

10
Finisterre
Ronaldsway
St Abb' s Head

11
Butt of Lewis

German Bight
North Utsire
Smith' s Knoll
South Utsire

14
Royal Sovereign

Over 15
Channel Light-Vessel
South-East Iceland

Signs of the Zodiac

3
Leo - Lion

5
Aries - Ram
Libra - Scales
Virgo - Virgin

6
Cancer - Crab
Gemini - Twins
Pisces - Fishes
Taurus - Bull

7
Scorpio - Scorpion

8
Aquarius - Watercar-rier

9
Capricorn - Goat

11
Sagittarius - Archer
Capricornus - Goat

Solomon Grundy

Born on Monday
Christened on Tuesday
Married on Wednesday
Took ill on Thursday
Got worse on Friday
Died on Saturday
Buried on Sunday ...
and that was the end of Solomon Grundy.

Sports and games

2 & 3

ace
bat
bar
bat
bet
bob
bow
box
bye
cox
cue
cup
dan
fly
gun
gym
jab
lap
lbw
let
lie
lob
mat
nap
net
oar
out
par
PE
pot
PT
put
rod
run
set
ski
sod
tag
tee

tie
TT
try
win

4

bail
ball
bars
barb
base
beam
bias
bike
boat
bout
bowl
buck
buoy
card
cast
chip
chop
club
coup
crew
dart
dash
dive
drag
duck
duel
épée
eyas
fall
flag
foil
fore
foul
gaff

game
goal
golf
grid
grip
hank
hare
heat
hold
hole
home
hook
hoop
hunt
iron
jack
jess
judo
jump
lane
lido
lift
line
lock
love
luge
lure
meet
mile
miss
nock
Oaks
oche
odds
Oval
over
pace
pack
play
pole
polo

pool
port
post
puck
punt
putt
race
reel
rest
ride
ring
rink
rope
sail
seed
shot
show
side
skip
slam
sled
slip
solo
spar
spin
spot
sumo
swim
tack
team
toss
tote
trap
trot
turf
walk
whip
wide
wing
wood
xyst

yoga

5

alley
arena
arrow
bails
baton
blade
board
bogey
bowls
boxer
break
bully
caber
caddy
carom
chalk
chase
check
chute
coach
coupé
court
crawl
cycle
darts
decoy
Derby
deuce
diver
divot
dormy
drive
dummy
eagle
evens
event

extra
fault
feint
field
final
fives
float
fluke
frame
green
guard
gully
horse
inner
jetty
joust
kayak
kendo
lasso
links
loose
loser
lunge
match
medal
mid on
miler
mount
pacer
pairs
parry
pilot
pitch
piton
point
pro-am
prize
racer
rally
range
reins

relay	borrow	header	riding	TT race
rider	boules	hiking	ringer	umpire
rifle	bowler	hockey	roll in	victor
rings	bowman	hooker	roquet	volley
rodeo	boxing	hunter	rowing	wicket
rough	bullet	hurdle	rugger	willow
round	bunker	ice axe	runner	winger
rugby	caddie	jesses	saddle	xystos
sabre	cannon	jockey	savate	xystus
scent	canter	jumper	scorer	yorker
score	caving	karate	sculls	
scuba	chukka	kicker	second	
scull	clinch	kung fu	shinny	**7**
silks	corner	lariat	shinty	
skate	course	leg bye	single	acrobat
skeet	crease	loader	skater	address
skier	crosse	mallet	skibob	also ran
slice	cup tie	manege	skiing	amateur
smash	curler	marker	slalom	angling
stalk	dedans	mashie	sledge	archery
stall	defeat	nelson	sleigh	arm lock
stick	discus	no-ball	snatch	assault
stump	diving	not out	soccer	athlete
sweep	dog leg	opener	spider	axe kick
swing	driver	outrun	spiral	barbell
sword	dry fly	paddle	sprint	batsman
thole	eleven	pelota	squash	batsmen
throw	etrier	pistol	stable	batting
touch	falcon	player	stakes	beagles
track	fencer	pocket	stalls	bicycle
train	finish	pommel	stance	bowling
vault	flight	punter	stands	brassie
wager	flying	putter	sticks	captain
wedge	fly rod	quarry	strike	catcher
yacht	gallop	quarte	string	century
	gambit	quiver	stroke	chicane
	gillie	quoits	stumps	chipper
6	glider	rabbit	stymie	chukker
	go-cart	racket	tackle	circuit
aikido	go-kart	rapids	target	classic
anchor	googly	rapier	tennis	compass
archer	gulley	record	torero	contest
birdie	gutter	remise	toss-up	couloir
bisque	hammer	replay	touché	crampon
blocks	hazard	result	trophy	cricket
bookie				croquet

cue ball	kick-off	scratch	aqualung	fast ball
curb bit	knock-up	sculler	aquatics	fielding
curling	last lap	service	armguard	finalist
cushion	line out	shin pad	away game	fish-hook
cutlass	long bow	shot put	backhand	flat race
cycling	love all	shuttle	backspin	flippers
cyclist	love set	singles	baseball	foilsman
decider	lugeing	skating	baseline	football
declare	matador	skid lid	biathlon	foothold
defence	midiron	ski jump	boat race	footwork
descent	netball	ski lift	body blow	forehand
diamond	net cord	ski pole	bonspiel	foul play
doubles	niblick	snaffle	boundary	foul shot
dribble	ninepin	snooker	bullring	foxhound
fairway	oarsman	snorkle	bull's eye	free kick
fencing	oarsmen	stadium	bully off	free shot
fielder	oassade	starter	canoeing	full back
fifteen	offside	stirrup	car rally	full time
fishing	on guard	St. Leger	champion	full toss
fixture	overarm	striker	chip shot	gauntlet
flipper	over par	stumped	climbing	glass jaw
fly half	own goal	sub-aqua	coursing	goal area
fly kick	paddock	surfing	coxswain	goal kick
fly line	penalty	tacking	crossbar	goal line
forward	picador	take-off	cup final	goal post
fox hunt	pinfall	tally-ho	dark blue	golf ball
frogman	pitcher	The Oaks	dead ball	golf club
gliding	pit stop	The Oval	dead heat	gridiron
goggles	play off	throw in	deadlock	gymkhana
golf-bag	press up	tilting	dead shot	half back
gymnast	putting	toe-hold	deck game	half-ball
hairpin	quarter	top spin	delivery	half-blue
harmony	rackets	tourney	drag hunt	half-mile
harness	racquet	trained	dragster	handball
harpoon	rebound	trainer	dressage	handicap
harrier	referee	trapeze	drop goal	hat trick
hunting	regatta	vaulter	drop kick	haymaker
hurling	reserve	walking	drop shot	head-lock
ice pick	ripcord	weights	duelling	helmsman
in field	riposte	whistle	dumb bell	high dive
innings	rosette	workout	even keel	high jump
javelin	rowlock	wrestle	eventing	holed out
jogging	running		exercise	home base
jujitsu	sailing	**8**	falconer	home game
karting	scoring	après ski	falconry	horseman

how's that
huntsman
hurdling
iron shot
jousting
joystick
knockout
korfball
lacrosse
left back
left half
left hook
left wing
leg break
leg guard
leg sweep
lifeline
linesman
long jump
long odds
long shot
long slip
long stop
lost ball
love game
marathon
marksman
natation
ninepins
nosedive
olympiad
olympics
opponent
outfield
outsider
oval ball
pall mall
pavilion
pétanque
pike dive
ping-pong
pole jump
polo pony
pony race
port tack

pugilism
pugilist
pushball
pyramids
quintain
racegoer
rambling
recovery
ricochet
ringside
rink polo
rounders
runner-up
sand iron
sand trap
scramble
sculling
set point
shooting
short leg
shot putt
side blow
sideline
side slip
skipping
ski slope
ski stick
skittles
sledding
slow ball
snow line
softball
southpaw
sparring
speedway
stand off
stock-car
stop shot
straddle
stumping
stun shot
swimming
teamwork
The Ashes
third man

tholepin
tie-break
toboggan
toreador
tracking
trailing
training
transfer
trial run
trotting
tug of war
tumbling
turf club
underarm
undercut
under par
upper cut
vaulting
walkover
wall bars
wall game
water ski
wing area
wood shot
yachting

9

abseiling
advantage
aiki-jutsu
all square
anchorman
apparatus
aquaboard
aquaplane
athletics
aunt sally
backswing
badminton
belly-flop
bicycling
billiards
black belt
black flag

black pawn
bladework
bobsleigh
bodycheck
body punch
bowstring
brown belt
bull fight
butterfly
caddie car
cannonball
camelspin
chair lift
challenge
clubhouse
cock fight
combatant
conqueror
crackshot
cricketer
crossjack
cup winner
cycle race
cycle tour
dartboard
decathlon
decoy duck
deep field
dirt track
disengage
dog racing
dolly drop
double top
drawn game
dumbbells
enclosure
en passant
equalizer
Eton fives
extra time
faceguard
favourite
field game
fieldsman
first base

first half	midwicket	spin parry	Boston crab
first seed	moto-cross	split shot	boxing ring
first slip	motorboat	square-leg	catch a crab
fisherman	Newmarket	stable boy	centre half
fixed odds	pacemaker	stable lad	centre spot
fletching	palaestra	stalemate	challenger
flight bow	pole vault	starboard	checkpoint
foot fault	pot holing	steersman	clay pigeon
forty love	pot hunter	stopwatch	competitor
free reach	programme	stroke oar	contestant
freestyle	puissance	surf board	corner flag
freewheel	punchball	sweat-band	counted out
game point	racehorse	swordplay	cover point
gate money	race track	swordsman	cricket bat
goal posts	racing cap	tennis net	crown green
golf clubs	relay race	test match	cyclo-cross
golf links	relay team	third base	deck quoits
golf range	right back	third slip	deck tennis
golf widow	right half	the sticks	diving bell
good sport	right hook	tight rein	dolly catch
grand prix	right wing	touch-down	double axle
grand slam	safety net	touch goal	drag racing
greyhound	sand wedge	touchline	draw stumps
gum shield	sand yacht	tracksuit	drop cannon
gymnasium	sauna bath	tramlines	drop volley
handstand	schnorkel	twist dive	eel fishing
hard court	score card	water jump	eliminator
hill climb	screw dive	water polo	equitation
infielder	screw shot	whipper-in	Eskimo roll
ice hockey	scrimmage	wrestling	fast bowler
in-fielder	scrum half	wrist lock	field event
jackknife	scrummage	yacht race	field games
judo throw	semi-final		field sport
kennelman	shin guard		first blood
king's rock	short stop	**10**	fishing net
lawn bowls	short slip		fishing rod
light blue	signal gun	acrobatics	fisticuffs
lob bowler	skindiver	aerobatics	fives court
long field	ski runner	agility mat	flat racing
loose ball	skydiving	back marker	fly-fishing
loose rein	sleighing	backstroke	flying mare
love match	small bore	ballooning	footballer
low volley	small slam	banderilla	forced move
match play	spectator	basketball	Formula One
mid mashie	speedboat	battledore	Formula Two
		binoculars	

full nelson	Monte Carlo	sidesaddle	athleticism
foxhunting	non-starter	side stroke	bear baiting
goal circle	opening bat	silly mid on	biased bowls
goal crease	open season	silly point	blood sports
goalkeeper	open target	ski-jumping	bobsledding
goal kicker	outfielder	ski-running	boxing glove
golf course	paper-chase	slow bowler	bull baiting
grandstand	par contest	somersault	canoe slalom
gymnastics	pari-mutuel	speed trial	casual water
half-nelson	passed pawn	spin bowler	Channel swim
half-volley	penalty try	sportswear	cheerleader
halved hole	point of aim	stable-mate	cinder track
handspring	polo ground	stake money	class racing
hard tackle	pony racing	stop thrust	close season
hazard side	pot hunting	strokeplay	competition
headhunter	prize fight	strokesman	county match
heel and toe	prize money	submission	coup de grâce
horsewoman	punch-drunk	substitute	crawl stroke
hunting bow	push stroke	surf riding	cricket pads
hurdle race	racecourse	suspension	croquet arch
ice dancing	real tennis	sweepstake	croquet ball
ice sailing	relegation	swerve shot	croquet hoop
ice skating	riding whip	switchback	curling rink
Indian club	rifle range	team spirit	cycle racing
indoor golf	right bower	tennis ball	daisy cutter
injury time	right innner	thrown goal	deep fine leg
inside lane	right swing	timekeeper	declaration
inside left	rowing boat	title fight	discus throw
inside lock	rugby fives	tournament	diving board
in the rough	rugby match	track event	double fault
in training	rugby pitch	trampoline	downhill run
isometrics	rugby union	tricycling	driving iron
Jockey club	run through	triple jump	fast bowling
jump the gun	rush stroke	tumble turn	fell walking
karate chop	safety play	twelfth man	fencing mask
landing net	safety shot	Vardon grip	fifteen-love
lawn tennis	scoreboard	volleyball	field hockey
league game	second base	weighing-in	first eleven
little slam	second half	white water	fishing line
lob bowling	second slip	win by a head	flick stroke
love thirty	seconds out	win by a nose	flying start
maiden over	second wind		forced error
marker buoy	seven-a-side	**11**	forward line
mashie iron	short tacks		forward pass
match point	show-jumper	accumulator	Fosbury flop

free skating
game fishing
grass skiing
hairpin bend
hammer throw
hang-gliding
hockey pitch
hockey stick
home stretch
horse racing
horse riding
horse trials
hunting crop
hunting horn
ice yachting
inside right
inter-county
lap of honour
league table
loop the loop
martial arts
medlay relay
motor racing
neck and neck
Olympic team
out of bounds
outside lane
outside left
pairs skating
parachuting
penalty area
penalty goal
penalty kick
penalty line
penalty spot
pentathalon
photo finish
pools coupon
prizewinner
prop-forward
protagonist
public stand
quarterback
rabbit punch
race meeting

regatta card
return match
rising block
rising punch
round of golf
royal tennis
rugby league
sand sailing
scuba diving
seam bowling
self-defence
service line
service side
show jumping
shuttlecock
silly mid-off
simple parry
skating rink
slow bowling
snowshoeing
soft landing
spade mashie
springboard
squash court
starting gun
striker ball
sudden death
swallow dive
sweep rowing
table tennis
target arrow
test cricket
tennis court
third player
tobogganing
track record
transfer fee
uncontested
walking race
water hazard
Western roll
water skiing
windsurfing
wing forward
winning post

winning side
winning team
win on points
wooden horse
world record
yacht racing

12

anchor cannon
approach shot
back straight
banger racing
batting order
billiard ball
boardsailing
bobsleighing
bowling alley
bowling green
breast stroke
bullfighting
caber tossing
century break
championship
change bowler
change of ends
climbing rope
cockfighting
crash barrier
cricket match
cricket pitch
croquet court
curling stone
cut and thrust
dead ball line
deer stalking
direct cannon
double sculls
doubles match
dressing room
electric hare
field glasses
figure skater
first defence
first innings

first reserve
first service
flying tackle
Eton wall game
gamesmanship
googly bowler
ground-stroke
handicap race
hare coursing
head scissors
home straight
hundred yards
in the running
long distance
loose forward
losing hazard
javelin throw
maiden stakes
marathon race
medicine ball
mixed doubles
National Hunt
netball match
nursery slope
Olympic games
Olympic torch
opposing side
orienteering
outside right
parellel bars
penalty bully
penalty throw
pigeon racing
pitch and toss
playing field
point-to-point
pole position
pole vaulting
pony trekking
postponement
prize fighter
professional
putting green
quarter-final
racing stable

receiving end
record holder
return crease
ride to hounds
ringside seat
rock climbing
rope climbing
rope spinning
rope throwing
running strip
running track
scissors jump
second eleven
service court
shadow boxing
sharpshooter
single combat
single sculls
singles match
skipping rope
slice service
speed skating
sport of kings
squash racket
stabbing blow
stand-off half
starting gate
starting grid
starting post
staying power
steeplechase
sticky wicket
straddle jump
strong finish
swimming gala
swimming pool
sword fencing
tennis racket
thoroughbred
trampolining
trap shooting
treble chance
wicket keeper
winter sports

13
aquatic sports
billiard table
bowling crease
centre forward
checkered flag
chequered flag
coarse fishing
counter attack
county cricket
cricket ground
cricket stumps
croquet mallet
figure of eight
figure skating
finishing line
finishing post
fishing tackle
follow-through
football pitch
Grand National
half-time score
harness racing
horizontal bar
hundred metres
isometric bars
mashie niblick
mixed foursome
mountaineering
nightwatchman
one-day cricket
pitch invasion
popping-crease
qualification
record breaker
return service
rifle shooting
roller-skating
scratch player
second innings
shooting range
skateboarding
sportsmanship
sports stadium

starting price
starting stall
swordsmanship
track and field
vaulting horse
victor ludorum
weight lifting
wicketkeeping

14

all-in wrestling
American karate
approach stroke
asymmetric bars
billiard marker
cauliflower ear
discus throwing
downhill skiing
football league
Gaelic football
glorius twelfth
greyhound Derby
grouse shooting
hammer throwing
league football
master of hounds
mountaineering
nineteenth hole
opening batsman
sheepdog trials
sporting chance
starting blocks
starting stalls
pistol shooting
starting pistol
stock-car racing
thousand metres
weight training

wrestling match

15

appearance money
badminton racket
bodyline bowling
bowl a maiden over
butterfly stroke
cannonball serve
football stadium
greyhound racing
nursery handicap
public enclosure
shooting gallery
sparring partner
stable companion

16 +

aggressive offence
American football
association football
Australian Rules football
freestyle wrestling
game, set and match
hit below the belt
hot-air ballooning
leg before wicket
modern pentathalon
motorcycle racing
odds-on favourite
parachute jumping
pipped at the post
Royal and Ancient
rugby league football
synchronized swimming
throw in the towel
volunteer snooker

Threes
Three Graces

Aglaia
Thalia
Euphrosyne

Three Musketeers

Athos
Aramis
Porthos

Three Wise Men

Gaspar or Casper
Melchior
Balthazar
who gave:
gold
myrrh
frankincense

Titles, officials and forms of address

1 & 2	3	4		5		6
HE	aga	agha	inca	ameer	imaum	archon
M	beg	aide	kadi	baboo	junta	ataman
Mr	bey	amir	khan	baron	junto	bailie
S	cid	amma	king	bedel	jurat	bashaw
	dey	babu	lady	begum	kalif	beadle
	Dom	cadi	lama	boyar	laird	bigwig
3	Don	cham	Lord	brenn	liege	bursar
aga	HRH	czar	Ma' am	calif	macer	caesar
beg	Mme	dame	Miss	chief	Madam	
bey	Mrs	dato	M' Lud	comte	mayor	
cid	mir	dean	naib	conte	mirza	
dey	ras	doge	naik	count	mogul	
Dom	rex	Doña	peer	dewan	mpret	
Don	Sir	ducé	raja	diwan	mufti	
HRH		duke	rana	Donna	nabob	
Mme		earl	rani	doyen	nawab	
Mrs		emir	shah	elder	negus	
mir		foud	Sire	emeer	nizam	
ras		graf	tsar	envoy	noble	
rex		heir	tzar	ephor	omrah	
Sir		imam	vali	hakam	pacha	
			wali		pasha	
			zaim		queen	

5 (cont.)
rajah
ranee
reeve
ruler
sagan
saheb
sahib
Señor
sheik
subah
thane
wazir

caliph	sherif	headman	subadar	heptarch
censor	shogun	hidalga	sultana	hierarch
chagan	sirdar	hidalgo	supremo	Highness
cherif	soldan	infanta	toparch	His Grace
consul	squire	infante	tribune	His Grace
daimio	sultan	jemadar	tsarina	hospodar
daimyo	tycoon	justice	tzarina	interrex
deputy	vidame	karling	vavasor	kingling
despot	vizier	khedive	viceroy	Ladyship
doctor	yeoman	kinglet	vaivode	Landgraf
duenna		Law Lord	voivode	laureate
dynast	**7**	maestro		lawgiver
exarch		magnate	**8**	lawmaker
Führer	akhoond	maharao		life peer
Gräfin	alcalde	mahatma	alderman	lordling
herald	armiger	Majesty	archduke	Lordship
hetman	attaché	marquis	atheline	maharaja
holkar	bailiff	marshal	autocrat	maharani
Junker	baronet	matgraf	banneret	manciple
kabaka	brenhin	monarch	baroness	mandarin
kaiser	burgess	Mr Mayor	Black Rod	marchesa
knight	cacique	notable	burgrave	marchese
legate	cazique	officer	cardinal	margrave
lictor	candace	padisha	caudillo	marquess
lucumo	comtess	paladin	chairman	marquise
Master	consort	peeress	cicerone	martinet
mikado	coroner	pharoah	contessa	mayoress
Mister	curator	podesta	co-regent	memsahib
mullah	czarina	praetor	countess	minister
My Lady	dauphin	prefect	czarevna	Mistress
My Lord	dowager	premier	dauphine	monocrat
notary	duchess	proctor	deemster	Monsieur
peshwa	duumvir	questor	delegate	nobility
pretor	effendi	royalty	dictator	nobleman
prince	elector	sea-king	diplomat	official
puisne	emperor	sea-lord	director	oligarch
rajput	empress	senator	dukeling	overlord
rector	equerry	shereef	emeritus	overseer
regent	esquire	sheriff	emissary	padishah
regina	Fuehrer	Signior	Eminence	palatine
sachem	gaekwar	Signora	ethnarch	placeman
satrap	gaikwar	Signore	eupatrid	pontifex
Senora	grafine	skipper	guardian	princess
shaikh	grandee	Speaker	Head Girl	quaestor
sheikh	Head Boy	steward	headsman	queenlet
				recorder

sagamore
Seigneur
Seignior
Señorita
squireen
subahdar
suzerain
talukdar
tetrarch
tipstaff
triumvir
tsarevna
tzarevna
vavasour
vavassor
verderer
viscomte
viscount
zamindar
zemindar

9

abimelech
authority
bodyguard
bretwalda
burggrave
castellan
catchpole
centurion
chevalier
chieftan
Chief Whip
commander
commadore
constable
custodian
dictatrix
dignitary
diplomate
electress
escheator
exciseman
executive

Gauleiter
Gold Stick
grand duke
His Honour
imperator
inspector
justiciar
Landgrave
liege-lord
liveryman
lord mayor
magnifico
maharajah
maharanee
maharawal
majordomo
matriarch
monsignor
ombudsman
palsgrave
patrician
pendragon
policeman
portreeve
president
pretender
princekin
princelet
principal
proconsul
registrar
secretary
Seigniore
seneschal
Signorina
sovereign
statesman
sub-beadle
sultaness
town clerk
town crier
treasurer
venerable
waldgrave
whipper-in

Your Grace

10

adelantado
aide-de-camp
ambassador
areopagite
aristocrat
baronetess
burgmaster
bumbailiff
chancellor
commandant
commissary
controller
councillor
crown agent
dauphiness
door-keeper
Excellency
headmaster
Honourable
inquisitor
King-at-Arms
legislator
lieutenant
mace-bearer
Madam Mayor
magistrate
margravine
mayor-elect
noblewoman
palsgravine
priest-king
princeling
procurator
ringmaster
tsarevitch
vice-consul
vice-regent
viscomtess
Your Honour

11

archduchess
aristocracy
burgomaster
cesarevitch
chamberlain
comptroller
crowned head
crown lawyer
crown prince
diplomatist
earl-marshal
functionary
grand master
grand vizier
His Eminence
Her Highness
His Highness
His Holiness
landgravine
life peeress
marchioness
Mister Mayor
Monseigneur
Mr President
My Lord Abbot
My Lord Mayor
palsgravine
policewoman
prince royal
Queen Mother
queen-regent
stadtholder
subordinate
sword-bearer
viscountess
waldgravine

12

agent-general
ambassadress
armour-bearer
chief justice

chief of staff
civil servant
commissioner
crown equerry
earl palatine
grand duchess
headmistress
heir-apparent
jack-in-office
knight errant
lady mayoress
lord temporal
maid of honour
Madamoiselle
Most Reverend
notary public
peace officer
price-bishop
prince regent
queen consort
queen dowager
queen-regnant
staff officer
temporal peer
Very Reverend
water bailiff
Your Eminence
Your Highness
Your Holiness

13

administrator
consul-general
count palatine
district judge
generalissimo
Grand-Seigneur
high constable
judge-advocate
lord spiritual
prime minister
prince consort
Prince of Wales
princess royal
public trustee
spititual peer
vice-president

14

archchancellor
auditor-General
chief constable
crown solicitor
dowager duchess
lord of the manor
hereditary peer
high court judge
king's messenger
knight-bachelor

knight-banneret
lord chancellor
lord lieutenant
My Lady Mayoress
prince imperial
provost-marshal
superintendent
town councillor
vice-chancellor
Your Excellency

15 +

advocate-general
attorney-general
cabinet minister
chargé d'affaires
district officer
governor general
heir-presumptive
hereditary peeress
Her Royal Highness
His Royal Highness
Mister President
plenipotentiary
privy councillor
queen's messenger
Right Honourable
Right Worshipful
vice-chamberlain
vice-chancellor
Your Royal Highness

Tools and implements

3	fan	zax	burr	hink	mole	rasp
adz	gad		cart	hook	mule	rule
awl	gin		celt	hose	nail	sock
axe	hod	**4**	crab	jack	pick	spud
bit	hoe	adze	file	last	pike	tool
die	jig	bill	fork	loom	plow	trug
dog	loy	bore	frow	mall	pump	vice
	saw	brog	gage	maul	rake	whim

Tools and implements

5

anvil
auger
beele
bench
besom
betty
bevel
blade
borer
brace
burin
chuck
churn
clamp
clams
clasp
cleat
cramp
crane
croom
croze
cupel
dolly
drill
flail
flang
forge
gauge
gavel
gouge
hoist
incus
jacks
jemmy
jimmy
knife
lathe
level
lever
mower
parer
plane
plumb

preen
prise
prong
punch
quern
quoin
ratch
razor
sarse
scoop
screw
spade
spike
spile
spill
swage
temse
tommy
tongs
tromp
trone
wedge
winch

6

barrow
beetle
bender
blower
bodkin
borcer
bow-saw
brayer
broach
burton
chaser
chisel
colter
crevet
cruset
dibber
dibble
digger
doffer

dredge
driver
eolith
fanner
faucet
ferret
folder
gadget
gimlet
grater
graver
hackle
heckle
hammer
harrow
jagger
jigger
jig saw
ladder
mallet
mortar
muller
oil gun
oliver
pallet
pencil
pestle
pitsaw
planer
pliers
plough
pontee
pooler
rammer
ramrod
rasper
reaper
riddle
ripsaw
roller
rubber
sander
saw-set
scales
screen

scythe
segger
shaver
shears
shovel
sickle
sifter
skewer
sledge
slicer
spigot
square
stiddy
stithy
strike
stylus
tackle
tedder
tenter
trepan
trowel
tubber
turrel
wimble
wrench

7

band saw
boaster
bradawl
buzz saw
capstan
catling
cautery
chamfer
chip-axe
chopper
cleaver
couloir
coulter
crampon
crisper
crowbar
cuvette

derrick
diamond
dog-belt
drudger
fistuca
forceps
fretsaw
fruggin
gradine
grainer
grapnel
gripper
grub axe
hacksaw
handsaw
hatchel
hatchet
hayfork
hayrake
jointer
mandrel
mattock
nippers
nut hook
pickaxe
piercer
pincers
plummet
pole axe
pounder
pricker
riffler
rotator
salt-pan
scalpel
scauper
scraper
screwer
scriber
seed lop
shuttle
spaddle
spanner
spatula
sprayer

stapler
strocal
tenoner
thimble
trestle
triblet
T-square
twibill
twister
whip-saw
whittle
wood saw
woolder

8

airbrush
andirons
bark mill
bar shear
beakiron
bench peg
billhook
bistoury
bloomary
blowlamp
blowpipe
boathook
bowdrill
bull nose
butteris
calender
calipers
canthook
chainsaw
chopness
cross bit
crow mill
crucible
die stock
dividers
dowel bit
drill bow
Dutch hoe
edge tool

filatory
fire kiln
flame gun
flat iron
flax comb
gavelock
gee cramp
handloom
handmill
handtool
hand vice
hay knife
haymaker
hoof pick
horse hoe
lapstone
lead mill
nitre box
molegrip
muck rake
nut screw
oilstone
paint pad
panel saw
penknife
picklock
pinchers
plumb bob
polisher
power saw
prong-hoe
puncheon
reap hook
saw knife
saw wrest
scissors
scuffler
shoehorn
slate axe
spray gun
stiletto
strickle
strimmer
tenon saw
throstle

tommy bar
tooth key
tweezers
twist bit
weed hook
windlass
windmill

9

air hammer
arc welder
belt punch
bench hook
blowtorch
bolt auger
boot crimp
callipers
can opener
cement gun
centre bit
compasses
corkscrew
cotter pin
cramp iron
curry comb
cutter bar
dog clutch
draw knife
draw-plate
drop forge
excavator
eyeleteer
fillister
fining pot
fork chuck
gas pliers
grease gun
hair dryer
hammer axe
hand brace
hand drill
handspike
holing axe
hummeller

implement
jackknife
jackplane
jackscrew
lace frame
lawnmower
mousetrap
nail punch
nut wrench
pitch fork
plane iron
planisher
plumbline
plumb-rule
road drill
screwjack
scribe awl
secateurs
shearlegs
sheep hook
staple gun
steam iron
steelyard
sugar mill
telescope
tin opener
try square
turf spade
turn bench
turnscrew
tyre lever
watermill

10

bowie knife
box spanner
bread knife
bush harrow
claspknife
clawhammer
coal shovel
cold chisel
crane's bill
cultivator

dray plough
drift bolts
drill press
drillstock
drop hammer
edging tool
emery wheel
fire engine
firing iron
fly swatter
garden fork
grindstone
instrument
keyhole saw
masonry bit
masticator
mitre block
motor mower
mould board
nail drawer
paintbrush
paper knife
perforator
pipe wrench
pointed awl
power drill
safety lamp
screw press
sleek stone
snowplough
spokeshave
steam press
stepladder
tenterhook
thumbscrew
thumbstall
tilt hammer
trip hammer
turf cutter
turnbuckle
twist drill
watercrane
watergauge
waterlevel
wheel brace

11

brace and bit
breast drill
butcher's saw
chaff cutter
chain blocks
chain wrench
cheese press
cigar cutter
circular saw
countersink
crisping pin
crosscut saw
dovetail saw
drill harrow
electric saw
fanning mill
garden spade
glass cutter
grubbing hoe
helvehammer
jagging iron
machine tool
monkey block
paring knife
paint roller
ploughshare
pocketknife
power shovel
pruning hook
rabbet plane
reaping-hook
ring spanner
rotary drill
safety razor
sanding disc
sawing stool
screwdriver
side-cutters
skim coulter
snatch block
spirit level
squaring rod
steam hammer
steam shovel

stone hammer
straw cutter
strike block
stubble rake
sward cutter
swingplough
tamping iron
tape measure
turfing iron
two-foot rule
warping hook
warping post
watering can
weeding fork
weeding hook
weeding rhim
wheelbarrow

12

barking irons
belt adjuster
branding iron
breastplough
carving knife
caulking tool
counter gauge
cradle scythe
cramping iron
crimping iron
crisping iron
curling tongs
drill grubber
driving shaft
driving wheel
electric iron
emery grinder
flour dresser
garden roller
garden shears
garden trowel
glass furnace
hedge trimmer
hydraulic ram

mandrel lathe
marline spike
masonry drill
monkey wrench
palette knife
pruning knife
pulley blocks
ratchet drill
running block
scribing iron
sledgehammer
sliding bevel
socket chisel
stone breaker
straightedge
swingle knife
touch needles
trench plough
turfing spade
turning lathe
two-handed saw
water bellows
weeding tongs

13

butcher's broom
chopping block
chopping knife
cylinder press
electric drill
grappling-iron
hydraulic jack
packing needle
pinking shears
scribing block
sewing machine
single-cut file
soldering bolt
soldering iron
sowing machine
spinning jenny
spinning wheel
stocking frame
subsoil plough
three-foot rule
two-hole pliers
weeding chisel

14

blowing machine
carding machine
draining engine
draining plough
pneumatic drill
reaping machine
shepherd's crook
smoothing plane
swingling knife
thrusting screw
weeding forceps

15

carpenter's bench
crimping machine
dredging machine
drilling machine
entrenching tool
pestle and mortar
pump screwdriver
weighing machine

Trades, professions and occupations

2

GP
MD
MO
MP
PA
PM

3

boy
cop

4

dip
doc
don
gyp
ham
lad
lag
pro
rep
spy
sub
tec
vet

alto
amah
ayah
baas
bard
bass
beak
boss
bull
cadi
char

chef
cook
dame
dean
dick
diva
doge
dyer
G-man
grip
hack
hand
head

help
herd
hind
hoer
hood
lead
maid
mate
mime
mute
page
peon
poet

seer
serf
sice
snip
snob
star
syce
temp
thug
tout
ward
whip

5

actor
ad-man
agent
baker
baler
bobby
bonze
boots
bosun
boxer
bride

buyer
cabby
caddy
chips
clerk
clown
coach
comic
crier
crimp
crook
curer
daily
dhobi
diver
druid
envoy
extra
fakir
fence
fifer
filer
finer
flier
fraud
gipsy
gluer
groom
guard
guide
hakim
heavy
helot
hewer
hirer
inker
judge
knave
layer
leech
liner
locum
luter
madam
mammy

mason
mayor
medic
mimer
mimic
miner
model
navvy
nazir
nurse
oiler
pasha
paver
pilot
piper
poser
pupil
quack
raker
reeve
rimer
roper
rover
saice
sawer
scout
screw
sewer
sepoy
shoer
slave
smith
sower
staff
super
sweep
tamer
tawer
taxer
tenor
thief
tiler
tuner
tutor
tyler

usher
valet
viner
walla
watch
waxer
wench
wirer

6

airman
archer
artist
au pair
aurist
author
bagman
bailee
bailer
bailie
bailor
balker
bandit
banker
barber
bargee
barker
barman
batman
beadle
beagle
bearer
bigwig
binder
boffin
bookie
bowman
bowyer
brewer
broker
buffer
bugler
bumble
burler

bursar
busker
busman
butler
cabbie
cabman
calker
canner
carter
carver
casual
censor
cleric
codist
coiner
comber
commis
conder
conman
consul
coolie
cooper
copper
corker
co-star
coster
cowboy
cowman
critic
culler
cupper
cutler
cutter
dacoit
dancer
dealer
deputy
digger
dipper
docker
doctor
dowser
draper
drawer
driver

drover
drudge
duenna
duffer
earner
editor
escort
etcher
fabler
factor
farmer
feller
fisher
fitter
flayer
fly-man
forger
flower
fluter
framer
fuller
gaffer
ganger
gaoler
garçon
gaucho
gauger
gelder
geisha
gigolo
gilder
gillie
glazer
glover
graver
grocer
grower
guider
guidon
gunman
gunner
guv'nor
harlot
harper
hatter

hawker
header
healer
heaver
hedger
helper
herald
hit-man
hodman
hooper
horner
hosier
hunter
husker
iceman
intern
ironer
issuer
jagger
jailer
jailor
jester
jobber
jockey
joiner
jurist
keeler
keeper
killer
lackey
lagger
lapper
lascar
lawman
lawyer
leader
lector
legate
leg-man
lender
lictor
loader
logger
logman
looter

lopper	pinder	sawyer	tiller	**7**
lumper	pin-man	scaler	tinker	
lutist	pirate	scribe	tinman	abettor
lyrist	pitman	sea-dog	tinner	abigail
mahout	planer	sealer	toiler	acolyte
marker	plater	seaman	toller	acolyth
master	player	seamer	tonsor	acrobat
matron	porter	seiner	tapman	actress
medico	pot-boy	seller	totter	acutary
mender	pot-man	server	touter	adviser
menial	potter	setter	tracer	advisor
mercer	priest	sexton	trader	alewife
milker	prover	shaman	trusty	almoner
miller	pruner	shaver	tubber	alnager
minter	purser	shroff	tubman	analyst
monger	pusher	singer	turner	arabist
mooter	querry	sister	tweeny	arbiter
mopper	racker	sitter	tycoon	artisan
mugger	ragman	skivvy	typist	artiste
muller	raider	slater	usurer	assayer
mummer	ranger	slaver	valuer	assizer
mystic	rapist	slavey	vamper	assurer
nailer	ratter	slayer	vandal	attaché
nailor	reader	sleuth	vassal	auditor
nautch	reaper	snarer	vender	aviator
notary	reever	socman	vendor	bailiff
nuncio	rector	sorter	verger	bandman
oboist	regent	soutar	verser	barmaid
oilman	relief	spicer	vibist	baulker
old lag	renter	squire	viewer	bell-boy
orator	rhymer	stager	vizier	bell-hop
ostler	rigger	stoker	waiter	bellman
outlaw	ringer	stooge	wallah	bencher
packer	robber	stoner	waller	best boy
parson	roofer	storer	warden	best man
pastor	rooter	sutler	warder	big-shot
patron	rozzer	tailor	warper	birdman
pavior	runner	tamper	washer	blaster
pedant	sacker	tanner	weaver	blender
pedlar	sailor	tapper	weeder	boatman
peeler	salter	tasker	welder	bondman
penman	salvor	taster	whaler	bookman
picker	sapper	taxman	worker	botcher
piecer	sartor	teller	wright	bottler
pieman	satrap	tester	writer	bouncer

Trades, professions and occupations

breeder	crooner	fuguist	knitter	patcher
brigand	cropper	furrier	lace-man	paviour
buffoon	curator	gateman	lineman	peatman
builder	currier	girdler	linkboy	peddler
burgess	danseur	glazier	linkman	pianist
burgher	daysman	gleaner	lockman	picador
burglar	dentist	gleeman	lorimer	pickler
butcher	dialist	glosser	maestro	pierrot
buttons	diarist	grafter	mailman	pig-herd
call-boy	dietist	grainer	maltman	pikeman
cambist	ditcher	granger	manager	pioneer
carrier	dobhash	grantor	mangler	planner
caseman	dominie	grazier	marbler	planter
cashier	doorman	greaser	mariner	pleader
caterer	dragman	grinder	marshal	plumber
caulker	drapier	gumshoe	masseur	poacher
cellist	drawboy	gymnast	matador	poetess
changer	drayman	hackler	matcher	pop star
chanter	dredger	haggler	matelot	postboy
chapman	dresser	handler	mealman	postman
checker	drifter	hangman	meatman	praetor
chemist	drummer	harpist	midwife	prefect
cleaner	dustman	haulier	mildman	premier
clicker	duumvir	heckler	milkman	presser
clippie	elegist	herbist	mobster	printer
clogger	equerry	herdman	modiste	proctor
coalman	famulus	heritor	moneyer	provost
cobbler	fancier	hobbler	monitor	puddler
cockler	farrier	hogherd	moulder	puncher
collier	fiddler	hoodlum	mountie	quilter
comique	firebug	hostler	mourner	rancher
commere	fireman	hurdler	needler	realtor
compère	flesher	indexer	newsboy	referee
convict	florist	inlayer	newsman	refiner
co-pilot	flunkey	insurer	oculist	reviser
copyist	flusher	janitor	officer	revisor
coroner	flutist	juggler	operant	riddler
corsair	footboy	junkman	orderer	riveter
counsel	footman	juryman	orderly	roadman
courier	footpad	justice	ostiary	roaster
cowgirl	foreman	keelman	packman	roper-in
cowhand	founder	khedive	pageboy	rouster
cowherd	friseur	knacker	painter	rustler
cowpoke	frogman	knapper	palmist	sacrist
crofter	fueller	kneader	partner	saddler

sampler	stylist	**8**	cabin boy	emissary
samurai	surgeon	abductor	call girl	employee
scanner	swabber	advocate	caroller	employer
scourer	sweeper	aeronaut	castrato	engineer
scraper	taborer	alderman	cellarer	engraver
sea-cook	tallier	alienist	chairman	enroller
securer	tapster	analyser	chandler	epic poet
senator	taxi-man	animator	charlady	essayist
servant	teacher	annalist	choirboy	examiner
settler	tipster	annealer	claqueur	executor
sharper	tracker	aphorist	clothier	exorcist
shearer	trainee	apiarist	coachman	explorer
sheller	trainer	aquarist	co-author	exponent
sheriff	traitor	arborist	codifier	exporter
shifter	trapper	armorist	collator	fabulist
shipper	trawler	armourer	comedian	factotum
shopboy	tribune	arsonist	compiler	falconer
shopman	trimmer	arrestor	composer	farcense
showman	trouper	assassin	conjurer	farmhand
shunter	trucker	assessor	convener	ferreter
simpler	trusser	attorney	conveyor	ferryman
skimmer	trustee	bagmaker	courtier	figurant
skinner	tumbler	bagpiper	coxswain	film star
skipper	turnkey	bandsman	cremator	finisher
slipper	viceroy	banjoist	criminal	fishwife
smelter	villain	bargeman	croupier	flatfoot
snuffer	vintner	baritone	cutpurse	flautist
socager	violist	beadsman	dairyman	fletcher
soldier	voyager	bedesman	danseuse	fodderer
soloist	wagoner	bedmaker	deckhand	forester
soprano	warbler	bigamist	deemster	forgeman
sounder	warrior	bit-maker	defender	front man
speaker	webster	Black Rod	delegate	fugitive
special	weigher	blazoner	diplomat	gangsman
spencer	whetter	bleacher	designer	pugleman
spinner	wireman	boatsman	director	gangster
spotter	woodman	bondmaid	domestic	gaol-bird
stainer	woolman	bondsman	doughboy	gardener
stamper	workman	botanist	dragoman	gavelman
stapler	wrapper	bothyman	druggist	gendarme
starlet	wrecker	bowmaker	druidess	geometer
statist	yardman	boxmaker	duettist	glassman
steerer		brewster	educator	goatherd
steward		broacher	embalmer	godsmith
sticker			embosser	governor

Trades, professions and occupations

guardian	lecturer	observer	provisor	servitor
gunmaker	libeller	offender	psalmist	shearman
gunsmith	licensee	official	publican	shepherd
hammerer	linesman	onion-man	pugilist	shipmate
handmaid	linguist	oologist	purveyor	ship's boy
handyman	logician	operator	quaestor	shopgirl
hatmaker	lumberer	optician	quarrier	showgirl
haymaker	lutanist	ordainer	rabbiter	sidesman
head chef	lyricist	ordinand	raftsman	sitter-in
head cook	magician	organist	ragtimer	sketcher
headsman	magister	outrider	ragwoman	smuggler
helmsman	maltster	overseer	ranchero	solderer
henchman	mameluke	palatine	rapperee	soldiery
herdsman	mandarin	paper-boy	receiver	songster
hijacker	man of law	pargeter	recorder	spaceman
hireling	map-maker	parodist	regrater	spearman
home help	marauder	penmaker	releaser	speed-cop
hotelier	marketer	penwoman	repairer	spurrier
houseboy	masseuse	perfumer	reporter	starcher
houseman	mayoress	perjurer	resetter	star turn
huckster	measurer	peterman	resident	stitcher
humorist	mechanic	pewterer	restorer	stockman
huntsman	medalist	picaroon	retailer	storeman
importer	mediator	pig-woman	retainer	streamer
improver	melodist	pilferer	reveiwer	stripper
inkmaker	merchant	pillager	rewriter	strummer
indentor	merryman	plateman	riverman	stuntman
inventor	metal-man	plougher	rivetter	supplier
jail-bird	milkmaid	poisoner	roadsman	surfacer
jet pilot	millhand	polisher	romancer	surveyor
jeweller	milliner	politico	rugmaker	swindler
jig-borer	mimester	portress	saboteur	tabourer
jongleur	mimicker	postiler	salesman	tallyman
kipperer	minister	potmaker	satirist	taverner
knife-boy	minstrel	preacher	sawbones	teamster
labourer	mistress	prefacer	scrubber	thatcher
landgirl	modeller	preluder	scullion	theorist
landlady	motorman	pressman	sculptor	thespian
landlord	muleteer	prisoner	seamster	thrasher
lapidary	muralist	procurer	searcher	thresher
larcener	murderer	producer	sea-rover	tin miner
larderer	musician	promoter	seasoner	tinsmith
law-giver	narrator	prompter	seedsman	tipstaff
law-maker	newshawk	prosaist	sempster	top-liner
leadsman	novelist	provider	sergeant	torturer

toymaker	anatomist	cameraman	cupbearer	film extra
trackman	anchorman	canvasser	custodian	film-maker
trencher	annotator	car driver	cut-throat	financier
triumvir	announcer	caretaker	cymbalist	fire-eater
truckman	antiquary	carpenter	daily help	fish-curer
turncock	appraiser	carvanner	dairymaid	fisherman
turnspit	arborator	casemaker	decorator	fish-woman
unionist	architect	catchpole	desk clerk	flag-maker
usheress	archivist	catechist	detective	flyfisher
valuator	art critic	celebrity	dice-maker	forewoman
veneerer	art dealer	cellarman	die-sinker	fraudster
verderer	art editor	cembalist	dietetist	freelance
vintager	artificer	charwoman	dietician	freighter
virtuoso	art master	chanteuse	dietitian	fripperer
vocalist	assembler	chauffeur	dignitary	fruiterer
volumist	assistant	cheapjack	dispenser	full-timer
waggoner	astronaut	Chief Whip	dissector	furbisher
waitress	attendant	chorister	distiller	furnisher
walker-on	authoress	citharist	draftsman	galvanist
wardress	auxiliary	clergyman	dramatist	gasfitter
warrener	balladeer	clinician	drum-maker	gazetteer
watchman	balladist	clogmaker	drysalter	gem-cutter
waterman	ballerina	coalminer	ecdysiast	geologist
water-rat	bar-keeper	collector	ecologist	gladiator
wet nurse	barrister	colourist	economist	gluemaker
whaleman	barrowboy	colourman	embezzler	goldminer
whiffler	bartender	columnist	enameller	goldsmith
whistler	beefeater	commissar	engineman	gondolier
whitener	beekeeper	companion	engrainer	gooseherd
wigmaker	biologist	concierge	engrosser	gospeller
winchman	boatswain	conductor	errand-boy	governess
winnower	bodyguard	conserver	estimator	guardsman
woodsman	boilerman	constable	excavator	guerrilla
wool-dyer	bondslave	contralto	excerptor	guitarist
wrestler	bondwoman	co-partner	exchanger	gun-runner
yodeller	bookmaker	corrector	exciseman	half-timer
	bootblack	cosmonaut	executive	harlequin
	bootmaker	cost clerk	exorciser	harmonist
9	brakes-man	costumier	eye doctor	harpooner
	buccaneer	courtisan	fabricant	harvester
absconder	burnisher	couturier	fagottist	herbalist
accessory	bus driver	cowfeeder	fan dancer	herbarian
adulterer	bush pilot	cowkeeper	fashioner	herborist
alchemist	cab driver	cracksman	felt-maker	herb-woman
analogist	café owner	craftsman	film actor	hired hand

hired help	lumberman	pantaloon	protector
historian	machinist	paramedic	psaltress
homeopath	major-domo	part-timer	publicist
hop-picker	make-up man	patrolman	publisher
horologer	male model	paymaster	pulpiteer
hosteller	male nurse	pedagogue	punctator
housemaid	man-at-arms	pen-pusher	puppeteer
housewife	Man Friday	performer	qualifier
hygienist	mannequin	physician	quarryman
hypnotist	mechanist	physicist	racketeer
incumbent	medallist	pierrette	railmaker
ingrafter	memoirist	pinkmaker	ransacker
innkeeper	mercenary	pin-up girl	recruiter
inscriber	mesmerist	pipe-layer	reformist
inspector	messenger	pit-sawyer	registrar
intendant	metallist	planisher	regulator
ironsmith	metrician	plasterer	rehearser
job-master	middleman	play-actor	repairman
joculator	mill-owner	ploughboy	retoucher
justiciar	mine owner	ploughman	ribbonman
kennel-man	model girl	plunderer	roadmaker
kidnapper	moderator	pluralist	rocketeer
kitchener	mortician	poetaster	ropemaker
knocker-up	muffin-man	pointsman	roundsman
lacemaker	murderess	policeman	rum-runner
lacquerer	musketeer	pop artist	sacristan
lady's maid	musketoon	pop singer	safemaker
lampooner	myologist	portrayer	sailmaker
land agent	navigator	portreeve	scarifier
landreeve	negotiant	postilion	scavenger
larcenist	neologian	postwoman	scenarist
launderer	neologist	poulterer	scholiast
laundress	newsagent	practiser	schoolman
legionary	newshound	precentor	scientist
librarian	nursemaid	preceptor	scribbler
lifeguard	odd-jobber	predicant	scrivener
life-saver	odd-job man	prelector	scytheman
linotyper	office boy	presenter	sea-robber
lion-tamer	ombudsman	president	second man
liveryman	operative	priestess	secretary
loan agent	ordinator	principal	seneschal
lockmaker	organiser	privateer	serenader
locksmith	osteopath	processer	shampooer
log-roller	otologist	proconsul	shantyman
Lord Mayor	outfitter	professor	shipowner

ship's mate	tic-tac man	accountant	bookseller
shoeblack	timberman	adulteress	bootlegger
shoemaker	timpanist	advertiser	boot-mender
shopwoman	tool-maker	aerologist	bricklayer
sightsman	toolsmith	agrologist	brickmaker
signalman	town clerk	agronomist	brushmaker
slanderer	town crier	air hostess	bryologist
soapmaker	tradesman	air steward	bumbailiff
solicitor	tragedian	algebraist	bureaucrat
songsmith	traveller	amanuensis	bushranger
sonneteer	treasurer	ambassador	butterwife
sorceress	trepanner	apothecary	career girl
soubrette	tributary	apprentice	cartoonist
spiderman	trumpeter	arbalister	cartwright
spokesman	tympanist	arbitrator	cash-keeper
stableboy	undercook	astrologer	cataloguer
stableman	usherette	astronomer	cat breeder
stagehand	van driver	atmologist	cat burglar
statesman	varnisher	auctioneer	ceramicist
stationer	versifier	audit clerk	chair-maker
stay-maker	vigilante	baby-farmer	chairwoman
steersman	violinist	baby-sitter	chancellor
stevedore	volcalist	balloonist	chargehand
strangler	wadsetter	ballplayer	charioteer
stud groom	waldgrave	bandleader	chauffeuse
sub-editor	warrantee	bandmaster	chirurgion
subwarden	warranter	baseballer	chorus girl
succentor	washerman	bassoonist	chronicler
sur-master	waxworker	beadswoman	chucker-out
swan-upper	wherryman	beautician	circuiteer
swineherd	whitester	bell-hanger	city editor
switchman	winemaker	bell-ringer	claim agent
swordsman	wood-reeve	billposter	clapper-boy
tablemaid	workwoman	biochemist	clockmaker
tactician	wrong-doer	biographer	clog-dancer
tailoress	zookeeper	blacksmith	cloth maker
tap-dancer	zoologist	bladesmith	clubmaster
tattooist		blockmaker	coachmaker
tea-taster	**10**	blue jacket	coal-backer
tentmaker	able seaman	bombardier	coal-fitter
test pilot	abstractor	bondswoman	coalheaver
theorbist	accomplice	bone-setter	coal-master
therapist	accomptant	bookbinder	co-assessor
theurgist	accoucheur	bookholder	coastguard
throwster		bookkeeper	collocutor

colloquist	drummer-boy	governante	law-breaker
colporteur	dry cleaner	grammarian	law officer
comedienne	emblazoner	groundsman	leading man
commissary	enamellist	gunslinger	legislator
compilator	ephemerist	hackney-man	librettist
compositor	epitaphist	hall porter	lighterman
compounder	epitomizer	handmaiden	lime-burner
concordist	ergonomist	harmonizer	linotypist
consultant	errand-girl	harvestman	liquidator
contractor	ethologist	hatcheller	lobsterman
controller	evangelist	hatchet man	lock-keeper
copyholder	eye-servant	headmaster	lumberjack
copywriter	fell-monger	head porter	mace-bearer
cordwainer	file-cutter	head waiter	machineman
cork-cutter	filibuster	hedge layer	magistrate
corn-cutter	film editor	hierophant	manageress
cornettist	firemaster	highwayman	manicurist
councillor	fire-raiser	homoeopath	manservant
counsellor	fire-walker	horn player	master-hand
couturiere	fire-worker	horologist	matchmaker
cowpuncher	fishmonger	horse-thief	meat-hawker
crop-duster	flight crew	house agent	medical man
Crown Agent	flowergirl	husbandman	merceriser
cultivator	folk-dancer	impressario	militiaman
customs man	folk-singer	incendiary	millwright
cytologist	folklorist	inoculator	mineralist
delineator	forecaster	inquisitor	mine worker
delinquent	frame-maker	institutor	missionary
deputy head	freebooter	instructor	moonshiner
dinner lady	fund raiser	interagent	mouthpiece
disc jockey	gamekeeper	ironmaster	naturalist
discounter	game warden	ironmonger	naturopath
discoverer	gatekeeper	ironworker	nautch girl
dishwasher	gear-cutter	journalist	negotiator
dispatcher	geisha girl	journeyman	newscaster
distrainer	gemologist	junk dealer	news editor
distrainor	geneticist	justiciary	newsmonger
dockmaster	geographer	kennelmaid	newsreader
dog breeder	glee-singer	keyboarder	newsvendor
dog-fancier	glossarist	knockabout	newswriter
doorkeeper	glue-boiler	lady doctor	night nurse
dope-pedlar	go-go dancer	lampoonist	nosologist
drag artist	gold-beater	land-worker	nurseryman
dramaturge	gold-digger	lapidarist	obituarist
dressmaker	gold-panner	laundryman	office girl

oil painter	quiz-master	soap-boiler	typesetter
one-man band	railwayman	songstress	understudy
osteologer	rat-catcher	sound-mixer	undertaker
overlooker	recidivist	specialist	unicyclist
panegyrist	recitalist	staff nurse	veterinary
pantrymaid	researcher	steersmate	vice consul
paper-maker	rheologist	stenciller	victualler
park-keeper	ringmaster	step-dancer	virologist
park-ranger	roadmender	stewardess	vivandière
pasquilant	rope-dancer	stipulator	vocabulist
pastry-cook	rope-walker	stocktaker	wage-earner
pathfinder	roughrider	stone-borer	wainwright
pawnbroker	roustabout	stonemason	ward sister
pearl-diver	safeblower	street-ward	watchmaker
pediatrist	saleswoman	sub-prefect	waterguard
pedicurist	scaffolder	supervisor	weather man
peltmonger	scat singer	surface-man	wharfinger
penologist	schoolmarm	swan-keeper	whipper-in
perruquier	scrutineer	symphonist	whitesmith
personator	sculptress	tally clerk	wholesaler
pharmacist	sea-captain	taskmaster	winegrower
philologer	seal-fisher	taxi-driver	wine taster
piano tuner	seamstress	taxonomist	wine-waiter
pickpocket	second mate	tea-blender	wire-dancer
platelayer	seminarist	tea planter	wire-drawer
playwright	sempstress	technician	wire-walker
polemicist	serologist	technocrat	wireworker
politician	serving-man	theogonist	woodcarver
postillion	sexologist	theologian	woodcutter
postmaster	ship-broker	theologist	wood-monger
practician	ship-holder	threnodist	woodworker
prescriber	shipmaster	timekeeper	wool-carder
press agent	shipwright	tractarian	wool-comber
prima donna	shire-reeve	traffic cop	wool-driver
print buyer	shopfitter	trafficker	wool-grower
private eye	shopkeeper	tram-driver	wool-sorter
procurator	shoplifter	transactor	wool-trader
programmer	shopwalker	translator	wool-winder
pronouncer	signwriter	trawlerman	working man
proprietor	silk-mercer	treasuress	yardmaster
prosecutor	silk-weaver	trespasser	zoographer
prospector	sinologist	trolley-man	zymologist
prostitute	skirmisher	trombonist	
protractor	slop seller	troubadour	
puncturist	sneak thief	type-cutter	

11

accompanist
accoucheuse
adjudicator
allopathist
annunciator
antiquarian
apple-grower
arch-villian
army officer
arquebusier
art mistress
assemblyman
audiologist
audio typist
backbencher
bank cashier
bank manager
bargemaster
barnstormer
basketmaker
batti-wallah
beachcomber
bell-founder
belly-dancer
bill-sticker
bird-catcher
bird-fancier
bird-watcher
blackmailer
boatbuilder
body servant
boilermaker
boilersmith
bondservant
boot-catcher
breadwinner
broadcaster
bullfighter
burgomaster
businessman
candlemaker
carol singer
car salesman

cattle thief
cat's-meat-
   man
chair-minder
chalk-cutter
chamberlain
chambermaid
charge nurse
chiffonnier
child minder
chirologist
chiromancer
chiropodist
choirmaster
chronologer
clairvoyant
clock-setter
cloth-worker
coffin-maker
cognoscente
collar-maker
commentator
comptroller
conciliator
condisciple
condottière
conductress
confederate
congressman
consecrator
conservator
conspirator
constituent
contributor
conveyancer
coppersmith
cosmologist
court jester
crane driver
crime writer
crown lawyer
cub reporter
cypher clerk
dancing girl
day labourer

delivery man
demographer
diplomatist
dispensator
distributor
double agent
draughtsman
duty officer
electrician
emblematist
embroiderer
entertainer
equilibrist
estate agent
ethnologist
etymologist
executioner
extortioner
factory hand
faith healer
field worker
figure-maker
filing clerk
finestiller
fier-fighter
fire insurer
fire-watcher
flax-dresser
flesh-monger
floorwalker
fourbisseur
fringe-maker
fruit picker
funambulist
funtionary
galley-slave
games master
gemmologist
genealogist
ghost writer
glass-bender
glass-blower
glass-cutter
glass-worker
grave-digger

greengrocer
green keeper
haberdasher
hagiologist
hairdresser
hair stylist
handicapper
hardwareman
heirologist
High Sheriff
histologist
homesteader
horse doctor
horse trader
hospitaller
hotel-keeper
housefather
housekeeper
housemaster
housemother
hydrologist
hymnologist
illuminator
illusionist
illustrator
infantryman
internuncio
interpreter
interviewer
invigilator
iron-founder
ivory-carver
ivory-turner
ivory-worker
kerb-crawler
kitchenmaid
lamplighter
land steward
laundrymaid
leading lady
ledger clerk
lifeboatman
lightkeeper
limbo dancer
linen draper

lithologist
lithotomist
lollipop man
Lord Provost
lorry driver
madrigalist
maidservant
mammalogist
master baker
matinée idol
mechanician
medicine man
memorialist
merchantman
metal worker
miniaturist
minnesinger
mole-catcher
money-broker
money-lender
monographer
monologuist
moonlighter
mule-spinner
music critic
music master
mythologist
necrologist
necromancer
needlewoman
neurologist
neurotomist
night porter
night sister
nightworker
nomenclator
numismatist
office staff
onion-seller
opera singer
ophiologist
orientalist
osteologist
pamphleteer
panel-beater

paperhanger
parlourmaid
pathologist
pearlfisher
petrologist
pettifogger
philatelist
philologist
phonologist
phthologist
piano player
piece-worker
play-actress
policewoman
polyphonist
pork butcher
print-seller
probationer
promulgator
proofreader
property man
questionary
radiologist
rag merchant
representer
republisher
rhetorician
rhinologist
roadsweeper
safebreaker
safe-cracker
salesperson
sandwich man
saxophonist
scoutmaster
scrap dealer
scripholder
secret agent
seditionary
secret agent
seditionary
semanticist
servant girl
serving maid
share-broker

sheep-farmer
shepherdess
shipbreaker
shipbuilder
ship's master
shopbreaker
shop steward
silversmith
slaughterer
slave-driver
slave-holder
smallholder
sociologist
stage-driver
steel-worker
steeplejack
stilt-walker
stockbroker
stockjobber
stonecutter
storekeeper
storyteller
straight man
strip-teaser
sundriesman
system-maker
talent scout
tax gatherer
taxidermist
telegrapher
telephonist
ticket agent
toastmaster
tobacconist
tooth-drawer
topographer
torch-bearer
torch-singer
touch-typist
town planner
tragedienne
train driver
transcriber
transporter
transhipper

travel agent
type founder
typographer
underbearer
underwriter
upholsterer
versemonger
vine-dresser
washerwoman
watchkeeper
watch-mender
wax-chandler
wheel-cutter
wheelwright
whitewasher
witch-doctor
witch-finder
wool-stapler
xylophonist

12

accordionist
actor-manager
ambulanceman
anaesthetist
animalculist
archeologist
artilleryman
artist's model
baby-snatcher
ballet dancer
ballet master
bellows-maker
bibliologist
body-snatcher
booking clerk
bottle-washer
bus conductor
cabinet-maker
calligrapher
cardiologist
caricaturist
carpet-fitter
cartograhper

cerographist
cheesemonger
chief cashier
chimney-sweep
chiropractor
chronologist
churchwarden
circuit judge
civil servant
clarinettist
clerk of works
cloth-shearer
coach-builder
coleopterist
commissioner
conchologist
confectioner
corn chandler
corn merchant
cosmographer
costermonger
counter-tenor
crafts-master
craniologist
cryptogamist
cryptologist
crystal gazer
dance hostess
deep-sea diver
demonologist
demonstrator
dendrologist
dock labourer
drama teacher
drug smuggler
ecclesiastic
educationist
egyptologist
electrotyper
elocutionist
embryologist
engine-driver
entomologist
entrepreneur
enzymologist

escapologist
ethnographer
experimenter
exterminator
family doctor
farm labourer
film director
film producer
first officer
flint-knapper
flying doctor
footplateman
front-bencher
funambulator
geometrician
glass-grinder
glossologist
grease monkey
guild brother
hagiographer
harness-maker
head gardener
head mistress
horse-breaker
horse-courser
horse-knacker
hotel manager
house-breaker
housepainter
house steward
house surgeon
hydrographer
immunologist
impersonator
instructress
investigator
invoice clerk
jerry-builder
joint-trustee
juvenile lead
King's Counsel
kitchen-wench
knife-grinder
knife-thrower
labouring man

land surveyor
lath-splitter
leader writer
lexicologist
lithographer
lollipop lady
longshoreman
loss adjuster
lumber-dealer
maid of honour
maître d' hotel
make-up artist
manual worker
manufacturer
mass producer
meat-salesman
messenger-boy
metallurgist
mezzo soprano
microscopist
mineralogist
miscellanist
money-changer
Morris-dancer
mosaic-artist
mosaic-worker
musicologist
mythographer
neurosurgeon
newspaperman
notary public
nutritionist
obstetrician
office junior
orchestrator
organ-builder
organ-grinder
orthodontist
orthographer
paper-stainer
pattern-maker
photographer
phrenologist
physiologist
plant manager

ploughwright
plumber's mate
plyer-for-hire
postmistress
practitioner
press officer
prestigiator
principal boy
prison warder
prize-fighter
professional
propagandist
proprietress
psephologist
psychiatrist
psychologist
publicity man
pupil-teacher
puppet-player
quarry master
racing driver
radiographer
receptionist
restaurateur
riding-master
right-hand man
rubber-grader
sales manager
scene-painter
scene-shifter
school doctor
schoolmaster
screenwriter
scriptwriter
scullery-maid
seed-merchant
seismologist
selenologist
senior master
serving-wench
sharecropper
sharpshooter
sheep-shearer
sheep-stealer
ship chandler

ship's husband
shoe-repairer
silver-beater
slaughterman
snake-charmer
social worker
soil mechanic
special agent
speechwriter
spice-blender
spokesperson
sportscaster
sports master
sportswriter
stage manager
stand-up comic
statistician
steel erector
stenographer
stonebreaker
stonedresser
street trader
street-walker
sugar-refiner
tax collector
technologist
telegraph boy
telegraphist
tenant farmer
test engineer
therapeutist
timber trader
toll-gatherer
tourist agent
toxicologist
tradespeople
transplanter
trichologist
trick cyclist
undermanager
underservant
veterinarian
vibraphonist
vice-chairman
waiting-woman

warehouseman
water diviner
wine merchant
wood-engraver
works manager
zincographer

13

administrator
agriculturist
antique dealer
arachnologist
archaeologist
arithmetician
articled clerk
barber-surgeon
basso-profundo
bibliographer
biology master
businesswoman
calico-printer
calypso singer
campanologist
chartographer
chicken-farmer
chirographist
choreographer
civil engineer
contortionist
contrabandist
contrapuntist
correspondent
cotton-spinner
counter-caster
counterfeiter
craniometrist
criminologist
cryptographer
dancing master
debt collector
dental surgeon
deipnosophist
dermatologist
diagnostician

diamond-cutter
district nurse
draughtswoman
drawing-master
dress designer
drill sergeant
dubbing editor
electroplater
electrotypist
encyclopedist
entozoologist
epigrammatist
estate manager
exhibitionist
fencing-master
fortune-teller
freight-broker
galvanologist
games mistress
glossographer
glyphographer
ground-bailiff
gynaecologist
haematologist
harbour master
heieroglyphist
High Constable
horse-milliner
hospital nurse
housemistress
ichthyologist
impressionist
industrialist
intelligencer
kettledrummer
lady-in-waiting
laryngologist
lepidopterist
letter-carrier
letter-founder
lexicographer
lighthouseman
literary agent
lollipop woman
machine-minder

maid-of-all-work
master builder
master mariner
mathematician
maths mistress
meistersinger
melodramatist
metaphysician
meteorologist
music mistress
night-watchman
oceanographer
old-clothes-man
ornithologist
orthographist
paediatrician
park attendant
peasant-farmer
periodicalist
pharmaceutist
physiognomist
physiographer
police officer
posture-master
poultry farmer
prime minister
printer's devil
prison officer
privateersman
process-server
projectionist
psalmographer
psychoanalyst
pteridologist
public speaker
Queen's Counsel
racing-tipster
rag-and-bone-man
rent collector
revolutionary
revolutionist
rubber-planter
sailing master
schoolteacher
science master

shop assistant
seismographer
selenographer
singing-master
sports teacher
stage-coachman
stationmaster
sterioscopist
straight actor
street-sweeper
sub-contractor
superintender
supernumerary
supply teacher
toll collector
trade unionist
traffic warden
tramcar-driver
tram conductor
trapeze artist
ventriloquist
vice-president
vice-principal
vulcanologist
welfare worker
violoncellist
window-cleaner
window-dresser
woollen-draper
writing-master
zoogeographer

14

anthropologist
astrophysicist
autobiographer
bacteriologist
ballet mistress
billiard-marker
billiard-player
black marketeer
bus conductress
casual labourer
chamber counsel

character actor
chief executive
chimney-sweeper
citizen-soldier
classics master
colour sergeant
commissionaire
cost accountant
customs officer
dancing partner
design engineer
discount-broker
ecclesiologist
educationalist
electrochemist
encyclopaedist
exhange-broker
fifth columnist
flamenco dancer
French polisher
general manager
handicraftsman
High Court Judge
horticulturist
house decorator
house furnisher
house physician
hydrotherapist
king's messenger
language master
leading counsel
leather-dresser
maître de ballet
manual labourer
market-gardener
marriage broker
medical officer
merchant-tailor
metallographer
money-scrivener
Mother Superior
music publisher
naval pensioner
painter-stainer
palaeobotanist

pavement artist
pharmacologist
plastic surgeon
pneumatologist
prima ballerina
property master
question master
reception clerk
representative
rheumatologist
schoolmistress
ship's carpenter
spectacle-maker
spectroscopist
sports mistress
station manager
store detective
superintendent
sword swallower
systems analyst
tallow chandler
timber merchant
tobacco planter
town councillor
traffic manager
troubleshooter
turf accountant
under-secretary
vice-chancellor
vivisectionist
water-colourist
weather prophet

15

agriculturalist
ambulance driver
ancillary worker
arboriculturist
assistant master
attorney general
Bow Street Runner
cabinet minister
casting director
charge d'affaires

Christy minstrel
cinematographer
commission agent
company director
crossing-sweeper
dancing mistress
diamond merchant
domestic servant
forwarding agent
funeral director
gentleman-farmer
geomorphologist
governor-general
graphic designer
hackney coachman
heart specialist
helminthologist
instrumentalist
insurance broker
jack-of-all-trades
musical director
numismatologist
ophthalmologist
palaeontologist
physiotherapist
platform-speaker
plenipotentiary
police constable
police inspector
portrait-painter
prestidigitator
professional man
programme seller
provision dealer
queen's messenger
railway engineer
recording artist
resurrectionist
school inspector
science mistress
scripture-reader
sleeping partner
song-and-dance man
speech therapist
stretcher-bearer

strolling player   ticket collector   vice-chamberlain
supporting actor   tight-rope walker

Trees and shrubs

2 & 3
ash
bay
ben
bo
box
elm
fig
fir
gum
koa
may
oak
yew

nipa
palm
pear
pine
plum
poon
rata
rose
shea
sloe
sorb
teak
toon
upas
whin

4
acer
aloe
anil
bael
bass
bush
coca
cola
date
dhak
dita
gean
holm
ilex
jute
kava
kola
lime
ling

5
abele
alder
apple
areca
aspen
babul
balsa
beech
birch
briar
brier
broom
cacao
caper
carob
cedar
chico
cubeb
ebony

elder
erica
furze
genip
gorse
guava
hazel
henna
holly
iroko
Judas
karri
kauri
larch
lemon
lilac
maple
mango
myrrh
olive
osier
papaw
peach
pecan
pipal
plane
roble
rowan
salix
savin
sumac
thorn
withy
yucca
zamia

6
acacia
acajou
almond
antiar
azalea
bamboo
banian
banyan
baobab
bog oak
bonsai
cashew
cassia
cherry
cohune
conker
daphne
datura
deodar
derris
durian
fustic
gingko
ginkgo
gomuti
jarrah
jujube
kalmiay
laurel
linden
locust
longan
loquat
mallee
manuka

mimosa
myrtle
nutmeg
orache
orange
pawpaw
papaya
peepul
platan
poplar
privet
protea
quince
raffia
rattan
redbud
red fir
red gum
red oak
sallow
sapele
sapota
spirea
spruce
sumach
tupelo
walnut
wattle
willow

7
althaea
ambatch
arbutus
bebeeru
big tree

blue gum
bramble
bullace
cajuput
cajeput
camelia
catalpa
champac
conifer
coquito
cork oak
cow tree
cypress
dogwood
durmast
fan palm
filbert
fuchsia
genipap
gum tree
heather
hemlock
hickory
holm oak
jasmine
juniper
madrona
oil palm
palmyra
red pine
redwood
robinia
rosebay
sequoia
sourgum
soursop
spiraea
syringa
talipot
tea tree
wax palm
wax tree
wych-elm

8

allspice
barberry
basswood
bayberry
beefwood
bergamot
box elder
buddleia
calabash
calamite
carnauba
chestnut
cinchona
coolabah
coolibah
cork tree
corkwood
date palm
dwarf box
euonymus
evonymus
gardenia
guaiacum
guaiocum
hardwood
hawthorn
holly oak
hornbeam
inkberry
ironwood
japonica
kingwood
laburnum
lavender
magnolia
mahogany
mangrove
manna ash
mesquite
mulberry
oleander
palm tree
pear tree

piassava
pinaster
plum tree
quandong
rain tree
rambutan
red cedar
rosemary
rosewood
sago palm
saltbush
shadbush
silky oak
sourwood
sugar gum
sweet bay
sweet gum
sweetsop
sycamore
tamarack
tamarind
tamarisk
viburnum
wisteria
witch-elm
woodbine

9

ailanthus
algorroba
auracaria
azedarach
balsawood
balsam fir
bearberry
blackjack
bog myrtle
buckthorn
butternut
carob tree
casuarina
China tree
chincapin
coco de mer

coral tree
crab apple
crowberry
deciduous
eaglewood
euphorbia
evergreen
firethorn
flame tree
forsythia
hydrangea
ivory palm
jacaranda
Judas tree
kalanchoe
kapok tree
launcewood
macadamia
mistletoe
paulownia
pitch pine
plane tree
poinciana
poison oak
poison ivy
quebracho
rose apple
royal palm
sagebrush
sapanwood
sapodilla
sassafras
satinwood
screw pine
sour gourd
stinkwood
stone pine
sugar bush
sugar pine
sweet gale
tallow wood
thorn tree
tree heath
tree tomato
tulip tree

tulipwood
wax myrtle
whitebeam
whitewood
wych hazel

10

almond tree
arbor vitae
bird cherry
blackthorn
bladdernut
bottle tree
brazilwood
breadfruit
bunya-bunya
butter tree
buttonwood
chinaberry
coffee tree
coniferous
coral tree
cotton bush
cottonwood
Douglas fir
dragon tree
durmast oak
eucalyptus
fiddlewood
frangipani
gopher-wood
gomuti palm
grease bush
greasewood
greenheart
Joshua tree
laurustimus
mangosteen
mock orange
pagoda tree
poinsettia
prickly ash
pyracantha
raffia palm

rose acacia
rubber tree
sappanwood
sessile oak
sorrel tree
sour cherry
sugar apple
sugar maple
weeping ash
white cedar
whitethorn
wild cherry
witch hazel
yellow-wood

11

Aaron's beard
black spruce
black walnut
bottlebrush
burning bush
cabbage palm
cabbage tree
camphor tree
chaulmoogra
coconut palm
copper beech
cotoneaster
crepe myrtle
crape myrtle
cryptomeria
cypress pine
dawn redwood
false acacia
feather palm
honey locust
honeysuckle
Japanese ivy
lacquer tree
mountain ash
native peach
Norway maple
purple heart
pussy willow

service tree
slippery elm
spindle tree
stephanotis
talipot palm
tulip poplar
varnish tree

12

balsam poplar
balsam spruce
blackcurrant
blackjack oak
cherry laurel
Christ's thorn
creosote bush
cucumber tree
custard apple
golden wattle
rhododendron
rose of Sharon
monkey puzzle
Norway spruce
philadelphius
sea buckthorn
snowball tree
snowdrop tree
Spanish cedar
St. John's bread
swamp cypress
tree of heaven
umbrella pine
umbrella tree
wellingtonia
white currant
yellow poplar

13

bougainvillea
butcher's-broom
cranberry bush
cranberry tree
hemlock spruce

horse chestnut
Japanese cedar
paper mulberry
poison hemlock
royal ponciana
spike lavender
sweet chestnut
wayfaring tree
weeping willow

14 +

African mahogany
bergamot orange

cedar of Lebanon
flamboyant tree
flame-of-the-forest
flowering currant
Japanese andromeda
Jerusalem cherry
Lombardy poplar
maidenhair tree
monkey bread tree
mountain laurel
red-osier dogwood
silk-cotton tree
strawberry tree
turpentine tree
virginia creeper

Twelve

Twelve apostles

Andrew
James
James, son of Alphaeus
John
Judas, brother of James
Judas Iscariot
Matthew (Levi)
Nathaniel (Bartholomew)
Peter (Simon)
Philip
Simon the Zealot
Thomas

Twelve tribes of Israel

Asher
Benjamin
Dan
Ephraim
Gad
Issachar
Judah
Levi
Manasseh
Naphtali
Reuben
Zebulun

United Nations members

2 &

Syria
Zaïre

3

UK
USA

4

Chad
Cuba
Fiji
Iran
Iraq
Laos
Mali
Oman
Peru
Togo
USSR

5

Benin
Chile
China
Congo
Egypt
Gabon
Ghana
Haiti
India
Italy
Japan
Kenya
Libya
Malta
Nepal
Niger
Qatar
Samoa
Spain
Sudan

6

Angola
Belize
Bhutan
Brazil
Brunei
Canada
Cyprus
France
Gambia
Greece
Guinea
Guyana
Israel
Jordan
Kuwait
Latvia
Malawi
Mexico
Monaco
Norway
Panama
Poland
Russia
Rwanda
Sweden
Turkey
Uganda
Zambia

7

Albania
Algeria
Andorra
Armenia
Austria
Bahamas

Bahrain
Belarus
Belgium
Bolivia
Burundi
Comoros
Croatia
Denmark
Ecuador
Eritrea
Estonia
Finland
Georgia
Germany
Grenada
Hungary
Iceland
Ireland
Jamaica
Lebanon
Lesotho
Liberia
Moldova
Morocco
Myanmar
Namibia
Nigeria
Romania
St. Lucia
Senegal
Somalia
Tunisia
Ukraine
Uruguay
Vanuatu
Vietnam

8

Barbados
Botswana

Bulgaria
Cambodia
Cameroon
Colombia
Djibouti
Dominica
Ethiopia
Honduras
Malaysia
Maldives
Mongolia
Pakistan
Paraquay
Portugal
Slovakia
Slovenia
Sri Lanka
Suriname
Tanzania
Thailand
Zimbabwe

9

Argentina
Australia
Cape Verde
Costa Rica
Guatemala
Indonesia
Kampuchea
Korea, North
Lithuania
Mauritius
Nicaragua
San Marino
Singapore
Swaziland
Venezuela

10

Azerbaijan
Bangladesh
El Salvador
Kazakhstan
Korea, South
Kyrgyzstan
Luxembourg
Madagascar
Mauritania
Micronesia
Mozambique
New Zealand
Seychelles
Tajikistan
Uzbekistan
Yugoslavia

11

Afghanistan
Burkina Faso
Côte d' Ivoire
Netherlands
Philippines
Saudi Arabia
Sierra Leone
South Africa

12

Guinea-Bissau
Turkmenistan

13

Czech Republic
Liechtenstein
United Kingdom

14

Papua New Guinea
Solomon Islands

15 +

Antigua and Barbuda
Central African Republic
Dominion Republic
Equatorial Guinea
Marshall Islands

St. Kitts and Nevis
St. Vincent and the Grenadines
Sao Tomé and Príncipé
Trinidad and Tobago
United Arab Emirates
United States of America

Weapons and armour

2 & 3
ABM
axe
bow
dag
das
gat
gun
gyn
ram
Sam
TNT
V1
wad

4
ammo
arms
ball
barb
bill
bolo
bolt
bomb
bren
butt
cane
club
colt
cosh
dart
dirk

épée
fang
flak
foil
gaff
ICBM
jack
helm
kora
kris
mace
mail
mere
mine
nuke
piat
pike
Scud
shot
slug
Sten
tank
tock
tuck
whip
Z-gun

5
A-bomb
aegis
ancus
ankus
armet

armor
arrow
aswar
bacyn
baton
bidag
bilbo
birch
bolas
boson
brand
buffe
crest
CS gas
culet
estoc
flail
fusée
fusil
gipon
grape
gupti
H-bomb
hobit
imber
jupel
jupon
keris
khora
kilig
kilij
knife
knout
kukri

kylie
lames
lance
lasso
latch
lathi
luger
Maxim
noose
pilum
poker
pouch
prodd
razor
rifle
royal
sabre
salet
salvo
shaft
shell
skean
skene
sling
spear
stake
staff
stave
stick
sword
tachi
targe
tasse
tawse

visor
vizor
waddy

6
ack-ack
air gun
aletes
amukta
anlace
armlet
barkal
barong
barrel
basnet
baston
bhanju
bodkin
Bofors
bonnet
bracer
bridle
brugne
buffer
bullet
calote
camail
cannon
carcas
carrel
casque
cassis
celate

cheeks
crenel
crinet
cudgel
cuello
cuisse
dagger
daisho
dragon
dualin
dum-dum
dusack
exocet
feltre
glaive
gorget
gusset
hanger
heaume
helmet
homing
jezail
katana
kerrie
khanda
kikuki
kodogu
lancet
lariat
lassoo
lorica
mascle
massue
Mauser

mazule	**7**	cutlass	oil bomb	attaghan
mesail		djerrid	panache	atom bomb
morian	ailetes	dualine	panoply	axe-knife
morion	anelace	dudgeon	patriot	balister
mortar	assagai	dussack	placard	ballista
musket	assegai	elf-bolt	poitrel	bardings
muzzle	ataghan	Encorder	Polaris	bascinet
napalm	awl-pike	espadon	pole-axe	baselard
pac one	bacinet	fauchon	poniard	basilard
pac two	balasan	fendace	punt gun	basilisk
parang	baldric	firearm	quarrel	baudrick
pellet	balista	fire-pot	rabinet	birdbolt
petard	barbute	frontal	roundel	blowpipe
pistol	bar-shot	garotte	scourge	bludgeon
pom-pom	basinet	garrote	Sea Dart	brassard
pop gun	baslard	Gatling	Sea Hawk	brassart
powder	bayonet	gauchet	shashqa	brayette
primer	bazooka	gouchet	shinken	broad-axe
qillij	belfrey	gunlock	shotgun	Browning
ramrod	biliong	greaves	side-arm	buckshot
rapier	blow gun	grenade	sjambok	buff coat
rocket	bombard	gunshot	Skybolt	burganet
salade	bourdon	halbert	Sten gun	burginot
sallet	brasset	halberd	surcoat	burgonet
saturn	Bren gun	hand gun	teargas	cabasset
scythe	buckler	harpoon	torpedo	calthrop
Sea Cat	calibre	hatchet	Trident	canister
semtex	caliver	hauberk	twibill	carabine
shield	caltrap	hoguine	vamplet	cartouch
sickle	carabin	holster	ventail	cascabel
stylet	carbine	javelin	visiere	case-shot
sumpit	carreau	kastane	Walther	catapult
swivel	chakram	kindjal	warhead	chacheka
tabard	chalcos	langrel	wind-gun	chamfron
talwar	chauces	laniers		champons
target	chopper	long bow	**8**	chanfron
tonite	cordite	Long Tom		chausses
tulwar	corslet	lyddite	allecret	cladibas
VGO gun	couteau	machete	amusette	claymore
umbril	crupper	missile	Anschutz	cod piece
Webley	cuirass	Mons Meg	armament	colleret
zipgun	cuisses	morglay	arbalest	colletin
	culeset	murrion	arbalist	corselet
	currier	mursail	arbalete	crinière
	curtana	musquet	arquebus	crossbow
	curtein			

culettes
culverin
damaskin
deringer
destrier
dynamite
eel-spear
elf-arrow
falchion
falconet
fauchard
field-gun
fireball
firelock
fireship
gadlings
garrotte
gauntlet
gavelock
gunflint
gunpaper
gunsight
gunstock
hackbutt
halecret
hail shot
half-pike
hand-pike
haquebut
hassegai
howitzer
jambeaux
jazerant
land mine
langrage
Lewisite
Lewis gun
magazine
mangonel
mantelet
Maxim gun
munition
oerlikon
ordnance
organ gun

paravane
paterero
pauldron
Pauly gun
pectoral
pederero
petronel
phosgene
pistolet
plastron
poignard
portfire
pyroxyle
querquer
radar gun
repeater
revolver
ricochet
ringmail
sabatons
scabbard
scimitar
scorpion
shamshir
shrapnel
siege-gun
solarets
solerets
spadroon
spontoon
springal
stiletto
stinkpot
stone axe
stonebow
sumpitan
The Baron
testière
tomahawk
Tommy gun
umbrière
vambrace
vamplate
volcanic
whin-yard

yataghan

9

ack-ack gun
aerial gun
angel-shot
arrowhead
artillery
automatic
aventaile
backpiece
badelaire
bainbergs
beinbergs
ballistic
bandeleer
bandolier
bannerole
bastinado
battleaxe
Big Bertha
Blue Water
boar-spear
Bofors gun
bomb-chest
bombshell
booby trap
boomerang
Brown Bess
cannonade
cartouche
cartridge
chain-mail
chain-shot
champfron
chassepot
chaussons
columbiad
defoliant
demi-lance
Derringer
detonator
doodle-bug
epaulette

espringal
face-guard
falcastra
fish-spear
flagellum
flamberge
flintlock
Francisca
garde-bras
gelignite
grapeshot
green fire
guncotton
gunpowder
habergeon
hand-staff
harquebus
hausse-col
headpiece
heelpiece
knobstick
Landridge
matchlock
mazzuelle
Mills bomb
minute man
munitions
musketoon
needle-gun
poison gas
pom-pom gun
pourpoint
quaker-gun
rerebrace
sabatynes
shillalah
slingshot
slung-shot
small-arms
small bore
spring-gun
starshell
stinkbomb
sword-cane
teeth arms

trebuchet
truncheon
turret gun
volley gun
ward staff
welsh-hook
wheel lock
xyloidine
zumbooruk

10

ammunition
arcubalist
artillator
aventaille
banded mail
banderolle
banderilla
barrel helm
battery gun
blind shell
Blue Streak
Bowie-knife
brandestoc
brichettes
brigandine
broad arrow
broadsword
burrel shot
cannonball
cannon shot
coat armour
coat of mail
colt python
cataphract
cross-arrow
demi-cannon
dive bomber
field-piece
fire-sticks
flanchards
flick knife
flying bomb
Gatling gun

grainstaff
harquebuse
hand cannon
hand mortar
iron bullet
iron cannon
knobkerrie
lambrequin
Lee-Enfield
letter bomb
limpet mine
machine gun
Minie rifle
mustard-gas
paixhan-gun
pea-shooter
powder horn
pyroxyline
rocket ball
Sidewinder
six-shooter
small sword
sticky bomb
sword stick
Winchester

11

anti-tank gun
basket sword
blunderbuss
bow and arrow
breastplate
breaststrap
brigandyron
brigantayle
chapel de fer
chlorine gas
contact-mine
Dahlgren gun
depth charge
elephant gun
espallières
grande-garde
gun carriage

gun howitzer
hand grenade
harping iron
hawk missile
Holstein gun
Jacob's staff
Kelver cable
khyber knife
Lochaber axe
misericorde
morning star
neutron bomb
nuclear bomb
plate armour
powder chest
safety-catch
scale-armour
Snider rifle
sporting gun
Steinbuchse
Thompson gun

12

Armstrong gun
battering ram
boarding pike
breech loader
bridle cutter
cartridge box
curved dagger
demi-culverin
fire carriage
flame-thrower
floating mine
fowling-piece
Hotchkiss gun
hydrogen bomb
Lancaster gun
magnetic mine
Mills grenade
mitrailleuse
muzzle-loader
poisoned dart
quarterstaff

revolving gun
rocket-mortar
sharp shooter
Stokes mortar
suicide plane
sword-bayonet
tracer bullet
trident spear
wheel-lock dag

13

aerial torpedo
arming doublet
ball-cartridge
brass knuckles
chiefton tank
Churchill tank
cruise missile
duelling sword
guided missile
high-explosive
holster pistol
Kentucky rifle
knuckleduster
leather cannon
mortar carbine
nuclear weapon
Orgelgesschutz
percussion cap
poisoned arrow
sharpened pole
sub-machine gun
submarine mine
throwing knife
two-edged sword

14

blank cartridge
Brunswick rifle
duelling pistol
incendiary bomb
miniature rifle
nitroglycerine

rocket launcher
sawn off shotgun
small-bore rifle
stone-head spear
two-handed sword

15

anti-aircraft gun
anti tank grenede
bolt action rifle
bulletproof vest
holster revolver
imbricate armour
lachrymatory gas
Mannlicher rifle
matchlock musket
Maxim machine gun
missile launcher
Molotov cocktail
Partridge mortar
pepperbox pistol
Perkins steam gun
Raytheon missile
swivel musketoon
wheellock pistol

16 +

anti-personnel mine
anti-satellite missile
automatic machine gun
ballistic missile
Der Grosse Pumbart Von Steyr
double-barrelled shotgun
double-edged knife
double-edged sabre
double-edged sword
heat-seeking missile
muzzle loading rifle
Nordenfeldt machine gun
Schofield Smith and Wesson
shoulder launcher
Springfield rifle
volitional repeater

Weather

3

col
dew
dry
eye
fog
hot
ice
icy
low
sky
sun
wet

4

bank
bise
bora
bore
calm
cold
cool
damp
dank
dark
dewy
dusk
dull
east
eddy
fair
flaw
föhn
fret
gale
gust
haar
hail
haze

hazy
heat
high
hoar
iris
knot
lour
melt
mild
mist
pelt
puff
puna
rain
rime
scud
smog
snap
snow
spit
thaw
vane
veer
warm
west
wind

5

balmy
blast
blink
blowy
brume
buran
chill
cirri
clear
cloud
draft
drift

dusty
eager
eagre
ether
Eurus
flake
flood
foehn
foggy
fresh
front
frost
gibli
gusty
humid
light
lower
misty
muggy
north
Notus
rains
rainy
sleet
slush
snowy
sonde
south
spate
spout
stone
storm
sunny
virga
windy

6

arctic
aurora
Auster

boreal
breeze
bright
buster
chilly
cirrus
cloudy
colder
deluge
floods
flurry
fogbow
fogdog
freeze
frosty
ghibli
hyetal
icicle
isobar
isohel
kamsin
mizzle
mizzly
nimbus
samiel
seadog
sea fog
serein
shower
simoom
simoon
squall
starry
stormy
sultry
sunbow
sunset
torrid
trades
trough
vortex

warmer
welkin
winter
wintry
zephyr

7

backing
blowing
bluster
broiler
cat's
 paw
Celsius
chinook
climate
clouded
cumulus
cyclone
dewdrop
drizzle
draught
drought
dry-bulb
etesian
fog bank
freshen
hailing
isogram
isohyet
isoline
kamseen
khamsin
meltemi
mistral
monsoon
pampero
pelting
pouring
rainbow

raining
sea fret
set fair
sea haar
sea mist
showery
sirocco
sizzler
snowing
squally
stratus
summery
sunglow
sunless
sunrise
sunspot
tempest
thawing
thermal
thunder
tornado
twister
typhoon
veering
wintery

8

aerology
autumnal
black ice
blizzard
clear day
clear sky
cloudlet
cold snap
cold wave
cumulous
dead calm
dewpoint
doldrums

downpour
easterly
east wind
elements
fireball
flooding
fogbound
fog patch
forecast
freezing
freeze-up
head wind
heat wave
high wind
iceblink
icebound
isobaric
isopleth
isotherm
levanter
libeccio
light air
lowering
millibar
overcast
rainfall
raindrop
rainy day
scorcher
sea storm
snowfall
snowbank
spitting
sunburst
sunlight
thundery
thermals
tropical
twilight
variably
velocity
westerly
west wind
white out
wildfire
williwaw

wind cone
windless
wind rose
windsock

9

advection
afterglow
anemology
anthelion
atmometer
barometer
barograph
baroscope
cloudbank
cloudless
cloud rack
cold front
crosswind
drizzling
dry season
dust devil
dust storm
fresh gale
hailstone
hailstorm
hard frost
harmattan
heavy rain
hoarfrost
hurricane
hygristor
ice needle
isallobar
isotheral
Jack Frost
lapse rate
libecchio
lightning
mare's tail
meltwater
moonlight
north-east
northerly
north-west

north wind
nor'wester
occlusion
pea-souper
pyrometer
raincloud
rained off
rained out
rain guage
rainstorm
sand storm
scorching
snowblink
snowbound
snow drift
snow eater
snowflake
snowstorm
solar wind
south-east
south-west
starlight
storm belt
tidal wave
trade wind
updraught
unsettled
warm front
whirlwind
whole gale
wind-chill
wind force
wind gauge
wind scale
windstorm

10

aerography
anemograph
anemometer
anemometry
anemoscope
antitrades
atmosphere
black frost

Cape doctor
centigrade
changeable
clear night
cloudburst
cloudscape
convection
cumuliform
depression
Euroclydon
Fahrenheit
hot climate
hyetograph
hygrograph
hygrometer
hygroscope
ice station
isopiestic
land breeze
March winds
mare's tails
radiosonde
Scotch mist
storm cloud
strong gale
sweltering
thundering
tramontana
tramontane
turbulence
visibility
warm sector
water cycle
waterspout
weather eye
weatherman
weather map
wet chinook
wet weather
white frost
willy-willy

11

altocumulus
altostratus

anemography
anticyclone
atmospheric
cats and dogs
cold climate
cold weather
downdraught
dull weather
equinoctial
etesian wind
freezing fog
fresh breeze
foul weather
ground frost
hyetography
lowering sky
low pressure
mackerel sky
meteorology
mild weather
rain or shine
rainy season
stiff breeze
storm centre
storm signal
sunny spells
temperature
tempestuous
thermometer
thunderbolt
thunderclap
tourbillion
troposphere
warm weather
weathercock
weather vane
white squall

12

April showers
atmospherics
cirrocumulus
cirrostratus
cumulonimbus
easterly wind

freezing rain
gentle breeze
high pressure
Indian summer
lightning rod
meteorograph
moonlit night
nimbostratus
slight breeze
starlit night
storm brewing
storm warning
strong breeze
thundercloud
thunderstorm
tropical heat
tropical rain
weather glass
weather house
westerly wind
white rainbow
wind velocity
windy weather

13

autumn weather
ball lightning
Beaufort scale
cumulostratus
electric storm
frosty weather
galeforce wind
heat lightning
magnetic storm
north-east wind
northerly wind
north-west wind
occluded front
peal of thunder
precipitation
roll of thunder
south-east wind
southerly wind
south-west wind

stratocumulus
summer weather
thundershower
torrential rain
weather report
weather symbol
wintry showers
wintry weather

14

air temperature
aurora borealis
blustery shower
chain lightning
freshening wind
mackerel breeze
meteorological
moderate breeze
Northern Lights
sheet lightning
southern lights
sunny intervals
torrential rain
weather station

15 +

aurora australis
barometric pressure
Beaufort wind scale
bolt of lightning
centigrade scale
come rain or (come)
  shine
Fahrenheit scale
forked lightning
lightning conductor
mean temperature
microclimatology
prevailing winds
radiometeorograph
southerly buster
tropical climate
wind-chill factor

Wedding anniversaries

3

tin   (10th)

4

gold   (50th)
iron   (4th)
lace   (13th)
ruby   (40th)
wood   (5th)
wool   (7th)

5

china   (20th)

coral   (35th)
fruit   (4th)
ivory   (14th)
paper   (2nd)
pearl   (30th)
steel   (11th)
sugar   (6th)

6

bronze   (8th)
copper   (9th)
cotton   (1st)
flower   (4th)
silver   (25th)

7

crystal   (15th)
diamond   (60th)
emerald   (55th)
leather   (3rd)

8

platinum   (70th)
sapphire   (45th)

15 +

silk and fine linen   (12th)

Wines

(including grape varieties and wine-producing regions)

3 & 4

asti
Aszu
brut
Bual
cru
Döle
fino
hock
port
sec
seco
sekt
vin
vino

5

aroma
Byrrh
Corvo
Crépy

cuvée
Fitou
Médoc
Mosel
Rioja
Rully
secco
Tavel
Tokay

6

Alsace
Bandol
Barolo
Barsac
Beaune
Ben Ean
Cahors
Cassis
Chénas
Chinon

Claret
Cornas
Corton
Dingac
Frangy
Graach
Graves
Málaga
Morgon
muscat
Quinta
Saumur
Volnay
Wehlen

7

acidity
Aligoté
auslese
Banyuls
Barbera

bouquet
Caldaro
Chablis
Chianti
Clairet
Cotnari
demi-sec
dry wine
Eiswein
Falerno
Fendant
Fleurie
Fronsac
Gaillac
Inferno
Lutomer
Madeira
Malmsey
Margaux
Marsala
Martini
Moselle

Musigny
Oloroso
Orvieto
Othello
Pomerol
Pommard
Pouilly
Recioto
red wine
Retsina
St. Amour
Sasselo
Schluck
Sercial
Vouvray

8

Bordeaux
Brouilly
Burgundy
Condrieu

Dubonnet
Echezaux
essencia
Frascati
Gigondas
Juliénas
Mercurey
Montagny
Montilla
muscadel
Muscadet
muscatel
Pauillac
Piesport
Pol Roger
Riesling
rosé wine
Sancerre
Santenay
Sauterne
spatlese
Sylvaner
tastevin
Valencay
Valgelia
Vaudesir
Verdelho
Vermouth
vin blanc
Vin Jaune
vin leger
vin rouge
Vin Santo

Clairette
Corbières
Côte-Rótie
Domestica
Est! Est! Est
Hermitage
Kreuznach
Lambrusco
Meursault
Minervois
Montlouis
pétillant
St. Emilion
St. Raphael
San Severo
Steinwein

Commanderia
Egri Bikaner
Maurodaphne
Monbazillac
Moulin-à-Vent
Nierstiener
Pouillly-Fumé
Saint Julien
Vega Cecilia
Vin de Paille
Vin de Graves
vin mousseux
vintage wine

9

abboccato
Anjou wine
Ayler Kupp
Bardolino
Blanc Fumé
Bollinger
Bourgogne
Bourgueil
Champagne
Chialetto

10

Barbaresco
Bernkastel
Beaujolais
Bull's Blood
Chambertin
Chiroubles
Lakes Folly
Mâcon Lugny
Manzanilla
Mateus Rosé
Montrachet
Rhine wines
Rhone wines
Richebourg
Rivesaltes
Taittinger
Vinho Verde

11

Aloxe-Corton
Amontillado
Bocksbeutal
Bonnes Mares
Chianti Putto
Clos-de-Bèzes
Clos St. Denis

12

Asti Spumante
Blanc de Noirs
Château Canon
Château Gazin
Château Pavie
Côtes-du-Rhône
Frecciarossa
Hickinbotham
Petit Chablis
Pouilly-loche
Romanée-Conti
Saint-Emilion
Saint Estephe
Saint Raphael
still Moselle
Valpolicella
vin ordinaire
Virginia Dare
Vosne-Romanée

13

Beerenauslese
Blanc of Blancs
Château Ausone
Château Bélair
Château Chalon
Château Coutet
Château Dauzac
Château d'Yquem

Château Figeac
Château Kirwan
Château Lafite
Château Lagune
Château Langoa
Château Latour
Château Meyney
Château Nissac
Château Palmer
Château Pouget
Coteau Dulayon
Clos de Vougeot
Entre-deux-mers
Liebfraumilch
Moselblumchen
Muscato Mabile
Pouilly-Fuissé
Qualitatswein
Rhine Riesling
Scharzhofberg
sparkling wine
Touraine wines
Wild Irish Rose

14

Château Boscaut
Château Caillou
Château Climens
Château Giscour
Château Grillet
Château Guiraud
Château Lamothe
Château la Tâche
Château Margaux
Côtes-du-Ventoux
Gamay de la Loire
Gewürztraminer
Henkell Trocken

Lacrima Christi
Moet and Chandon
Quarts de Chaume
Rothbury Estate
Santa Maddelena

15

Château Belgrave
Château Rieussec
Clos de Jacobins
Côtes-de-Provence
Côtes-du-Vivarais
Crozes-Hermitage
Gruner Veltliner
haut poitou wines
Mersault Charmes
Morey-Saint-Denis
Passe-tout-Grains
Sacramental wine
Saumurchampigny

16

Chambolle Musigny
Château Batailley
Château Desmirail
Château Haut Brion
Château Lascombes
Cremant de Cramant
Gevrey-Chambertin
La Roche Aux Moines
Les Forts de la
   Tour
Monteé de Tonnerre
Muscato de Setubal
Pouilly Vinzelles
Savigny-les-Beaune
Schloss Schunburn

Zinfandel Essense

17

Charmes-Chambertin
Château Beausejour
Château Calon-Segur
Château Magdelaine
Corton-Charlemagne
Côtes-du-Roussillon
Nuits-Saint-Georges
Ockfener Bockstein
Wehlener Sunnenhuhr

18

Blanquette de Limoux
Château Cheval Blanc
Château Lafon-Rochet
Domaine de Chavalier
Muscat de Frontenac
Schloss-Rockelheim
Zeller Schart-Katze

19 +

Brunello de Montalcino
Chassagne-Montrachet
Château de Brane-Can-
   tenac
Château Carbonnieux
Château Chasse-Spleen
Château la Fleur Petrus
Château la Gaffelière
Château Latour-Figeac
Château Mouton Roth-
   schild
Sauvignon de Touraine
Vernaccia de Oristano
Trockenbeeren Auslese

Grape varieties

3 & 5	KWV	**6**	Saumur	**7**
	Steen		Shiraz	
Flora	Syrah	Merlot		Aligoté
Gamay		Muscat		Catawba

Chelois
Cinsaul
~~Fendant~~
Gutedel

Sylvaner
Viognier

Ugni Blanc
Vernaccia
Zinfandel

13

Cabernet Blanc
Cabernet Franc
Montepulciano
Müller-Thurgau

8

Baco Noir
Carignan
Charbond
Delaware
Malvasia
Nebbiolo
Rulander

9

Chasselas
Columbard
Clairette
Nederburg
Pinot Gris
Pinot Noir
Trebbiano

10

Chardonnay
Fleur du Cap
San Giovesi

14 +

Gewürztraminer
Emerald Riesling
Thompson seedless

11 & 12

Chenin Blanc
Fulle Blanc

Wine-producing regions

3 & 4

Ahr
Alba
Aude
Dao
Jura
Nahe
Ohio
Saar

Cognac
Cyprus
Graves
Greece
Limoux
Marche
Oregon
Sicily
Umbria

Burgundy
Bulgaria
Dalmatia
Gigondas
La Mancha
Lombardy
Mersault
Monterey
Piedmont
Provence
Slovenia

Côte de Nuit
Napa Valley
Rheinpfalz
Santa Clara
Valdepenas

11

Finger Lakes
Württemburg

5

Anjou
Baden
Blaye
Bourg
Loire
Mâcon
Medoc
Mosel
Paarl

7

Almaden
Côte d' Or
Fronsac
Hérault
Penedès
Pomerol
Romania

9

Alto Adige
Alto Douro
Bourgueil
Champagne
Corbières
Hawkes Bay
Lake Garda
Languedoc
Mendocino

12

Amador County
Barosa County
Hunter Valley
New York State
Yakima Valley

8

Abbruzzi
Auckland
Bergerac
Blenheim
Bordeaux

6

Alsace
Apulia
Bandol

10

California

13 +

Alameda County
Castell di Jesi
Emilia Romagna
Entre-Deux-Mers
Pleasant Valley
Washington State

Index and cross-references

Acknowledgements

I would like to acknowledge the help of the following people in the preparation of this book. For their contributions to the research that made possible the inclusion of so many specialist terms in the compilation, I would like to thank Betty Bawden, Muriel Hoadley and, in particular, Gwyneth and John Machin. I would like also to thank Julia Pickles for her help in keying some of the longer lists. Finally I must thank my mentors John Clark and David Skinner whose advice, criticism and support helped to see the book through to completion. I hope the finished work will prove to be helpful and add to the enjoyment of fellow crossword fanatics and other puzzle solvers.

G.C. - Oxford 2007